YOUTH *IN*JUSTICE

YOUTH *IN*JUSTICE

Canadian Perspectives

2nd edition

Edited by

Thomas Fleming

Patricia O'Reilly

and

Barry Clark

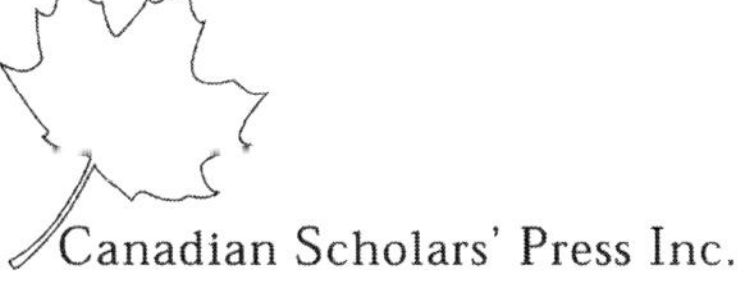

Canadian Scholars' Press Inc.

Youth Injustice: Canadian Perspectives, 2nd edition
Edited by Thomas Fleming, Patricia O'Reilly, and Barry Clark

First published in 2001 by
Canadian Scholars' Press Inc.
180 Bloor Street West, Suite 1202
Toronto, Ontario
M5S 2V6

www.cspi.org

Canadian Scholars' Press gratefully acknowledges financial assistance for our publishing activities from the Ontario Arts Council, The Canada Council for the Arts, and the Government of Canada through the Book Publishing Industry Development Program.

Canadian Cataloguing in Publication Data

National Library of Canada Cataloguing in Publication Data

Main entry under title:

Youth injustice : Canadian perspectives

2nd ed.
Includes bibliographical references.
ISBN 1-55130-139-3

1. Juvenile justice, Administration of—Canada. 2. Juvenile delinquency—Canada. I. Fleming, Thomas, 1951- II. O'Reilly, Patricia, 1950- III. Clark, Barry, 1944-

KE9445.Y69 2001 345.71'08 C2001-902239-5

Managing Editor: Ruth Bradley-St-Cyr
Proofreading: Cheryl Isaacs
Production Editor: Rebecka Sheffield
Page Layout: Brad Horning
Cover Design: Rebecka Sheffield
Cover Image: Greg Varano

01 02 03 04 05 06 07 7 6 5 4 3 2 1

Printed and bound in Canada by AGMV Marquis

For Patrick, Tom, and Kate

For Elaine and Sam

"Let the Deed Show"

ACKNOWLEDGEMENTS

The editors wish to acknowledge the support and assistance of Jack Wayne of Canadian Scholars' Press. Our editor Ruth Bradley-St-Cyr made the compilation of this collection an enjoyable task. Murray Pomerance, Marino Tuzi, Howard Doughty, Fred Sureet, Heather Dockeray, Livy Visano, Andria Turner, Michelle Irvine and John Yocom deserve a special thanks for their support and assistance.

ABOUT THE EDITORS

Patricia O'Reilly, L.L.B. of Injured Workers Consultants, Toronto, is a community activist, author, and former college professor.

Dr. Thomas Fleming is Chair, Applied Arts and Health Sciences, Seneca College of Arts and Technology.

Barry Clark is Executive Director, John Howard Society of Windsor and Essex County and Adjunct Professor, University of Windsor.

CONTENTS

PART FOUR
YOUNG PERSONS AND THE COURTS

PART FIVE
TRENDS AND ISSUES IN YOUTH INJUSTICE

INTRODUCTION

Almost a decade has elapsed since the publication of the first edition of *Youth Injustice*. In 1992, we recognized that there were no academic readers available on this important subject despite intense interest in the area. The success of that reader and significant development in law, policy, and public debate have led to this completely revised edition. The majority of the chapters in this book have been drawn from *The Canadian Journal of Criminology*, reflecting the cutting edge of theory and research in Canada. This edition brings together those articles in a format that is readily accessible to students and their instructors. It also provides a broader exposure for writers and *The Canadian Journal of Criminology* in an era of declining library budgets. Because this is the last remaining criminology journal in the country, we wanted to support its efforts to provide a forum for the exchange of ideas in the field.

In building the contributions for this edition, we were cognizant that many different research paradigms would be encapsulated in the book. In this context, we believe the chapters chronicle, regardless of these differences, the erosion of youth justice in Canada and its acceleration through the rise of law and order government. Globalization and its impact on rights and employment, the effect of free trade upon the life chances of Canadian youth, the increasing use of private imprisonment, and reversion to punitive forms of justice, are all issues that have become the core of contemporary debate. Similarly, governments have increasingly turned to the confinement model, despite its escalating cost, eschewing the need for effective alternative programs. Finally, the view that children should be transferred to adult court at ever earlier ages has signaled a reversal in a century of movement toward enlightenment in our treatment of youth crime.

Not every criminologist whose work appears in this book would support our contentions on the state of youth crime and its treatment under the Canadian criminal justice system. We do not want to suggest that a critical approach is one that they would personally espouse in their work. The views are our own; however, we invite readers to contemplate both the partial and sum total of all of the changes to our society and the treatment of youthful deviance that is reflected in the writing in this book. No reader could claim that the increasingly Draconian approach to young people in trouble is helping to reduce the amount of juvenile crime, or that it has proven more effective than past efforts. Despite cries from some quarters to criminalize toddlers and treat fourteen-year-old children as adults, there is no evidence that these measures will ameliorate the effect of youth crime on society. Indeed, the American experience underscores the futility of hard line approaches when socio-cultural and economic problems are ignored. While education and economic well-being have an impact on many areas of youthful offending, there is little doubt that government efforts in Ontario, for example, have resulted in cuts to social support systems that have has serious ramifications for youth and their families. Similarly, the lean budget of Toronto has resulted in the removal of breakfast programs in schools where children will now "simply" go hungry. Do we really believe that justifying deeper cuts to our social programs while at the same time emphasizing responsibility and punishment, will actually result in improvements to our youth offense rates? Will it build a better society for future Canadians? It is apparent that these social developments will yield fruit of a poisoned vine, leaving yet another generation of young Canadians to suffer under a law and order regime.

Justice for youth is not easy to deliver. As we already indicated, forces both within and outside of our control have gathered to create an atmosphere where *injustice* is presented as justice. This is a reflection of the political environment which predominates in Canada particularly in reference to youth crime. The push for increasing use of punishment, severe forms of punishment, and transferring younger children into adult court, have replaced reasoned approaches to rehabilitating our youth. It is common for politicians to refer to youth as Canada's greatest natural resource. In this case, we argue that the protection of this resource demands a much greater effort. It is no exaggeration to suggest that the treatment of Canada's young people will determine the quality of our future as a society, and as individuals within this society. We hope this book is one step toward a better future for all.

PART ONE

The State of Research and Practice

CHAPTER ONE

Youth justice research in Canada: An assessment

Anthony N. Doob
Centre of Criminology
University of Toronto
Toronto, Ontario

IN THE FALL OF 1994, THREE OF US WERE ASKED, BY THE DEPARTMENT of Justice, Canada, to spend a month producing "a summary review of criminological research, potentially relevant and useful to the Standing Committee on Justice and Legal Affairs [of the House of Commons] in... their review of the *Young Offenders Act*." We decided that one way to produce a report that would be useful for the committee (and, we hoped, to others) would be to divide the field into a set of questions and do searches for relevant (largely Canadian) research addressing each of these questions.

The result (Doob, Marinos, and Varma 1995) was a report that included a fair amount of Canadian research which allowed us to give (at least tentative) answers to more than fifty policy-related questions concerning the youth justice system in Canada. I am not suggesting that "all is fine" in youth justice research in Canada, but I am suggesting that our experience four years ago convinced me that we knew quite a bit about the youth justice system and, in the four years since, we have extended our knowledge.

Delinquency research

As with many areas of criminological research, there are some topics within the broad area of "youth crime" where one can

Canadian Journal of Criminology/Revue canadienne de criminologie, April/avril 1999, pp. 217 – 224.

be reasonably comfortable relying on research from other countries. When one looks at the work on the development or treatment of serious delinquency or of the impact of criminal justice (or community) interventions on offending, international research is quite relevant. Few of the findings on the development of serious delinquency that are examined in other countries contradict the extensive work carried out in Canada. It is not surprising that, in reviews written by Canadian researchers, Canadian research is reviewed along side research in other countries (e.g., LeBlanc and Loeber 1998; Tremblay and Craig 1995).

On the other hand, it is important to examine youthful offending in Canada in part because cultural differences and differences in social programs that exist in different countries may affect the relative importance of different factors. Thus, projects like the National Longitudinal Study of Children and Youth which follows Canadian children from birth to adulthood (and which started with a cross-section of children from birth to age 11) should provide useful data on the development of delinquency. This, of course, is predicated on the assumption that reasonable "delinquency measures" will continue to be part of the data that are collected every two years. Unlike some longitudinal studies that focus on delinquency, this survey's focus is elsewhere; hence given the fierce competition for survey time, the survival of delinquency questions is by no means certain. If "delinquency measures" do continue to be included in the survey, the challenge for the criminology community will be to ensure that these data are used sufficiently to justify the considerable cost in collecting them.

I do not want to suggest that we can rely solely on foreign data and these broad Canadian surveys: obviously there are many very specific Canadian issues that need to be looked at within the Canadian context and which are best understood by way of more normal local studies. The apparently large increase in very serious violent youth crime that took place in the late 1980's in the United States (Cook and Laub 1998) but not in Canada serves to remind us of the problems of assuming that crime in one community can be understood by looking at another. But generally speaking, the factors that increase the likelihood that young people will be violent or which increase the likelihood that a youth will come in contact with a youth justice system are going to be similar in many countries.

The operation of the youth justice system

When one looks at the operation of the youth justice system, however, the situation is quite different. Many knowledgeable Canadians, including a couple of recent Ministers of Justice, have stated that Canada imprisons too many young people (see, for example, the Minister of Justice's *Strategy for a renewal of youth justice*, May 1998). Two policy questions arise out of such concerns: "How do we know what we think we know" and "What can we do about it?" It turns out that we know a lot about the youth justice system and, when we don't know the answer to a specific question, data often exist that would allow us to answer the question.

Looking at the "overuse of imprisonment," for example, we know that the 25,278 cases sent to custody in 1996-7 are not equitably distributed across provinces. A Quebec youth is much less likely to be sent to prison than is a youth from other provinces. Why is this? It appears to be largely (but not exclusively) a result of decisions not to bring youth into the youth justice system in the first place. But why does this happen? We do not know. Understanding variation like this is important, but the answers will not be found in official reports of court processing.

We still do have large numbers of kids given custodial sentences in Canada. It turns out that we know that seven offences(1) are responsible for about three quarters of the committals to custody for youth. And we know that, for minor offences, the real crime is to get caught twice or more: the likelihood of being imprisoned for a minor offence goes up dramatically as a youth accumulates a criminal record (Stevenson, Tufts, Hendrick, and Kowalski 1998: 53). We know that the majority of these sentences are very short and we havc data on why short sentences are sometimes combined with community service orders for some offences (Marinos 1998).

Canadian Centre for Justice Statistics (CCJS) data

Our information in these areas comes largely from the youth court data collected from the provinces by the CCJS. These data are extremely important for anyone interested in how Canada treats youths charged with offences. Detailed analyses of provincial variation or variation across offences can be carried out. These data are more or less complete from 1991-2 to the present. The challenge for researchers is to figure out how to use these data in an efficient and effective manner. Much of the information is published in the form of an annual Juristat and the full "youth court survey" publication (e.g., CCJS 1998). More detailed information is available, with costs, from what are often referred to as "shelf tables" – tables that are routinely produced but not published.

More importantly, for certain research purposes, are the specialized data sets which the people at CCJS have developed. These allow researchers to do more complex analyses of the data and yet, because they are not "individual record" data, can be made available to researchers without violating confidentiality agreements. There are some costs associated with the creation of these special data sets. My experience, however, is that the production costs are very reasonable but not necessarily low. Finally "special runs" – where the analysts at the CCJS produce specialized tables are typically produced very quickly to the researcher's specifications, though once again there are costs. The specialized data sets or special runs can allow for quite detailed analyses For example, Naomi Lee at the Department of Justice has examined the full detailed youth court histories of a group of young offenders from their first youth court appearance to age 18. Such data allow one to answer such questions as whether the disposition a young person receives at a particular age affects the likelihood of the youth reappearing in youth court at some later point in their lives.

The CCJS data are enormously useful and, given the level of expertise and cooperation that I have experienced, can be very helpful in understanding a wide range of issues in the youth justice system. But not all questions related to youth courts can be answered with these data. And access to the data for special purposes assumes that the researcher has funds to pay the costs. A charge of $40 per hour is reasonable but may be impossible for many researchers unless they have some form of external funding. These special data sets can be used to examine such matters as combinations of sanctions imposed on offenders or the impact of criminal record on youth court sentencing. For policy purposes they could be useful in defining who, under the new legislation for young offenders, might qualify as a "serious repeat" young offender.

Data gaps in official court data

But what if you want to know something more about some special group of cases. What if you need something beyond such characteristics as age, gender, criminal record, and what court they are in? There is almost no information about these offenders in the system. We can find out with a reasonable level of accuracy whether they have been in court before. But we cannot find out anything about race or ethnicity, economic situation, whether they were held in custody awaiting trial, or a range of other things. We can get a fair amount of information about cases that have actually been transferred to adult court for trials, but we cannot identify the cases where the Crown attempted to have a case transferred but where the transfer hearing was not successful. Hence, we do not know whether the small number of cases transferred each year (92 out of 110,065 cases in 1996-7) is due to few transfer applications being brought or youth court judges being reluctant to deem young people to be adults. Equally important, when a youth is transferred to adult court "and dealt with as an adult," we do not know what happens when they arrive in adult court. Do youths who are transferred receive sentences that could not be given in the youth system, or do they receive treatment that is available only in the adult system? We simply do not know.

Transfers are not the only gap in our knowledge. The youth justice *Strategy* released by the Minister of Justice in May 1998 suggested that too many youths are being brought to court rather than being dealt with informally outside of the court. Although we have some estimates of the number of youths dealt with informally (from the police statistics of "youths not charged"), these data are not published for very good reasons: nobody really knows what they mean. Some large police forces do not record "youths not charged" and some may include those under 12 years old in the category. Furthermore, we do not know much about pre- or post-charge use of alternative measures since such data are not systematically, at this point, collected. Given the legitimate concern about the over-use of the youth justice system, these gaps are unfortunate. But these gaps should be kept in perspective. Compared to the situation in the adult courts, the youth court data are very complete.(2)

Funding

Does this mean that we are in good shape as far as knowledge about youth crime and the youth justice system goes? Not at all. We have certain large sets of data. But the research community that is looking at these data in detail is very small. Furthermore, of course, there is no sustained research funding for work in this area, just as there is no sustained research funding for work in any other area of crime or criminal justice. The public may be concerned with "violence" or with "youth crime" or with the effects of certain kinds of interventions or programs. But, in general, other than the Social Science and Humanities Research Council (SSHRC), nobody funds – except on an ad hoc basis – work in this area. In other words, the independent university based researcher without funds from the SSHRC has almost nowhere to go – even to help pay for getting access to data that have cost hundreds of thousands of dollars to collect.

SSHRC is, of course, the only relatively predictable funding source for much of the work that is done in criminology. If federal funding of social sciences and the humanities were given a higher level of priority, this would not be too bad. But without any sustained funds from governments, it is unlikely that we will ever address the wide range of questions that SSHRC chooses not to fund. In a country that finds money enough to bring 1 in 36 young people to court (one or more times) each year and which finds enough money to impose a custodial sentence in 34% of cases each year at a cost of about $125-$250 per day per youth, it is remarkable that we do not know much about how this whole process affects the children it processes. But then priorities are always difficult to get right. Obviously other sources sometimes exist: we received funding from Operation Springboard, a community corrections organization in Ontario, for a province-wide survey of public attitudes relating to adult and youth crime (Doob, Sprott, Marinos, and Varma 1998). Without Springboard's funding, we simply could not have carried out the survey. At that particular point in time, I could not find any government department that was interested in understanding public views of youth (and adult) crime and justice. Of course the Department of Justice, Canada, does fund some research, though it appears to be focused on the immediate short term policy needs of the Department or on program evaluation rather than on the broad accumulation of knowledge and understanding of problems related to youth crime.

Conclusion

In the end, then, there are some contradictions. We have very good data in certain areas (largely those where we can depend on government budgets to collect the basic data). But we have no predictable funding other than SSHRC to get access to or to take advantage of these data. This would appear to ensure that the expensive data that are collected will be under-used. In other areas, we have knowledge based on studies done in Canada and in other countries. And, when there are questions that need to be answered with either small or large amounts of data collection, unless someone can convince a government department that it is in their immediate short-term interests to do the research, or unless a researcher has SSHRC funds for this purpose, or unless one is extraordinarily lucky in finding some other unusual source, the question will not be addressed.

Notes

1. Thefts, break-and-enters, mischief/vandalism, minor assaults, failure to comply with a disposition, failure to appear, possession of stolen property.
2. See Stevenson *et al.* (1998) for a sampling of the kind of information that is available on youth justice. A similar publication for adult crime could not be as complete.

References

Canadian Centre for Justice Statistics, Statistics Canada
1998 Youth Court Statistics: 1996-97. Ottawa: Statistics Canada.

Cook, Philip J. and John H. Laub
1998 The unprecedented epidemic in youth violence. In Michael Tonry and Mark H. Moore (eds.), Crime and Justice: A Review of Research. Volume 24. Chicago: University of Chicago Press.

Doob, Anthony N., Voula Marinos, and Kimberly N. Varma
1995 Youth Crime and the Youth Justice System in Canada: A Research Perspective. Toronto: Centre of Criminology, University of Toronto.

Doob, Anthony N., Jane B. Sprott, Voula Marinos, and Kimberly N. Varma
1998 An Exploration of Ontario Residents' Views of Crime and the Criminal Justice System. Toronto: Centre of Criminology, University of Toronto.

LeBlanc, Marc and Rolf Loeber
1998 Developmental criminology updated. In Michael Tonry (ed.), Crime and Justice: A Review of Research. Volume 23. Chicago: University of Chicago Press.

Marinos, Voula
1998 What's intermediate about "intermediate" sanctions? The case of young offender dispositions in Canada. Canadian Journal of Criminology 40(4): 355-376.

Stevenson, Kathryn, Jennifer Tufts, Dianne Hendrick, and Melanie Kowalski
1998 A Profile of Youth Justice in Canada. Ottawa: Canadian Centre for Justice Statistics, Statistics Canada.

Tremblay, Richard E. and Wendy M. Craig
1995 Developmental crime prevention. In Michael Tonry and David P. Farrington (eds.), Building a Safer Society: Strategic Approaches to Crime Prevention [Crime and Justice: A Review of Research. Volume 19]. Chicago: University of Chicago Press.

CHAPTER TWO

Changes in police charging of young offenders in Ontario and Saskatchewan after 1984[1]

Peter J. Carrington
University of Waterloo
Waterloo, Ontario

CARRINGTON AND MOYER (1994) ANALYSED PER CAPITA RATES OF young offenders apprehended and charged in Canada from 1980 to 1990, and found that the proportion of apprehended youth who were charged (the "charge ratio") increased from 53 percent during the last 4 years of the *Juvenile Delinquents Act* (1980 to 1983) to 64 percent in the first six years of the *Young Offenders Act* (1985 to 1990). This increase was confined to seven of the eight provinces and territories in which the Uniform Maximum Age (UMA) provision of the YOA caused 16- and 17-year-olds to be added to the jurisdiction of the youth justice system.[2] In the other 4 provinces – Quebec and Manitoba, in which 16- and 17-year-olds were already under the jurisdiction of the JDA, and Newfoundland and British Columbia, in which only 17-year-olds were added by UMA – there was no significant difference between the pre- and post-YOA periods in the proportion of accused youth who were charged. After testing and rejecting other possible explanations for this change, they suggested that it could have been due to the addition of 16- and 17-year-olds to the jurisdiction of youth justice in these provinces: that police were continuing to charge relatively low proportions of 12- to 15-year-olds, as they did under the JDA, but were charging 16- and 17-year-olds in higher proportions, which resulted in higher overall proportions

Canadian Journal of Criminology/Revue canadienne de criminologie, April/avril 1998, pp. 153–164.

of apprehended young offenders who were charged. This hypothesis implies the tantalizing possibility that police might not have changed their charging practices at all after 1984, but that the observed higher proportion of apprehended youths who were charged could have been an artifact of the re-definition of 16- and 17-year-olds as young offenders, with the resulting importation of their hypothesized pre-existing higher charge ratios into young offender statistics after 1984.

The Carrington and Moyer hypothesis rests on three assumptions concerning charging of young offender accused in the seven provinces experiencing an increase in proportion charged after 1984:

- that 12- to 15-year-olds apprehended by police continued to be charged in approximately the same proportions as under the JDA,
- that 16- and 17-year-olds who were apprehended were charged after (and possibly before) 1984 in substantially higher proportions than 12- to 15-year-olds, and
- that the numbers of 16- and 17-year-old youth apprehended after 1984 were sufficiently large relative to the numbers of 12- to 15-year-olds apprehended that their hypothesized higher charge ratios could offset the lower charge ratios of 12- to 15-year-olds.

Data

None of these assumptions could be tested when Carrington and Moyer did their research, because the UCR Survey did not capture the age of offenders. In the late 1980's, the Canadian Centre for Justice Statistics began phasing in a "Revised" UCR Survey that does capture the age of apprehended persons. By 1995, police forces with caseloads representing almost half (47 percent) of reported crime in Canada, distributed over 6 provinces, were reporting to the Revised UCR Survey. Data from the Revised UCR Survey for 1995 are analysed here to test the Carrington and Moyer hypothesis.

Of course, data for 1995 cannot tell us what was happening during 1985 to 1990. Furthermore, data from the UCR are generally believed to be unreliable as a basis for comparisons across jurisdictions, because of variations in police administrative practices that affect their reports to the UCR (Hackler and Paranjape 1983), and doubts have been raised as to whether changes over time in UCR crime rates within jurisdictions are due to real changes in crime rates, or rather to changes in police strength and/or police reporting practices (Kennedy and Veitch 1997; O'Brien 1996; Marvell and Moody 1996). On the other hand, it is reasonable to presume that UCR data are reliable enough for comparisons over time of certain phenomena within the same jurisdiction (Silverman and Teevan 1986; Carrington and Moyer 1994), and we believe that the ratio of young persons charged to young persons apprehended, and the relationship of this ratio to the age of the accused, are among these phenomena. At the very least, these data can tell us whether higher charge ratios for 16- and 17-year-olds can explain the difference between overall charge ratios for young offenders apprehended in 1995, and those in the last years under the JDA.

Of the seven provinces and territories that experienced substantial increases in police charging of young offenders after 1984, only Ontario and Saskatchewan were covered sufficiently by the Revised UCR of 1995 to be analysed here.[3] Can much be learned by looking at only two of seven jurisdictions? On the one hand, it is a truism that Canada has not one, but twelve, youth justice systems – even after the *Young Offenders Act* came into effect. With respect to police charging, we know, for example, that in three provinces – New Brunswick, Quebec, and British Columbia – the decision to charge young offenders is made not by the police, but by the Crown on the advice of the police. In Quebec, this is complicated by the provisions of the *Youth Protection Act* of 1979, particularly the role of the Youth Protection Director. Provincial variations affect the meaning of UCR statistics: in New Brunswick and Quebec, police adjust their records concerning clearance of an incident after the Crown decides whether charges will be laid, so UCR data for these provinces reflect both police and Crown decision-making. In British Columbia, police report persons as charged in the UCR returns on the basis of the police recommendation to charge, regardless of the eventual Crown decision (Canadian Centre for Justice Statistics 1994). The Metropolitan Toronto police include very few suspects who are not charged in their counts of "(young) persons apprehended": so their reported charge ratio is close to 100 percent (Carrington 1996). The police officer's decision to "write up" an incident that does not result in charges is highly discretionary (Ericson 1982), and this discretion is probably exercised in widely varying ways in different Canadian police forces, with significant implications for the comparability of UCR statistics on "young persons apprehended".

On the other hand, Ontario and Saskatchewan together represent approximately 75 percent by volume (67 percent for Ontario and 8 percent for Saskatchewan) of all crime reported by police in the seven provinces and territories in which we are interested (Hendrick 1996: Table 7). Thus, understanding what happened in Ontario goes a long way towards understanding what happened in the aggregate of these seven provinces – even if the other provinces turn out to be quite different from Ontario – simply on the basis of Ontario's numerical preponderance. Furthermore, these two provinces experienced the most extreme manifestation of the phenomenon we are investigating, the increase in police charging of young offenders after 1984: in Ontario, the average charge ratio almost doubled from 32 percent during 1980 to 1984 to 58 percent during 1985 to 1990; in Saskatchewan, it more than doubled, from 25 percent for 1980 to 1984 to 61 percent for the period 1985 to 1990, and had reached 82 percent (in our sample of Saskatchewan communities) by 1995 (Table 1).

Police forces responsible for about 50 percent of reported crime in Ontario and 48 percent in Saskatchewan reported to the Revised UCR in 1995.[4] Data from the Metropolitan Toronto police could not be used in this analysis, because they omit from their UCR returns most young persons who are

Table 1
Proportion of apprehended youth charged, by age, Ontario and Saskatchewan

Period	Age	Ontario			Saskatchewan		
		Number apprehended[1]	Age group as a percentage of total apprehended	Percent charged	Number apprehended[1]	Age group as a percentage of total apprehended	Percent charged
1980-84[2]	12-15	8320	100.0	31.6	9604	100.0	25.2
1985-90[2]	12-17	8316	100.0	58.0	13764	100.0	60.9
1995[3]	12-17	28964	100.0	58.3	8651	100.0	82.2
1995[3]	12	1537	5.3	34.9	574	6.6	58.9
	13	2756	9.5	47.2	928	10.7	68.8
	14	4282	14.8	55.0	1476	17.1	77.8
	15	6057	20.9	58.1	1663	19.2	84.1
	16	7231	25.0	61.3	1972	22.8	87.8
	17	7101	24.5	66.7	2038	23.6	91.1
	12-15	14632	50.5	52.7	4641	53.6	75.9
	16-17	14332	49.5	63.9	4010	46.4	89.5

1 For 1980-84 and 1985-90, this is the mean rate per 100,000 for the entire province; for 1995, it is the actual number apprehended in the sampled jurisdictions.
2 Source: Carrington and Moyer (1994), Table 1.
3 Source: Revised UCR Survey, Canadian Centre for Justice Statistics.

apprehended but not charged. This reduces the coverage of Ontario in our analysis to approximately 36 percent.

Results

The third assumption listed above is essentially correct for both Ontario and Saskatchewan: in both provinces[5] in 1995, 16- and 17-year-olds made up approximately half of young offenders apprehended by police (Table 1).

The second assumption – the crux of the Carrington and Moyer hypothesis – that 16- and 17-year-olds apprehended by police were and are charged in substantially higher proportions than 12- to 15-year-olds, is only weakly supported in both provinces. Table 1 shows that in Ontario, the charge ratio for 16- and 17-year-olds in 1995 was 11 percent higher than for 12- to 15-year-olds, and "pulled up" the overall charge ratio for young offenders by 5 percent; in Saskatchewan, it was 13 percent higher and "pulled up" the overall charge ratio for young offenders by 6 percent (Table 1 and Figures 1 and 2).

Finally, the first assumption – that charge ratios for 12- to 15-year-olds remained fairly constant after the YOA came into force – is clearly incorrect for both provinces. In Ontario, 32 percent of 12- to 15-year-olds who were apprehended by police during 1980 to 1984 were charged; this had increased by 1995 to 53 percent (Table 1). In Saskatchewan, the charge ratio for 12- to 15-year-olds was 25 percent in 1980 to 1984 and 76 percent in 1995. The differences between the hypothesized and observed distributions by age group of charge ratios can be seen in Figures 1 and 2.

Discussion

These age-specific police-reported data for parts of Ontario and Saskatchewan in 1995 show that the increase after 1985 in the proportions of apprehended young offenders who were charged cannot be entirely explained by the higher charge ratios applicable to the 16- and 17-year-olds who were added to the jurisdiction of the youth justice system in 1985 by the

Figure 1
Observed charge ratios in Ontario, and the charge ratios expected under the Carrington and Moyer hypothesis

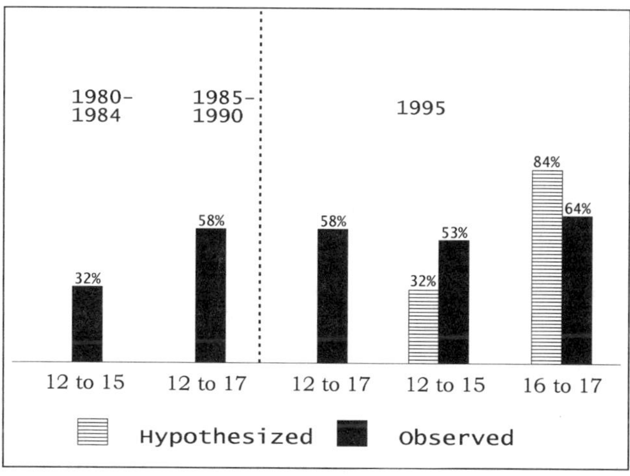

Sources: Carrington and Moyer (1994) for observed charge ratios in 1980-84 and 1985-90; Revised UCR Survey, Canadian Centre for Justice Statistics, for 1995 observed charge ratios

Figure 2
Observed charge ratios in Saskatchewan, and the charge ratios expected under the Carrington and Moyer hypothesis

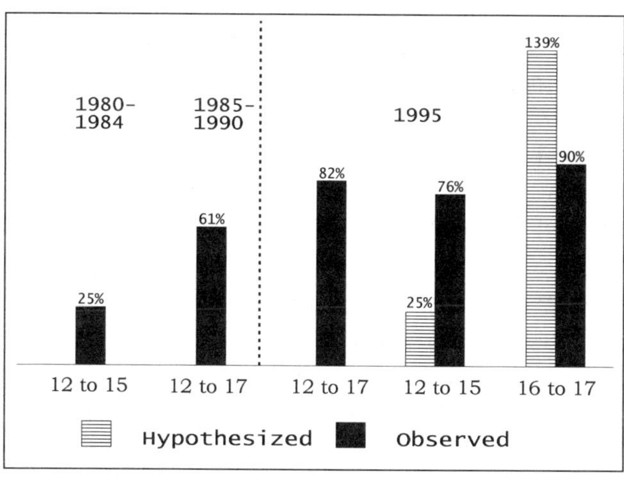

Sources: Carrington and Moyer (1994) for observed charge ratios in 1980-84 and 1985-90; Revised UCR Survey, Canadian Centre for Justice Statistics, for 1995 observed charge ratios.

UMA provision of the YOA. Rather, the increase in charge ratios can bc broken down into two components: part of the increase was due to the increase in the proportion of apprehended 12- to 15-year-olds who were charged, and part was due to the addition of 16- and 17-year-olds, who were charged in higher proportions than 12- to 15-year-olds.

A rough estimate of the relative importance of each of these components, based on our samples for Ontario and Saskatchewan, is developed in Table 2. Imagine that in the Ontario sample, the charge ratio for all apprehended young offenders in 1995 had been the same as the average level for 12- to 15-year-olds during 1980 to 1984: 31.6 percent. Now contrast that with the actual charge ratios for 1995: 52.7 percent for 12- to 15-year-olds, and 63.9 percent for 16- and 17-year-olds. The differences are 21.1 percent for the former group, and 32.3 percent for the latter. For the entire 12- to 17-year-old group, the difference between the actual 1995 charge ratio (58.3 percent) and the 1980-84 charge ratio for 12- to 15-year-olds (31.6 percent) is 26.7 percent. Multiplying these differences in charge ratios by the number in each age group who were apprehended in 1995, we find that, of the difference between the number of young persons actually charged and the number that would have been charged if conditions had remained the same as in 1980 to 1984, 40 percent was due to increased charging of apprehended 12- to 15-year-olds, and 60 percent was due to the addition of 16- and 17-year-olds. In Saskatchewan, increased charging of 12- to 15-year-olds accounted for 48 percent of the increase in charge ratio, and the addition of 16- and 17-year-olds accounted for the other 52 percent.

In summary, we can conclude that about half of the increase from 1980-84 to 1995 in police charging of apprehended young persons in Ontario and Saskatchewan was due to the higher charge ratios for 16- and 17-year-olds; and that about half was due to increased charging of 12- to 15-year-olds. It should be emphasized that we cannot determine to what extent the higher observed charge ratios for 16- and 17-year-olds were "pre-existing" (i.e., existed prior to 1985),

Table 2
Breakdown by age group of the increase from 1980-84 to 1995 in charge ratios, Ontario and Saskatchewan (selected police forces)

	Ontario			Saskatchewan		
	12-15 years	16-17 years	Total	12-15 years	16-17 years	Total
Number apprehended, 1995	14632	14332	28964	4641	4010	8651
Charge ratio, 1995	52.7%	63.9%	58.3%	75.9%	89.5%	82.2%
1980-84 charge ratio for 12- to 15-year-olds	31.6%	31.6%[1]	31.6%	25.2%	25.2%[1]	25.2%
Difference between 1995 and 1980-84 charge ratios	+21.1%	+32.3%	+26.7%	+50.7%	+64.3%	+57.0%
Proportion of difference[2]	40%	60%	100%	48%	52%	100%

Source: Revised UCR Survey, Canadian Centre for Justice Statistics.

1 Of course, the actual charge ratio for 16- and 17-year-olds in 1980-84 is unknown; here it is set to the ratio for 12- to 15-year-olds, in order to estimate the impact of adding these 16- and 17-year-olds to the 12- to 15-year-olds, whose charge ratio in 1980-84 is known.
2 Using 12- to 15-year-olds in Ontario as an example, the calculation is: (.211*14632)/(.267*28964) = .399.

and to what extent they, like the charge ratios for 12- to 15-year olds, increased after 1984 – because we have no data on charge ratios for 16- and 17-year-olds prior to 1985. For example, charge ratios for 16- and 17-year-olds in Ontario during 1980 to 1984 could conceivably have been as high as 64 percent (their level in 1995) or as low as 32 percent (the level for 12- to 15-year-olds during 1980 to 1984).

Thus, we are justified only in concluding that somewhere between none and about half of the increase in Ontario and Saskatchewan in observed charge ratios for apprehended young offenders can be explained by the continuation of a possibly pre-existing police practice of charging 16- and 17-year-olds in higher proportions than 12- to 15-year-olds; and somewhere between about half and all of the observed increase was due to an actual change in police charging practices, namely an actual increase in the charging of apprehended young persons (of all ages). The reasons for this increase in police charging remain unknown, although researchers have suggested that the increased procedural formality under the YOA (Moyer 1996: 21) or the need to lay charges in order to make young persons eligible for post-charge alternative measures programmes in Ontario (John Howard Society 1994), may have played a role.

Notes

1. This is a revised version of an argument which I first made, using data for 1992 and 1993, as part of research performed under contract to the Department of Justice Canada (Carrington 1996: 148-152). Preparation of this paper was supported by Social Sciences and Humanities Research Council Research Grant No. 410-95-0661. I gratefully acknowledge the assistance of Peter Greenberg and Alison Scott of the Canadian Centre for Justice Statistics, who prepared the data from the 1995 Incident-Based UCR Survey that are reported here; and the helpful comments of an anonymous referee.
2. There was no change in the charge ratio in the eighth province, New Brunswick.
3. Although Alberta was covered by the Revised UCR in 1995, this coverage was concentrated in the two largest cities – Calgary and Edmonton – which were evidently not representative of the province as a whole with respect to police practices, since 81 percent of apprehended youth were charged in these two cities, compared with 69 percent in the province as a whole. Police forces in the other four

jurisdictions of interest – Prince Edward Island, Nova Scotia, Yukon and Northwest Territories – were not yet reporting to the revised UCR in 1995.

4. Unless otherwise noted, statistics from the Revised UCR Survey were calculated by the author from tabulations specially prepared by the Canadian Centre for Justice Statistics.
5. Unless otherwise noted, "Ontario" and "Saskatchewan" refer hereafter to the parts of these provinces covered by the 1995 Revised UCR Survey, excluding Metropolitan Toronto.

References

Canadian Centre for Justice Statistics
1994 Canadian Crime Statistics 1993. Catalogue No. 85-205. Ottawa: Canadian Centre for Justice Statistics, Statistics Canada.

Carrington, Peter J.
1996 Age and Youth Crime in Canada. Working Document No. 1996-1E. Ottawa: Department of Justice Canada.

Carrington, Peter J. and Sharon Moyer
1994 Trends in youth crime and police response, pre- and post-YOA. Canadian Journal of Criminology 36(1): 1-28.

Ericson, Richard V.
1982 Reproducing Order: A Study of Police Patrol Work. Toronto: University of Toronto Press.

Hackler, Jim and Wasanti Paranjape
1983 Juvenile justice statistics: Mythmaking or measure of system response? Canadian Journal of Criminology 25(2): 209-226.

Hendrick, Diane
1996 Canadian Crime Statistics 1995. Juristat. Vol. 16 No. 10. Catalogue No. 85-002-XPE. Ottawa: Canadian Centre for Justice Statistics, Statistics Canada.

John Howard Society of Ontario
1994 Youth Crime: Sorting fact from fiction. Fact Sheet #3. Toronto: The John Howard Society of Ontario.

Kennedy, Leslie W. and David Veitch
1997 Why are crime rates going down? A case study in Edmonton. Canadian Journal of Criminology 39(1): 51-69.

Marvell, Thomas B. and Carlisle E. Moody
1996 Specification problems, police levels, and crime rates. Criminology 34: 609-646.

Moyer, Sharon
1996 A Profile of the Juvenile Justice System in Canada. Report to the Federal-Provincial-Territorial Task Force on Youth Justice. Ottawa: Department of Justice Canada.

O'Brien, Robert M.
1996 Police productivity and crime rates: 1973-1992. Criminology 34: 183-207.

Silverman, Robert A. and James J. Teevan, Jr.
1986 Crime in Canadian Society. 3rd ed. Toronto: Butterworths.

CHAPTER THREE

Trends in youth crime in Canada, 1977-1996[1]

Peter J. Carrington
University of Waterloo
Waterloo, Ontario

IN 1991, POLICE-REPORTED YOUTH CRIME IN CANADA REACHED THE highest level ever recorded. This peak followed increases in five of the six years since the *Young Offenders Act* came into force in 1985. Not surprisingly, the long climb from 1985 to 1991 in the level of youth crime, immediately following the inception of the YOA, aroused considerable adverse comment in the media, and contributed to public disenchantment with the YOA (Corrado and Markwart 1992: 160-163; Bala 1994: 248-251; Hylton 1994: 236-239; Task Force on Youth Justice 1996: 14-19). By 1996, the rate of youth crime had returned to the same level as in 1983, prior to the YOA, after falling for four of the five years since 1991; this decrease seems to have received less public attention.

Although scholarly commentators did not attribute the rise in youth crime to the YOA, it did occasion debate about the extent to which youth crime was increasing, and the extent to which its level exceeded that under the *Juvenile Delinquents Act.* Answers to these questions were conditioned by the range of years selected for study by researchers, although most writers cautioned that insufficient time had elapsed since the inception of the YOA to draw definite conclusions about post-YOA trends.

More than a decade has now elapsed since the YOA came into effect. At the time of writing (August, 1998), the federal

Canadian Journal of Criminology/Revue canadienne de criminologie, January/janvier 1999, pp. 1–32.

government is once more considering changes to the Canadian youth justice system in response to public concern about youth crime (Department of Justice Canada n.d. [1998]). This is therefore an opportune time to review the fluctuations in youth crime over the past twenty years, and to assess the change, if any, in its post-YOA level, and the extent to which any change that has occurred is due to the YOA.

Previous research

Has the level of youth crime in Canada increased since 1984?

Carrington and Moyer (1994: 8-11) compared quarterly data from the Uniform Crime Reporting (UCR) Survey on rates of young persons apprehended and charged for the periods 1980-84 (under the JDA) and 1985-90 (under the YOA),(2) and concluded that the average per capita rate of police-reported youth crime(3) during 1985-90 was the same as during 1980-84, but that the average rate of young persons *charged* was 21 percent higher in the post-YOA period. They also noted that there was no upward or downward trend in either rate during 1980-84, but that there appeared to be slight upward trends, which were not statistically significant, in both rates during 1985-90, especially during 1989-90.

Corrado and Markwart (1994: 350-51) concluded from analysis of annual UCR data on young persons charged with *Criminal Code* offences from 1986 to 1992 that there was a "relatively modest 25 percent increase" over the period. Comparing annual UCR data for 1986-92 with 1980-83, Carrington (1995: 63-64) found a statistically non-significant increase of 5 percent in the per capita rate of young persons apprehended, and an increase of 29 percent in the rate of young persons charged. He also reported an apparent upward trend in both rates from 1986 to 1992, which he said required further data for confirmation. Markwart and Corrado (1995: 77-79) compared UCR data on rates of young persons apprehended during 1990-93 and 1980-83, and found a 10 percent increase.

They estimated that, after correcting for inflation in the per capita rates for 1980-83, the post-YOA increase was "more likely in the range of 20%". Using annual UCR data for 1980 to 1993, Moyer (1996: 16) noted a "steady climb" in rates of young persons apprehended and charged from 1986 to a peak in 1991, followed by declines in 1992 and 1993. Comparing the level in 1993 with the average level in 1980-83, she reported an increase of 5 percent in the rate of young persons apprehended and of 32 percent in the rate of young persons charged.

In summary, there is agreement that the per capita rate of young persons charged has increased significantly since the inception of the YOA, but disagreement as to the size and interpretation of the change, if any, in the per capita rate of young persons apprehended.

What has caused the increase, if any, in youth crime? Is it the YOA?

After comparing the 1985-90 period with 1980-84, Carrington and Moyer (1994) concluded that the observed increase in the per capita rate of young persons charged with offences reflected a change in the police propensity to charge young persons, rather than in the criminal behaviour of young persons, since the average rate of young persons *apprehended* by police did not change. Furthermore, they speculated that this change in police propensity to charge young persons might be statistical rather than "real": that is, that it might reflect a change in statistical categories rather than in police behaviour. After examining this phenomenon on a province-by-province basis, they suggested that the observed post-YOA increase in police charging could be due to a possibly pre-existing practice of charging 16- and 17-year-old suspects in higher proportions than 12- to 15-year-olds; when these 16- and 17-year-olds were added, in many provinces, to the youth justice system and, therefore, the statistics on youth crime by the Uniform Maximum Age provision of the YOA, the average per capita rate of young persons charged would increase: more "young persons" per capita would be charged (although no more people would actually be charged), due to the legal redefinition of 16- and 17-year-olds as "young persons". Carrington (1998) analysed age-specific data for Ontario and Saskatchewan and concluded that a substantial part – between one-half and all – of the observed increase in police charging of young offenders in at least those two provinces is not a statistical artifact, and reflects a change in actual police behaviour.

None of these writers attributes the observed changes in youth crime since 1985 to the effect of the YOA on the criminal behaviour of young persons. DuWors (1997) and Kong (1997) note that peaks in the early 1990s in overall police-reported crime in Canada are mirrored by similar trends in other countries. As Markwart and Corrado (1995: 84) put it,

> ...the international evidence seems quite clear that crime control changes in law alone will not have any significant effect on youth crime rates, changes to which, of course, arise as a result of far broader social factors...

The present study

The logic of this study is that of the interrupted time series experiment. It attempts to detect the effects, if any, of the YOA on youth crime by comparing the level and direction of time series of crime data before and after the legislation came into effect. This "natural experiment" has serious weaknesses as a design for establishing cause-and-effect (Cook and Campbell 1979). In order to attribute any observed changes to the YOA, it is necessary to rule out other possible causes and to establish a plausible conceptual connection with the YOA. This can never be done with certainty. Nevertheless, we believe that a *prima facie* case for an effect of the YOA can be made on the basis of evidence of sudden changes occurring immediately after 1985 which cannot be attributed to other events. More gradual changes during the period are more likely to be due to the "broader social factors" referred to in the quotation above.

The analyses presented here are based on annual UCR data on young persons apprehended and charged during 1977 to 1996, omitting 1984-85.[4] Differences in average levels under the YOA and the JDA were tested for statistical significance using t-tests, in order not to attribute significance to results that could well be due to random year-to-year fluctuations. Trends over time were estimated by regressing the annual rate per 100,000 on the year, separately for the JDA and YOA periods.

Data from the UCR Survey cannot be taken at face value as an indicator of the level of youth crime.[5] The UCR Survey collects its data from police forces, and is therefore limited to criminal activity known to police and considered by police to be worth recording. Furthermore, counts of young persons implicated and charged in connection with criminal incidents, which are used in the present study, are necessarily limited to incidents which have been "cleared": that is, to incidents in which the offender(s) have been identified, or "apprehended", by police. Thus, the very substantial number of incidents that are known to and recorded by police, but not cleared, are omitted: in 1996, for example, only about 38 percent of incidents known to police in Canada were cleared.

The UCR Survey reports counts of both "young persons charged" and "young persons not charged". Counts of "young persons charged" are probably a very accurate indicator of *the charging* of young persons, since the laying of charges is an official act which must be carefully recorded as the first step in court process.[6] As an indicator of the amount of youth crime, it has the major disadvantage of omitting the substantial number of persons – especially young persons – who are apprehended but not charged: that is, levels of "young persons charged" reflect both criminal activity by young persons (and its detection and recording by police) and the exercise of police discretion to charge or to deal with the apprehended youth by other means.[7] Thus, changes in numbers of young persons charged may confound changes in youth crime with changes in police charging practices. The analyses presented below show that the use of "young persons charged" as an indicator of youth crime (which is a common practice) would lead to seriously erroneous conclusions concerning changes in the level of youth crime after the YOA came into effect. Therefore, in this study, "young persons charged" is interpreted as precisely that: an indicator of the charging of young persons by police.

For an indicator of changes over time in the amount of youth crime, this study uses UCR data on "young persons apprehended" – that is, the sum of police-reported "young persons charged" and "young persons not charged". Numbers of young persons apprehended are a more valid indicator of changes in the level of youth crime than numbers of young persons charged, since they are not filtered by the decision to charge, but they are less reliable – that is, consistent – because the criteria for classifying a person as "[apprehended but] not charged" are much less precise than for "charged", and vary considerably among police forces reporting to the UCR (Hackler and Paranjape 1983; 1984).[(8)] Data on young persons apprehended (and, *a fortiori*, on young persons charged) also systematically underestimate the amount of youth crime known to the police, because police tend to under-report minor incidents involving young persons (Doob and Chan 1982).[(9)]

On the other hand, UCR data are probably reliable enough to be useful for certain purposes. After reviewing research on the production, interpretation, and reliability of police crime statistics, Scanlon (1986: 94-95) concludes:

> ...Despite these serious limitations, which are associated with the crime *rates* for any given year, official crime *trends* may accurately reflect relative changes in crime over time. Finally, while differences in crime rates between police jurisdictions may be confounded to an unknown extent by differences in levels of police activity and reporting procedures, there is some empirical evidence to suggest that regional comparisons may be valid.

In this study, UCR data are used primarily to trace trends over time, and to compare changes over time across regions.

In order to make meaningful comparisons of levels of crime over time or across jurisdictions, population-standardized rates such as the rate per 100,000 population must be used. This is a difficult problem in the comparison of youth crime during the periods under the JDA and the YOA, because the populations defined as "juveniles" under the JDA and as "young persons" under the YOA differ. The age jurisdiction of the YOA is 12 to 17 years inclusive, everywhere in Canada. The age jurisdiction of the juvenile courts under the JDA varied by province: 7 to 17 years inclusive in Quebec and Manitoba, 7 to 16 years in Newfoundland and British Columbia, and 7 to 15 years in the other provinces and the territories.(10)

One obvious approach to defining youth crime and the corresponding populations would be to use the legal definitions given above: that is, to compare the number of persons apprehended or charged by police who were aged 7 to 15 (or 16 or 17, depending on the province) during the JDA period with the number aged 12 to 17 during the YOA period. This results in the technically correct but rather spurious conclusion that there was a huge jump in youth crime after the YOA came into effect: the jump in the population standardized rate is due to the inclusion of the very low crime rates of 7- to 11-year-olds in the rates for the JDA period, and the inclusion of the relatively high crime rates of 16- and 17-year-olds in the rates for the YOA period.(11)

To avoid this artificial jump in rates, Carrington and Moyer (1994; Carrington 1995; Moyer 1996) excluded -7 to 11-year-olds from the populations which they used to standardize their juvenile crime data for the JDA period. They justified this procedure by arguing that, in practice, few children under 12 were charged under the JDA: in other words, since these children were largely omitted from the numbers of juvenile offenders (the numerator in the calculation of the population-standardized rate), they should also be omitted from the standardizing populations (the denominator in the rate calculation). This procedure resulted in estimated juvenile crime rates under the JDA that were remarkably similar in level to those under the YOA. As Markwart and Corrado (1995: 77-79) pointed out, while Carrington and Moyer were able to eliminate children under 12 from the standardizing population estimates, because Statistics Canada publishes age-specific population data, they could not eliminate them from their juvenile crime data, since the UCR data are not age-specific. This resulted in inflation of their population-standardized juvenile crime rates under the JDA, and, therefore, under-estimation of increases under the YOA. This inflation would be more acute in data on juveniles apprehended than on juveniles charged, since many more children under 12 were probably apprehended than charged under the JDA.

One solution to this problem, which Markwart and Corrado adopted in order to evaluate Carrington and Moyer's findings, is to estimate the number of children under 12 included in the UCR data on young persons apprehended and charged for the JDA period, and adjust the calculated rates downward to offset the resulting inflation. This is easier in the case of data on children charged than on children apprehended, since age-specific data are available from Statistics Canada's publication *Juvenile Court Statistics* for persons appearing in juvenile court before 1984. According to Bala and Mahoney (1994: 12), in 1983 "just under 2% of all J.D.A. charges against juveniles were laid against children ages 7 to 11". Bala and Corrado (1985: 17-19 and note 21) report that some provinces had statutory or policy restrictions on charging children under 12 or under 14, which resulted in very low charge rates: for example, in 1981, only 3 children under 12 were charged in Quebec, only 53 in Manitoba, and only 110 in Alberta, out of a total of 24,406 juveniles charged in those provinces.

No such data are available for children *apprehended* during the JDA period. One source of age-specific data on apprehended youth is the Revised, or Incident-Based, Uniform Crime Reporting Survey: a new annual census of police-reported crime in Canada, which captures detailed information on criminal incidents, including the age of the accused. The Revised UCR was initiated in 1988 with reporting by only a few police forces, and continues to increase its coverage each year. The numbers in Table 1 are taken from a summary by DuWors (1992: 3) of the sample of apprehended persons in the Revised UCR Survey for 1988-92, and suggest that children aged 7 to 11 years constituted about 5 percent of apprehended youth under 18.[(12)] The estimate of 5.3 percent shown in the table is slightly inflated by the inclusion of accused under 7 years old.

Table 1
Numbers and percentages of persons apprehended by police, by age group, police forces reporting to the Revised UCR Survey, 1988-92

Age of the accused	Number	% of accused under 18	% of total
Under 12 years	4,757	5.3	1.2
12 to 17 years	84,701	94.7	20.8
Subtotal under 18 years	89,458	100.0	22.0
18 years and older	317,194		78.0
Total	406,662		100.0

Source: DuWors (1992: 3), based on data from the Revised UCR Survey.

This estimate is corroborated by a sample of apprehended persons from the Incident-Based UCR Survey, obtained by the author from the Canadian Centre for Justice Statistics. This sample includes all accused reported by police forces participating in the Revised UCR Survey in 1992 and 1993 – covering parts of five provinces and about one-third of all police-reported crime in Canada in those years. Table 2 shows that children aged 7 to 11 made up 4.5 percent of accused aged 7 to 17 in this sample.

The inflation of per capita rates of juvenile crime for the JDA period which was caused by inclusion of accused aged 7 to 11 years would actually have been somewhat greater than the 5 percent suggested by Tables 1 and 2, since the numbers

Table 2
Numbers and percentages of persons apprehended by police, by age group, police forces reporting to the Revised UCR Survey, 1992-93

Age of the accused	Number	% of accused aged 7-17	% of total
7 to 11 years	5,510	4.5	0.8
12 to 17 years	117,456	95.5	17.4
Subtotal 7 to 17 years	122,966	100.0	18.2
Under 7 years	315		0.0
18 years and older	550,929		81.7
Total	674,210		100.0

Source: tabulations supplied by the Canadian Centre for Justice Statistics.

of young offenders shown in those tables include accused aged 16 and 17 years, who were excluded from the jurisdiction of the JDA, and, therefore, from the UCR counts of apprehended juveniles, in most provinces (Markwart and Corrado 1995: 76). Therefore, the estimate of inflation has been further adjusted in Table 3, which uses the same definition of "juvenile" as that used by each province and, therefore, by the UCR Survey, prior to 1984.

Overall, 7- to 11-year-olds made up 6 percent of accused in this sample in the age groups which would have been under the jurisdiction of the JDA. One would expect the proportion of juveniles 7- to 11-years-old to be least in Quebec, since it treated persons as old as 17 years as juveniles, and to be highest in those provinces with the lowest maximum age of jurisdiction: New Brunswick, Ontario, and Saskatchewan. In fact, the proportions vary considerably, and are, contrary to expectations, above average in Quebec and below average in Ontario and New Brunswick.

This sample is not nationally representative, since it includes only parts of five provinces, and is strongly skewed toward Quebec, which makes up approximately 60 percent of apprehended youth in the sample, but only about 15 percent of apprehended youth in Canada in 1992-93 (Carrington 1996: Table III.1). The numbers in Table 3 can be adjusted to simulate a national census of youth crime by making the further, somewhat tenuous, assumption that the sample from Quebec is representative of all youth crime in provinces with an age limit under the JDA of 17 (that is, all of Quebec and Manitoba), and that the samples from British Columbia and from the other three provinces are representative of youth crime in all provinces and territories with JDA age limits of 16 and 15 respectively. This is done in Table 4. The result suggests that children aged 7 to 11 would constitute 5.3 percent of a national sample of "juvenile" offenders in 1992-93, using the provincially-specific definitions of "juvenile" which were in

Table 3
Numbers and percentages of apprehended persons aged 7 years to the provincial maximum age of jurisdiction of the JDA, by province, police forces reporting to the Revised UCR Survey, 1992-93

		Age of the accused				
		7 to 11 years		12 years to the JDA maximum age		
Province*	Age limits	Number	%	Number	%	Total
New Brunswick	7 - 15	25	4.0	600	96.0	625
Ontario	7 - 15	844	3.5	23,257	96.5	24,101
Saskatchewan	7 - 15	909	10.1	8,121	89.9	9,030
British Columbia	7 - 16	115	3.7	3,023	96.3	3,138
Quebec	7 - 17	3,617	6.6	51,584	93.4	55,201
Total		5,510	6.0	86,585	94.0	92,095

* Note: does not include all police forces in each province.

Source: tabulations supplied by the Canadian Centre for Justice Statistics.

Table 4
Simulated national numbers and percentages of apprehended persons aged 7 years to the provincial maximum age of jurisdiction of the JDA, 1992-93

		Age of the accused				
		7 to 11 years		12 years to the JDA maximum age		
Provinces/ territories	Age limits	Number	%	Number	%	Total
Quebec, Manitoba	7 - 17	5,414	6.6	77,207	93.4	82,621
B.C., Newfoundland	7 - 16	2,144	3.7	56,353	96.3	58,497
All others	7 - 15	12,894	5.3	231,910	94.7	244,804
Canada		20,452	5.3	365,470	94.7	385,922

Source: Table 3 above and Carrington (1996: Table III.1).

effect under the JDA and which determined the classification of accused persons in the UCR Survey during the JDA period.

In summary, this attempt to develop a method to adjust the estimated rates per 100,000 of juveniles apprehended during 1977-83 to make them more comparable with rates under the YOA rests on the assumption that the proportions of 7- to 11-year-olds reported as apprehended by police forces participating in the Revised UCR during 1988 to 1995 were similar to those of 7- to 11-year-olds in the UCR Surveys of 1977 to 1983. If that is true, then to exclude 7- to 11-year-olds from the numbers of apprehended juveniles in the UCR for 1977-83, one should adjust the numbers downward by 5.3 percent. Juvenile court statistics suggest that rates of juveniles *charged* should be deflated by 2 percent. These adjustments are incorporated in the following analyses.

Analysis and Results

Young persons apprehended by police

As Figure 1 shows, the per capita rate of youth apprehended by police increased rapidly during the late 1970s, which were the last years of a rising trend in officially recorded crime in Canada extending throughout the 1960s and 1970s (Brantingham 1991: 399). From 1980 to 1988, youth crime remained at about the same level, then it rose to a peak in 1991, and fell back almost to its former level by 1996. During the period of stable rates under the JDA – 1980 to 1983 – the average annual rate of juveniles[(13)] apprehended was approximately 7,891 per 100,000. During 1986-96, the average annual rate of young persons (aged 12 to 17) apprehended was 8,413 per 100,000 – a statistically significant[(14)] increase of 522 per 100,000, or 7 percent, over the annual rate under the JDA.

Thus, the rate of police-reported youth crime was a little higher during the first decade under the YOA than during the last few years under the JDA. Was this increase due to the

Figure 1
Rates per 100,000 of juveniles/young persons apprehended and charged by police, Canada, 1977-1996

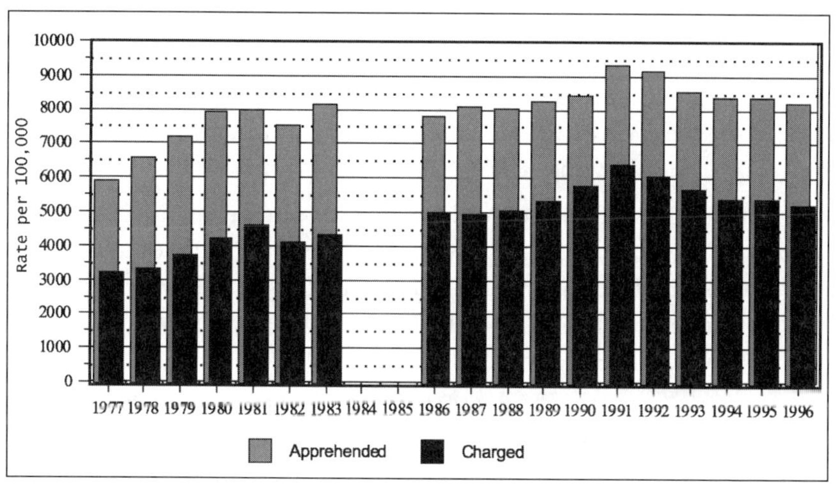

YOA itself? If the YOA had affected rates of youth crime, we would expect to see one or both of the following phenomena: a jump in level after 1984-85, or a rising trend after 1984-85 that had not existed previously. Changes such as these would indicate that something had happened that affected the rate of youth crime around 1984-85, and if other causes could be ruled out, the changes could be attributed to the YOA.

In fact, there was no jump after 1985, as can be seen from Figure 1. There was a slight change in the trend over time. During 1980-83, the trend was an annual increase of 25 per 100,000, but this was not statistically significant – that is, it could represent random fluctuations, rather than a "real" trend. During 1986-96, the rising trend increased to 46 per 100,000, but it remained statistically non-significant. Thus, we cannot be confident that any real change in trend took place after 1986. The only noteworthy change in the level of youth crime that took place after 1984-85 was the "hump" in the early 1990s, and this is highly unlikely to have been caused by the YOA, since it occurred several years later, and was mirrored by similar "humps" in crime in other countries, that could not be related to the YOA.

Another way of looking for changes in youth crime due to the YOA is to examine data for individual provinces and territories, since some underwent large changes in age jurisdiction, due to the addition of 16- and 17-year-olds, and others underwent smaller or no change in age jurisdiction. It is in the provinces and territories that added 16- and 17-year-olds that we would most expect to see changes in the rate of youth crime following 1984-85 (Carrington and Moyer 1994).

The results of this examination are shown in Figure 2 and Table 5. Figure 2 has been simplified by aggregating the provinces and territories having similar levels and trends, based on the detailed results presented in Table 5, and by smoothing with 3 year moving averages.[15]

In the four Atlantic provinces, there appears to have been a rising trend in youth crime during the entire period, 1977-

Figure 2
Rates per 100,000 of juveniles/young persons apprehended, by region, 1977-1996

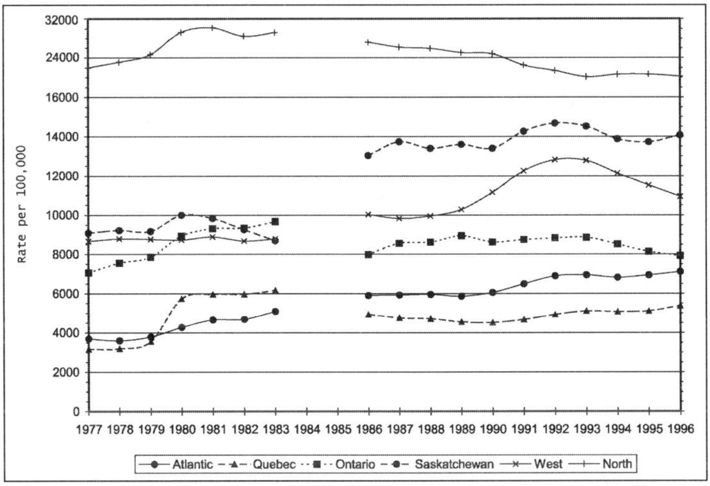

Notes: rates are modified 3 year moving averages; the upper part of the Y-axis is not linear.

96, with a temporary peak in the early 1990s. This is suggested in Table 5 by positive trend parameters for both the JDA and YOA periods, and higher average levels during 1986-96 than during 1980-83. New Brunswick is the only province in which there was a (small) jump after 1984-85.(16) Thus, the rate of police-reported youth crime in the Atlantic provinces was much higher during 1986-96 than during 1977-83, but this appears to be due to a pre-existing trend, not to the YOA.

In Quebec, the rate of youth crime was significantly *lower* during 1986-96 than during 1980-83. This decrease was due to a sudden drop, not to a falling trend: in fact, there was a slight *rising* trend during both periods (Table 5). We would speculate that this drop in official youth crime reflects not a sudden change in actual youth crime, but rather a change made by the Quebec government in 1984 in the screening procedure for young offenders (LeBlanc and Beaumont 1992) which could have affected the numbers of young persons reported to the UCR as apprehended offenders.

Table 5
Changes over time in rates per 100,000 of young persons apprehended by police, by province, 1980 to 1996

			Mean level					Trend	
Region / province	% of young offenders	Ages added by the YOA	JDA 1980-83 adjusted)	YOA 1986-96	Difference between mean levels	Difference (as % of JDA rate)	Jump after 1985?	JDA 1980-83 (adjusted)	YOA 1986-96
Canada	100.0		7,891	8,413	+522	+7%	no	+25	+46
Atlantic	6.9								
Newfoundland		17	5,885	6,329	+444	+8%	no	+469	+105 *
P.E.I.		16-17	4,651	6,675	+2,024 **	+44%	no	+727 *	+181
Nova Scotia		16-17	5,016	7,021	+2,005 ***	+40%	no	+270 **	+164 *
New Brunswick		16-17	3,553	6,226	+2,673 ***	+75%	yes	+191	+173 ***
Quebec	17.5	—	6,062	4,955	-1,107 **	-18%	drop	+164	+94 **
Ontario	35.6	16-17	9,486	8,487	-999 **	-11%	drop	+267	-76
Saskatchewan	5.9	16-17	9,020	13,950	+4,930 ***	+55%	yes	-661	+84
West	33.0								
Manitoba		—	9,256	10,763	+1,507 *	+16%	no	-33	+164
Alberta		16-17	7,753	11,051	+3,298 **	+43%	no	+237	+125
B.C.		17	9,234	11,702	+2,468 ***	+27%	yes	-13	+103
North	1.1								
Yukon		16-17	23,018	20,701	-2,317	-10%	no	-2,839	-194
N.W.T.		16-17	31,571	23,228	-8,343 **	-26%	no	+1,040	-946 **

Note: significance levels: *p < .05; **p < .01; ***p < .001.

Source: tabulations supplied by the Canadian Centre for Justice Statistics; the adjustment for 1980-83 is explained in the text.

There was also a substantial drop in Ontario in police-reported youth crime in 1986, and little trend thereafter. As a result, the average rate of youth crime in Ontario was 999 per 100,000 *lower* during 1986-96 than during 1980-83: a statistically significant decrease of 11 percent. Perhaps some or all of this was due to the YOA, but we are unable to say how.

In Manitoba, Alberta, and British Columbia, rates of police-reported youth crime were fairly stable from 1980 to 1983, then rose steadily from 1988 to peaks in the early 1990s, from which they declined through 1996. In British Columbia, there was a jump in 1986. The large "hump" in youth crime rates during 1986-96 (Figure 2), and the post-1985 jump in British Columbia, resulted in average rates for the period that were significantly (16 to 27 percent) higher than during 1980-83. With the possible exception of the jump in 1986 in British Columbia, the timing of these phenomena suggests that they are not related to the YOA.

Saskatchewan is shown separately in Figure 2, because of the unique, and spectacular, one-time jump in its rate of official youth crime after 1986, which resulted[(17)] in an average rate during 1986-96 that was 55 percent higher than during 1980-83, and the highest among the ten provinces. Since this coincided with the introduction of the YOA, it may well have been related to it; however, we are unable to determine from these data to what extent this sudden increase of more than 50 percent reflects a change in the criminal behaviour of young persons, and to what extent it reflects a change in police enforcement activity and reporting practices.

Beginning at very high levels, both the Yukon and the Northwest Territories experienced somewhat erratic downward trends in police-reported youth crime from 1980 to 1996,[(18)] and no jump after 1984-85.

This survey of trends over two decades in police-reported youth crime in the provinces and territories confirms once again the diversity of patterns of criminal behaviour in Canada. With the exception of Quebec, regional youth crime rates rise from east to west and are far higher in the territories.

Saskatchewan and British Columbia are the only provinces in which there was a substantial increase in recorded youth crime immediately after the YOA was introduced.[(19)] Ontario and Quebec experienced *drops* in police-reported youth crime immediately after 1984-85; this could have been due to changes in the *Youth Protection Act* (YPA) in Quebec, and may have been related somehow to the introduction of the YOA in Ontario. In the other provinces and territories, there were rising or falling trends, or both, that appear to be unrelated to the YOA.

Young persons charged by police

Figure 1 shows that the rate per 100,000 of young persons charged (the "charge rate") tracked the rate of young persons apprehended fairly consistently over the period 1977 to 1996, with one important exception: there was a jump in charging in 1986 that did not occur in apprehensions of young persons. As a result of this jump, the average charge rate during 1986-96 was 27 percent higher than during 1980-83, compared with the 7 percent increase in young persons apprehended. There was practically no rising or falling trend in the charge rate, either before or after 1984-85.

Since the rate of young persons apprehended increased by only 7 percent after 1985, most of the 27 percent increase in the charge rate was due to an increase in the proportion of apprehended young persons who were charged (the "charge ratio"), and a corresponding reduction in the use by police of informal means – that is, in police discretion (Carrington and Moyer 1994). This is shown in Figure 3, in which the proportion of apprehended youth who were charged fluctuated around 55 percent prior to 1984, jumped to about 65 percent in 1986, and fluctuated around that level through 1996. There was practically no trend over time in the charge ratio either before or after 1984-85.

It seems likely that this jump in charging of apprehended youth was due to the YOA, since it occurred immediately after the YOA came into effect, and the charge ratio was stable over

Figure 3
Percent of apprehended youth who were charged, Canada, 1977-1996

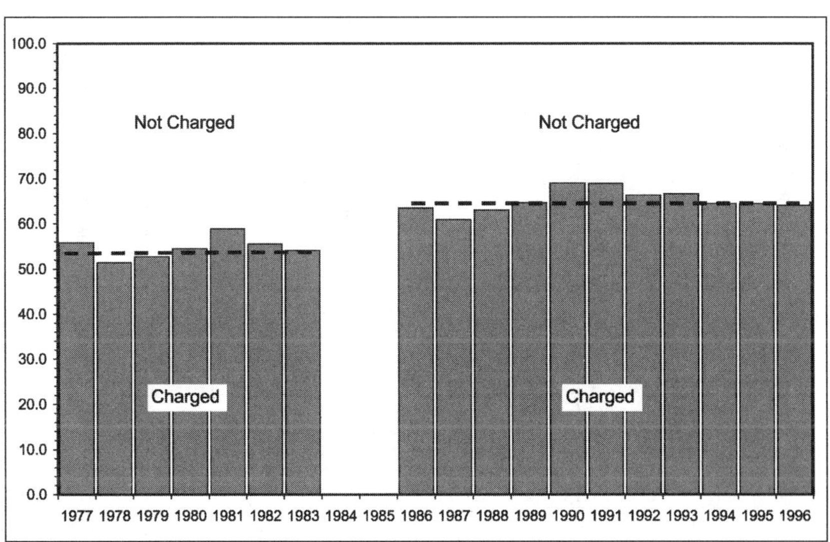

the rest of the two decades examined.[20] The following section examines changes in charging of young persons by province, to see if the changes were more pronounced in the eight provinces and territories which experienced the greatest expansion of their youth justice systems due to the addition of 16- and 17-year-olds, as Carrington and Moyer (1994) suggested.

Table 6 shows the average level and trends in rates of young persons charged, by province. In Figure 4, these data are aggregated into regions with similar levels and trends, and are smoothed using 3-year moving averages (see note 13). Table 7 shows similar information for charge ratios, which are charted in Figures 5a and 5b.[21]

Quebec is the only province in which fewer young persons per capita were charged after 1984-85 than during 1980-83. There was an immediate drop after 1985, similar to the drop in the rate of apprehensions, but then the charge rate declined

Table 6
Changes over time in rates per 100,000 of young persons charged by police, by province, 1980 to 1996

		Mean level					Trend	
Province	Ages added by the YOA	JDA 1980-83 (adjusted)	YOA 1986-96	Difference between mean levels	Difference (as % of (JDA rate)	Jump after 1985?	JDA 1980-83 (adjusted)	YOA 1986-96
Canada		4,302	5,483	+1,181 ***	+27%	yes	-22	+46
Quebec	—	4,930	3,375	-1,555 ***	-32%	drop	+127	-112 ***
Manitoba	—	6,987	8,429	+1,442 **	+21%	no	-80	+210 *
Newfoundland	17	3,520	4,687	+1,167 *	+33%	no	-41	+226 *
B.C.	17	5,832	6,466	+634 *	+11%	no	+6	-45
P.E.I	16-17	2,084	4,391	+2,307 **	+111%	no	+149	+109
Nova Scotia	16-17	2,646	5,379	+2,733 ***	+103%	yes	-36	+184 **
New Brunswick	16-17	2,539	4,391	+1,852 ***	+73%	yes	-59	+145 ***
Ontario	16-17	3,105	5,450	+2,345 ***	+76%	yes	-153	+94
Saskatchewan	16-17	2,306	9,290	+6,984 ***	+303%	yes	-117	+236 **
Alberta	16-17	4,358	7,366	+3,008 ***	+69%	small	-24	+120
Yukon	16-17	11,616	12,986	+1,370	+12%	no	-1,856	+266
N.W.T.	16-17	11,063	14,486	+3,423	+31%	yes	-788	-883 ***

Note: significance levels: *p < .05; **p < .01; ***p < .001.

Source: tabulations supplied by the Canadian Centre for Justice Statistics; the adjustment for 1980-83 is explained in the text.

Figure 4
Rates per 100,000 of juveniles/young persons charged, by region, 1977-1996

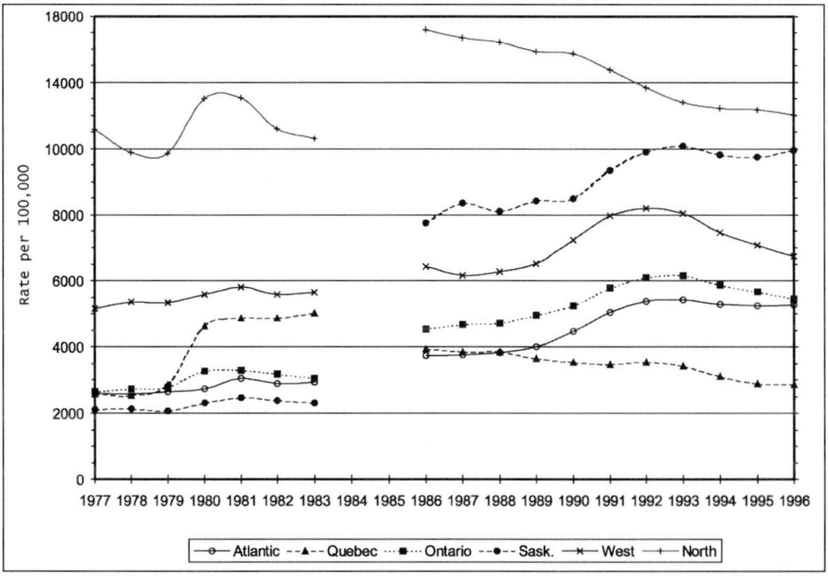

Note: rates are modified 3 year moving averages; the upper part of the Y-axis is not linear.

slowly through 1996; whereas the rate of apprehensions rose slightly in Quebec during 1986-96 (Figure 2). This divergence in the rates of apprehensions and charging is reflected in a strong downward trend in the charge ratio – the proportion of apprehended youth who were charged – from 80 percent in 1986 to 51 percent in 1996 (Figure 5b and Table 7). Quebec moved from being the province having the highest proportion of apprehended youth charged during 1980 to 1988, to having the lowest proportion charged, and by far the lowest per capita rate of young persons charged, by 1996. Since these trends are unique to Quebec, it seems likely that they are due to its unique system of diversion for young persons, which was implemented in 1979 by the provincial *Youth Protection Act*, and whose operation was not greatly changed by supersession of the YPA by the YOA in 1984 (LeBlanc and Beaumont 1988; 1992).

Table 7
Changes over time in proportions of apprehended youth who were charged by police, by province, 1977 to 1996

Province	Ages added by the YOA	Mean level					Trend	
		JDA 1977-83 %	YOA 1986-96 %	Difference between mean levels	Difference (as % of JDA level)	Jump after 1985?	JDA 1977-83 %	YOA 1986-96 %
Canada		53.5	65.1	+11.6 ***	+22%	yes	+0.3	+0.2
Quebec	—	80.9	68.8	-12.1 **	-15%	no	+0.2	-3.5 ***
Manitoba	—	77.2	78.1	+0.9	+1%	no	-1.2 *	+0.8 *
New Brunswick	16-17	74.8	70.5	-4.3	-6%	no	-2.8 *	+0.4
Newfoundland	17	65.8	73.5	+7.7	+12%	no	-3.9 *	+2.5 *
British Columbia	17	55.1	55.3	+0.2	+0%	no	+2.9 *	-0.9 ***
P.E.I	16-17	44.2	65.3	+21.1 ***	+48%	yes	+0.3	-0.1
Nova Scotia	16-17	58.6	76.5	+17.9 **	+31%	yes	-3.8 **	+0.9 *
Ontario	16-17	34.0	64.4	+30.4 ***	+89%	yes	-1.2 *	+1.7 **
Saskatchewan	16-17	24.3	66.5	+42.2 ***	+174%	yes	+0.7	+1.3 ***
Alberta	16-17	56.1	66.4	+10.3 *	+18%	small	-1.8	+0.5
Yukon	16-17	46.2	63.1	+16.9 ***	+37%	no	+1.1	+1.8 *
N.W.T.	16-17	36.9	61.9	+25.0 ***	+68%	yes	-2.4 *	-1.3 *
Coefficient of variation	0.33	0.10						

Note: significance levels: *p < .05; **p < .01; ***p < .001.

Source: tabulations supplied by the Canadian Centre for Justice Statistics; the adjustment for 1977-83 is explained in the text.

Figure 5
Percent of apprehended youth who were charged, 1977-1996.

(a) Provinces in which the charge ratio jumped in 1986

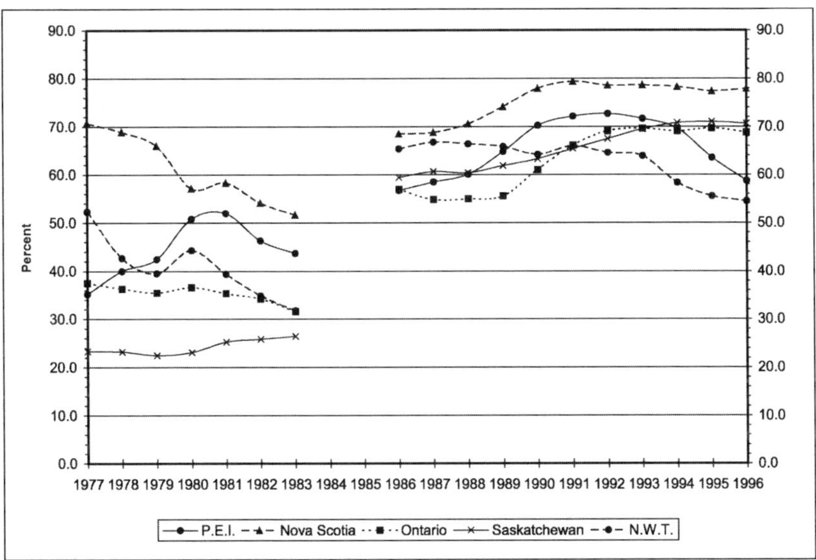

(b) Other provinces

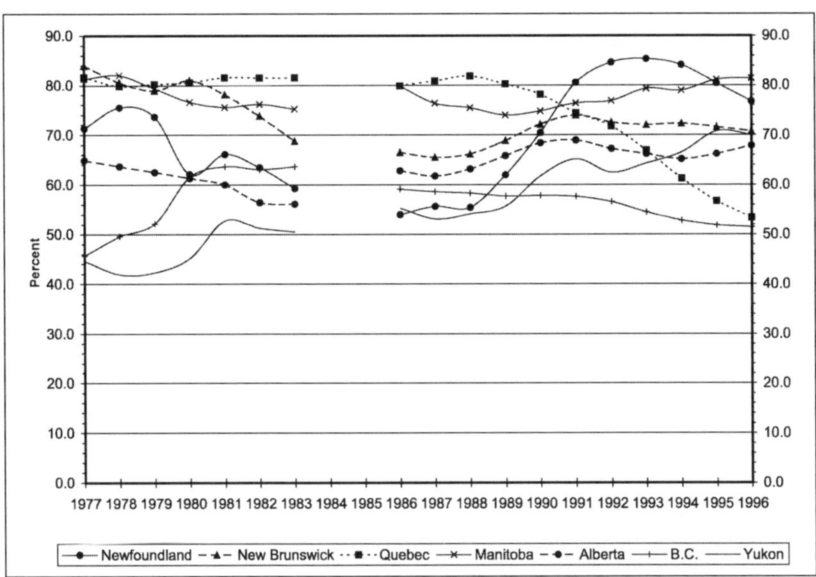

Note: percentages are modified 3-year moving averages

The other provinces and territories all experienced increases after 1985 in rates of young persons charged: in the range of 10 to 30 percent in British Columbia, Newfoundland, Manitoba, the Yukon, and the Northwest Territories, and 70 to 110 percent in the other provinces, except Saskatchewan, in which the rate of young persons charged tripled after 1985. Saskatchewan moved from having the second-lowest rate of youth charged in the country during 1980-83 to having the highest rate, except for the territories, during 1987-96. This spectacular increase was due both to the large increase in the rate of young persons apprehended (Figure 2) and to the large increase after 1985 in the proportions of these apprehended youth who were charged: from around 25 percent in 1977-83 to 60 to 70 percent in 1986-96 (Table 7). Both of these increases were mainly in the form of large jumps in 1986, but there were also upward trends after 1986 (Figure 5a).

Ontario also experienced a large increase – about 75 percent – after 1985 in the rate of young persons charged, due to a jump from about 3,000 per 100,000 in the early 1980s to about 4,500 in 1986, rising to 5-6,000 per 100,000 in the early 1990s. This was not due to an increase in apprehensions – which actually declined during the period (Figure 2) – but to a jump in the proportion of these apprehended youth who were charged, from about 30 percent in 1983 to about 55 percent in 1986, followed by a steady increase to about 70 percent in the early 1990s (Figure 5a).

Indeed, one of the most striking aspects of the transition from the JDA to the YOA in five of the eight provinces and territories that had a maximum age of 15 years under the JDA, and therefore added 16- and 17-year-olds under the Uniform Maximum Age provision of the YOA, is the sudden transition in 1986 from charging relatively low proportions of apprehended youth – that is, high use of police discretion – to charging high proportions. This has resulted in greater national homogeneity in police charging practices.[22] This sudden change was particularly pronounced in Saskatchewan and Ontario, but also occurred in Prince Edward Island, Nova Scotia, and the Northwest Territories (Figure 5a and Table 7). The timing suggests the influence of the YOA. Previous research suggests that the increase in proportions charged in Ontario and Saskatchewan applied over the entire YOA age range (12 to 17 years inclusive), and was therefore not simply due to the addition of 16- and 17-year-olds to the jurisdiction of the youth justice system (Carrington 1998).

In Prince Edward Island and Nova Scotia, this increase in charge ratios, combined with the rising trends in both the rate of apprehensions and charge ratios, resulted in rising trends after 1986 in the rates of young persons charged, and in average rates of young persons charged that were twice as high as during 1980-83 (Table 6). In the Northwest Territories, the large jump in charge ratio in 1986 (Figure 5a) was offset to some extent by a decrease in the rate of apprehensions (Table 5), resulting in a moderate, statistically non-significant, increase in the rate of young persons charged (Table 6).

On the other hand, the higher average charge ratios for 1986-96 in Alberta and the Yukon are due to rising trends rather than large jumps in 1986, and may be unrelated to the YOA.

In New Brunswick and Manitoba, there were fairly stable, high proportions of apprehended youth charged throughout 1977-96 (Figure 5b and Table 7), so the rate of young persons charged followed the rate of apprehensions.

In Newfoundland, the charge ratio decreased steeply during 1977-83, rose sharply from 1988 to 1993, then fell (Figure 5b). Similarly, the rate of young persons charged rose from a rather low level of about 3,200 per 100,000 in 1986 to a peak of about 6,000 in 1991, then fell to about 5,300 in 1996. In British Columbia – the other province in which 17-year-olds were added to the youth justice system by the YOA – the charge ratio and the rate of young persons charged increased from 1977 to 1983, then decreased from 1986 to 1996. In neither province was there a significant change in level in 1986, and it is difficult to know to what extent the changes in charging in these provinces might have been affected by the YOA.

Discussion

This paper has shown that there is no basis in fact for public concern about increased levels of youth crime or the supposed failure of the YOA to control youth crime. Apart from a temporary peak in the early 1990s, the level of police-reported youth crime in Canada has changed very little since 1980. The average per capita rate of police-reported youth crime was 7 percent higher during the first 11 years under the YOA than during the last 4 years under the JDA.[23] This increase does not appear to be due to the YOA, since it did not occur immediately after 1985, but is largely accounted for by a temporary "hump" in youth crime during the early 1990s, mainly in the Western provinces. There were jumps in police-reported youth crime in Saskatchewan and British Columbia immediately after 1985, which may have been due to the YOA, possibly because of changes in police recording practices rather than the criminal behaviour of young persons. On the other hand, police-reported youth crime was *lower* under the YOA than during 1980-83 in Quebec and Ontario. Although the drop in Quebec was probably at least partly due to the provincial youth diversion system, which predated the YOA by 5 years, we cannot account for the drop in 1986 in Ontario.

The average rate of young persons *charged* by police was 27 percent higher during 1986-96 than 1980-83 (see note 23). Unlike the rate of young persons apprehended, the charge rate jumped immediately after the YOA came into effect. Before and after this, the charge rate followed the rate of apprehensions quite closely.

The jump in 1986 in young persons charged reflects a jump in the proportion of identified young offenders who were charged – that is, to a sudden drop in police diversion of young offenders. This sudden change in the charge ratio, a time series that is otherwise quite stable, suggests the effect of a discrete event: presumably the YOA. The jump in police charging was especially pronounced in Saskatchewan and Ontario, but also occurred in Prince Edward Island, Nova Scotia, and the Northwest Territories. All of these jurisdictions were characterized, prior to the YOA, by the charging of relatively low proportions of apprehended youth – that is, by the use of relatively high levels of police discretion. On the other hand, Quebec – which had the highest proportion of apprehended youth charged prior to the YOA – experienced a continuous decline in the charge ratio after 1988. The charging of apprehended youth in the other six jurisdictions appears not to have been affected by the YOA.

During the decade after the YOA came into effect, the rate of police-reported youth crime in Canada has increased slightly, but probably not because of the YOA. It has decreased in Ontario, Quebec, and the Yukon, and increased elsewhere. The YOA does appear to have caused a substantial increase in the rate of young persons charged in Canada, by causing an increase in the proportion of apprehended youth who are charged – that is, a reduction in the use of police discretion – in some jurisdictions. In other jurisdictions, the rate of young persons charged has also increased, but apparently not because of the YOA. Quebec is the only province in which the rate of young persons charged has declined since 1985.

In its Declaration of Principle, the YOA recognizes the right to the "least possible interference" in the lives of young persons accused of crimes. It encourages the use of informal processing in preference to formal proceedings against young persons. Quebec is the only province in which formal charging of apprehended young persons has decreased under the YOA. It is difficult to see how the increase in the laying of charges against young persons in Ontario, Saskatchewan, Prince Edward Island, Nova Scotia, and the Northwest Territories is consistent with the intent of the YOA. The federal government is currently considering changes to the youth justice system to encourage more use of police discretion and other innovative alternatives to formal charging (Department of Justice Canada n.d. [1998]: 19-24). The findings reported in this paper suggest that such measures are needed.

Notes

1. I am indebted to Jim Hackler, Julian Roberts, and Jean Trépanier for comments on an earlier version. Preparation of this article was supported by Social Sciences and Humanities Research Council Research Grant No. 410-95-0661.
2. They excluded the four quarters from April, 1984 to March, 1985, because the Uniform Maximum Age provision of the YOA was phased in during that period, making per capita rates of youth crime rather unreliable (Carrington and Moyer 1994: 7).
3. That is, the rate of young persons apprehended but not necessarily charged by police.
4. 1977 is the first year for which reliable detailed data are available from the UCR Survey. See note 2 re the omission of 1984 and 1985.
5. Details of the methodology of the UCR Survey are provided annually in the *Canadian Crime Statistics* series; see, e.g. Canadian Centre for Justice Statistics (1996).
6. The category "persons charged" in the UCR Survey actually refers to persons "charged or recommended for charges by police," since, in some jurisdictions, such as New Brunswick, Quebec, and British Columbia, the laying of charges against young persons is subject to approval by the Crown. It appears that in UCR returns from New Brunswick and Quebec, if the Crown does not approve the recommendation to charge, the apprehended person is counted as "not charged"; but that in British Columbia, the person recommended for charges is counted as charged whether or not the Crown approves the charges (Canadian Centre for Justice Statistics 1994: 14-15).
7. Police in Canada have discretion to use "other means" in dealing with apprehended offenders, such as taking no action at all, or none beyond an informal warning or notification of the parents; they may also refer the apprehended youth to a pre-charge alternative measures programme. Police discretion not to charge in Canada is discussed at length in Hornick, Caputo, Hastings, Knoll, Bertrand, Paetsch, Stroeder, and Maguire (1996); for discussion of the relative values of the UCR Survey's "persons charged" and "persons apprehended," see Carrington (1995: 62), Markwart and Corrado (1995: 74-75), and Task Force on Youth Justice (1996: 146-147).
8. According to Hackler, the UCR category "juveniles not charged" was used particularly inconsistently by individual police departments prior to the YOA, varying "from 0 to a very large figure" (private communication; see also Hackler and Don 1990). However, even very large inconsistencies among individual police departments in a given year do not invalidate inferences concerning changes over time aggregated to the provincial or regional level, as long as the inconsistencies are reasonably consistent over time.
9. In addition to the underestimation due to crime that the police are unaware of, or are aware of but do not record, and incidents that are not cleared (see above).
10. Some provinces used a minimum age of 12 or 14, rather than 7 years, for juvenile court proceedings (Bala and Corrado 1985: 17-19).

11. For an example of this approach, see Schissel (1993: Chapter 3). Silverman (1990) illustrates the pitfalls of using the "legal" definition of juveniles in studying youth homicide, and cautions against making comparisons when definitions are unstable; however, to eschew such pre-post comparisons would severely restrict evaluation of many legislative initiatives, and, more generally, the study of many social phenomena over time.
12. Clark and O'Reilly-Fleming (1994: 308) calculated from these data that children under 12 made up "roughly 2% of total national offences" during 1988-92. Using this estimate of 2 percent, and knowing that accused aged between 12 and 17 made up 21 percent of the total, Markwart and Corrado (1995: 76) concluded that children under 12 made up about 10 percent [2/(2+21)] of accused under 18. However, Clark and O'Reilly-Fleming appear to have miscalculated the percentage of the national total made up by children under 12, which is 1.2 percent, not 2 percent (Table 1 above; see also DuWors 1992: 3). This estimate is corroborated by the official annual reports on crime in Canada, which reported that children under 12 accounted for 1.2 percent of all apprehended offenders in each of 1994 and 1995; that is, 5.6 percent of accused under 12 in 1994 and 4.9 percent in 1995 (Canadian Centre for Justice Statistics 1995; 1996).
13. At least 12 years old; this estimate was obtained by using the adjustment for inflation discussed above.
14. That is, there is less than a 5 percent chance that this increase could be due to random annual fluctuations. Actually, the increase is barely significant: the p value is .047.
15. Charts for individual provinces and territories for 1980-93 are in Moyer (1996: 13-15); and are available from the author for 1977-96. The data for 1977, 1980, and 1986 were not smoothed. The plotted points for 1978, 1981, and 1987 are 2-year moving averages (i.e. the averages of 1977-78, 1980-81 and 1986-87 respectively). All other plotted points are 3-year moving averages.
16. See the previous note. There was also a small, but short-lived, jump in Nova Scotia.
17. Along with a very small, and statistically non-significant, upward trend during 1986-96.
18. The non-significant positive trend value of 1,040 for 1980-83 for the Northwest Territories is due to an anomalous high value for 1983: the rates for 1980-82 decline consistently.
19. The increases in 1986 in Nova Scotia and Manitoba appear to be part of a trend that existed prior to 1984.
20. Except for the temporary peak in the early 1990s, which is characteristic of many indicators of crime and police activity.
21. The entire 7-year period, 1977-83, is used in the analyses in Table 7, since charge ratios – unlike rates of young persons apprehended and charged – had relatively consistent trends during this period.
22. This is indicated by the reduction in the coefficient of variation in the last line of Table 7.

23. Assuming that the adjustment for inflation of rates under the JDA is correct.

References

Bala, Nicholas
1994 What's wrong with YOA bashing? What's wrong with the YOA? - Recognizing the limits of the law. Canadian Journal of Criminology 36(3): 247-270.

Bala, Nicholas and Raymond R. Corrado
1985 Juvenile Justice in Canada: A Comparative Study. Technical Report TRS No. 5. Ottawa: Solicitor General Canada.

Bala, Nicholas and D'Arcy Mahoney
1994 Responding to Criminal Behaviour of Children Under 12: An Analysis of Canadian Law & Practice. Ottawa: Department of Justice Canada.

Brantingham, Paul J.
1991 Patterns in Canadian crime. In Margaret A. Jackson and Curt T. Griffiths (eds.), Canadian Criminology. Toronto: Harcourt Brace Jovanovich, Canada.

Canadian Centre for Justice Statistics
1994 Canadian Crime Statistics 1993. Ottawa: Canadian Centre for Justice Statistics, Statistics Canada.

Canadian Centre for Justice Statistics
1995 Canadian Crime Statistics 1994. Ottawa: Canadian Centre for Justice Statistics, Statistics Canada.

Canadian Centre for Justice Statistics
1996 Canadian Crime Statistics 1995. Ottawa: Canadian Centre for Justice Statistics, Statistics Canada.

Carrington, Peter J.
1995 Has violent youth crime increased? Comment on Corrado and Markwart. Canadian Journal of Criminology 37(1): 61-73.

Carrington, Peter J.
1996 Age and Youth Crime in Canada. Working Document No. 1996-1e. Ottawa: Department of Justice Canada.

Carrington, Peter J.
1998 Changes in police charging of young offenders in Ontario and Saskatchewan after 1984. Canadian Journal of Criminology 40(2): 153-164.

Carrington, Peter J. and Sharon Moyer
1994 Trends in youth crime and police response, pre- and post-YOA. Canadian Journal of Criminology 36(1): 1-28.

Clark, Barry M. and Thomas O'Reilly-Fleming
1994 Out of the carceral straightjacket: Under twelves and the law. Canadian Journal of Criminology 36(3): 305-327.

Cook, Thomas D. and Donald T. Campbell
1979 Quasi-Experimentation. Boston: Houghton Mifflin.

Corrado, Raymond R. and Alan Markwart
1992 The evolution and implementation of a new era of juvenile justice in Canada. In Raymond R. Corrado, Nicholas Bala, Rick Linden, and Marc LeBlanc (eds.), Juvenile Justice in Canada. Toronto: Butterworths.

Corrado, Raymond R. and Alan Markwart
1994 The need to reform the YOA in response to violent young offenders: Confusion, reality or myth? Canadian Journal of Criminology 36(3): 343-378.

Department of Justice Canada
n.d. [1998] A Strategy for the Renewal of Youth Justice. Ottawa: Department of Justice Canada.

Doob, Anthony N. and Janet B.L. Chan
1982 Factors affecting police decisions to take juveniles to court. Canadian Journal of Criminology 24: 25-37.

DuWors, Richard
1992 Report on the Involvement of Children Under 12 in Criminal Behaviour. Ottawa: Canadian Centre for Justice Statistics, Statistics Canada.

DuWors, Richard
1997 The Justice Data Factfinder. Juristat Vol. 17, No. 13. Ottawa: Canadian Centre for Justice Statistics, Statistics Canada.

Hackler, Jim and Kim Don
1990 Estimating system biases: Crime indices that permit comparison across provinces. Canadian Journal of Criminology 32(2): 243-264.

Hackler, Jim and Wasanti Paranjape
1983 Juvenile justice statistics: Mythmaking or measure of system response? Canadian Journal of Criminology 25(1): 209-226.

Hackler, Jim and Wasanti Paranjape
1984 Official reaction to juvenile theft: Comparison across provinces. Canadian Journal of Criminology 26(1): 179-198.

Hornick, Joseph P., Tullio Caputo, Ross Hastings, Patrick J. Knoll, Lorne D. Bertrand, Joanne J. Paetsch, Lyle Stroeder, and A. Owen Maguire
1996 A Police Reference Manual on Crime Prevention and Diversion with Youth. Ottawa: Solicitor General Canada.

Hylton, John H.
1994 Get tough or get smart? Options for Canada's youth justice system in the twenty-first century. Canadian Journal of Criminology 36(3): 229-246.

Kong, Rebecca
1997 Canadian Crime Statistics, 1996. Juristat Vol. 17, No. 8.

Ottawa: Canadian Centre for Justice Statistics, Statistics Canada.

LeBlanc, Marc and Hélène Beaumont
1988 The Quebec perspective on the Young Offenders Act: Implementation before adoption. In Joe Hudson, Joseph P. Hornick, and Barbara A. Burrows (eds.), Justice and the Young Offender in Canada. Toronto: Wall and Thompson.

LeBlanc, M. and Hélène Beaumont
1992 The effectiveness of juvenile justice in Quebec: A natural experiment in implementing formal diversion and a justice model. In Raymond R. Corrado, Nicholas Bala, Rick Linden, and Marc LeBlanc (eds.), Juvenile Justice in Canada. Toronto: Butterworths.

Markwart, Alan and Raymond R. Corrado
1995 A response to Carrington. Canadian Journal of Criminology 37(1): 74-87.

Moyer, Sharon
1996 A Profile of the Juvenile Justice System in Canada. Report to the Federal-Provincial-Territorial Task Force on Youth Justice. Ottawa: Department of Justice Canada.

Schissel, Bernard
1993 Social Dimensions of Canadian Youth Justice. Toronto: Oxford U. Press.

Silverman, Robert A.
1990 Trends in Canadian youth homicide: Some unanticipated consequences of a change to the law. Canadian Journal of Criminology 32: 651-656.

Scanlon, R. Lorcan
1986 Canadian crime trends. In Robert A. Silverman and James J. Teevan, Jr. (eds.), Crime in Canadian Society. 3rd ed. Toronto: Butterworths.

Task Force on Youth Justice
1996 A Review of the Young Offenders Act and the Youth Justice System in Canada. Report of the Federal-Provincial-Territorial Task Force on Youth Justice. Ottawa: Department of Justice Canada.

CHAPTER FOUR

Trends in youth crime: Some evidence pointing to increases in the severity and volume of violence on the part of young people

Thomas Gabor
Department of Criminology
University of Ottawa
Ottawa, Ontario

IN RECENT ISSUES OF THE *CANADIAN JOURNAL OF CRIMINOLOGY*, SEVERAL articles have appeared on the subject of youth crime. The articles by Peter Carrington (April, 1998; January, 1999) and that by Tony Doob and Jane Sprott (April, 1998), in particular, caught my attention because they concluded that youth violence had not increased in recent years and attributed evidence to the contrary to an increasing tendency to lay charges against youth under the *Young Offenders Act* and under "zero tolerance" policies. My aim herein is not to engage these authors in a debate – their analyses have been carefully and competently done – but to raise a concern I have with basing our conclusions, in relation to such a complex question, exclusively on quantitative analyses of police and court data, including the Uniform Crime Reporting Survey (UCR). While I may, on occasion, refer to the aforementioned studies, my comments are intended to be broader in scope.

It is widely recognized that justice system data offer just a glimpse of crime due to the failure of citizens to report many infractions and the discretion exercised by police forces in the recording of infractions that are reported to them. One might

Canadian Journal of Criminology/Revue canadienne de criminologie, July/juillet 1999, pp. 385–392.

conjecture that the picture of youth crime we obtain from the justice system is even more skewed than is the case with adults, as the violations of young people may be more easily forgiven by victims, witnesses, and the police, resulting in a larger "dark figure" of crime (Doob and Chan 1982; Bynum and Thompson 1996: 346). Carrington (1998), in fact, has shown that age is a factor in the response of the justice system, as older youth (16-17-year-olds) are dealt with more harshly than those between 12 and 15 years of age, in that they are more likely to be charged when apprehended.

If the societal and justice system response does escalate with the age of the suspect/offender, it may also follow that the threshold, in terms of the gravity of misconduct, for reporting and recording infractions is higher for youths than for adults. Thus, even where zero tolerance policies are present, the actions of a young person, generally, may need to be quite serious for the police to be notified and the act to be recorded as a crime. Lower level acts of extortion and intimidation in and around school grounds will continue to go unreported (Smith, Hornick, Copple, and Graham 1995: 4); these are precisely the types of acts that have been said to have increased in recent years (Walker 1994).

Analyses of official trends in youth crime are vulnerable to a number of additional pitfalls. Demographic changes involving an aging population may, for example, obscure heightened criminal activity among youth. Sagi and Wellford (1968) pointed out years ago that such changes could account for a substantial proportion of the variation in crime rates. Simply observing that youth are committing offences at a lower or stable rate, over a period of time, tells us little if we fail to consider the changing size of the youthful segment of the population. Age-specific crime rates, which take into account the number of young people in the population between the ages of 12 and 17 (those within the potential jurisdiction of the *Young Offenders Act*), ought to be tallied in comparisons over time or across geographic areas. Demographers project that a large cohort of youth is in the process of reaching their most crime-prone years as the millenium draws to a close (Foot and Stoffman 1996).

The time frame of a study, too, is critical. Analyses of the violent crime rate in Canada can furnish us with virtually any result we seek. In the 1980's, the official rate increased every year; while in the last few years it has been in decline. Studies comparing crime rates over several decades are vulnerable to a myriad of contemporaneous legislative, policy, and attitudinal changes that may undermine their validity. Conversely, studies adopting a very short time frame may fail to capture underlying social trends. In examining the important question as to whether youth violence is becoming more serious, Doob and Sprott (1998) compared the number of youth court cases in Canada from 1991 through 1995. While acknowledging that "inferences about crime trends from reported crime rates and charge rates are... very risky", Doob and Sprott calculated the percentage change in youth court cases by comparing just two years – 1991 and 1995. The authors undoubtedly selected this short time frame because national youth court data have only been forwarded to the Canadian Centre for Justice Statistics since 1991. The short time frame nevertheless precludes comparisons with the 1970's and 1980's.

Problematic, also, are the different time frames used by different researchers. While Doob and Sprott compared 1991 and 1995, Carrington (1999) drew conclusions from a 20-year comparison (1977-96). An earlier debate involving Carrington (1995) and Corrado and Markwart (1994) was based on yet a different time frame – 1986-1992.

Another concern is the frequent use of aggregated national crime statistics. Increases in youth crime in Canada's large urban areas may be obscured by greater stability in smaller communities or rural areas. The analyses conducted thus far have tended to overlook the role of community size. There are indications, for example, that the problem of school violence has grown more serious, particularly in our larger cities (Gabor 1995). Also, in Metro Toronto, data drawn from Statistics

Canada has revealed that the number of reported incidents of violent crime by males aged 12-17 rose by 64% and more than doubled for females during the decade beginning in 1987 and ending in 1997 (Shephard 1998). Weapons were used in 36% of 1997 violent incidents as opposed to 23% of 1987 incidents. In Ottawa, the number of youths charged for violent crimes more than doubled from 1988 to 1993. Lest one attribute this entire increase to a growing propensity of the police in Ottawa to lay charges, how does one explain a tripling of car thefts during the same period (Gabor 1994)? Motor vehicle thefts are among the most consistently reported incidents and about half are committed by youth (Statistics Canada 1997). Indeed, the rate of motor vehicle theft across Canada has almost doubled from 1986-1996 (Statistics Canada 1997).

Given the limitations of official crime data, survey results and the impressions formed by those in close contact with youths (educators, clinicians, school liaison officers) may be instructive.

A study commissioned by the Calgary Police Service during 1994 revealed fairly high levels of apprehension among high school students about violence, gangs, and the use of weapons against them (Smith, Bertrand, Arnold, and Hornick 1995). This survey of students from 20 junior and senior high schools also suggested that weapons possession is quite commonplace among youth, at least in urban Canada. Between one-third and one-quarter of students surveyed indicated that they had carried some form of weapon at school during the previous year. More than half the students who had an opinion on the issue felt that youth crime had increased over the previous five years, whereas about a third felt it was the same, and less than 10 percent believed that youth crime had decreased during that time.

Similar findings emerged from a survey of adults conducted under the auspices of the same Calgary study (Smith *et al.* 1995). About one-half of adult Calgarians surveyed felt that crime had increased within their community during the previous five years, whereas only 3.7 percent thought it had decreased. Moreover, close to one-half felt that there was a youth crime and violence problem in their community. Studies by the Teachers Federations of Ontario and British Columbia have provided further evidence suggesting substantial increases in physical and verbal assaults in schools have taken place (MacDougall 1993). A study conducted in Southern Ontario, exploring student perceptions of violence in the schools, revealed significant levels of fear relating to possible victimization (Ryan, Mathews, and Banner 1993).

A national study of weapons use in Canadian schools, involving focus groups and interviews with police personnel and school administrators, found that weapons use in schools had increased from the late 1980's to the mid 1990's (Walker 1994). The study also revealed that weapons and violent behaviour, on the part of younger children (including those in elementary school) and girls, increased during the same period.

My own national study of violence in the schools lends further support to the notion that violence and intimidation among our youth rose from the mid-1980's to the mid-1990's (Gabor 1995). Officials from 260 school boards and 250 police departments were surveyed across the country (including the Northwest Territories and Yukon). Close to 80 percent of both police personnel and educators contacted felt that the problem of violence in the schools had grown over the ten-year period leading up to the survey. Most of the remaining respondents felt the problem had remained about the same over the ten-year period. Not one police official and just two percent of the educators felt that the problem was less serious than it had been a decade earlier.

Alternative data sources tapping the perceptions of students, educators, and criminal justice professionals, therefore, suggest that, at the very least, concern over youth violence ought not be dismissed. UCR data not only fail to provide an accurate and complete tally of the incidence of violence, they also provide little information about the extremity of violence. Participants in a number of surveys and focus groups, including the two studies just mentioned, have commented on the growing viciousness of youth violence. The murders of Sylvain Leduc in Ottawa and Reena Virk in Victoria were particularly brutal. There may be few precedents to the torture and degradation seen in these cases. Then, there are random slayings, such as the drive-by shooting of Nicholas Battersby in Ottawa. While certainly not epidemic, drive-by shootings were virtually unknown in Canada prior to the 1990's. There have also been many reports by journalists and specialists in youth violence of particularly vicious school yard beatings and swarmings of young people. The clear ethnic/racial undertones of the Leduc and Virk slayings, as well as other incidents, are also of concern. Such evidence may be dismissed as anecdotal; however, the argument that these incidents, along with the recent massacre of students in Littleton, Colorado, and other murders on school property, are mere aberrations, rather than a reflection of wider social trends, defies credibility.

Is a social problem merely being constructed or has there been a real change in the quantity and quality of violence among our youth? The evidence, while somewhat contradictory, suggests that real changes are taking place in some areas. There is certainly no reason to be complacent. Youth crime is diverse and it is likely that new forms have emerged and increases have occurred in some forms. Doob, Marinos, and Varma (1995: 19), for example, note that the term "swarming" is a new addition to our lexicon and that swarmings probably represent some new forms of crime committed by groups of youth. In my view, dismissing or minimizing these changes does a disservice to our attempts to deal with interpersonal violence.

In future assessments of youth crime trends, I would suggest that we diversify our data sources. UCR data may be even less reliable indicators of youth than of adult crime. Apart from unreported crime, they fail to include the types of extortion, threats, and intimidation faced by thousands of public school students every day. UCR data are also highly sensitive to changing justice system practices and enforcement measures in schools. Furthermore, they are highly sensitive to attitudinal changes among our young that may alter the views of young victims as to what constitutes violence. Much has been written of late about the notion that many young people today have a higher tolerance, than did their counterparts a few decades ago, for violent images, abusive language and behaviour. They may be less likely, therefore, than in the past, to define certain acts as violent and, hence, to report such incidents. Trend analyses that fail to consider demographic changes are also problematic, as are blanket statements that ignore regional differences and variables such as community size. The implementation of appropriate policies entails that we be extremely prudent in our analyses of trends, as there are risks involved in either over-dramatizing or minimizing the issue of youth violence.

References

Bynum, J.E. and W.E. Thompson
1996 Juvenile Delinquency: A Sociological Approach. Third Edition. Boston: Allyn and Bacon.

Carrington, P.J.
1995 Has violent youth crime increased? Comment on Corrado and Markwart. Canadian Journal of Criminology 37(1): 61-73.

Carrington, P.J.
1998 Changes in police charging of young offenders in Ontario and Saskatchewan after 1984. Canadian Journal of Criminology 40(2): 153-164.

Carrington, P.J.
1999 Trends in youth crime in Canada 1977-1996. Canadian Journal of Criminology 41(1): 1-32.

Corrado, R.R. and A. Markwart
1994 The need to reform the YOA in response to violent young offenders: Confusion, reality, or myth? Canadian Journal of Criminology 36(3): 343-378.

Doob, A.N. and J.B.L. Chan
1982 Factors affecting police decisions to take juveniles to court. Canadian Journal of Criminology 24(1): 25-37.

Doob, A.N., V. Marinos, and K. Varma
1995 Youth Crime and the Youth Justice System in Canada: A Research Perspective. Toronto: Centre of Criminology.

Doob, A.N. and J.B. Sprott
1998 Is the “quality” of youth violence becoming more serious? Canadian Journal of Criminology 40(2): 185-194.

Foot, D.K. and D. Stoffman
1996 Boom, Bust, and Echo. Toronto: Macfarlane Walter & Ross.

Gabor, T.
1994 Ottawa's crime rate rising dramatically. The Ottawa Citizen. November 4: p.A13.

Gabor, T.
1995 Responding to School Violence: An Assessment of Zero Tolerance and Related Policies. Ottawa: Solicitor General Canada.

MacDougall, J.
1993 Violence in the Schools: Programs and Policies for Prevention. Toronto: Canadian Education Association.

Ryan, C., F. Mathews, and J. Banner
1994 The Anti-Violence Community School: A Police/School Partnership Model. Toronto: Central Toronto Youth Services.

Sagi, P.C. and C.F. Wellford
1968 Age composition and patterns of change in criminal statistics. Journal of Criminal Law, Criminology and Police Science 59: 29-36.

Shephard, M.
1998 Teen gangs: fear in our schools. Toronto Star. October 24, p. A1.

Smith, R.B., J.P. Hornick, P. Copple, and J. Graham
1995 A Community-based Strategy for Dealing with Youth Crime and Violence in Calgary. Calgary: Calgary Police Service.

Smith, R.B., L.D. Bertrand, B.L. Arnold, and J.P. Hornick
1995 A Study of the Level and Nature of Youth Crime and Violence in Calgary. Calgary: Calgary Police Service.

Statistics Canada
1997 Motor Vehicle Theft – 1996. Juristat. Vol. 18, No.1.

Walker, S.G.
1994 Weapons Use in Canadian Schools. Ottawa: Solicitor General Canada.

CHAPTER FIVE

Interprovincial variation in the use of the youth court[1]

Anthony N. Doob
and ***Jane B. Sprott***
Centre of Criminology
University of Toronto
Toronto, Ontario

IT WOULD PROBABLY COME AS NO SURPRISE TO CANADIANS THAT THERE are enormous variations in the rate at which youths in the United States are arrested and brought to court for offending. Looking at property crimes, for example, Mississippi apparently arrests juveniles (age 10 to 17) at a rate that is roughly twice that of Alabama (2236 vs. 1069 per 100,000 youths). New Hampshire's rate of arresting juveniles is more than twice that of neighbouring Vermont (1789 vs. 691 per 100,000 youths) (Snyder and Sickmund 1995: 114). Violent crime arrests show similar dramatic differences. Vermont arrests only about 36 juveniles per 100,000 juveniles in the state, as compared to New Hampshire's rate of 101, Massachusetts' rate of 545, or Rhode Island's rate of 613 (Snyder and Sickmund, 1995: 102).

Such variation is not surprising for a number of reasons among them being an obvious fact: each state has its own laws that deal with juveniles and each state makes its own policies on how those laws are to be enforced. Hence it is difficult to know whether the dramatic differences that we see across states relate to the behaviour of juveniles, the behaviour of the law enforcement community, or the behaviour of the state legislatures, or some combination of all of them.

Canadian Journal of Criminology/Revue canadienne de criminologie, October/octobre 1996, pp. 401–412.

In Canada, however, the law is the same across the country. The provinces and territories administer the *Young Offenders Act,* and it is well known that they administer it differently. A survey carried out a few years ago by the Canadian Centre for Justice Statistics on the administration of *alternative measures* under the *Young Offenders Act* demonstrated that in this important part of the *Act* there was variation in how it was administered (Canadian Centre for Justice Statistics 1990).

In a more general vein, it is well known that Quebec administers the *Young Offenders Act* in a manner that differs from that used in the rest of the country. For example, Quebec had implemented a form of formal diversion of young people from the youth justice system long before the *Young Offenders Act* was made law (LeBlanc and Beaumont 1992). In the 1970's, Quebec passed legislation – the *Youth Protection Act* – to protect abused children from their abusers and from the *Juvenile Delinquents Act* and, subsequently, from the *Young Offenders Act.* Even though a young person may have been brought to the attention of the police because of an offence, such a youth would be diverted from the criminal justice stream if it was felt that, in essence, the case could best be handled by way of the *Youth Protection Act.*

Variation between Quebec, on the one hand, and the rest of Canada, on the other, in terms of whether a young person is brought into the criminal justice system has often been recognized. A careful look at interprovincial variation demonstrates, however, that the variation is *not* adequately characterized by suggesting *only* that Quebec is different. For example, Carrington and Moyer (1994) examined variation across all provinces in the number of youths suspected and charged with offences before and after the implementation of a uniform maximum age in 1985. They suggest that the inclusion of older youths into the youth system in provinces that previously had a maximum age for the youth system of 16 or 17 may have affected the likelihood that youths would end up in court. In addition to changes in the rate at which cases were brought to youth court before and after 1985, their data show a good deal of interprovincial variation.

The variation across provinces is important in understanding how the *Young Offenders Act* is being administered. We suggest that there are now dramatic interprovincial differences that go beyond Quebec and that there are "local cultures" on how best to deal with young offenders that may bear no relationship to the behaviour of young people. In looking at interprovincial variation in the use of the youth justice system, one must keep in mind one important fact about youth crime. Most young people commit crimes (Doob, Marinos, and Varma 1995). In fact, most young people in Canada do numerous things in any given year that could land them in youth court if they were caught and someone was thoughtless enough to bring them to court. Young people steal, vandalize, fight, threaten their friends and others, use public transportation without paying, and other things that, if taken seriously, could land them in custody. One might suggest, therefore, that the best way of thinking about youth crime and the official processing of it is that there is an infinite supply of youth crime in the community that could be processed by the courts. Hence differences among provinces are best thought of as reflecting explicit or implicit decisions of those running the youth justice system.

We have chosen to look at five provinces – Newfoundland, Quebec, Ontario, Saskatchewan, and British Columbia. These provinces include about 79% of the young offender age people in Canada. We decided to focus on a subset of provinces since they are sufficient to illustrate the nature of the problem. The three largest provinces (Quebec, Ontario, and British Columbia) are examined, as are two of the provinces (one each from Canada's other two regions) with relatively smaller populations.

As shown in Table 1, the rates of reported *Criminal Code* offences (excluding driving offences such as impaired driving) go up quite dramatically across these five provinces as one moves from east to west. Looking at reported violent offences, there is also some variability, but it is not as orderly as one goes from east to west.

Overall rates of reported and police recorded crime do not appear, however, to explain adequately the variation that exists in bringing cases to youth court. Ontario and Saskatchewan apparently bring dramatically more cases to court per 100 young offender age people in the province than do either Newfoundland and British Columbia. All four provinces bring dramatically more young people to court (per 100 juveniles in the province) than does Quebec. These are not trivial differences. Looking at the extremes, there was one case being brought to the Saskatchewan youth courts that year (1993-4) for every 11 young people in the province. The rate for Quebec is one case for every 57 young people in the province.

Table 1
Differential use of the youth court in five provinces (and Canada): 1993-1994

	Canada	Nfld.	Quebec	Ontario	Sask.	B.C.
Crime rate	9,516	5,711	7,336	8,978	10,937	14,575
Violent crime rate	1,079	1,160	744	1,046	1,224	1,527
Cases to court	4.97	3.68	1.74	6.01	8.71	3.88
Guilty findings	3.35	3.13	1.45	3.68	6.08	2.79
Custody rate	11.0	10.2	4.6	14.1	17.1	8.3
% cases with guilty finding	67.3%	84.9%	83.1%	61.2%	69.8%	71.8%

Notes:

- "Crime rate" and "violent crime rate" are police reported *Criminal Code* incidents reported in 1993 per 100,000 in the population and derive from Canadian Centre for Justice Statistics, 1994, Table 2. Youth court data in all the tables derive from the Youth Court Statistics, 1993-1994 and tables produced by the Canadian Centre for Justice Statistics listed in that publication, but not included in it.
- "Cases to court" is the rate per 100 youths age 12-17 in the jurisdiction.
- "Guilty findings" is the number of cases where a young person is found guilty per 100 youths age 12-17 in the jurisdiction
- "Custody rate" is the number of cases where a young person is sent to custody (open or secure) per 1000 youths age 12-17 in the jurisdiction.

It seems unlikely that young people in Saskatchewan are really that much worse than their counterparts in Quebec.

It could be argued that much of this variation relates to the screening of youths for alternative measures. A better measure of the use of youth court, therefore, may be the rate at which youths in each province are found guilty of an offence. Once again, the differences are enormous. These data are shown in Table 1. Ontario finds a dramatically higher proportion of its young people guilty (per 100 young offender age youth) than does Quebec and finds slightly more young people guilty than does British Columbia. It should be remembered that British Columbia's official reported crime rate is about 50% higher than that of Ontario, yet Ontario brings in more youth court cases and finds more young people guilty. Those provinces that bring more cases to court also tend to carry through and have more cases at the disposition stage. There is some variation, of course. For Ontario, only 61% of the cases get as far as the disposition stage of proceedings. At the other extreme (among these five provinces) is Newfoundland where 85% of the cases brought to court end up with dispositions being handed down. This differential attrition does not, however, obliterate differences among the provinces. Saskatchewan still has more than twice as many cases (per 100 young offender age youth) at the disposition stage of proceedings as does British Columbia and more than four times the rate of Quebec. Ontario and Newfoundland have rates somewhat higher than British Columbia.

Perhaps the variation disappears when one gets down to real business: placing young people into custody. Here, once again, dramatic interprovincial differences exist. As shown in Table 1, Saskatchewan and Ontario seem to excel in the rate at which they lock up their 12- through 17-year-olds. Assuming that those placed in custody are those whom the province sees as "really bad", it is clear that Ontario has about three times as many "really bad" youth as does Quebec.

The variation across provinces appears to exist for a wide range of different kinds of offences. Ontario, with an officially recorded violent crime rate about 40% higher than that of Quebec, finds young people guilty of violent crimes at a rate that is more than twice that of Quebec, and places them in custody for violent offences at a rate close to three times that of Quebec (Table 2). British Columbia, on the other hand, has a reported violent crime rate that is about 25% higher than the rate in Saskatchewan and about 46% higher than the rate in Ontario. However, British Columbia finds young people guilty of violent crimes at a rate that is much lower than that of Saskatchewan or Ontario. Moreover, when it comes to locking up youths for violence, the British Columbia custody rate (per 1000 youths age 12-17 in the province) is considerably lower than that of Ontario and Saskatchewan.

Table 2
Violence cases in youth court in five provinces (and Canada): 1993-1994

	Canada	Nfld.	Quebec	Ontario	Sask.	B.C.
Guilty findings	6.17	4.92	2.98	7.73	8.49	4.69
Custody rate	1.92	1.44	0.93	2.73	2.59	1.36

Notes:

- "Guilty findings" is the number of cases with violence as the most significant charge at the disposition stage of proceedings per 1000 youths age 12-17 in the jurisdiction.
- "Custody rate" is the number of cases with violence as the most significant charge where a young person is sent to custody (open or secure) per 1000 youths age 12-17 in the jurisdiction.

More than half of the cases in Canada at the disposition stage of proceedings in youth court have a property offence as the most significant charge. Once again, Quebec brings relatively few cases through to this stage of the proceedings (Table 3). The rate of findings of guilt in Saskatchewan is roughly four times that of Quebec. Newfoundland, Ontario, and British Columbia fall between these two extremes. The variation across provinces in placing young people in custody

Table 3
Property cases in youth court in five provinces (and Canada): 1993-1994

	Canada	Nfld.	Quebec	Ontario	Sask.	B.C.
Guilty findings	17.26	18.09	7.40	18.05	31.82	15.41
Custody rate	4.90	4.35	2.16	5.60	8.19	3.62

Notes:

- "Guilty findings" is the number of cases with a property offence as the most significant charge at the disposition stage of proceedings per 1000 youths age 12-17 in the jurisdiction.
- "Custody rate" is the number of cases with a property offence as the most significant charge where a young person is sent to custody (open or secure) per 1000 youths age 12-17 in the jurisdiction.

for property offences follows the same pattern. The rate of placing young people in custody for property offences in Saskatchewan is almost four times that of Quebec. The other provinces fall between those two extremes.

When one looks within the categories of property offences, there is also dramatic variation in the use of the youth court and of custody for minor property offences (theft under $1000 and possession of stolen property). Ontario's rate of custody (per 1000 young people age 12-17 in the province) for these youths is almost five times that of Quebec (Table 4). Saskatchewan's custody rate for minor property crime is more than five times that of Quebec. When one turns to property crime *other than* minor theft and possession, one finds that Ontario's rate for sending young people to custody is almost twice that of Quebec, and Saskatchewan's is about three times that of Quebec. Generally, it seems that the variation across these provinces is greater for the less serious property offences.

Within the category of violent offences we see a similar pattern: interprovincial variation is greatest for the least serious cases. Ontario is finding youths guilty of minor assaults at a rate (per thousand young people age 12-17 in the province) that is four times that of Quebec and is sending youths to custody at a rate that is seven times that of Quebec

Table 4
Minor and less minor property offences in youth court in five provinces (and Canada): 1993-1994

	Canada	Nfld.	Quebec	Ontario	Sask.	B.C.
Guilty findings for minor property offences	7.75	6.66	2.33	8.87	12.94	8.07
Custody rate for minor property offences	1.80	1.30	0.47	2.33	2.68	1.64
Guilty findings for "other property" offences	9.51	11.44	5.07	9.18	18.88	7.34
Custody rate for "other property" offences	3.10	3.05	1.69	3.27	5.51	1.98

Notes:

- "Minor property" includes theft under $1000 and possession of stolen property.
- "Other property" are the rest of the property offences.
- "Guilty findings" is the number of cases with this kind of offence as the most significant charge at the disposition stage of proceedings per 1000 youths age 12-17 in the jurisdiction.
- "Custody rate" is the number of cases with this kind of offence as the most significant charge where a young person is sent to custody (open or secure) per 1000 youths age 12-17 in the jurisdiction.

(Table 5). The other provinces fall between those two extremes. For other kinds of violence, there is still variation, but it is not so marked. Quebec and British Columbia are finding fewer youths guilty of non-minor violence. The rate of custody decisions for Newfoundland, Quebec, and British Columbia are lower than the rates for Ontario and Saskatchewan. There is, however, less variability across provinces for these more serious cases than there is for the minor ones.

What can one conclude from this evidence of variability across provinces? First of all, as we pointed out earlier, we doubt very much that the variation that we have illustrated is due to the behaviour of young people. Quebec may be distinct,

Table 5
Minor assault and other violent cases in youth court in five provinces (and Canada): 1993-1994

	Canada	Nfld.	Quebec	Ontario	Sask.	B.C.
Guilty findings for minor assaults	3.15	2.67	0.85	4.35	3.92	2.55
Custody rates for minor assaults	7.25	6.76	1.66	12.11	8.61	5.16
Guilty findings for other violence	3.02	2.25	2.13	3.37	4.57	2.14
Custody rates for other violence	11.93	7.63	7.69	15.15	17.33	8.45

Notes:

- "Other violence" includes all violent offences other than "minor assault".
- "Guilty findings" is the number of cases with this kind of offence as the most significant charge at the disposition stage of proceedings per 1000 youths age 12-17 in the jurisdiction.
- "Custody rate" is the number of cases with this kind of offence as the most significant charge where a young person is sent to custody (open or secure) per 10,000 youths age 12-17 in the jurisdiction.

and British Columbia may claim to be special, but it is unlikely that the youths in these two provinces are angels in comparison to those found in Newfoundland, Ontario, and Saskatchewan.

When looking at the cases at the disposition stage of proceedings, it would seem that the proportion of those found guilty of an offence who are sentenced to custody is more or less the same across provinces, notwithstanding the dramatically different rates of bringing cases to this stage. Thus, for example, as we have shown in Table 1, Saskatchewan has about twice as many cases being sentenced per 100 youths in the province as does British Columbia. Nevertheless, the proportion of those at the sentencing stage getting custody is almost the same. In both provinces, close to 30 cases end up with custodial dispositions for every 100 cases where dispositions are being handed down. These figures are remarkably similar to the Quebec figure where about 32 young people receive a custodial disposition per 100 cases being sentenced. When one looks at different categories of offences, one sees remarkable consistency across provinces in rate of custodial dispositions per 100 cases being sentenced (Table 6). Although it is true that in Ontario the proportion of those sentenced going to custody is higher than in the other four provinces, the interprovincial variation in the use of custody at the disposition stage of proceedings is minor compared to the different rates of bringing young people to court in the first place.

Table 6
Rate at which cases at disposition stage receive custody in five provinces (and Canada) 1993-1994

	Canada	Nfld.	Quebec	Ontario	Sask.	B.C.
All violent cases	31.1	29.2	31.3	35.3	30.5	29.0
Minor assaults	23.0	25.3	19.4	27.8	22.0	20.2
Other violence	39.6	33.8	36.1	44.9	37.9	39.5
All property cases	28.4	24.0	29.2	31.0	25.7	23.5
Minor property	23.2	19.5	20.0	26.3	20.7	20.3
Other property	32.6	26.7	33.4	35.6	29.2	27.0

Notes:

- Tabled figures are the rates per 100 cases at the disposition stage of proceedings of getting a disposition that includes custody (secure or open).
- "Other violence" includes all violent offences other than "minor assault".
- "Minor property" includes theft under $1000 and possession of stolen property.
- "Other property" are the rest of the property offences.

Conclusion

Provinces bring cases to court at dramatically different rates. It would appear that some provinces such as Ontario and Saskatchewan want high proportions of their 12-17-year-old youths to benefit from the youth court experience. Other provinces such as British Columbia and Quebec appear to have policies or procedures that reflect the view that courts are not the best place to deal with all youthful offenders. Once in court, however, the court systems seem to treat young people in a remarkably similar fashion, placing a similar proportion of those found guilty into custody.

In understanding the interprovincial variation, it is worth noting that the variation appears to be greatest for the *least* serious offences. The variation in the rates of finding young people guilty (and, therefore, of sending them to custody) appears to be greater for minor assaults than for other violent offences. Similarly, there is more interprovincial variation in the number of young people at the sentencing stage or being sent to custody for minor property crimes than there is for other property crimes. These differences suggest, once again, that the interprovincial variation in youth court processing is less likely to be caused by differential behaviour of youth across provinces than it is to the behaviour of provincial criminal justice personnel. The more serious cases probably go to court in all provinces, and the variation across provinces in the rates of these offences is less than for the cases involving less serious offences.

These data should be interpreted with another finding in mind. More than forty percent of all custodial dispositions in Canada are for property offences and, across Canada, another 15% are used for the *Young Offenders Act* offence of failure to comply with a disposition. Hence, if a province were interested in reducing the use of custody, it might start by looking at the volume of cases – particularly the less serious cases – it is bringing to court. One can obviously also look at what is happening in the youth court and at the choices of dispositions that are available to the court. But, if one is interested in understanding where the variability lies at present, one need look no further than the court house door.

Note

1. The production of this paper was supported in part by a Social Sciences and Humanities Research Council of Canada grant to A. N. Doob.

References

Canadian Centre for Justice Statistics
1990 National Summary of Alternative Measures Services for Young Persons. Jurist Service Bulletin, Volume 10, Number 2, February 1990.

Canadian Centre for Justice Statistics
1995 Youth Court Statistics, 1993-1994. Ottawa: Statistics Canada.

Canadian Centre for Justice Statistics
1994 Canadian Crime Statistics, 1993. Ottawa: Statistics Canada.

Carrington, Peter J. and Sharon Moyer
1994 Trends in youth crime and police response, pre and post-YOA. Canadian Journal of Criminology 36: 1-28.

Doob, Anthony N., Voula Marinos, and Kimberly N. Varma
1995 Youth crime and the youth justice system in Canada: A research perspective. Toronto: Centre of Criminology.

LeBlanc, Marc and Hélène Beaumont
1992 The effectiveness of juvenile justice in Quebec: A natural experiment in implementing formal diversion in a justice model. In Ray Corrado, Nicholas Bala, Rick Linden, and Marc LeBlanc (eds.), Juvenile Justice in Canada: A Theoretical and Analytic Assessment. Toronto: Butterworths.

Snyder, Howard N., and Melissa Sickmund
1995 Juvenile Offenders and Victims: A National Report. Washington, D.C.: Office of Juvenile Justice and Delinquency Prevention, U.S. Department of Justice.

PART TWO

Youth Deviance and the State

CHAPTER SIX

Marijuana, juveniles, and the police: What high-school students believe about detection and enforcement[1]

Jessica Warner
Benedikt Fischer
Ricardo Albanes
Oren Amitay
Addiction Research Foundation
Toronto, Ontario

THIS PAPER EXAMINES HOW HIGH-SCHOOL STUDENTS CALCULATE THE risks of being caught and punished for possessing an illegal substance or for using it. The illegal substance is marijuana, and our focus is on how students categorize the motives and practices of the police officers with whom they or their peers might come into contact. The results come from a larger project examining attitudes toward marijuana and its use among young people in Ontario. The methodology is qualitative, and uses as its data the comments of high-school students who participated in focus groups. Our interest is twofold: what are the perceived legal risks associated with using or possessing marijuana, and what are the strategies for reducing those risks?

The paper starts with a review of research relevant to our topic, and then looks specifically at the beliefs and practices that police officers observe in enforcing laws against marijuana and its use. This is followed by a discussion of the methods that we used in conducting our focus groups. We conclude by presenting and then discussing our results.

Canadian Journal of Criminology/Revue canadienne de criminologie, October/octobre 1998, pp. 401–420.

Background

Researchers who study how the police do their work are apt to assume that interactions between police officers and offenders are essentially dialectical in nature. In this scenario, the offender challenges the established order, and it is the primary task of the police to reassert the primacy of that order. Hence, the importance of deference on the part of the offender. By the same token, exchanges of this sort are often assumed to be invested with an element of ritualized drama. In this scenario, the police play one role and their offenders play another, and in so doing the social order is challenged, negotiated, and ultimately reproduced in miniature. Manning (1988), for example, found that exchanges between offenders and the police serve to reaffirm order and authority, and that they do so through a dramaturgical "display of symbols that serve to draw the bounds of the permissible, the possible and the deviant."

Offenses involving marijuana are for the most part very minor, and as such can be expected to conform to what researchers have observed more generally about how the police respond to trivial violations of public order. As far as marijuana is concerned, the usual assumption is that it poses a particular threat to the maintenance of order in public settings, and that its use by youths is especially threatening to the status of the police as the "boss of the social situation" (Skolnick 1975). The reasons for the assumption are threefold. First, marijuana is very often used in public places or venues where large numbers of people are gathered. Second, its use in public places has, until recently at least, constituted a highly visible and intentional form of deviance in the form of a challenge to order and authority. And finally, its use by young people in particular is also a flashpoint. This is because the police tend to view young people as the likeliest and most natural challengers to order and authority, even in the absence of overt acts of rebellion. As such, young people who use marijuana may be viewed as posing a critical challenge to the ways in which the police are assumed to identify with middle-class morality and operationalize the symbolic-normative structure of "respectable citizens" (Ericson 1982).

Specific studies

The literature on what police officers think about marijuana and about their role in enforcing laws against it is thin. The same observation applies when it comes to determining what young users think about the police, and whether the latter's practices in enforcing laws against possession and use influence users in their strategies and behaviour. What has been published so far suggests that individual police officers vary both in their attitudes toward marijuana and in the extent to which they enforce laws banning it. California provides an example. In 1976, the state reduced penalties for possession, and these, in turn, had the practical effect of reducing incentives for the police to charge individuals found in possession of small amounts of marijuana (Gibson 1987). Sommer (1988) found that reduced penalties also resulted in greater tolerance toward marijuana on the part of law enforcement personnel. Two studies of police officers in Maryland also suggested that the police are by no means monolithic or even especially conservative in their attitudes toward marijuana or in their responses to individuals found in possession of it. The majority of his respondents believed that their colleagues were not actively enforcing the state's strict penalties for possession, and most also believed that although marijuana has harmful effects, it is no more harmful than alcohol (Beck, Kavelak, and Summons 1982; Beck and Summons 1984).

The studies that we have just cited suggest that the police are in fact highly ambivalent in both their beliefs and practices, and this raises an interesting question: are young users aware of this ambivalence, and if so, do perceptions of this sort influence how they calculate the legal risks associated with the use and possession of marijuana? This raises another question: do young people look upon the police as flawed messengers in the official campaign against marijuana? The question is highly topical, as it has a direct bearing on the effectiveness of using police officers in drug education programs.

Methods

Ethical constraints

The project's protocol, inclusive of the moderator's script and procedures for recruiting participants, was reviewed and approved by the Ethics Review Board of the Addiction Research Foundation and the University of Toronto. Additionally, one school board required review and approval by its own research review committee. Names, whether of individuals or of institutions, were deleted in the course of transcribing tapes of the sessions, and the tapes, in turn, were destroyed upon transcription.

Study group

We conducted 49 focus groups, consisting of 22 in the spring semester of 1996, 21 in the fall of the same year, and six in January of 1997. The total number of participants was 278, with 155 males and 123 females. There were 14 focus groups consisting of students in grade nine, 13 of students in grade 11, and 17 of graduating seniors only. Participants recruited at high schools totalled 252. We also conducted five focus groups made up entirely of Hispanic youths. The latter numbered 26, and consisted of one student in grade nine, three students in grade 10, 11 students in grade 11, and nine graduating seniors, in addition to two individuals not currently attending high school.

The nine high schools were chosen in an attempt to get a dispersed study group of high-school students in Ontario, with an emphasis on recruiting a study group as representative as possible of the geographical and socioeconomic distribution of the overall population of the province. Two of the schools were single-sex private schools, one for males, the other for females, in both schools, approximately 20 percent of the students were boarders. The remaining seven schools were public and coeducational, although in two of the urban schools males outnumbered females by a significant margin. Two schools were located in rural districts, and two others were located in the remote and relatively unpopulated northern region of the province. The remaining five schools, including the two private schools, were all located in greater metropolitan Toronto.

The five focus groups with Hispanic youths were conducted in Spanish, with an Hispanic liaison as the moderator. The remaining 44 focus groups were conducted in English. The students attending schools A and B were ethnically diverse, and included numerous first-generation immigrants from Portugal and several different Asian countries. All of the Hispanic participants, in turn, were first-generation immigrants to Canada; their provenance, like that of the larger Hispanic population of Canada, was highly diverse, being fairly evenly distributed between countries in South and Central America. Approximately one third of the students attending one of the two northern schools consisted of Aboriginal Canadians. Our transcripts do not allow us to identify the race or ethnicity of individual speakers; the gap is in part compensated for by the project's field notes, which include detailed observations on how members of racial or ethnic minorities responded to our questions.

We recruited participants in individual classrooms as well as in assemblies. In each instance, we described the project and reinforced our message by handing out one-page flyers that also described the project. Potential participants knew in advance that we would be asking them about their attitudes toward marijuana and its use, and that actual participants would each receive an honorarium worth approximately $15.00. Potential participants were additionally informed that participation was voluntary and that the anonymity of both the participants and of their respective schools would be safeguarded in any presentation of the results. We also emphasized that we were equally interested in talking with non-users, light users, and heavy users. Participants 18 years of age or older were allowed to sign consent forms on their own behalf, while younger participants had to obtain the signed consent of a parent or guardian. All signed consent forms were returned in sealed and unmarked envelopes, and in instances where there was a surplus of volunteers, names were randomly drawn from the box in which the envelopes were collected. It was our experience that the honorarium, in addition to the prospect of time off from class, was a strong inducement to participate, and attracted users and non-users alike.

There were four pilot focus groups in which we tested our script, after which we modified our questions and their phrasing in light of what we had learned. The focus groups were standardized to the extent that each moderator asked the same questions; at the same time, however, moderators were free to pose supplementary questions in response to points raised by participants.

Each focus group lasted for about an hour and a half. The moderators, of whom there were seven, worked on their own in each instance, and each focus group was tape-recorded for subsequent transcription. Moderators also recorded field notes immediately after recruitment as well as after each focus group, with a particular emphasis on identifying intra-group dynamics, as well as any non-verbal interactions.

We relied on the procedures of Zemke and Kramlinger (1985) in analyzing our data. Toward that end we read through our transcripts and from them generated a list of key ideas, words, phrases, and relevant quotations. From these we identified categories for further organizing sub-topics within which we grouped quotations and relevant observations from the project's field notes. These same procedures rely heavily on using representative quotes from the transcripts in illustrating the results. The transcripts were also analyzed for any intra- and inter-group variations, with a particular emphasis on any variations by gender, geographical location of individual high schools, and ethnicity. It should, however, be noted that focus groups represent an imperfect means of gathering data, and that this limits the extent to which our results can be generalized. In particular, it is impossible to measure the depth and sincerity of beliefs expressed by participants; nor is it possible to measure the extent to which the dominant members of a group influence the behaviour and remarks of other participants. As such, focus groups are an unreliable instrument for gauging the prevalence of a particular opinion in the larger population. At the same time, however, the views expressed by any one participant are subject to comment or challenge by the other participants in the group, with the result that comments tend to be influenced by what the participants collectively perceive to be the norms of their peers.

Results

We asked participants how marijuana compares to other illicit drugs, alcohol, and tobacco, and included in this set of questions specific questions about the effects of each on behaviour and functioning. We also asked participants what adults, inclusive of parents, teachers, and police officers, think about marijuana, and how they respond to adolescents who use it. From the participants' responses to these questions, we were able to identify four working assumptions that inform their beliefs about detection and enforcement. These concern: (1) marijuana's effects on demeanor, and how these effects, in turn, influence the odds of an individual's being singled out by the police; (2) the odds of being charged for use or possession once an individual has been singled out by one or more police officers; (3) the motives of police officers who confiscate marijuana; and (4) the extent to which a young person's ethnicity and social class influence individual police officers in the enforcement of laws against possession and use.

1. Beliefs about marijuana's effects on demeanor

Many of the students with whom we spoke believed that marijuana's effects on demeanor are so slight that the police cannot tell when an individual is under its influence. "The cops are so stupid around here," a female in grade 11 told us. "They have no clue." A male in grade nine at another high school told us that "they'd have to be really looking at the kid to notice if he's high or not. They'd probably tell . . . right away if he seemed drunk."

Most of our participants also believed that individuals who are high on marijuana are essentially innocuous in their demeanor, and are as a result less likely to be singled out by the police than are individuals who are drunk or otherwise out of control. A remark made by a graduating senior male illustrates the point: "I don't see how they can really tell unless you, like, have a joint in your hand." The remark was credible to the other members of the focus group. "There's some people that are really good at being stoned," said one. "Like, you can barely tell." "People can hide it," added another. A female in grade nine claimed that "some people can hide alcohol," and further claimed that these same people "can be real straight walking down the street." The other members of the group strongly disagreed. People who are drunk are "less aware of what they're doing," explained one. "You can walk down the street when you're drunk and do something stupid and you don't know. But if you're on weed, you could most likely control it." "You know what you're doing when you're on weed," added another.

The same distinctions were maintained when we asked students to compare marijuana to other illegal drugs. The latter they associated with obsessive and unpredictable behaviour, that is, with behaviour that might either be disruptive or otherwise require the intervention of the police. "People who do cocaine, heroin, speed, ... all the huge uppers, they have more of a craving for it," explained a graduating senior male. "It's like their lifestyle drastically changes to adapt to this drug." "Your lifestyle doesn't really change that much" with marijuana, he added. And a male in grade 11 told us that "you don't see people robbing a store or beating up somebody for a piece of marijuana, but you see people doing that for crack, heroin, ecstasy, whatever else."

2. *Beliefs about the probability of actually being charged*

Most of our participants believed that the police are neither systematic nor active in enforcing laws against possession. "It really depends on the cop, ... like, what their personality is," explained a female in grade 11. "It depends if the cop is ... a cranky asshole or if the cop is nice," explained a male in grade nine. A graduating senior male believed that luck determined the outcome of an exchange with the police. "If they are acting like they want to make a difference that day then they will make a big thing out of it," he said, adding that "it's all an attitude and what kind of cop you're dealing with ..."

Most of the purported incidents described in our transcripts did not result in arrest, consistent with studies that show the probability of arrest is very low when the offender is a juvenile and the presumed offense is minor (Black and Reiss 1970; Lundman, Sykes, and Clark 1978). In the stories that our participants told, police officers typically confiscated marijuana, and only some of the officers in question also issued a warning. A female in grade 11 told us that the police "don't really do anything about drugs because my brother and his friends got pulled over and they found a bag of marijuana in the glove compartment and they just dumped it out and said, 'don't do this' ..." A male in grade 11 told us what happened when he and some friends were pulled over by a police officer at four in the morning: "... we're driving and it was ... a lot of smoke and we opened the windows and ... he came and he said he knew what we were doing, and he said, 'give me the stuff,' and we gave it, and he dumped it, and he goes, 'I can't really let you have it.'" A graduating senior male told us that when he had been "caught with pot" the police officer threw it away and "just said to me, 'go home.' And I hear that that happens ... all the time ..."

Moreover, many of our participants were able to cite instances in which the police temporarily detained suspects, but did not press charges. In each of these instances the suspect was released after he or she had, for all intents and purposes, been "scared straight." A male in grade nine, for example, told the story of an acquaintance who had been arrested for possession, only to be released after "a slap on the wrist." "They talked to him. They gave him a slap on the wrist and said don't do it again and let him go." A graduating senior male told the story of a friend who "happened to have a bag of hash on him." The police, he claimed, "handcuffed him and they put him in the car and they're ... scaring him and stuff. Like, 'you're under arrest, blah, blah, blah ...' Ten minutes later they dumped it into the drain and let us go. Just gave us a warning."

In most of the incidents described in our transcripts, actual arrests occurred only when an individual was suspected of trafficking in marijuana. Individuals carrying large quantities of marijuana were thus believed to be at a higher risk of arrest than were casual users. The same was true of individuals carrying units potentially packaged for resale. As a consequence, most casual users felt that they could act with relative impunity in the presence of the police. There were two reasons for this assumption. First, as we have already seen, most participants believed that marijuana has very little effect on demeanor. And second, most participants believed that the probability of being charged for possession is very low, provided that an individual is carrying marijuana in quantities too small for resale. In the words of a male in grade 11, "if you have a little," and it "looks like a cigarette, they ain't gonna do nothing 'cause, like, it's ... your own personal use ..." A female in grade 11 told us that the chances of being arrested depend "on how much you have" and "on how you have it." They "let you off a lot of times if ... you just have it in a bag ... If you have it ... in foil or whatever and you have all different sizes and stuff you get charged with trafficking."

The distinctions reported by our participants correspond very closely to those contained in Canada's *Narcotic Control Act* and in the pending *Controlled Drugs and Substances Act*. Both acts mandate up to seven years' imprisonment for trafficking in marijuana; first-time offenders, by contrast, can be imprisoned for no more than six months, and may also be subject to a fine of no more than $1,000, provided that they were found in possession of less than 30 grams of marijuana or less than one gram of hashish (Fischer, Erickson, and Smart 1996). The discrepancy between the penalties for the two offenses was very clearly a factor in how our participants calculated the odds of being charged for an offense involving marijuana. In particular, they believed that the police were likely to press charges only when the severity of the penalties associated with the crime outweighed the loss of time to paperwork and other procedural details, or when the offender could also be charged with some other crime that would justify time away from the beat. In the words of one graduating senior male, "they have to do, like, three hours of paper work to arrest a student for this type of thing. And they think, 'well, it's not going to do them any good, so if I dump it I'll save myself some paper work; it's not a big deal ..." The participants may also have calculated that their odds of actually being convicted and punished were also very low, as has been documented by Erickson and Murray (1988), but the topic did not arise in the course of our focus groups.

An additional factor concerns the extent to which individual police officers are invested in helping young people who are enrolled in high school complete their education and enter adulthood without the stigma of a criminal record. This topic, however, came up only once over the course of the focus groups with non-Hispanic participants, and was, perhaps not surprisingly, raised by a male in his final year at an exclusive private school:

> I figured that cops don't want to bust kids for having drugs. And if they run into a kid who does and they check up on him and find out that he's never really gotten into any trouble with the law before, then they'll let him off because they don't want to see a kid's future get potentially ruined by something so they'll try to scare him and, you know, make it so he's more careful and won't do it again.

In most of the examples given by our participants, the police took it upon themselves to punish offenders, whether by confiscating their marijuana, or by temporarily detaining them. Offenders in this class were never formally charged, but they were subjected to a form of extra-legal justice, consistent with Reiss' (1971) claim that, in each encounter with a suspect, police officers stage a trial to determine who is guilty and who is not, and then assign punishment as appropriate.

The participants' accounts also show a keen understanding of the extent to which the police exercise discretion in determining both an offender's intent and possible involvement in other criminal activities, as inferred from the amount of marijuana found in his or her possession, the ways in which it is packaged, or by more impressionistic visual cues, most notably, race or ethnicity, and clothing. The latter two cues were especially important in the case of Hispanic youths, but were also understood by their peers elsewhere in the province. This observation, for example, comes from a female in grade 11 at high school E, which is located in one of Toronto's more affluent neighbourhoods:

> You'd be walking down the street and if you're wearing, like, nice clothes ... they won't stop and talk to you ... They'll categorize by the clothes you're wearing. You may not be doing anything wrong. You may be waiting at ... a bus stop for a bus, and they'll come up and start yelling at you and screaming at you. "Empty out your bag! What are you doing?"

Our results also suggest that many students believe that possession alone constitutes grounds for arrest. A graduating senior male thus claimed that he could "walk into a police station high 'cause I know my rights and I know exactly what they can do and what they can't do to me." The police, said one graduating senior male, might "try to harass you for a bit, but that's about all they can do ... sit there and laugh." Another graduating senior male told us that he thought that "it's a lot more difficult to test that you're high. I mean, they may be able to smell it but . . . what are they going to say to a judge? 'Yeah, I smelt it on him.' That's not going to go very far."(2)

Most of the students in our study group reported that they tend to be more circumspect in where and when they use marijuana than they are when using alcohol, and that this caution, in turn, reduces the odds of their coming into contact with the police. This was especially true of female participants, who reported that they tend to use marijuana in settings that offer privacy and, with it, a certain degree of security from exposure and possible arrest. This is consistent with what Johnson and his colleagues (Johnson, Peterson, and Wells 1977) found, namely, that females were arrested in much lower numbers than were males, in part because their levels of use were lower, and in part because they tended to use marijuana indoors and on private property. By the same token, males were likelier to be arrested by patrolmen in the course of routinely policing public areas, while females were likelier to be arrested in the course of investigative or proactive policing. As a female in grade 11 observed, "if you're going to smoke it just ... don't make it where it's obvious."

3. *Beliefs about the motives of police officers who confiscate marijuana*

Many students believed that police officers confiscate marijuana in order to use it themselves. "Finders keepers," explained a graduating senior male. Another graduating senior male speculated that "they might take it from you and smoke it themselves." "It happens," he added. According to a male in grade 11, police officers "confiscate it and go smoke it themselves." Another male in the same focus group agreed. "I've seen that happen," he said. And a male in grade nine told us this: "Cops smoke it. Like, if there's ... a van full of weed or something, you can't tell me that they don't take bricks of that ... And then, like, all the rest of the cops ... have it down their pants or something."

These beliefs are interesting on two levels. First, they serve to diminish the moral authority of the police by ascribing to them the desires and values of the young people whom they monitor and control. This is implicit in the belief that police officers themselves use marijuana, which is to say that they are believed to see marijuana much as young users see it, namely, as a substance whose effects are desirable and whose use does not especially threaten public order and decorum. The second level of interest also involves an element of projection on the part of our participants. In particular, stories about police officers who confiscate marijuana in order to use it themselves very closely resemble a practice known to high-school students as "taxing." "Taxing" occurs when a dealer or individual user is attacked by other adolescents and is robbed of his or her drugs and money. Here, the victim is without recourse, and can complain neither to the police nor to teachers or parents. In the words of one female in grade nine, "you get taxed, what are you going to say? 'Oh, they stole my pot!'"

4. Beliefs about ethnicity and social class

The reports of Hispanic participants were very different from those of our other participants, and also differed significantly from those of their peers in the two inner-city high schools where we conducted our focus groups. Most Hispanic participants believed that the use of marijuana is likelier to get an individual into trouble with the police than is the use of alcohol, although a sizable minority believed that the use of alcohol can also be highly risky, especially in conjunction with driving. This is in direct contrast to the remarks of our other participants, who believed that the use of alcohol incurs greater risk. An Hispanic female, for example, told us that the police react more strongly when they find an underage youth in possession of marijuana than they do when he or she is drunk or in possession of alcohol; she qualified the observation by adding that driving under the influence of alcohol is a more serious offense than being caught high on marijuana.

Because questions about the police made many of our Hispanic participants uneasy, we opted to turn off the tape recorder while asking for examples of their interactions with the police. Field notes recorded immediately after these sessions revealed the following assumptions:

I. The police, it was widely believed, tend to discriminate against Hispanic youths on the basis of ethnicity and clothing, and make no effort to distinguish youths who use marijuana from those who do not. This is most dramatically the case when the police confront groups of Hispanic youths in public places such as parks. Only some members of the groups may use marijuana or have criminal records, and yet all are treated with the utmost suspicion by the police. This, in the eyes of our participants, amounts to guilt by association. Moreover, numerous Hispanic participants believed that the police single out Hispanic youths, and use simple possession as a pretext for arresting them. Their non-Hispanic peers, by contrast, were believed to receive much better treatment at the hands of the police.

II. The participants believed that the police frequently exceed their authority in their dealings with young Hispanic users. As examples they mentioned planting evidence in the form of marijuana and beating Hispanic suspects. Moreover, Hispanic youths who claimed to have done nothing illegal were nonetheless perceived to be at a higher risk of being arrested and charged for simple possession or trafficking than were their non-Hispanic counterparts.

III. Youths who have been formally charged or who already have criminal records felt that they continued to be treated with suspicion by the police upon completing their sentences. They claimed that the police continue to monitor them closely, and make it difficult for them to associate with other Hispanic youths or even to go out in public. The underlying assumption was that former offenders need the support of the police if they are to be rehabilitated and reintegrated into the larger society. This support, it was widely felt, is not forthcoming.

Discussion

A regime of discretionary enforcement

Most of the students with whom we spoke were under the impression that the police are lax in enforcing laws against marijuana. The fact that most participants told stories not about their own close brushes with the law but about those of friends or acquaintances is also revealing. At the very least, it suggests that large numbers of high-school students are able to smoke marijuana without ever coming into contact with the police, and that the effectiveness of the police as a deterrent is, as has already been more generally observed by Gibbs (1975), Homel (1988), and Schneider (1990), very much diminished in the eyes of both potential and actual offenders.

Most participants also believed that police officers will, in most instances, stop short of imposing formal legal sanctions on young users. The impression is broadly consistent with what Skolnick (1975) described in *Justice without Trial.* Skolnick reported that police officers exercise considerable discretion in how they enforce laws, especially those designed to control vice. Police officers, he claimed, effectively dispense a sort of street justice that often circumvents the courts altogether. In the case of offenses involving marijuana, this may reflect a reluctance to process the paperwork associated with each such offense, as was noted by Manning (1980); it may reflect that the police are generally reluctant to take formal actions against minor offenses, and prefer instead to do nothing at all, give some form of advice, or impose informal sanctions (Bayley 1994); it may reflect the fact that the majority of the officers in question belong to a generation that has already come to terms with marijuana; or it may, more plausibly, reflect a bit of each.

The exercise of discretionary enforcement on the part of individual police officers led many of our participants to impugn the motives of all police officers. Police officers who enforce the law and charge offenders were thus widely regarded as overzealous, in large part because so many of their colleagues choose not to press charges. For their part, officers who confiscate marijuana without pressing charges were also regarded with considerable suspicion, on the assumption that they intend to use it themselves. The dilemma is not dissimilar to that described by Cressey (1975) in his study of traffic enforcement. The policeman, he wrote, is a player "in a game that he cannot win." He "is damned for being inhumanly zealous" if "he enforces the law in a routine and efficient way," and "he is damned for operationalizing discriminatory attitudes" if he instead exercises discretion in enforcing the law.

The variables of social class and ethnicity were a further source of cynicism among our participants. Middle-class adolescents reported that they are able to exploit the variables of social class and ethnicity to their advantage; Hispanic adolescents reported just the opposite. The remarks of our Hispanic participants are broadly consistent with what Johnson and his colleagues (1977) found in investigating racial differences in arrests in Cook County, Illinois. The team found that blacks were likelier to be arrested in the course of routine patrols, whether as a result of simply coming into contact with the police, or as a result of being suspected of committing offenses not involving illicit drugs. Their reported experiences may also reflect the fact that different social classes have differential access to what Chambliss and Seidman (1971) described as "the institution of privacy." In practical terms, the odds of being arrested increase to the extent that an individual inhabits public spaces or is otherwise visible (Spradley 1970), whether by choice or by necessity. Johnson and his colleagues (1977) speculated that the two factors in combination, namely, the social location of use *and* the suspicion cued by certain sociodemographic characteristics of users, account for significant differentials in the probability of being arrested for offenses involving marijuana.

By the same token, adolescents who are easily identified as high-school students may also enjoy certain advantages in their interactions with the police. Their status as students is relevant on two levels. First, young people who manage to stay in high school are fulfilling the role that their society expects of them at their age, and this, by itself, implies a certain level of deference to the social norms that the police are presumed to believe in and uphold (Ericson 1982; Goffman 1971). And second, staying in high school requires that an individual master the art of deferring to adults in a position of authority, if only on a minimal or token level, and this, in turn, is a skill that can also be used to influence the outcome of an encounter with the police. The comment of a police officer in Fletcher's (1991) study illustrates the point: "People write their own tickets. Your conduct to me will predict how I'll act to you. Your attitude writes your ticket." And indeed, most of our middle-class participants felt that they could exercise considerable control over the outcome of a chance encounter with the police, depending on how well they comported themselves and otherwise played their role in the ensuing exchange.

Marijuana and authority

A few of the inner-city males with whom we spoke almost seemed disappointed by the sheer banality of their purported encounters with the police. Their disappointment and our more general findings suggest to us that marijuana has lost much of its symbolic value, and that it has ceased to afford an opportunity to confront authority in its most obvious form, again excepting our Hispanic participants. Still less did its use afford our participants the opportunity to create the sorts of heroic images of themselves that Chandra Mukerji (1978) found among young male hitchhikers back in the early 1970s. A story told by a male in grade 11 illustrates the point:

> ... I'm going to work and smoking a spliff and he's coming out on his bike and I put it in my mouth just to see whether they would come over and ask me what I'm doing with that

> stuff. I'm smoking it, you know, so he said, "OK, I'm supposed to throw it away," and I'm like, "no, I can't throw it away." So he took it from me and stepped on it. So I say, "so you're not going to charge me?" and he said no.

By the same token, our results suggest that minor offenses involving marijuana have ceased to afford police officers the opportunity to reaffirm authority, provided that the offenders are middle-class and otherwise inconspicuous. Rather, we are looking at symbolic interactions that are in fact increasingly devoid of any larger meaning or dialectical imperative. This is in line with Hathaway's (1997) claim that the use of marijuana has "become a lifestyle choice rather than the mark of a subculture."

Our findings further suggest that there is a tacit agreement linking casual middle-class users and police officers. Neither group is especially threatened by the other, and neither equates marijuana with a breakdown in public order, or with an assault on the middle-class respectability which the police are presumed to believe in and uphold (Ericson 1982). This equation continues to exclude dealers, as well as minorities whose culture and values are rejected by the police. Hence, the very different experiences of the Hispanic youths with whom we spoke. The same equation also casts serious doubt on the appropriateness of assigning police officers to the educational vanguard of the war on drugs. While our findings do not allow us to generalize about drugs other than marijuana, they do suggest that the police and young middle-class users may see marijuana in very similar terms, and that, under the circumstances, it makes little sense to have police officers deliver messages that are at variance with what they are presumed to believe and do.

Notes

1. Special thanks go to Birgitta Pavic, Cindy Smythe, Phil Lange, and Tamara Blitz-Miller for their hard work and resourcefulness in recruiting participants and in conducting focus groups.
2. The statement is inaccurate. In Canadian case law, the smell of marijuana on a suspect can constitute reasonable grounds for arrest.

References

Bayley, David H.
1994 Police for the Future. Oxford: Oxford University Press.

Beck, Kenneth H., Anthony L. Kavelak, and Terry G. Summons
1982 Police officer attitudes toward marijuana: a descriptive analysis. American Journal of Drug and Alcohol Abuse 9: 183-193.

Beck, Kenneth H. and Terry G. Summons
1984 Police officer attitudes toward marijuana: a replication and confirmation. American Journal of Drug and Alcohol Abuse 10: 519-528.

Black, Donald and Albert J. Reiss
1970 Police control of juveniles. American Sociological Review 35: 63-77.

Chambliss, W. and R. Seidman
1971 Law, Order and Power. Reading, Massachusetts: Addison-Wesley.

Cressey, Donald
1975 Law, order and the motorist. In Roger Hood (ed.), Crime, Criminality and Public Policy. New York: The Free Press.

Erickson, Patricia G. and Glenn F. Murray
1988 Cannabis criminals revisited. In Judith C. Blackwell and Patricia G. Erickson (eds.), Illicit Drugs in Canada. A Risky Business. Scarborough, Ontario: Nelson Canada.

Ericson, Richard V.
1982 Reproducing Order: a Study of Police Patrol Work. Toronto: University of Toronto Press.

Fischer, Benedikt, Patricia G. Erickson, and Reginald Smart
1996 The new Canadian drug law: One step forward, two steps backward. The International Journal of Drug Policy 7: 172-179.

Fletcher, Connie
1991 Pure Cop. New York: Villard Books.

Gibbs, J.P.
1975 Crime, Punishment and Deterrence. New York: Elsevier.

Gibson, S.
1987 Arresting pot smokers often 'not worth the time'. Sacramento Bee. August 2: A1.

Goffman, Erving
1971 Insanity of Place. In Erving Goffman (ed.), Relations in Public. Microstudies of the Public Order. New York: Basic Books, Inc.

Hathaway, Andrew D.
1997 Marijuana and tolerance: Revisiting Becker's sources of control. Deviant Behavior 18: 103-124.

Homel, Ross
1988 Policing and Punishing the Drinking Driver. A Study of General and Specific Deterrence. London: Springer-Verlag.

Johnson, Weldon T., Robert E. Peterson, and L.Edward Wells
1977 Arrest probabilities for marijuana users as indicators of selective law enforcement. American Journal of Sociology 83: 681-699.

Lundman, Richard J., Richard E. Sykes, and John P. Clark
1978 Police control of juveniles: A replication. Journal of Research in Crime and Delinquency 15: 127-141.

Manning, Peter K.
1980 The Narcs' Game. Organizational and Informational Limits on Drug Law Enforcement. Cambridge, Massachusetts: The MIT Press.

Manning, Peter K.
1988 Community policing as a drama of control. In Jack R. Greene, and Stephen D. Mastrofski (eds.), Community Policing. Rhetoric or Reality. New York: Praeger.

Mukerji, Chandra
1978 Bullshitting: Road lore among hitchhikers. Social Problems 25: 241-252.

Reiss, Albert J.
1971 The Police and the Public. New Haven: Yale University Press.

Schneider, Anne L.
1990 Deterrence and Juvenile Crime. Results from a National Policy Experiment. New York: Springer-Verlag.

Skolnick, Jerome H.
1975 Justice without Trial: Law Enforcement in a Democratic Society. Second ed. New York: John Wiley and Sons.

Sommer, Robert
1988 Two decades of marijuana attitudes: The more it changes, the more it stays the same. Journal of Psychoactive Drugs 20: 67-70.

Spradley, James P.
1970 You Owe yourself a Drunk. An Ethnography of Urban Nomads. Boston: Little, Brown and Company.

Zemke, Ron and T. Kramlinger
1985 Figuring it out. Reading, Massachusetts: Addison Wesley.

CHAPTER SEVEN

Criminal business organizations, street gangs and 'wanna-be' groups: A Vancouver perspective[1]

Robert M. Gordon
School of Criminology,
Simon Fraser University,
Burnaby, B.C.

THOSE INTERESTED IN THE "GANG" PHENOMENON IN CANADA ARE frequently surprised by the absence of a body of research that is distinctively Canadian and publicly available. The first recorded piece of work was a study of juveniles in street gangs in Toronto in the 1940's undertaken by Rogers (Rogers 1945), and there is an occasional reference to street gangs and youth gangs in other publications (e.g., Ley 1975). Some research was also conducted by Joe and Robinson on street gangs in the "Chinatown" area of Vancouver in the late 1970's (Joe and Robinson 1980). Apart from this, no organized and systematic research was undertaken, and nothing was published, until quite recently.

The same appears to be true for the research and literature on criminal organizations. Beare's (1996) recently published book on organized crime (or criminal enterprises) in Canada is the first major contribution to the field. A host of important definitional, policy, and legislative issues are canvassed (especially with respect to money laundering) and help pave the way for new empirical research. Dubro's (1985; 1992) journalistic accounts of the Mafia, and of Asian organized crime in Canada are illuminating, and the nature and form of

Canadian Journal of Criminology/Revue canadienne de criminologie, January/janvier 2000, pp. 39–60.

Canadian organized crime is usefully clarified in a recently released report of a pilot survey of organized criminal activity conducted by the Canadian Centre for Justice Statistics (1999). Wolf's (1991) ethnography of biker gangs in Alberta still stands as the only insider's account of what, for some analysts, is a criminal organization (e.g., Beare 1996; Canadian Centre for Justice Statistics 1999) but which, in Wolf's view, is a subculture of rebels – a brotherhood of outlaws – for whom crime is a casual rather than entrenched activity. It is clear that the debate over the nature of biker gangs will continue for some time and that an accurate picture is often blurred by regional and other variations. As Wolf (1991: 268) points out, there are tremendous differences between clubs and between chapters, and those involved in the "full gamut of crime remain a distinct minority". This is supported by one of the findings in the report of the Centre for Justice Statistics (1999: 19) which acknowledges that "among all the motorcycle associations, only 1% fall into the underworld of organized crime".

Several pieces of Canadian gang research were coincidentally released in 1993. Three reports, each written for either the federal or the provincial levels of government (Fasiolo and Leckie 1993; Gordon 1993; Mathews 1993), and an unpublished M.A. thesis (Young 1993) examined different aspects of the gang phenomenon. In addition, Kennedy and Baron (1993) and Baron and Tindall (1993) published their studies of groups of street youth in part to understand better an apparent increase in youth violence. All of this work provided not only the answers to some pressing policy questions (e.g., to what extent are Canadian street gangs dominated by the members of visible ethnic minorities?) but also the building blocks for more comprehensive research such as the Greater Vancouver Gang Study.

Fasilio and Leckie's work (1993) on the coverage of gangs and gang activity by the Canadian media made an extremely valuable contribution to what was, at the time, a lively debate over news media amplification of the nation's street gang "problem." The authors undertook a content analysis of major national news magazines and the major daily newspapers published in urban centres such as Vancouver, Winnipeg, Toronto, and Montreal between July and October 1992. They found that the media characterized gangs and gang activity as widespread, a significant threat to society, and as a relatively new phenomenon. Gangs were depicted as a subject of "growing social concern" and the product of an ailing society; themes which, according to Young (1993), have been trumpeted by Canadian newspapers during every wave of urban street gang activity since at least 1945.

Fasilio and Leckie noted the absence of any historical reference or perspective in the stories and a focus that accentuated polarization along ethnic lines: "Asian gangs" were a particular menace. One consequence, the authors argued, was an unjustified increase in the fear of gangs and gang activity, and a similarly unwarranted concern over the extent to which immigrants who were members of visible ethnic minorities were responsible for gang related crimes. The reasons why gangs emerged were largely ignored apart from some vague references to the consequences of immigration policies and practices. Generally, in the authors' view, the media were contributing to a moral panic.

Gordon's (1993) preliminary study of gang members in British Columbia correctional centres provided something of a counterfoil to the news media's pre-occupation with "Asian gangs" and "youth gangs." The files of 41 male inmates (adult and youth) who were identified as active gang members by the police and corrections personnel were examined and the inmates were asked to participate in interviews. Ten adults and 24 young offenders were interviewed, the goal being to obtain information about the activities and membership of gangs in the province (especially the Greater Vancouver area) and the reasons why young people, in particular, became involved with gangs. A secondary objective was to design and test some research definitions and instruments for use in a later study (i.e., the Greater Vancouver Gang Study).

The majority of incarcerated gang members were young adult males (the mean age was 19), rather than young offenders. This finding was of importance in combating the false perceptions created by the news media's use of the term "youth gangs." Also of importance was the finding that the largest single group of incarcerated gang members were individuals of European ethnic origin born in Canada (40 percent). The next largest group were individuals of Asian ethnic origin (34 per cent), the majority having been born in Canada. There were very few gang members of East Indian, aboriginal, and Hispanic origin, and only one black gang member in the sample. Overall, 32 per cent of incarcerated gang members were not born in Canada; a proportion higher than the proportion of immigrants in the provincial population and, therefore, the expected percentage (22 percent). This finding lent support to an hypothesized relationship between immigration and gang membership. As Gordon and Nelson (2000) have pointed out, however, the actual numbers of gang members in the study who were not born in Canada (14) is extremely small, especially when compared with the size of the immigrant population in the province as a whole (approximately 750,000 people).

The gang members who were interviewed indicated that they were not coerced or otherwise pressured into joining gangs and that the process of becoming involved was a gradual, rather than abrupt event. There was a slow drift towards involvement that was often initiated by a close relative or a friend who was already a member of a gang or who knew a gang member. A prospective member would spend time on the periphery of the group but might eventually be drawn in, undergo an initiation ceremony, and then become a full member. As Gordon (1993; 1995) points out, the process was neither strange nor surprising and was similar to the experiences of a young person joining a legitimate "gang" such as the boy scouts or a baseball team.

According to Gordon (1993), the availability of choices is a key to understanding a person's involvement in gangs. If an individual has no access to, or is not encouraged to join, a mainstream group, an "illegitimate" group may be chosen instead, an hypothesis reflecting the seminal work of Cloward and Ohlin (1960) that was supported, in part, by the research data. Nearly one half of the subjects had backgrounds filled with domestic problems including drug, alcohol, and physical abuse in the family coupled with school records of truancy, fighting, suspensions, and expulsions. The picture was one of troubled individuals from troubled backgrounds. When these problems were related to the reasons why the subjects became involved with gangs (as stated in interviews), it was clear that the choice of an illegitimate, rather than legitimate, group was a function of the absence of alternatives. The reasons why other subjects became involved with gangs were not so clear. Some became involved primarily to continue associations with friends, to make money, and for the relief of boredom, considerations that could not be satisfied by membership in a legitimate "gang".

Mathews' (1993) preliminary research in Toronto also involved interviews with youth gang members. The study was intended to allow young people a voice in the emerging debate on gangs and groups. Youth involved in gang activity were approached by experienced social services and police personnel and asked to participate in the study. Twelve young people aged from 14 to 21 years agreed and were interviewed. Interviews were also conducted with social workers, police officers, school officials, the parents of gang members, and some victims of gang activity.

Mathews recognized that the term "gang" can be misleading and that the term "gang/group" is a better way of describing the different kinds of gatherings of young people. Analysts and policy-makers should view the phenomenon along a continuum ranging from groups of friends who spend time together and who occasionally get into trouble, to more serious, organized criminal groups or gangs. Mathews also developed an exploratory "gang/group involvement cycle" and a multivariate causal model. The model accounts for the process of joining, remaining with, and leaving a gang by reference to several variables including individual vulnerability factors that can drive a young person into a gang/group (e.g., an abusive family environment), situational factors, the larger social context, and the nature of the responses to the youth's behaviour.

Young's (1993) study of the history of gangs in Vancouver filled a significant gap in Canadian gang research by providing the first socio-historical analysis of youth gang activity. Young scrutinized each daily edition of a major Vancouver newspaper for an 85-year period and, when articles reporting gang activity were found, these were cross checked against stories in other newspapers. Young argues that the first significant wave of street gang activity occurred between 1948 and 1959: the era of the "Hoodlum Gangs". These street gangs included the "Alma Dukes" and the "Vic Gang", and the characteristics and activities of these gangs were similar to those of street gangs in more recent times. The second wave of street gang activity occurred between 1970 and 1975 and consisted of two, seemingly unrelated clusters of gangs: the "Park Gangs" (e.g., the *Riley Park Gang* and the *Clark Park Gang*), and the "Chinatown Gangs" discussed by Joe and Robinson (1980). The Chinatown gangs of the early 1970's included some gangs that may have eventually evolved into criminal business organizations. The third, and most recent, wave of street gang activity began in 1985 and began to dissipate in the mid-1990's.

Young attempted to explain the wavelike pattern during the post 1945 period by focusing on two independent variables: inward migration; and unemployment rates. A preliminary analysis of these variables indicated a slight positive relationship between inward migration rates and reported fluctuations in gang activity. Unemployment rates and fluctuations in gang activity were inversely related but Young cautions against the use of these results, beyond the development of hypotheses for future research.

The Greater Vancouver Gang Study

Method

The Greater Vancouver Gang Study was designed to build upon the existing but limited pool of knowledge about gangs and similar groups in Canada, and to inform policy and practice in British Columbia. The Study had four main goals: to develop profile data on known gang members (e.g., age, gender, and ethnicity); to test the validity of the classifications and definitions of gangs and groups proposed and discussed in preliminary studies; and to determine why individuals became involved with and left gangs. This third goal included identifying the processes of involvement and disengagement, with a particular emphasis on the psychological and sociological factors that propel individuals into gangs. The fourth goal was to examine the organization, composition, and activities of gangs, from the perspectives of those involved with, and those working with, gangs.

The research subjects were all adults and youth on the caseloads of corrections personnel in the Greater Vancouver area in January 1995, and those who were added to their caseloads during the following six months, who were identified by these personnel as being involved with "gangs". The group included individuals sentenced to terms of imprisonment and probation or those undertaking other forms of supervised community service. The main portion of the research took place during the first six months of 1995 and involved reviewing and extracting information from client files, interviewing clients who were willing to participate, and discussing individual cases with probation officers and police officers. The purpose was to obtain as many perspectives on a client as possible. A total of 128 subjects were included in the research and 33 agreed to be interviewed, in some cases with the assistance of a social worker or probation officer who spoke the subject's first language. The interviews were conducted in probation offices, "natural settings" in the community (c.g., coffee shops), and in correctional centres. In addition, there were 11 family visits and interviews each conducted by a qualified and experienced family therapist assisted by an experienced social worker who spoke the languages of the families.

Although the subjects were the entire population of "gang members" known to the provincial Corrections Branch at the time, they were not the entire population of gang members in the Vancouver area. The extent to which the subjects are representative of the larger gang population is impossible to determine (no "gang census" was available), and the proportion of the larger gang population represented by the research subjects is similarly impossible to ascertain. The estimated numbers of gangs and gang members varies considerably at any given moment, and from year to year, and even the best estimates offered by authoritative sources such as the police are only ever educated guesses. Communication breakdowns, rivalries, and territoriality affecting the police departments in the Greater Vancouver area also means that no single police unit has a comprehensive overview of the situation.

The status of the gang members involved in the research could not be determined with certainty. Police and probation officers offered their best opinions but it was not always clear whether a subject was a core member of a gang, an associate, or a peripheral (or wanna-be) member. In addition, the gang members involved in the research were those who had been caught, charged, and convicted, and this must be borne in mind when interpreting the results. Further challenges were posed by the perennial problem of defining gangs.

Defining "gangs"

One of the initial problems for the Study was finding an accurate and widely accepted definition of a "gang", and a "gang member". Similar difficulties are reported consistently in research reports and other literature on gangs, regardless of the location and objectives of the research, and the methods used by the researchers (e.g., Goldstein and Huff 1993; Mathews 1993; Klein, Maxson, and Miller 1995; Spergel 1995; Curry and

Decker 1998). A valid and reliable answer to the question "what is a gang?" has been elusive and depends upon who is asked. Different police departments and individual police officers have different conceptions and definitions (formal and informal), as do probation officers, corrections centre staff, researchers, policy-makers, and the members of "gangs" and criminal groups.

As the research proceeded, it became clear that small groups of offenders were being referred to as "gangs" when the members of these groups did not see themselves that way. Perhaps predictably, the primary offenders seemed to be the news media who used a range of inaccurate terms to describe groups (e.g., Asian gangs, and youth gangs), thereby generally distorting and amplifying the "gang" problem. In one case, a daily newspaper actually constructed a name for a small group of young offenders who, for several weeks, had been bullying high school students into parting with cash and possessions, and then began to refer to this group as a "gang". The name given by the newspaper – the "Back Alley Boys" – reflected both the chosen scene of crime (alleyways at the rear of houses) and the membership of the group (teenage males), but it was an imposed name.

Another example of the problem of construction involved both the media and the police. The so-called "626 gang" was a group of eight youth and young adults who committed a series of armed robberies of banks, stores, and credit unions in the Greater Vancouver area, over a four month period in 1992. The group was named the "626 gang" by the police because they consistently used stolen Mazda 626 automobiles to drive to and escape from the scenes of their robberies. When members of the "gang" were interviewed it became clear that they had not chosen the "gang" name and did not see themselves as a "gang"; they were simply a group drawn together by friendship and a common interest in crime that decided to try its luck at armed robbery.(2)

Attaining a common and accurate understanding of a phenomenon (or phenomena) being studied, and about which policy and programming are being developed, is important. In the absence of common and widely accepted conceptions and definitions research, policy development, program development, and even police operations, both within and between jurisdictions, will be confused and confusing. The Greater Vancouver Gang Study took a grounded approach to the development of gang classifications and definitions. A typology was developed and tested prior to the main research and a great deal of time and effort was expended on this component. Six main types of groups that seemed to attract the label "gang" were identified: youth movements; youth groups; criminal groups; wanna-be groups; street gangs; and criminal business organizations.(3) The research concentrated on the last three types.

Criminal business organizations are organized groups that exhibit a formal structure and a high degree of sophistication. Organizations are comprised primarily of adults, including older adults. They engage in criminal activity primarily for economic reasons and almost invariably maintain a low profile, which is a characteristic that distinguishes them most clearly from street gangs. Organizations may have a name, examples being *Lotus, The Flying Dragons,* and *The Big Circle Boys (Dai Huen Jai).* There were 24 members of criminal business organizations in the research, representing both the organizations named above and three other organizations.

Street gangs are groups of young people, mainly young adults, who band together to form a semi-structured organization the primary purpose of which is to engage in planned and profitable criminal behaviour or organized violence against rival street gangs. They can be distinguished from other groups (especially wanna-be groups) by a self-perception of the group as a gang; a name selected and used by gang members; and some kind of identifying marks such as clothing and colours. The members will openly acknowledge gang membership because they want to be seen as gang members by others. Street gangs will tend to be less visible but more structured, better organized, and more permanent than wanna-be groups. Examples include *Persian Pride, Midnight Rockers,* and the quintessential Vancouver street gang of the 1980's and 1990's: *Los Diablos.* There were 35 members of street gangs in the research, representing both the gangs named above and ten other gangs.

Wanna-be groups are clusters of young people who band together in a loosely structured group to engage in spontaneous social activity and exciting, impulsive, criminal activity including collective violence against other groups of youths. A wanna-be group will be highly visible and its members will openly acknowledge their "gang" involvement because they want to be seen by others as gang members. The group will have a local gathering area and a name, selected and used by its members, which may be a modified version of the name of either a local or an American street gang. The group may use clothing, colours, or some other kind of identifying marks. The group's name, meeting ground, and colours may fluctuate. Examples include a suburban wanna-be group known as *Los Cholos* that was active in Greater Vancouver during the early 1990's. There were 25 members of wanna-be groups in the research, representing *Los Cholos* and six other groups.

The categories and definitions are not perfect, partly because of inter-relationships between the groups that tend to blur boundaries. Some street gangs were allied to criminal business organizations, one example being the link between the street gang known as *Los Diablos* and the criminal business organization known as *Lotus* (Gordon 1998). During the late 1980's and early 1990's, *Los Diablos* acted as the drug retail and enforcement arm of *Lotus,* some key members of *Los Diablos* also being *Lotus* associates. Some criminal groups are affiliated with criminal business organizations, many of which have a cell-like (rather than pyramidal) organizational structure, each cell being potentially independent. Some wanna-be groups may have been created (in part) by former street gang members and may exhibit more gang-like characteristics than other wanna-be groups. Despite these overlaps and connections, the typology and its associated definitions reflected a reality that was recognized and endorsed by a variety of criminal justice practitioners and policy-makers.

Results: Why individuals become involved with organizations, gangs and groups

There is no single and simple answer to the frequently posed question, "why do individuals become involved with gangs?" This, in part, is because the question itself is not terribly useful. It makes more sense to ask why people become involved with criminal business organizations, or with street gangs, or with wanna-be groups. The answers differ.

In the case of criminal business organizations, answers begin to appear once the basic characteristics of their memberships are examined. Organization members included in the Study tended to be older males (mean age 27.8 years) who were better educated than the members of street gangs. They were less likely to be economically disadvantaged, primarily because of the lucrative nature of their work with an organization. Criminal business organizations engage primarily in the supply of illegal goods and services (e.g., drugs), areas of commerce in which significant profits are made. Organization members were more likely to have migrated to Canada than, for example, street gang members (21 out of the 24), and more likely to be members of a visible ethnic minority (21 out of the 24). Sixteen of the 24 were of Vietnamese or Chinese ethnic origin.

Members of criminal business organizations and the corrections personnel responsible for their cases (e.g., probation officers) indicated that there was a social and cultural bond which attracted individuals to organizations and that addressed their sense of ethnic and cultural marginality in a predominantly Euro-Canadian environment. The importance of a shared language and a sense of belonging accounted for their continued involvement with organizations. Members consistently stated that, on arriving in Canada, there was a lack of resources and employment opportunities available to them. They had few marketable skills, and experienced significant difficulties in obtaining rewarding, legitimate employment because of significant language barriers. In order to overcome their economic marginality and achieve the economic status valued by the larger Canadian society, organization members were drawn into illegal activities. In short, and perhaps not surprisingly, membership of criminal business organizations (in Greater Vancouver) is ethnically shaped and meets the economic and social needs of both organization members and their families.

Particularly telling were the responses given to questions about leaving (as opposed to joining) criminal business organizations. Members were asked about the process of leaving, and any associated problems such as fear of retaliation. Two subjects stated that they had considered leaving but could not afford to do so, and the loss of significant income was a factor for most individuals. Organization members reported earning from $2,500 per week to up to $30,000 per month (tax-free) and members, police officers and probation officers all agreed that membership of a criminal business organization was a lucrative endeavour. The majority of subjects had minimal work skills and could not expect to earn a comparable income in a legitimate field. As one organization member put it, "what else could I do and make this kind of cash... I speak little English, and legal work means no money" (Gordon and Foley 1998: 34).

Understanding why individuals became involved with street gangs proved to be less straightforward. Thirty-five street gang members were included in the research (only one was female) and they tended to be much younger than the members of criminal business organizations (the mean age of street gang members was 18 years). Education levels were lower and they were more likely to be from economically disadvantaged backgrounds. More than 60 percent were born in Canada, although 85 percent were members of visible ethnic minorities – a significant over-representation.[4] These included individuals of Indo-Canadian (Fijian), Hispanic, Iranian, Chinese, and Vietnamese ethnic origin.

Discussions with street gang members and their probation officers indicated that individuals became involved with gangs for a variety of interconnected reasons. Although the prospect of material gain cannot be discounted as an explanation, the members of gangs were more likely to become involved as a result of peer group attraction. They wanted to belong to a friendly, supportive group that included their friends or close relatives and this included a desire to be with individuals from the same cultural and ethnic group; gang members felt ethnically marginalized.

Many street gang members wanted to escape from, and find rewarding alternatives to, exceedingly unpleasant family lives. Their recent domestic histories and current circumstances reflected common characteristics that transcended, in particular, ethnicity. Most had physically abusive parents resulting in a lack of bonding, fear, and frequent absences from home (to avoid abuse). Parents seemed unable to control or otherwise influence the behaviour of their children without recourse to ineffective and extreme physical discipline which, in some cases, had resulted in child protection interventions by the (then) Ministry for Social Services. Another common factor was poverty, resulting from a combination of single parenthood, an absent or unemployed father, additional dependant siblings, and an inability to obtain employment due to a combination of parental commitment to the dependants and a lack of English. In the case of some immigrant and ethnic minority families, these problems were compounded by isolation from the larger, surrounding community, and even from individuals and families within that community who shared the same ethnic background (Gordon and Foley, 1998: 52-53).

The relationships among variables such as ethnicity, family circumstances, and peer group attraction could not be measured precisely but, arguably, they are closely related.(5) A young person or young adult experiencing abuse or neglect in his family – and this seemed to be present in the case of most street gang members – will probably be strongly attracted to a welcoming, supportive, and accessible alternative which simultaneously improves his material well being. The choice of alternative is likely a product of availability and opportunity and, for some young males living in the inner urban areas of Vancouver in the late 1980's and early 1990's, a viable alternative existed in the form of street gangs. The peer group attraction that is evidently responsible for young males becoming involved with street gangs is probably no different than the attraction of other socially legitimate groups such as hockey teams and the boy scouts. There is a common tendency on the part of adolescents and young adults to group together and the main difference with respect to street gang members appeared to be their choice of "gang". This choice is, to some extent, a function of the opportunities available in communities.

Understanding why individuals became involved with wanna-be groups was clearer than in the case of street gang members. Twenty-five wanna-be group members were included in the research (only one was female) and they tended to be much younger than the members of criminal business organizations and street gangs (the mean age of wanna-be group members was 16.8 years). About 60 percent were born in Canada, and 68 percent were members of visible ethnic minorities. Although there was an over-representation of subjects from visible minorities,[(4)] the largest single ethnic group found amongst wanna-be group members was Canadian born individuals of European descent (28 percent).

Individuals involved with wanna-be groups tended to be involved in less serious and less organized forms of crime – shoplifting, thefts from vehicles, and minor assaults. The members of *Los Cholos*, for example, spent most of their time in the suburbs of Burnaby and Coquitlam bullying other adolescents. *Los Cholos* members wore purple clothing and their primary mission in life appeared to be persuading other teenagers to part with any items of purple clothing they happened to be wearing. The group did not have any particular objectives (or significant organization) and would occasionally attack adolescents and groups of adolescents for no apparent reason other than as a response to a comment, a glance, or an appearance.

Wanna-be group members tended to fit the profile of hard core young offenders. They came from economically disadvantaged circumstances and exhibited behavioral and scholastic problems at school due, primarily, to the distractions of their adverse family circumstances. A disproportionate number attended alternate schools and other learning centres. They became involved with wanna-be groups primarily because of their distressing family backgrounds, most of which were characterized by physical and sexual abuse, as well as neglect. The Case of “B” provides a good illustration.

> B was a 17-year-old Canadian born subject of Aboriginal ethnic origin. He had a severe conduct disorder, severe anger management needs, and fetal alcohol syndrome. He was permanently removed from his home at age three. Prior to this he experienced physical and sexual abuse and was frequently neglected by his mother who had significant substance abuse problems (drugs and alcohol). B had been placed in more than 20 foster homes before the age of three. His adoptive parents divorced, at which point he became unable to control the anger he felt and expressed. According to B’s probation officer, his involvement in a wanna-be group seemed to meet his need to belong to a family.

In many cases, the wanna-be group was a replacement for the families that the members did not have, or that had rejected them. The group satisfied a variety of unmet emotional needs, especially the need for attachment – for a sense of belonging.

Discussion

The Greater Vancouver Gang Study was designed to expand the existing pool of knowledge of gangs and similar groups in Canada. The Study explored several possible explanations for “gangs” (inclusively defined), some of which were not supported by the data. The idea that the involvement of individuals in "gangs" was a function of their experiences with racism was not supported. Another hypothesis – that the involvement of individuals in "gangs" was a function of the messages and role models transmitted by the news and entertainment media – was also not supported. When the leaders and core members of criminal business organizations and street gangs were asked, in interviews, about the possibility that their behaviour had been shaped by the media (or words to that effect) most dismissed the idea as a joke.

There was some evidence to suggest that the *entertainment* media may shape the behaviour of individuals involved with wanna-be groups but only as an intervening, rather than an independent, variable. For example, police and probation officers reported that after the release of the popular movie *Colors* the behaviour and activities of young people who were already involved with gangs began to reflect the images portrayed in the film. Graffitti began to appear on walls and fences, wanna-be group members began to dress in "colours", and individuals and groups began to use the language – especially the idiom – of the actors in the film (e.g., the term "homes"). Other films may have had a similar impact, but *Colors* appears to have been the primary influence, for a while.

It is clear that membership of a visible ethnic minority is related to involvement in criminal business organizations, street gangs and, to a lesser extent, wanna-be groups. It is also evident that ethnicity is possibly more significant than whether or not a person was born in Canada (i.e., whether or not he is an immigrant). The problem lies in determining the role that ethnicity plays.

It is possible that the data used in the Greater Vancouver Gang Study were skewed or inaccurate in some way. In particular, it is possible that individuals from visible ethnic minorities are more easily caught and prosecuted, or are singled out for attention by a consciously or unconsciously biased criminal justice system. By definition, such individuals are more visible than individuals of Euro-Canadian ethnic origin, and their ethnicity may be (falsely) associated with "gang" involvement, primarily because of media-generated and other images. Alternatively, it is only individuals from visible ethnic minorities who are caught and prosecuted, while Euro-Canadian gang members remain undetected.

This is an important consideration and there is probably some negative labeling taking place on the part of some individuals working within the criminal justice system. However, police and probation officers in the Greater Vancouver area are generally sensitized to biases of this kind and labeling, alone, cannot account for the disproportionate representation of individuals from visible ethnic minorities who are identified as "gang" involved. In addition, there is concrete evidence in the form of police surveillance photographs and other hard data to confirm the involvement of such individuals in organizations and street gangs.

Another possibility is that the disproportionate number of individuals from visible ethnic minorities is a product of the lack of rewarding (materially and emotionally) economic opportunities for these individuals. This is an especially compelling explanation in the cases of those who were not born in Canada and who face significant language and skills barriers when they try to enter the legitimate job market. It may well be that experiencing the frustrations of attempting, but failing, to achieve material success in a highly materialistic society, results in a rejection of conventional ways of succeeding and an embracing of the unconventional ways. This may be especially prevalent amongst adolescents and young adults who are bombarded with achievement messages and who are raised on the idea of instant gratification for minimal effort (the so-called "MacDonald's Syndrome").

While the idea of "impatience" may be dismissed as unsubstantiated, there is ample evidence from the current research to underscore the importance of economic and, equally importantly, ethnic marginality as significant causal factors. Above all else, it is the economics of immigration and of ethnicity that seem to account best for a person's involvement in criminal business organizations and this should be explored in future research.

Conclusion

There are significant differences between criminal business organizations, street gangs, and wanna-be groups, with implications for policy and programme development. Dealing with a criminal business organization like *Lotus* requires a different strategy from one aimed at a street gang such as *Los Diablos,* or a wanna-be group such as *Los Cholos.* Unlike street gangs and wanna-be groups which tend to appear and disappear in waves (Young 1993), criminal business organizations are relatively constant (Dubro 1992). They are comprised of adult males of primarily Chinese or Vietnamese ethnic origin who migrated to Canada, and are involved in the provision of illegal goods and services. Clearly, organizations and their members are quite different from street gangs. And street gangs and organizations are quite different from wanna-be groups – a highly visible, noisy, and suburban phenomenon consisting of adolescent males from a variety of ethnic backgrounds who engage in random acts of collective violence and theft, some of which seemed quite pointless to all but the participants.

Although the development of specific recommendations for new policy and programming was not within the mandate of the Greater Vancouver Gang Study, the work did produce insights. It is clear that careful definition and classification of organizations, gangs and groups, and of their members, is critical to any effective policy and programming, but this may be hard to achieve. Policy and programming developments must address the needs of individuals from visible ethnic minorities who have recently migrated to Canada and who experience ethnic and economic marginality. The lack of language, and a lack of both money and the means to obtain money and material goods legitimately may result in individuals clustering in supportive groups where they are understood and can make money, albeit illegally. Whatever is being provided in the way of settlement services for immigrants is not reaching some individuals and families. This may be a function of the length of time during which services are provided for newly arrived immigrants, and especially those who are refugees.

Lastly, existing community-based anti-gang programming should be continued as an important preventative strategy, but must be expanded during the onset of a wave of street gang and wanna-be group activity. Anti-gang programming appears to be most effective when it is aimed at the supply of new gang and group members, rather than existing and well-established street gang members. Programs in high schools can reduce fear and intimidation, dry up the source of gang personnel, and help generate a broader, negative perspective of gang membership, especially amongst younger adolescents. A great deal is accomplished once gang membership is defined as "uncool" by the adolescent subculture (Danesi 1994).

Further research into Greater Vancouver's street gangs started in May 1999. Phase 2 of the Greater Vancouver Gang Study is concentrating on the emergence, growth, activities, and eventually decline of three street gangs from the most recent period of gang activity: *Los Diablos;* the *East Vancouver Saints;* and *Gum Wah.* In each case, key issues of ethnicity and immigration will be considered (e.g., the impact of ethnic marginality) along with an examination of the relationships among the gangs, criminal business organizations, and wanna-be groups. A more detailed analysis of the factors responsible for the beginning of a wave of street gang (and wanna-be group) activity will also be undertaken.

Notes

1. The research associated with this article was funded by the British Columbia Ministry of the Attorney-General and the Department of Justice, Canada. The author gratefully acknowledges the support and encouragement of these government agencies and of the British Columbia Inter-Ministry Committee on Youth Violence and Crime. The principal researcher was Sheri Fabian, M.A. Major contributions were made by Jacquelyn Nelson, Ph.D., Lynda Fletcher-Gordon,

M.S.W., Sergeant Jim Fisher of the Vancouver Police Department, and Mike White of the British Columbia Ministry for Children and Families.

2. Other examples of police constructed "gang" names surfaced during the research. These included the *"The Goof Troop"*, a name given by the police to a wanna-be group; *"The Ethnic Viets"*, a name given by the police to a conglomerate of criminal groups affiliated with a criminal business organization; and, *"The Pin-Heads"*, a name used by the police to identify the members of a criminal group led by one Mr. Pin.
3. Youth movements are extensive national, and often international, social movements characterized by a distinctive mode of dress or other bodily adornments, a leisure time preference, and other distinguishing features. The vagaries of adolescent fashion and other larger social and economic developments tend to determine the life spans of these movements. To the extent that birds of a feather will flock together, adolescents who subscribe to a movement often accumulate in groups and may be erroneously referred to, usually by the media, as a "gang". Examples include, the "zoot-suiters" (the 1940's and 1950's), the "mods and the rockers" (the 1960's); "skin-heads" (the 1970's and 1980's); and "punkers" (the 1980's and 1990's). Youth groups are sometimes referred to as "social gangs" insofar as they are comprised of small clusters of young people who "hang out" together in public places such as shopping malls, fast food outlets, and large convenience stores. They are often quite visible, noisy, and energetic and can seem intimidating. At one time, in the Vancouver area, these groups were referred to as "Mallies" because of their frequent appearance in large shopping malls. Criminal groups are small clusters of friends who band together, usually for a short period of time (no more than one year), to commit crime primarily for financial gain. They can be composed of young people and/or young (and not so young) adults and may be mistakenly, or carelessly, referred to as a gang.
4. More than three quarters of the research sample were members of visible ethnic minorities (78.0 percent). According to a 1994 projection for the Vancouver Metropolitan Area, approximately 59.0 percent of the general population of the Area were members of visible ethnic minorities (Gordon and Foley 1998; and Gordon and Nelson 1993).
5. The relationships among economic disadvantage and marginality, ethnicity and other variables will be examined more thoroughly during Phase 2 of the Greater Vancouver Gang Study, begun in the Spring of 1999.

References

Baron, S. and D. Tindall
1993 Network structure and delinquent attitudes within a juvenile gang. Social Networks 15: 255 - 273.

Beare, M.
1996 Criminal Conspiracies: Organized Crime in Canada. Toronto: Nelson Canada.

Canadian Centre for Justice Statistics
1999 Organized Crime Activity in Canada, 1998. Ottawa: Statistics Canada.

Cloward, R.A. and L.E. Ohlin
1960 Delinquency and Opportunity: A Theory of Delinquent Gangs. Glencoe, Il: Free Press.

Curry, D. and S. Decker
1998 Confronting Gangs: Crime and Community. Los Angeles: Roxbury.

Danesi, M.
1994 Cool: The Signs and Meanings of Adolescence. Toronto: University of Toronto Press.

Dubro, J.
1985 Mob Rule: Inside the Canadian Mafia. Toronto: MacMillan.

Dubro, J.
1992 The Dragons of Crime: Inside the Asian Underworld. Markham: Octopus Publishing.

Fasilio, R. and S. Leckie
1993 Canadian Media Coverage of Gangs: A Content Analysis. Users Report 1993-14. Ottawa: Ministry of the Solicitor General.

Goldstein, A. and C.R. Huff (eds.)
1993 The Gang Intervention Handbook. Champaign: Research Press.

Gordon, R.M.
1993 Incarcerated Gang Members in British Columbia: A Preliminary Study. Victoria: Ministry of Attorney General.

Gordon, R.M.
1995 Street gangs in Vancouver. In J. Creechan and R. Silverman (eds.), Canadian Delinquency. Toronto: Prentice Hall.

Gordon, R.M.
1998 Street gangs and criminal business organizations: A Canadian perspective. In K. Hazlehurst and C. Hazlehurst (eds.), Gangs and Youth Subcultures: International Explorations. Transaction: New Brunswick.

Gordon, R.M. and S. Foley
1998 Criminal Business Organizations, Street Gangs and Related Groups in Vancouver: The Report of the Greater Vancouver Gang Study. Victoria: Ministry of Attorney General.

Gordon, R.M. and J. Nelson
1993 Census '93: The Report of the 1993 Census of Provincial Correctional Centres. Victoria: Ministry of Attorney General.

Gordon, R.M. and J. Nelson
2000 Crime, ethnicity and immigration. In R. Silverman, James J. Teevan, and Vincent F. Sacco (eds.), Crime in Canadian Society (6th edition). Toronto: Harcourt Brace.

Joe, D. and N. Robinson
1980 Chinatown's immigrant gangs. Criminology 18: 337 - 345.

Kennedy, L. and S. Baron
1993 Routine activities and a subculture of violence: A study of violence on the street. Journal of Research in Crime and Delinquency 30: 88 - 112.

Klein, M., C. Maxson, and J. Miller (eds.)
1995 The Modern Gang Reader. Los Angeles: Roxbury Publishing.

Ley, D.
1975 The street gang in its milieu. In G. Gappert and H. Rose (eds.), The Social Economy of Cities: Vol. 9 Urban Affairs Annual Review. Beverly Hills: Sage Publications.

Mathews, F.
1993 Youth Gangs on Youth Gangs. Ottawa: Department of Justice.

Rogers, K.H.
1945 Street Gangs in Toronto: A Study of the Forgotten Boy. Toronto: Ryerson Press.

Spergel, I.
1995 The Youth Gang Problem: A Community Approach. New York: Oxford University Press.

Wolf, D.R.
1991 The Rebels: A Brotherhood of Outlaw Bikers. Toronto: University of Toronto Press.

Young, M.
1993 The History of Vancouver Youth Gangs: 1900 - 1985. Burnaby: Simon Fraser University, School of Criminology. Unpublished M.A. thesis.

CHAPTER EIGHT

The selling of innocence: The gestalt of danger in the lives of youth prostitutes

Bernard Schissel
and ***Kari Fedec***[1]
Department of Sociology
University of Saskatchewan
Saskatoon, SK

CRUELTY INFLICTED UPON CHILDREN, ESPECIALLY IN THE FORM OF SEXUAL exploitation, has the power to generate passionate public disapproval. Despite public indignation, the sex business continues to flourish: sex has become a multibillion-dollar industry, and today, children are bought, sold, and traded like any other mass-produced article (Sachs 1994). Various inquiries and studies have been commissioned at both the federal and local levels (Badgley 1984; Fraser 1985; Brannigan, Knafla, and Levy 1989; Brannigan and Caputo 1993; Mayor's Task Force 1996; McCarthy 1996), as social policy proponents continue to focus their attentions on the centuries-old problem of child prostitution. But the dilemma they face in addressing the exploitation of children from a causal paradigm is that the majority of research has focused on the factors that force youth to become and stay in the sex trade. What is missing, in a sensitive and complex understanding of the youth sex trade, is a focus on the detrimental effects that young people's participation in such a trade has on their overall well-being, not only on their prospects for escaping a life on the streets but also on their prospects for actual physical survival.

Canadian Journal of Criminology/Revue canadienne de criminologie, January/janvier 1999, pp. 33–56.

Previous research has addressed the general state of danger in which street prostitutes live (Badgley 1984; Canadian Panel on Violence Against Women 1993; Lowman and Fraser 1995; Boritch 1997; McNairn 1997); much of the focus for youth has been on violence by pimps and, for adults, on violence on the streets. Further, recent research on adult prostitution suggests that, in some cases, prostitution is a profession of choice and that street prostitute cultures develop occupational practices which minimize the dangers of the sex trade (Shaver 1996; Fraser 1985). While these foci are important, they tend to circumvent the direct danger to well-being that the sex trade poses to children and youth. In cities like Saskatoon and Regina, because youth prostitution is neither routine nor is there a well-developed youth sex trade culture, the conventions of protection are generally absent. The dangers for such children and youth go well beyond those described in contemporary research.

We focus, therefore, on two dimensions of youth prostitution: first, on previously identified factors that directly influence youth involvement in prostitution as an empirical test of the causation literature. Second, we examine the effects that being involved in the sex trade has on multiple dimensions of well-being. It is our intention to document and test an oft forgotten reality of research on youth prostitution: that involvement in the sex trade has dire consequences for an individual's physical, emotional, and social well-being.

Hypothetical issues relating to youth prostitution

a. Family trauma

The majority of recent literature concerning the topic of youth involvement in prostitution revolves around two issues: runaway behaviour and child sexual abuse as the most significant precursors to involvement in the sex-trade (Badgley 1984; Lowman 1987; Seng 1989; Chesney-Lind and Shelden 1992; Van Brunschot 1995; Brannigan 1996). Although child sexual abuse is regarded by some as a direct link to youth engagement in prostitution (Brannigan, Knafla, and Levy 1989; Van Brunschot 1995; McCarthy 1996; Boritch 1997), runaway behaviour is believed by some theorists to be an intervening or mediating variable (Seng 1989). In an attempt to escape a home where parents do not seem to care or where long term conflict occurs, some children may view the streets as their only option for survival as they seek to obtain food, shelter, and financial capital. Furthermore, a large proportion of youth who run away do so to escape sexual abuse at home (Chesney-Lind and Shelden 1992; Webber 1991). Once on the street, their only means of survival becomes routine engagement in criminal activities such as prostitution. According to Webber, "ironically, they run to save themselves, yet typically end up in as much, if not more, trouble than they were in at home. While most kids come to the street as victims, many can survive only by becoming perpetrators of crime" (Webber 1991: 31). The grim reality is that "their lives on the streets are almost always even more abusive in nature because they often become trapped in the sordid trafficking of children for sexual gratification" (Chesney-Lind and Shelden 1992: 37). We hypothesize that runaway behaviour does directly influence prostitution involvement; runaway kids end up in conditions that are conducive to engagement in the sex trade.

The direct causal link between childhood physical and sexual abuse and the decision to enter the sex trade has been well-documented (McMullen 1987; Seng 1989; Simons and Whitbeck 1991; Chesney-Lind and Shelden 1992; Van Brunschot 1995; Boritch 1997). The basic thesis is that childhood victimization, especially in terms of sexual abuse, leads to the future sexual exploitation of youth who have been made vulnerable to sexual advances. According to McMullen (1987), there is a psychological connection between child sexual abuse and prostitution: when youth have been abused in the past by family members, they are more likely to believe that strangers can use and abuse them also. The reasoning is that abusive families normalize abusive treatment in the minds of victimized youth. Furthermore, as a result of their sexual abuse, they may perceive themselves to be debased sexual objects. They often hold a "distorted image of their own bodies" which may "lead them to expect that their worth will only be acknowledged when they permit sexual access" (Boyer and James 1982, quoted in Chesney-Lind and Shelden 1992: 38). In effect, they may see themselves as commodities which can be bought and sold at the whim of those who have the financial capital (Simons and Whitbeck 1991; Boyer and James 1982). In addition, as they are used as sexual objects by men, they learn that they have the ability to manipulate men through sexual contact (McGinnes 1994). Because of socio-cultural factors, the level of abuse and its damaging effects may not be experienced equally by all prostitutes. For example, Lowman states that First Nations girls face many of the same problems which other teen prostitutes experience, but they encounter them in accentuated form. Not only do they enter into the sex trade at younger ages, they are also "more likely to be the victims of both family violence and trick or pimp violence" (Lowman 1986:36). We argue, as a result, that childhood physical and sexual abuse are strong precursors to involvement in prostitution (McCarthy 1996; Chesney-Lind and Shelden 1992), and the effects of abuse on involvement in prostitution differ across racial categories.

b. Personal and educational success

Since many of the youth who are involved in the sex trade have less than adequate educational backgrounds, their access to the job market is restricted, often positioning prostitution as the only logical way by which runaways have the ability to secure an income (Badgley 1984; Gibson-Ainyette, Templer, and Brown 1988; Seng 1989; Boritch 1997). We argue that poor educational achievement is due primarily to the fact that these youth have dropped out of school at an early age and that lack of educational achievement is coincident with negative attitudes toward education (Badgley 1984; Sullivan 1987). Because the majority of these young people have negative attitudes towards school, their escape from the street is jeopardized, for they have no means to obtain the marketable skills which will secure employment. We test to see if indifference to education and low educational achievement foster engagement in prostitution-related activities.

As related issues, personal capabilities may influence decisions about career choices and life chances. The developmental psychology literature in criminology is inundated with research that links abilities like self-esteem and social skills to conventional success (Hill, Soriano, Chen, and LaFramboise 1996; Campagna and Poffenberger 1988; Boyer and James 1982). Personal competencies and adequate self-concepts affect life outcomes either directly (as matters of personal empowerment) or indirectly through occupational and educational success. The reasoning is that such personal characteristics ultimately affect choices about engaging in conventional avenues of support or in unconventional activities like the sex trade.

c. *High risk behaviour, victimization and self-injury*

The incidence of drug use and addiction (including alcohol as well as other illegal drugs) are inordinately high among street prostitutes (Shaver 1993; Boritch 1997). One explanation for this is that substance abuse causes prostitution when youth turn to alcohol and drugs as a way of dealing with stressful life problems such as coping with prior physical and sexual abuse. In order to support a drug habit that helps them cope with life, they turn to prostitution as a means of financial support (Brannigan, Knafla, and Levy 1989; Gibson-Ainyette *et al.* 1988; Inciardi, Pottieger, Forwey, Chitwood, and McBride 1991). In contradistinction, it is also plausible that some prostitutes use drugs and alcohol as an escape, to help them endure the humiliation and negative consequences of their work (Fraser 1985; Lowman 1987; Lau 1989; Inciardi *et al.* 1991; Heinrich 1995). We analyze substance abuse and prostitution as coterminous and hypothesize that substance abuse is associated with youth involvement in the sex-trade.

We are also concerned in this research with exploring the psychologically and physically damaging effects of the sexual exploitation of youth. We argue that self-injurious dispositions like suicidal thoughts are associated with involvement in prostitution (Seng 1989; McMullen 1987; Griffin and Sheehan 1994). The reasoning is that children and youth are deeply traumatized by their experiences on the streets, and perhaps due to despair or humiliation, are prone to suicide. We hypothesize that involvement in prostitution increases the chance of suicidal thoughts and actual suicide attempts.

We extend this analysis by investigating whether the trauma of life in the sex trade leads to other forms of high risk and self-injurious behaviour, specifically, slashing and teen pregnancy. Slashing has been studied primarily in the context of women in prison. The conventional wisdom is that the psychic damage of prison isolation, especially isolation from family, compels some women inmates to self-injure in an attempt to mask their emotional pain (Boritch 1997; Schissel 1995; Faith 1993). Using the same reasoning, we test whether youth prostitutes engage in the same emotion-masking behaviour.

We also analyze the sexual risks that youth in the sex trade take by testing the effects of prostitution on pregnancy. Unprotected sex is a valuable commodity in the sex trade and the highest profits are obtained from the prostitution of young girls who are willing to engage in unprotected sex (Chesney-Lind and Shelden 1992; Sachs 1994; Nyland 1995). We measure the exposure to the dangers of unprotected sex by analyzing whether female youth prostitutes have a higher incidence of pregnancy than other youth in the survey. We do not have measures of incidence of sexually transmitted diseases, and, therefore, are restricted to utilizing pregnancy as the sole indicator of high risk sexual activity.

The last two issues relate to direct external victimization of youth in the sex trade. We analyze youth prostitute victimization by assessing the degree to which they have been both physically and sexually assaulted. A wealth of research addresses issues of risky lifestyles and victimization (Cohen and Felson 1979; Kennedy and Forde 1990; Lowman and Fraser 1995) and we test the degree to which a lifestyle of prostitution places youth at risk from violent assailants.

d. Race

Especially in the cities of Saskatoon, Winnipeg, and Regina, the majority of youth prostitutes are believed to be of First Nations background (Fraser 1985; Lowman 1987; Brannigan, Knafla, and Levy 1989; Webber 1991; Shaver 1993; Goulding 1994; Mayor's Task Force 1996; Boritch 1997). Based on the widespread acknowledgment of this fact, we analyze the causal origins of youth prostitution in the context of culture, indicated by youth of Aboriginal versus non-Aboriginal ancestry.

III. Methodology

a. Data description

The data were gathered from youth probation files on young offenders compiled by the Department of Social Services in both Regina and Saskatoon. Although the files are only from these two cities, youth from throughout the province come under the jurisdiction of both urban social services bureaus and are therefore represented in the final results. The files cover the years from 1980 to 1996 and were randomly selected from all files on youth who had at least some contact with the young offender system. Involvement in the legal system included any act for which the individual was required to report to a probation officer. The offenses ranged from break and entry and driving while impaired to armed robbery. Several files contained offenses related to soliciting for the purposes of prostitution. Additional files on individuals who had been involved in prostitution-related activities but had been charged with other offenses were supplied by probation officers upon request.

The official court documents were relied upon as much as possible as they indicated not only the offense but also other information such as the type of facility (open, closed, or group home custody), the type of sentence, and background information documented in the predisposition reports (family biographies and previous involvement in the justice system). Unofficial reports which were documented in the written reports of the probation officers were accessed for additional biographical and legal information including school performance, details about family life, pregnancy, personal feelings, and employment activity.

As a result, the data set covers a wide array of social, legal, and psychological variables and we use only those which directly relate to this project. Because the data set contains mostly nominal level data, the analysis is based primarily on multivariate contingency tables.

The sample consists of 401 youths, 52 of whom have been involved in the sex trade. Of the 52 youth involved in prostitution, 7 are male and 45 female. Of these same youth, 38 are aboriginal and 14 are non-Aboriginal. The age range of onset of prostitution for the 52 is from 9 to 18. Lastly, of the 52 youths involved in prostitution, 16 were at one time or another connected with a pimp/boyfriend.

b. *Variables in the analysis*

i. Dependent variables

Involvement in prostitution is the first dependent variable in this paper (Tables 1 and 2) and is defined as engagement at any time in the sex trade, even if the youth has not been charged. The variables that we examine as associated with involvement in the sex trade (Table 3) include:

(a) substance abuse (which groups all types of illegal and non-prescription chemicals into the category of drugs while also including alcohol in a separate category);
(b) severity of alcohol use as an assessment of the degree to which the young offender is dependent on alcohol;
(c) suicidal thoughts defined as the degree to which the youth thinks of committing a suicidal act;
(d) suicide attempts as whether or not the young offender has attempted suicide and been hospitalized as a result;

Tabl[illegible]
Percentages of youth in [illegible]
by childhoo[illegible]

Predetermined variables	Inv[illegible] Yes (N=14)	[illegible] (I[illegible]	[illegible]	[illegible]
Childhood physical abuse				
none	1.6	9[illegible]	[illegible]	[illegible]
some	3.8	96[illegible]	[illegible]	[illegible]
severe	6.5	93.[illegible]	[illegible]	[illegible]
chi-square	2.78		[illegible]	
Childhood psychological abuse				
none	2.4	97.6	[illegible]	75.8
some		100.0	66.7	33.3
severe	8.3	91.7	28.6	71.4
chi-square	2.13		7.64*	
Childhood sexual abuse				
none	1.0	99.0	18.5	81.5
some		100.0	47.1	52.9
severe	16.0	84.0	44.4	55.6
chi-square	21.15*		10.97*	
Childhood neglect				
none	2.0	98.0	15.3	84.7
some	5.3	94.7	41.3	58.7
chi-square	1.40		11.41*	
Runaway from home				
none		100.0	13.2	86.8
some	6.5	93.5	24.3	75.7
often	14.8	85.2	51.4	48.6
chi-square	23.188*		16.15*	

Note: * chi-square significant at the .05 level

(e) self-abuse defined as whether the subject has slashed or injured him/herself to the point of requiring medical intervention;

(f) physical health based on the social worker's rating of the actual physical health of the youth;

(g) teen pregnancy, whether or not the youth has been pregnant (including full term pregnancy, abortion, and miscarriage);

Table 2
Percentages of youth involved in prostitution by educational and personal attributes

	Involvement in prostitution			
Predetermined variables	Yes (N=14)	No (N=240)	Yes (N=38)	No (N=100)
Attitudes to education				
negative		100.0	30.8	69.2
neutral	3.1	96.9	28.6	71.4
positive	3.4	96.6	20.0	80.0
chi-square	1.26		1.52	
Educational achievement				
expelled	6.7	93.3	25	75
droppped out	6.8	93.2	42.5	57.5
failing		100.0	26.3	73.7
doing well	1.4	98.6	14.3	85.7
doing very well	3.2	96.8	33.3	66.7
returned to school	4.2	95.8	6.7	93.3
chi-square	4.58		10.60*	
Social skills				
loner		100.0	20.0	80.0
poor		100.0	9.1	90.9
moderate	1.7	98.3	26.8	73.2
very good	4.7	95.3	35.1	64.9
chi-square	3.03		3.12	
Self-esteem				
low	3.2	96.8	33.0	66.1
med	2.0	97.1	22.2	77.8
high		100.0		100.0
chi-square	1.46		4.84*	

Note: chi-square significant at the .05 level

(h) physical assault based on whether or not the youth has been physically assaulted outside the home; and,
(i) sexual assault as a recorded incident of sexual assault outside the home.

All of these variables are presented as direct correlations with involvement in the sex trade

Table 3
The effects of prostitution on high-risk behaviour, self-destructive behaviour, and violent victimization

	Involvement in prostitution			
Predetermined variables	Yes (N=14)	No (N=240)	Yes (N=38)	No (N=100)
Substance abuse				
None	12.5	48.1	7.9	28.3
Alcohol	25.0	75.0		8.1
Alcohol/drugs	62.5	34.3	92.1	63.6
chi-square	4.08		11.23	
Severity of alcohol abuse				
Not severe		50.6	13.5	33.7
Somewhat severe	41.9	35.1	40.5	30.6
Severe	57.1	14.2	45.9	35.7
chi-square	11.77*		5.40*	
Suicidal tendencies				
None	78.2	50.0	52.6	75.8
Some	15.1	50.0	13.1	11.1
severe	6.7		24.2	13.1
chi-square	5.49*		8.65*	
Suicide attempts				
No	30.8	90.8	57.9	81.0
Yes	69.2	9.2	42.1	19.0
chi-square	41.40*		7.77*	
Self abuse/slashing				
No	38.5	93.3	68.4	92.0
Yes	61.5	6.7	31.6	8.0
chi-square	43.24*		12.35*	
Physical health				
Poor	33.3	5.0	17.1	4.1
Moderate	16.7	24.3	42.9	42.9
very good	50.0	70.7	40.0	53.0
chi-square	8.71*		6.53*	
Teen pregnancy				
No	37.5	71.4	55.9	64.3
Yes	62.5	28.6	44.1	35.7
chi-square	3.10*		.288	
Physical assault (outside of home)				
No	83.3	90.6	58.3	78.4
Yes	16.7	9.4	41.7	21.6
chi-square	.362		5.33*	
Sexual assault (outside of home)				
No	50.0	89.4	62.9	87.4
Yes	50.0	10.6	37.1	12.6
chi-square	8.83*		9.89*	

Note: * chi-square significant at the .05 level

ii. Independent variables

There are a number of independent variables which are used in Tables 1 and 2 and are presented as direct causal influences on involvement in the sex trade. Their inclusion in the analyses is based on the relevant literature (which has been discussed in the previous section), obvious relevant issues concerning youth prostitution, and availability of data from the social services data set. The independent variables utilized in this analysis are based on ratings by social service youth workers and the categories of assessment are indicated in Tables 1 and 2. The variables for the analysis in Table 1 include:

(a) child physical abuse (which may have been inflicted by a parent, stranger, or other family member);
(b) childhood psychological abuse (psychological ratings by youth workers and doctors regarding family experiences);
(c) child sexual abuse (also inflicted by a parent, family member, or non-family member);
(d) childhood neglect by families or guardians; and,
(e) the prevalence of running away from home.

The variables for Table 2 include:

(a) educational attitudes (based on youth worker assessments of how the youth defines her/his feelings towards schooling);
(b) educational achievement (based on information from the social service files, which tracks the behaviour of youth only while involved in the system, not once they are released); and,

(c) social skills and self-esteem assessments based on social services rating scales for young offenders.

Finally, the factor of race has been included in all of the analyses as a control variable, based on prior findings from a number of cross Canada studies (Badgley 1984; Fraser 1985; Lowman 1987; Brannigan, Knafla, and Levy 1989; Shaver 1993;

McCarthy 1996; Mayor's Task Force 1996; Boritch 1997). Race has been divided into two categories, including First Nations (which includes individuals who are either Status Indian or Metis ancestry), and non-Aboriginal (which includes individuals who are Caucasian, or are from other ethnic minorities – the vast majority in this category self-define as Caucasian, i.e.95.7%).

IV. Results

Childhood Trauma

Table 1 presents the results for the childhood trauma variables including indicators of abuse and neglect. The causal variables are listed on the left side of the table. The table is presented in the contexts of Aboriginal and non-Aboriginal ancestry.

Most noticeable, in general, in this table is the strong consistent effects of forms of abuse on involvement in prostitution. For example, for both Aboriginal and non-Aboriginal youth, greater levels of childhood physical abuse are associated with greater involvement in prostitution. Although the relationship for non-Aboriginal youth is not significant, the percentage differences illustrate the nature of the association which is significant for Aboriginal youth; simply put, childhood physical abuse increases the likelihood of involvement in prostitution. Similar results occur for childhood sexual abuse. Important here, however, are the similar effects on prostitution for the categories of some and severe sexual abuse for Aboriginal youth. These findings suggest quite clearly that it is the act of sexual violation that predisposes children to prostitution, rather than the severity or the amount, especially for Aboriginal youth. For non-Aboriginal youth, it is primarily severe sexual abuse that leads to involvement in prostitution. Despite these racial differences, it is manifest that childhood sexual abuse has a large influence on future involvement in prostitution.

The results for psychological abuse are much less convincing than are those for the two previous physical forms of abuse. For example, for Aboriginal youth, 66.7% of those who suffer some degree of psychological abuse are involved in prostitution compared to 28.6% who suffer severe abuse. In contradistinction, non-Aboriginal youth who suffer severe abuse have the greatest degree of involvement in prostitution (8.3%) as would be expected. These ambiguous results may, in part, be a function of the inability of youth workers to identify and categorize psychological abuse, which is certainly a problem in social research on family violence (Storrie and Poon 1996; Dekeseredy and Hinch 1991). The categorizations of abuse are based on how the youth characterizes abusive situations when providing information to probation officers. While these categorizations may be somewhat subjective, they are corroborated by psychiatric assessments based on information supplied to the doctor by the young offender.

The last two variables present a most convincing argument for influence of childhood trauma on prostitution. For Aboriginal youth especially, the effect of childhood neglect on involvement in prostitution is strong, and, as expected, indicates that high levels of neglect result in high involvement in prostitution (41.3% of Aboriginal youth involved in the sex trade experience some neglect compared to 5.3% of non-Aboriginal youth). One of the behavioral manifestations of neglect, running away, also influences prostitution; 13.2% percent of the Aboriginal youth who never run away become involved in prostitution, compared to 44.4% of those who do run away. Similarly for non-Aboriginal youth, those who run the most often have the highest levels of involvement in the sex trade. As Seng (1989) has hypothesized, however, runaway behaviour may in fact have an indirect effect on prostitution-related activities, with actual engagement resulting from other factors such as abuse.

Overall these findings regarding abuse and home context are not unexpected. They do, however, paint a convincing picture that youth and child prostitutes generally suffer family-based childhood trauma; their victimization on the streets is preceded by victimization in the home. The connections between homelife and streetlife are complex, but certainly must involve the reality that abused children may internalize their abuse as normal. If so, they are much more psychologically disposed to accept further abuse than those who have not suffered similar childhood trauma.

Personal development

Table 2 presents the influences that psychological and educational deficits have on engagement in prostitution. We argue that personal and psychological success will dispose children and youth to resist prostitution as a debasing although somewhat lucrative activity in the face of economic despair.

It is unclear from the two education variables, whether success in school does prevent, to some extent, involvement in prostitution. For example, the effect of attitudes to education on prostitution for both racial categories is not significant and not terribly strong. On turning to educational achievement, however, we see that for Aboriginal youth, being expelled from, dropping out of, or failing school does increase the chances of being involved in prostitution. So does doing very well in school. Both of these variables present inconclusive results regarding the connection between school and prostitution. The one exception to this is the expected finding that returning to school results in low involvement in prostitution for both non-Aboriginal and Aboriginal youth (95.8% and 93.3% non-involvement respectively).

The psychological measures of self-esteem and social skills reveal some interesting and somewhat perplexing findings. The youth in this study with the best social skills were those most involved in prostitution, and this is the case for both racial categories of youth. Although the findings are not statistically significant, the percentage differences reveal trends that indicate that low social skills prevent or discourage youths from the sex trade. The results for the self-esteem variable, on the other hand, reveal associations that are more consistent with the literature on psychic well-being and vulnerability. For both Aboriginal and non-Aboriginal youth, high levels of self-esteem tend to prevent involvement in prostitution; in fact, no youth in this study who was assessed with high self-esteem was involved in prostitution at any time, as compared to 33% of Aboriginal youth with low self-esteem who were involved in the sex trade.

Effects of involvement in prostitution

This last table illustrates the behavioral manifestations of the psychic trauma produced by involvement in the youth sex trade. Essentially, we analyze the effects of engagement in prostitution on victimization, both self-imposed and perpetrated by predators.

As we maintain in this paper, youth prostitutes use drugs and alcohol, in part to help them bear the humiliation and potential danger of their work (Fraser 1985; Lowman 1987; Lau 1989; Inciardi *et al.* 1991; Heinrich 1995). The two substance abuse variables show quite consistently that alcohol and drug abuse are high for those youth engaged in prostitution. Alcohol alone, however, does not seem to be the crutch that youths use. For example, almost all Aboriginal youth (92.1%) involved in prostitution use a combination of drugs and alcohol as do a majority of non-Aboriginal youth (62.5%). These figures are appreciably higher than those for the youth not involved in prostitution. As for alcohol use alone, the most severe use of alcohol occurs for youth involved in prostitution and this is found in both racial categories. These results indicate quite clearly that prostitution is associated with indirect self-imposed harm as measured by exposure to high risk substance abuse.

On turning to the variables that measure the degree to which youth are exposed to direct self-imposed harm, we observe that, first of all, involvement in prostitution is related to greater suicidal tendencies and to more suicide attempts. Most strikingly, 69.2% of non-Aboriginal youth involved in prostitution have attempted suicide compared to 9.2% who are not involved. Although not as dramatic a contrast, similar results appear for Aboriginal youth (42.1% and 19.0% respectively). These findings suggest that involvement in prostitution is correlated with suicidal tendencies and is also strongly correlated with suicide attempts for all youth, but especially so for non-Aboriginal youth.

We also use slashing or self-abusive behaviour as another indicator of direct self-imposed harm and obviously as a proxy measure of emotional well-being. Much like the findings for suicide, the results here suggest a severe effect of prostitution on well-being. For non-Aboriginal youth, slashing seems to be a reality primarily for youth involved in prostitution (61.5% compared to 6.7% not involved in prostitution). The results for Aboriginal youth are similar although the relationship is less strong (31.6% compared to 8.0%). The stronger effect of prostitution on well-being for non-Aboriginal youth is consistent with the findings for suicide.

The physical health variable endorses the findings from the previous discussions on well-being. For both racial categories of youth, poorer health is characteristic of most youth involved in prostitution. For example, for non-Aboriginal youth involved in prostitution, 33.3% are assessed with poor physical health compared to 5% of those not involved. The results are similar for Aboriginal youth (17.1% and 4.1% respectively) but less pronounced.

While the outcome variables in this table to this point have shown the indirect effects of prostitution on well-being, the last two variables measure direct victimization. As mentioned previously, one of the dire realities of prostitution is that johns will pay more for sex without the use of protective measures. The teen pregnancy variable illustrates quite clearly that non-aboriginal youth involved in prostitution are being coerced or encouraged to engage in unsafe sex, or, possibly, they are unaware or indifferent to the consequences of unsafe sexual practices. Such youth involved in prostitution are much more likely to have been pregnant than their counterparts not involved in the sex trade (62.5% compared to 28.6%) Interestingly, the relationship between prostitution and pregnancy is not significant for Aboriginal youth, essentially showing little effect.

The physical and sexual assault variables illustrate directly the physical vulnerability of youths involved in the sex trade. For physical assault, unlike several of the previous variables, the dangerous effect of prostitution on well-being occurs primarily for Aboriginal youth. Here, 41.7% of youth involved in prostitution have been physically assaulted compared to 21.6% not involved. For non-Aboriginal youth, the relationship is not significant and the percentage differences indicate little or no effect. For sexual assault, on the other hand, the vulnerability of youth is apparent for both racial groups. The youth involved in prostitution are more prone to sexual assault than their counterparts who are not involved in the sex trade. This finding, we contend, is indicative not only of the dangerousness of the sex trade but also of the inherent danger of the street life that attends involvement in prostitution.

V. Conclusions

In this research, we have sought, firstly, to understand some of the experiential and psychic circumstances of youth involved in the sex trade. Secondly, we have analyzed how prostitution may endanger the well-being of youth both directly through victimization and indirectly through creating the opportunities and pre-conditions for self-destructive behaviour. In summary, this research is an attempt to understand the gestalt of danger that encompasses the lives of youth involved in prostitution as it examines the context of non-Aboriginal and Aboriginal young offenders.

The results show clearly that, in the first instance, youth are involved in prostitution partly because their early lives were characterized by neglect and abuse. The question remains whether such early damage traumatizes children who are then unable to cope in a conventional world, or if such damage normalizes abuse and sexual exploitation in the minds of these young victims. A partial answer to this question can be found in the results on psychological skills and education. Our evidence suggests that a child's self-concept and affective abilities, likely associated with early sexual and/or physical abuse, determine involvement in the sex trade. Part of our reasoning is that, with some ambiguity, prostitution is the result of lack of conventional psychic tools that lead to conventional avenues of success, such as success in the education system. Furthermore, childhood abuse damages self-perception that allows children and youth to resist exploitation (Finkelhor 1987; Finkelhor and Browne 1988) and it patterns behaviour that exposes individuals to dangerous individuals and events (Simons and Whitbeck 1991).

Most importantly, for this paper, however, are the results surrounding the dangers inherent in the sex trade. Quite clearly, teenage prostitution is enhanced by acute sexual and physical victimization and the sex trade is related to predispositions to self-destructive behaviour. Prostitution creates a context in which those youth who are involved will run a high risk of being damaged by a predator or by themselves – either directly through assault and self-injury or indirectly through high-risk behaviour. These findings are offered in a street context, in which sub-cultural norms for protection are absent and in which children and youth are coerced and trapped in the sex trade and are not there by choice (Chesney-Lind and Shelden 1992; Campagna and Poffenberger 1988).

It is important to stress that the correlations between prostitution and social, physical, and psychological well-being are somewhat different depending on whether the youth is Aboriginal or non-Aboriginal. In this regard, there is some evidence to suggest that although prostitution predisposes all youth to self-injury, it does so especially for the non-Aboriginal youth in this sample. On the other hand, while all youth involved in the sex trade are especially vulnerable to direct victimization, young Aboriginal prostitutes are more vulnerable to stranger violence than are non-Aboriginal youth prostitutes. These conclusions are offered in a context in which First Nations and Metis youth are more vulnerable to sexual exploitation on the streets than their non-Aboriginal counterparts (Badgley 1984, Lowman 1987, McCarthy 1996, and the Mayor's Task Force 1996).

The social policy implications that emanate from research such as this are clear. Young prostitutes develop and live in contexts of constant danger. Without caring intervention, the risk that these youth run, probably unparalleled anywhere else in society, will shorten their lives. Given that their supposed criminality is not one of choice but of coercion and victimization, an immediate, non-legalistic, non-condemnatory intervention strategy is crucial, not only for the welfare of the youth involved but also for the integrity of a society that so far has failed to stop adult predators of children and youth.

The specific types of caring intervention need to include not only safe houses where street youth can find sanctuary but also attendant counselling programs which deal with issues of health and safety, personal trauma, family problems, and financial and educational opportunity. Obviously, what we are advocating here is not just token shelters but ongoing, well-financed programs of one-to-one support as well as educational and employment programs which obviate the need to prostitute. Government policy needs to make it easier for destitute and disaffiliated youth to access financial and physical resources. Schools need to provide flexible education models that account for the remedial needs of street youth, physical spaces in which marginalized youth feel safe and secure, and a non-punitive, non-authoritarian model of learning and development in which the wishes and opinions of street youth are considered in school policy development. They also need to address issues of sexual exploitation of children, the social problem of destitute children and youth, and the reality of street life.

A most important step is intervention within the school setting, especially in inner city neighbourhoods. Schools with at-risk children and youth may, for example, address the issues directly by bringing in ex-prostitutes who are able to tell youths the reality and dangers of street life and not a glamorized portrait of riches and money. As for outreach and intervention, programs and services must be culturally significant especially in cities where the majority of children and youth in the sex trade are of Aboriginal ancestry. As stated in the 1996 Royal Commission on Aboriginal Peoples, Aboriginal street youth look for Aboriginal faces in helping agencies (Canada 1996). In light of our research and the Royal Commission (Canada 1996), more trusting and effective helping relationships occur when services and programs are culturally relevant.

Lastly, and probably most importantly, the police need to assume the mandate of frontline social workers as well as peace and crime control officers. Street youths need to trust police officers as guardians and protectors, and it is obvious from our research that they need the protection that should be afforded to all citizens. At present, the "policing of child prostitution" role is anathema to the needs of vulnerable youths. Inner-city police officers understand street life and the inherent dangers and they are on the front lines. It is certainly within the realm of possibility for officers to be advocates for children and youth involved in the sex trade. This, however, would involve changing the mandate and training of the police, allowing them to create and work in an atmosphere of trust of and by street children and youth.

Note

1. The authors are indebted to the Social Sciences and Humanities Research Council of Canada (Grant number 41-095-1532) for funding for the Saskatchewan Youth Attitudes Survey (1996). They are grateful to the Departments of Social Services of Saskatoon and Regina for their cooperation in this research. Please address all correspondence and offprint requests to Professor Bernard Schissel, Department of Sociology, University of Saskatchewan, 9 Campus Drive, Saskatoon, Saskatchewan, S7N 5A5. e-mail: schissel@sask.usask.ca fax: 306-966-6950.

References

Badgley, R. (Chair)
1984 Committee on Sexual Offenses Against Children and Youth. Ottawa: Supply and Services Canada.

Boritch, H.
1997 Fallen Women. Female Crime and Criminal Justice in Canada. Toronto: ITP Nelson.

Boyer, D. and J. James
1982 Easy money: Adolescent involvement in prostitution. In S. Davidson (ed.), Justice for Young Women. Seattle: New Directions for Young Women.

Brannigan, A.
1996 The adolescent prostitute: Policing delinquency or treating pathology? In J.A. Winterdyck (ed.), Issues and Perspectives on Young Offenders in Canada. Toronto: HBJ.

Brannigan, A., L. Knafla, and C. Levy
1989 Street Prostitution: Assessing the Impact of the Law, Calgary, Regina, Winnipeg. Ottawa: Supply and Services Canada.

Brannigan, A. and T. Caputo
1993 Studying Runaways and Street Youth in Canada: Conceptual and Research Design Issues. Ottawa: Supply and Services Canada.

Campagna, D.S. and D.L. Poffenberger
1988 The Sexual Trafficking in Children. Dover, Mass: Auburn House.

Canada
1996 Report of the Royal Commission on Aboriginal Peoples: Gathering Strength. Ottawa: Minister of Supply and Services Canada.

Canadian Panel on Violence Against Women
1993 Changing the Landscape: Ending Violence and Achieving Equality. Ottawa: Minister of Supply and Services.

Chesney-Lind, Meda and Randall Shelden
1992 Girls, Delinquency and Juvenile Justice. Pacific Grove, CA: Brooks/Cole Publishing.

Cohen, Lawrence E. and Marcus Felson
1979 Social change and crime rate trends: A routine activity approach. American Sociological Review 44: 588-608.

Dekeseredy, Walter and Ron Hinch
1991 Woman Abuse: Sociological Perspectives. New York: Thompson Educational Publishing, Inc.

Faith, Karlene
1993 Unruly Women: The Politics of Confinement and Resistance. Vancouver: Press Gang Publishers.

Finkelhor, David
1987 New myth about child sexual abuse. Address presented at the symposium on child sexual abuse. RIFAS: Ottawa.

Finkelhor, David and Angela Browne
1988 Impact of Child Sexual Abuse: A Review of the Research. Ottawa: Supply and Services.

Fraser, P. (Chair)
1985 Special Committee on Pornography and Prostitution. Pornography and Prostitution in Canada. Ottawa: Supply and Services Canada.

Gibson-Ainyette, I., D.I. Templer, and R. Brown
1988 Adolescent female prostitutes. Archives of Sexual Behaviour 17(5): 431-438.

Goulding, W.
1994 Younger hookers oblivious to danger. StarPhoenix. 26 Oct: A1.

Griffin, K. and A. Sheehan
1994 Children in the sex trade. Vancouver Sun. 15 Nov: A8.

Heinrich, K.
1995 Law fails to protect child prostitutes, expert charges. Calgary Herald. 30 Aug: B2.

Hill, Hope, Fernando Soriano, S. Andrew Chen, and Teresa LaFramboise
1996 Sociocultural factors in the etiology and prevention of violence among ethnic minority youth. In L. Eron, J. Gentry, and P. Schlegel (eds.), Reason to Hope: A Psychosocial Perspective on Violence and Youth. Washington: American Psychological Association.

Inciardi, J., A.E. Pottieger, M.A. Forwey, D.D. Chitwood, and D.C. McBride
1991 Prostitution, IV drug use, and sex-for-crack exchanges among serious delinquents: Risks for HIV infection. Criminology 29(2): 221-235.

Kennedy, Les and David Forde
1991 Routine activities and crime: An analysis of victimization in Canada. Criminology 28: 137-52.

Lau, E.
1989 Runaway: Diary of a Street Kid. Toronto: Harper and Collins.

Lowman, J.
1986 Prostitution in Canada. Resources for Feminist Research 14(4): 35-37.

Lowman, J. and L. Fraser
1995 Violence Against Persons Who Prostitute: The Experience in British Columbia. Vancouver: Departments of Justice and Solicitor General Canada.

Lowman, J.
1987 Taking young prostitutes seriously. Canadian Review of Sociology and Anthropology 24(1): 99-115.

Mayor's Task Force on Child Prostitution
1996 Action Plan For the Elimination of Child Prostitution in the City of Saskatoon. Saskatoon.

McCarthy, B.
1996 On the Streets: Youth in Vancouver. Victoria: Queen's Printer.

McGinnes, R.
1994 High Heels and Teddy Bears. Calgary: Street Teams.

McMullen, R. J.
1987 Youth prostitution: A balance of power. Journal of Adolescence, 10(1): 35-43.

McNairn, K.
1997 Child prostitutes need support, say ex-hookers." Saskatoon Star Phoenix. Oct 6: A1.

Nyland, B.
1995 Child prostitution, and the new Australian legislation on paedophiles in Asia. Journal of Contemporary Asia. 25(4): 546-560.

Sachs, A.
1994 The last commodity: Child prostitution in the developing world. World Watch, July/August: 24-30.

Schissel, Bernard
1995 Degradation, social deprivation and violence: Health risks for women prisoners. In B. Singh Bolaria and Rosemary Bolaria (eds.), Women, Minorities and Health. Halifax: Fernwood Books.

Seng, M. J.
1989 Child Sexual Abuse and Adolescent Prostitution: A Comparative Analysis. Adolescence 24(95): 664-675.

Shaver, F. M.
1993 Prostitution: A female crime?" In E. Adelberg and C. Currie (eds.), In Conflict With the Law: Women and the Canadian Justice System. Vancouver: Press Gang.

Shaver, F.M.
1996 The regulation of prostitution: Setting the morality trap. In B. Schissel and L. Mahood (eds.), Social Control in Canada: Issues in the Social Construction of Deviance. Don Mill, ON: Oxford University Press.

Simons, R. L. and L.B. Whitbeck
1991 Sexual abuse as a precursor to prostitution and victimization among adolescent and adult homeless women. Journal of Family Issues 12(3): 361-379.

Storrie, Kathy and Nancy Poon
1996 Deconstructing spousal violence: A socialist feminist perspective. In Bernard Schissel and Linda Mahood (eds.), Social Control in Canada: Issues in the Social Construction of Deviance. Don Mills, ON: Oxford University Press.

Sullivan, T.
1987 Juvenile prostitution: A critical perspective. Marriage and Family Review 12(1&2): 113-134.

Van Brunschot, E.G.
1995 Youth involvement in prostitution. Canadian Delinquency. In R.A. Silverman and J.H. Creechan (eds.), Canadian Delinquency. Scarborough: Prentice Hall.

Webber, M.
1991 Street Kids: The Tragedy of Canada's Runaways. Toronto: University of Toronto Press.

CHAPTER NINE

Deterrence and homeless male street youths

Stephen W. Baron(1)
University of Windsor
Windsor, Ontario
and ***Leslie W. Kennedy***
University of Alberta
Edmonton, Alberta

RECENT RESEARCH SUGGESTS THAT THE CANADIAN PUBLIC BELIEVES THE criminal justice system is too lenient in its punishment of both young and adult offenders (Baron and Hartnagel 1996; Hartnagel and Baron 1995; Roberts 1992; Sacco and Johnson 1990; Sprott 1996). Hartnagel and Baron (1995; Baron and Hartnagel 1996) suggest that these punitive attitudes may be linked to the deterrent value of punishment where the public believes that the threat of penalties serves to inhibit actors from engaging in illegal activities.

Set in the context of the ever-strengthening public demand for more and tougher punishments is the observation that a small number of chronic or "serious offenders" are responsible for a considerable amount of the criminal activity (Baron 1995; Hamparian, Schuster, Dinitz, and Conrad 1978; Sorrells 1977; Strasburg 1978; Wolfgang, Figlio, and Sellin 1972). Baron (1995) notes that many of these chronic offenders are drawn from the street youth population and, in contrast to public belief, there is speculation that these street-oriented boys do not fear the police or carceral punishments (Anderson 1994: 94). Zimring and Hawkins (1973) imply that living on the margins of society can alter perceptions of punishment and suggest

Canadian Journal of Criminology/Revue canadienne de criminologie, January/janvier 1998, pp. 27–60.

that deterrence does not threaten many of those who live in impoverished conditions since these people have little or nothing to lose if apprehended by the law.

Despite these insights, past research on deterrence has restricted its focus to high school and college samples (see Anderson, Chiricos, and Waldo 1977; Bishop 1984; Burkett and Carrithers 1980; Meier, Burkett, and Hickman 1984; Jensen, Erickson, and Gibbs 1978; Paternoster 1988; 1989a; 1989b; Paternoster, Saltzman, Waldo, and Chiricos 1983; Paternoster and Iovanni 1986), groups that tend to lack economically marginal respondents (McCarthy and Hagan 1992). Further, Decker, Wright, and Logie (1993) suggest that this prior work suffers from its failure to include known offenders in its evidence (Decker et al. 1993; Paternoster 1987) and likely emphasizes a bias towards the conforming aspects of the influence of sanctions. In sum, prior empirical work in the deterrence area ignores how criminally "at risk" populations react to the threats of sanctions and how their living circumstances might influence their perceptions of punishment.

In the paper that follows we explore the perceptions of punishment among homeless male street youths paying particular attention to how their perceived threats of formal sanctions influence their criminal behaviour and how these threats are shaped by their living conditions and other factors in their lifestyles.

Review of the literature

Fundamental to the concept of deterrence is the idea that law-abiding behaviour is produced and maintained by the threat of negative legal sanctions (Rankin and Wells 1982). As a perceptual theory (Paternoster et al. 1983; Waldo and Chiricos 1972; Williams and Hawkins 1986), the major proposition of deterrence is that certain and severe sanctions will keep actors from committing illegal behaviour (Anderson et al. 1977; Cook 1977; Grasmick and Appleton 1977; Grasmick and Green 1981; Jensen et al. 1978; Meier and Johnson 1977; Schneider

1990; Silberman 1976; Williams and Hawkins 1986). Empirical tests of this proposition generally suggest that the perceived certainty of legal punishment does provide a moderate deterrent effect (Anderson et al. 1977; Cook 1977; Grasmick and Appleton 1977; Grasmick and Green 1981; Jensen et al. 1978; Meier and Johnson 1977; Silberman 1976; Williams and Hawkins 1986) while the perceived severity of punishment does not (Anderson et al. 1977; Meier and Johnson 1977; Silberman 1976; Paternoster et al. 1983) although there are some indications that severity is important to the extent that it is certain (Geerkin and Gove 1975; Grasmick and McLaughlin 1978). This later finding suggests severity may be contingent upon certainty and it is the interaction between the two that reduces criminal behaviour. However, standing in contrast to this research are Schneider's (1990) findings based on adjudicated delinquents that perceptions of greater certainty and severity increase criminal behaviour.

In light of these findings a number of scholars have argued that formal deterrence is insufficient to prevent crime (Anderson et al. 1977; Burkett and Jensen 1975; Grasmick and Appleton 1977; Meier and Johnson 1977; Paternoster and Iovanni 1986; Williams and Hawkins 1986; 1989). Williams and Hawkins (1986) suggest that informal sanctions, including the fear of losing the support of close friends and relatives, and the fear of jeopardizing past and future accomplishments, are the prime inhibitors of criminal activity, not the threat of formal sanctions (see also McCarthy 1995). They suggest that these informal sanctions not only have a direct effect on criminal behaviour but can also indirectly affect illegal activities through their influence on formal sanctions. Here the perceived "costs" of informal sanctions may work to increase the "costs" of legal punishments by making actors more sensitive to their threat.

Others (Bishop 1984; Burkett and Ward 1993; Schneider 1990; Tittle and Rowe 1973) note that the fear of formal sanctions are probably secondary for most people because they have developed normative constraints and moral commitments to conventional values that compel them to conformity irrespective of sanctions. Again, there are indications that the presence of strongly internalized norms can decrease involvement in criminal activities directly while at the same time indirectly increase responsiveness to the threats of formal sanctions (Bishop 1984; Schneider 1990; Zimring and Hawkins 1973).

What all of this research ignores is the possibility that perceptions of sanctions differ depending upon one's position in the social structure. Zimring and Hawkins (1973) argue that resource availability can influence sanction calculation. They suggest that the maximum threat influence of formal sanctions is greater for those actors from higher status backgrounds since they may have the most to lose if subjected to formal punishment. On the other hand, the negative living conditions of those on the margins of society may reduce the threats of formal sanctions. In fact, formal sanctions may well be lost on those with little or nothing to lose if apprehended by the law. Zimring and Hawkins (1973) go so far as to state that deterrence does not threaten those whose lives can be characterized as miserable. Roshier (1989) notes that societies which are unable to provide conventional avenues of achieving personal goals to certain sections of the community leave themselves open to criminal behaviour (Roshier 1989; Zimring and Hawkins 1973). Thus, poverty may lead to criminal behaviour regardless of threats of punishment.

Beyond the issue of economic position are other variables that might serve to alter actors' perceptions of certainty and severity. A number of researchers suggest that perceptions of punishments can be altered by peers. Stafford and Warr (1993) note that offenders can draw on the experiences of peers who have committed offenses without detection or apprehension, thus reducing the fear of negative sanctions (Burkett and Jensen 1975; Meier et al. 1984; Paternoster 1988; 1989a; 1989b). Further, peer support and peer participation in criminal activities are consistent findings in the criminological literature on offending behaviour (Reiss and Farrington 1991).

It has also been suggested that the use of drugs and alcohol can impinge on sanction calculations (Inciardi, Horowitz, and Pottieger 1993). Being under the influence of drugs and/or alcohol prior to and during criminal activities can serve to neutralize or alter actors' calculations of risk and directly affect crime by making risky or otherwise difficult offenses easier (Inciardi and Russe 1977). Inciardi et al. (1993) note that being under the influence while committing a crime is something to be expected for those heavily involved in a street lifestyle. In fact, they go so far as to speculate that substance use is a major requirement for successfully participating in this lifestyle.

In light of this review, we believe that the study of street youths provides an important test for the strength of formal sanctions in deterring criminal behaviour. First, these homeless youths live in conditions of extreme poverty that might serve to negate the influence of official sanctions and lead to criminal behaviour. (Brennan, Huizinga, and Elliott 1978; Hagan and McCarthy 1992; Inciardi et al. 1993; Kufeldt and Nimmo 1987a; 1987b; McCarthy and Hagan 1991; 1992; Palenski 1984; Radford, King, and Warren 1989; Rothman 1991; Smart, Adlaf, Porterfield, and Canale 1990; Webber 1991). Second, many of the inhabitants of the street are caught up in a lifestyle involving crime, drugs, and criminal peers (Inciardi et al. 1993) which again might influence perceived threats of sanctions and lead to illegal activities. Third, research indicates that these youths tend to have severed attachments to parents and other important sources of informal sanctioning and conformity producing conventional commitments, including employment that might serve to influence the strength of formal sanctions (Brennan et al. 1978; Hagan and McCarthy 1992; Kufeldt and Nimmo 1987a; 1987b; McCarthy and Hagan 1991; 1992; Palenski 1984; Webber 1991). Further, all of the above mentioned factors might lead directly to criminal behaviour in addition to any influence they might have on the strength of formal sanctions. Finally, street youths provide us with a population that contains "serious offenders" thus addressing a further weakness of past work (Decker et al. 1993).

Hypotheses

The literature reviewed above suggests that the threat of formal sanction is important to inhibiting illegal behaviour. We argue that the perceived certainty of formal justice punishment will have a negative effect on criminality while perceived severity will have at best a smaller negative effect. Further, since these two perceptions may be contingent upon one another, we expect that the interaction between certainty and severity will have a negative effect on the amount of criminal activity.

Therefore, we argue:

1A) The greater the perceived certainty of formal punishments the greater the deterrent effect.
1B) The greater the perceived severity of formal punishments the greater the deterrent effect.
1C) The greater the perceived certainty and severity of formal punishments the greater the deterrent effect.

Similarly, we would expect that informal sources of social control such as parental attachments and future goals can deter youths from criminal behaviour. Further, we would argue that the internalization of morality would lessen criminality. Therefore:

2A) The greater the amount of informal social control and the greater the moral belief that an action is wrong, the less criminal behaviour.

We also expect that the realities of poverty, homelessness, and unemployment may lead to criminal behaviour independently of our other variables. Criminal peers and the use of drugs and alcohol may also have direct effects on crime. Therefore, we argue:

3) The greater the length of homelessness the greater the criminal activity; the longer the period of

unemployment the greater the criminal activity; the lower the legal income the greater the criminal activity; the more criminal peers who approve of criminal behaviour the greater the criminal activity; and the greater the use of drugs and alcohol the greater the criminal activity.

As we have observed, there are a number of factors that can contribute to perceptions of formal punishments. These can include both the informal mechanisms noted above as well as the various structural, peer, and substance use variables. We argue that:

4A) The greater the amount of informal social control and the greater the moral commitment to the conventional order the greater the perceived certainty and severity of formal sanctions.

4B) The greater the length of homelessness and unemployment the lower the perceived certainty and severity of formal sanctions. The lower the legal income the lower the certainty and severity of formal sanctions. The more criminal peers who support criminal behaviour and the greater the use of drugs and alcohol the lower the perceived certainty and severity of formal sanctions.

The hypotheses outlined above can be generally summarized by the model illustrated in Figure 1. We see here first the potential effects of our various measures on perceptions of certainty and severity and second the influence of these variables with the addition of the perceived threats of formal sanctions directly on criminal behaviour.

Methods

Street youth as a term has rarely been well defined, but usually refers to youth who have run away or been expelled from their homes and/or who spend some or all of their time in various public locations. Often utilizing "service" definitions, research has focused on youths ranging in age from 12 to 24 (Caputo

Figure 1
Theoretical model

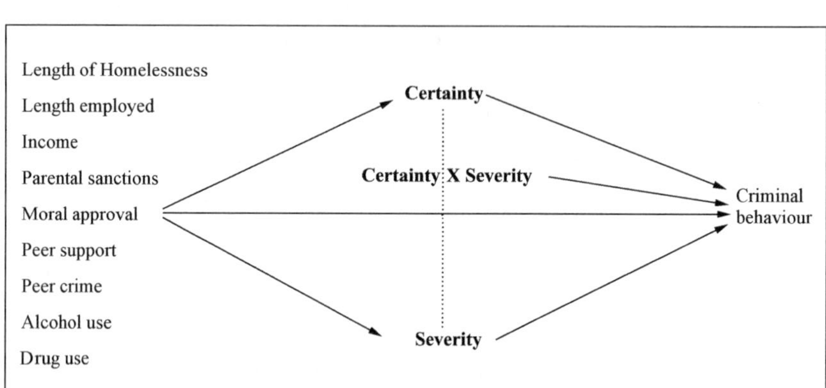

and Ryan 1991) and reveals a heterogeneity of street lifestyles and street youths as groups. The street population is made up both of youth who "hang out" on the street on a regular and permanent basis, and youth whose street life participation is more sporadic. It contains those who attend school and those who have dropped out. Some live at home, others on their own, and others on the street. Some work full-time or part-time, others rely on state assistance, social agencies, or crime to support themselves. Thus, street involvement can be characterized as a continuum rather than a categorical entity.

One hundred twenty five male respondents were identified based on four sampling criteria.

1. participants must be male;
2. they must be aged 24 and under;
3. they must have left or finished school
4. they must spend at least 3 hours a day, three days a week "hanging around" on the street or in a mall.

The rationales for these criteria were 1) to avoid potential ethical methodological problems of a male researcher inquiring about intimate areas of female respondents' lives[(2)]

(sexual abuse, sexual assault and prostitution); 2) to cover the age range of those described as street youth (Caputo and Ryan 1991); 3) to eliminate those who were not candidates for full-time employment; and 4) to obtain a sample of "serious" "at risk" youth and avoid the "weekend warriors." Although criteria four left the door open for the inclusion of respondents who were employed, lived at home, and spent minimal time on the street, the data show that only four of the respondents had lived at home for the entire twelve months and all but eight respondents had spent time living on the street in the prior year. The fact that the average respondent had spent over five months in prior year without a fixed address indicates that the sample was essentially on the street full-time.

Data collection

The data were collected in Edmonton, Alberta, a large western Canadian city (Canada's fifth largest) with a population of 800,000. The data were gathered from May 1995 through July of 1995 and focused on more serious property crimes and violent offenses. Data collection took place in and around the downtown business core of the city which is bordered by the local skid row and the "inner city." Thus, the area contained a mix of commercial and financial establishments surrounded by bars, pawnshops, hotels, shelters, detox centres, rooming houses, rundown residential units, and abandoned buildings.

Sample selection began with the interviewer situating himself in geographical areas known to be frequented by street youths. Potential respondents were approached, alerted to the project, and screened for study eligibility. Those youths meeting the selection criteria were then provided more information on the study and asked to participate.(3) After granting consent, the youths were taken to be interviewed in the comfortable and sheltered conditions of one of the food courts that dot the many malls in the downtown core. These interviews averaged around 45 – 50 minutes. Upon completion, the respondents were awarded $20 in food coupons at a popular fast food restaurant for their participation.

Once intial entrance into networks had been successful, youths who interacted with prior respondents were also targeted. About 35 of the 125 contacts were initiated by youths who had learned of the researcher's presence and solicited interviews or through introductions from previously interviewed members. Following these advances, informed consent was obtained from each new respondent who was then interviewed and rewarded[(4)].

The researcher began and ended each day by returning to the locations where he had come into contact with previous respondents. This allowed him to follow up on the youths' situations and observe and gather more information on their behaviours, which was recorded in field notes at the end of each day. This process also filled periods of down time when there were no new people to be approached or found.

Dependent variables

Information on a number of measures of criminal involvement was obtained via self report. An extensive literature has developed on the self report methodology indicating that its use with serious drug/crime participants consistently reveals findings that are "surprisingly truthful and accurate."(Inciardi et al. 1993; Johnson, Goldstein, Preble, Schmeidler, Lipton, Spunt, and Miller 1985). Research has determined that the most accurate self-reported delinquency measures do not restrict response categories, do not request information beyond a one year period, and utilize face to face interviews as opposed to paper-and-pencil written questionnaires (Huizinga and Elliott 1986). The present research contained all of these characteristics.

The respondents were asked how many times in the past year they had: "broken into a car; broken into a house; attacked someone with a weapon or fists/feet injuring them so badly they probably needed a doctor?" These measures provided somewhat skewed distributions due to the fact that the majority of respondents had committed only a few offenses while a minority were heavily involved in these behaviours. For example, the average respondent had broken into a house six times in the prior year. The standard deviation for this offense was over 23. This pattern was replicated in each of the offenses examined (broken into a car X = 56.36; SD = 202; injured someone with a weapon or fists X = 11.62 SD = 81.97). To remedy this skewness, each of the crime measures was subject to a natural log transformation that substantially reduced this problem (see Table 1).

Table 1
Mean and standard deviations

Variable	Mean	Std. dev.	min.	max.
Length of homelessness	5.34	3.84	0	12
Length employed	1.68	2.39	0	11
Income	1.88	1.28	0	3
Parental sanctions (prop crime)	2.75	.47	1	3
Job commitment (prop crime)	1.91	.93	1	3
Moral approval (prop crime)	3.32	.87	1	4
Peer support (prop crime)	2.55	1.04	1	4
Peer crime (prop crime))	2.97	1.18	1	5
Parental sanctions (viol crime)	2.71	.58	1	3
Job commitment (viol crime)	2.23	.92	1	3
Moral approval (viol crime)	3.14	.92	1	4
Peer support (viol crime)	2.37	1.02	1	4
Peer crime (viol crime)	3.77	1.17	1	5
Alcohol use	4.13	1.60	1	7
Drug use	5.00	2.24	1	7
Certainty (prop crime)	1.83	.93	1	4
Severity (prop crime)	2.41	.74	1	3
Certainty (viol crime)	2.23	1.04	1	4
Severity (viol crime)	2.49	.69	1	3
Log break into cars	1.31	1.95	0	7
Log break into buildings	.72	1.16	0	5.3
Aggravated assault	.86	1.17	0	6.8

These distributions demonstrate that the sample contains both low rate and high rate offenders across a range of offenses. Therefore, the sample provides us with substantial variation that will enable us to obtain a more accurate understanding of the role various factors play in the generation of property crime and aggravated assaults.

Independent variables

— *Formal sanctions*

The concepts of certainty and severity of formal punishments are central to the deterrence doctrine. The measures of perceived certainty and severity used here are similar to those employed in other deterrence research (Burkett and Carrithers 1980; Paternoster 1988; 1989a; 1989b; Paternoster et al. 1983; Paternoster and Iovanni 1986). To obtain the certainty measure, respondents were asked "If you were to (break and enter/stab someone in a street fight), how likely is it that you would be caught by the police?" Four response options ranged from "Very unlikely (=1)" to "Very Likely (=4)." To obtain the severity measure respondents were asked, "If you were caught (break and entering/after this street fight), by the police, taken to court, and punished, how much of a problem would that create for your life?" The three response options ranged from "no problem at all (=1)" to "a large problem (=3)." Consistent with theoretical insight, an interaction effect between certainty and severity was created by multiplying the two variables representing certainty and severity in each type of offense together.

— *Informal control*

One of the central tenets of the informal sanction argument is that people refrain from criminal activities because they fear the rejection of people to whom they are close. Since the youths of this sample primarily live outside of the parental home, on the street, they are not subject to the traditional types of parental supervision and parental attachment typical of other deterrence research examining the role of informal sanctions. As both Roshier (1989) and Hirschi (1969) argue, the presence, or even the existence, of people we care about may not be necessary for their influence to apply. It may be the case that we retain the desire to be the type of person who would have gained the affection and approval of the absent person by behaving in a certain fashion. To explore for this possibility respondents were asked "Which best describes how your parents would feel if they knew you had break and entered/stabbed someone in a street fight?" Response categories ranged from "approve but do not encourage me (=1)" to "strongly disapprove under any circumstances (=3)."

Similarly, one may be committed to conformity because future prospects could be put in jeopardy should deviance be exposed. One is committed to conformity by what one hopes to obtain. To examine the role of conventional commitments in deterring the criminal activities of street youth, the respondents were asked "How much would your chances of getting a good job be hurt if you were arrested for break and entering/stabbing someone in a street fight?" The available response categories ranged from "not at all (=1)" to "quite a bit (=3)."

Another important consideration in deciding to participate in delinquency is the respondents' moral position regarding criminal infractions. This emphasizes the importance of an internalized conscience and negative moral evaluations of behaviour in influencing potential offenders' choice of action. To explore the importance of the respondents' moral beliefs in explaining criminal behaviour, they were asked "How wrong do you think it is to break and enter/hit or threaten to hit someone?" Here four response categories were available ranging from "very wrong (=1)" to "not wrong at all (=4)."

Research suggests that peer approval of, and peer participation in illegal activities may increase offending behaviour (Hindelang 1973; Krohn and Massey 1980). To tap into the potential importance of peers' sanctions in the control of criminal activities, respondents were asked "how wrong do your friends think it is to break and enter/get into knife fights?" Again, response categories ranged from "very wrong (=1)" to "not wrong at all (=4)." To gauge peer participation in property crime, respondents were asked "how many of your friends steal things or money (none = 1, a few = 2, some = 3, most = 4, or all = 5). To gauge their participation in violent crime, respondents were asked "how many of your friends have hit or threatened to hit someone" (none = 1, a few = 2, some = 3, most = 4, or all = 5).

Theorists have also alluded to the importance of social status in deterring potential offenders. They assume that actors living in poverty have less to lose from criminal behaviour and that their perceptions of the benefits of criminal activity are altered. To explore the effect of poverty on criminal behaviour, respondents were asked for their monthly legal income, be it from employment or state assistance.(5) The respondents were also requested to determine the length of time they had been without a fixed address in the prior twelve months, and how long they had worked fulltime.

Finally, to examine the role of drugs and alcohol in perceptions of punishment and offending behaviour, the respondents were queried as to "How many times in the past 30 days did you drink alcohol/ smoke marijuana or hashish." (Never = 1, 1-2 times a months = 2, 3-4 times a month = 3, once a week = 4, 2-3 times a week = 5, 4-6 times a week = 6, everyday = 7). Table 1 provides a summary of the means and standard deviations of the various independent variables.

Table 1 illustrates that these procedures provided us with a sample of street youth with an average age of almost nineteen (mean = 18.84). About 38% of the sample were legally young offenders (under 18 years of age) at the time of the interview. Most of these (30% of the total sample) were 16 and 17 years of age. The other 62% of the sample were over 18 at the time of the interview. Over half of these (38% of the total sample) were between 18 and 20 years of age. Thus, the bulk of our sample is between 16 and 20 years of age. The respondents reported being homeless slightly over 5 months (mean = 5.34) in the 12 months prior to the interview and the average legal monthly income for the sample was 247 dollars (see footnote 4).

A further examination of Table 1 reveals that the sample as a whole perceives the certainty of punishment for both property and violent offenses to be low to midrange (means of 1.83 and 2.23 out of a 1-4 range). The respondents' perceptions of the severity of punishment if apprehended appears to be somewhat higher (means of 2.41 and 2.49 out of a 1-3 range). This suggests that there is some fear of legal sanctions in the sample. There also appears to be some recognition of informal sanctions in terms of job commitment and parental sanctions. This group of youths has few moral restrictions against criminal behaviours and appear to spend most of their time in the company of criminal peers who support these illegal activities.

The correlation matrix of all predictor variables(6) revealed few problems of collinearity (i.e., r>.4). An examination of Variance Inflation Factors(7) (below 1.6 in each case) suggested that any collinearity between independent variables would not significantly affect the estimates of other independent variables.

Results

— *Property crime*

We begin our statistical analysis by examining the model outlined in Figure 1 as it applies to property crime. Utilizing OLS regression, we first explore how the various factors identified in our literature review influence perceptions of formal sanctions. We then examine how all of our variables, including perceptions of formal sanctions, affect our respondents' property offending.

The first column in Table 2 summarizes the effects of our various indicators on perceptions of certainty. These results reveal, consistent with our hypotheses, that the internalization of conventional norms increases the perceived certainty of formal sanctions. Those youths who felt that break and entering was wrong were more likely to believe they would be caught if they undertook this type of offense. Thus, a strong

Table 2
Property crime model

Variable	Certainty of sanction prop crime	Severity of sanction prop crime	Break into cars	Break into blds
Length of homelessness	-.0670	.0761	.0050	-.0729
Length employed	-.1019	.0477	-.0394	.0923
Income	.1157	.0815	.0289	.0092
Parental sanctions	-.0368	.0317	.1493	.1594*
Job commitment	-.0070	.0115	.0518	-.1365
Moral approval crime	-.1817**	-.2550***	.0583	.1025
Peer support	-.0611	-.2498***	-.0282	.0368
Peer crime	-.0746	.0219	.2541***	.1958**
Alcohol use	-.1480	.1489*	.0516	-.0260
Drug use	-.1833**	.0276	.2206**	.2037**
Certainty	-	-	-.5713*	-.6401**
Severity	-	-	-.4128**	-.3684*
Certainty X severity	-	-	.6221*	.6331*
R2	.1150	.2130	.2095	.2364
N=	125	125	125	125

* Sig .10
** Sig .05
*** Sig .01

moral condemnation towards crime serves to increase the threat of formal sanctions. Alternatively, the lack of moral commitment serves to decrease the threat of formal punishment. While moral commitment increases perceptions of certainty, drug use decreases perceptions of certainty. Respondents who reported regular drug use also reported lower levels of perceived certainty of arrest for breaking and entering, suggesting that being under the influence of drugs can neutralize or alter actors' calculations of risk (Inciardi and Russe 1977). If substance use is a general requirement of the street lifestyle (Inciardi et al. 1993), then this lifestyle appears to reduce the threat of legal sanctions.

Moving to severity (see Table 2 column 2), we again see that a strong moral condemnation towards crime serves to increase the perceived threat of formal sanctions. Youths who have developed normative constraints are more threatened by the severity of punishment. Those respondents who saw nothing wrong with break and entering tended to view the punishments for this type of offense as minimal.

Table 2 also suggests that perceptions of severity are increased for heavy users of alcohol. We might speculate that the depressant effect of this substance leads respondents to alter their estimates of punishment severity upwards. Nevertheless, alcohol appears to have a different directional impact on punishment perception than drug use.

In contrast, the results suggest that perceptions of severity can be undermined by peers who support criminal behaviour. Peers who approve of breaking and entering minimize our respondents' perceptions of sanction severity for this type of property offense. The rewards gained from peer approval and the information on punishment gained from peers may outweigh the potential costs of punishment.

Moving now to the direct effects of our variables on property crime, Table 2 reveals that the perceived threat of formal sanctions are significant predictors of breaking into cars (see column 3) and breaking into houses (see column 4). First, the less certain these youths were of punishment, the more houses and the more cars they broke into. Second, the less severe they perceived the threatened formal sanctions the more houses and the more cars they broke into. Finally, our interaction term indicates that the combination of low certainty with low severity leaves street youths significantly more likely to break into cars and houses. Alternatively, what this suggests is that those youths on the street who felt punishments to be certain and severe were significantly less likely to undertake these activities.

In terms of informal sanctions, we discover that the fear of parental disapproval still holds weight for some street youths.

Those youths who thought parents would disapprove of their breaking into houses reported fewer offenses of this type.

In contrast, we find that the criminal behaviour of peers is related to greater participation in both types of property crime. Respondents who indicated most of their peers engaged in property crime reported breaking into cars and houses more than those youths without criminal peers. We also discover that respondents who report heavy drug use are at greater risk for breaking into cars and houses. Again these two variables may be linked to the street lifestyle. The availability of criminal partners who engage and assist in criminal activities makes for a criminogenic environment. Further, some of the criminal activity may be undertaken to fund drug habits. As Inciardi et al. (1993) note, within this lifestyle crime is more than simply a method of getting substances. Crime finances and facilitates use, and use encourages more profit making crimes to support an ever growing pattern of use (Inciardi et al. 1993: 111; see also Austin and Lettierri 1976; Faupel 1996; Gandossy, Williams, Cohen, and Harwood 1980; Inciardi 1992; McBride and McCoy 1982; Weissman 1978) while, as we have seen above, making risky and otherwise difficult offenses psychologically easier by reducing the perceived severity of punishment (Inciardi et al. 1993; Goldstein 1985; Inciardi and Russe 1977).

The last two equations in Table 2 also reveal that, outside of drug use, the variables that influence perceptions of sanctions do not have direct effects on criminal behaviour. Instead, it appears that moral commitment, peer support, and alcohol use make their presence felt through certainty and severity, both of which are significant predictors of breaking into cars and buildings. Thus, peer support and a lack of moral commitment lower perceptions of punishment which in turn increases the likelihood of property offending. In contrast, heavy alcohol use increases perceptions of threat which in turn decreases the likelihood of property crime.

Violent crime

Replicating the procedure used above, we move now to examine the model in Figure 1 as it applies to violent crime. Looking at

Table 3 (see column 1), we find that extended homelessness increases perceptions of probable apprehension for stabbing someone in a street fight. It is likely these youths recognize that spending considerable amounts of time on the street increases their exposure and familiarity to police officers. Sherman (1993) notes that youths on the street are prime targets for the police because they are viewed as probable offenders for certain offenses. This phenomenon leads to regular interaction between the police and youths on the street and appears to increase youths' perceptions of certainty of apprehension if involved in a stabbing.

Table 3
Violent crime model

Variable	Certainty of sanction violent crime	Severity of sanction violent crime	Aggravated assault
Length of homelessness	.1841**	-.0418	.0896
Length employed	-.0658	.0037	.0326
Income	.0988	.1928*	.1764*
Parental sanctions	-.0454	.1096	-.0215
Job commitment	-.0574	.2088***	.0354
Moral approval crime	-.1101	.0387	-.0590
Peer support	-.2527***	-.2013**	.0274
Peer crime	-.0465	-.1419	.1954**
Alcohol use	.0217	.1301	.0580
Drug use	-.1269	.0532	.1471
Certainty	-	-	.0903
Severity	-	-	.3618
Certainty X severity	-	-	-.4226
R2	.1345	.1983	.2621
N=	125	125	124

* Sig .10
** Sig .05
*** Sig .01

In contrast, we discover that peer support for stabbing someone in a knife fight decreases our respondents' perceptions of certainty. Thus, peers offer a sense of protection against the certainty of arrest for this serious violent offense. As alluded to above, it may be that peer support provides a type of reward that counteracts or overrides the potential costs of committing a crime. A popular explanation for the violent behaviour of youths has drawn from a subculture of violence perspective. Some have suggested that the violent crime in these groups is a product of conformity to a distinctive culture. Those who are in intimate contact with groups organized in favour of violent criminal activities become exposed to definitions favourable to this unlawful behaviour and, given their extensive associations with such definitions, such individuals are likely to act in terms of them, committing violent crimes (Curtis 1975; Wolfgang and Ferracuti 1967). It appears that part and parcel of this culture is information that overrides threats of formal sanctions.

Just as peers reduce the perceived certainty of punishment so do they reduce the perceived threat of severity (see Table 3, column 2). Peers who support violent behaviour, minimize our respondents' perceptions of sanction severity for stabbing someone in a knife fight.

Table 3 also reveals that youths who indicate more positive economic circumstances view the penalties for criminal behaviour to be more severe. Thus, consistent with our hypotheses, living on the most extreme margins of society serves to decrease the threats of legal sanctions. At the same time, this suggests that given the adverse circumstances of the majority of our sample, even minimal financial support appears to create some fear of formal sanctions.

Table 3 also indicates that youths, who felt that stabbing someone in a knife fight would destroy their chances of gaining desirable employment, also believed that the punishment for their actions would be severe. Alternatively, those youths who have lost hope for gaining employment do not view the potential legal sanctions for stabbing someone in a knife fight as potentially severe. Again it appears that some link to conventional society can increase the threat of formal sanctions.

Moving to the direct effects equations (see Table 3, column 3), we discover that none of our measures of threatened formal sanctions are significantly related to our measure of aggravated assault. Instead, the strongest predictor of aggravated assault is the association with violent peers. Respondents who indicated that many of their friends had hit or threatened to hit others were more likely to have higher aggravated assault totals. Returning to a subculture of violence perspective, Fagan and Jones (1984) note that the highest rates of aggressive behaviour are located in environments where aggressive role models are abundant and where aggressiveness is a positive attribute. The violent peer group offers a climate where violent behaviours are modeled, practised, and reinforced. Felson and Steadman (1983) suggest that violent peers can also influence altercations by acting as "third parties." Peers can engage in physical and verbal attacks themselves, acting as allies for one of the antagonists, and may instigate conflict by defining a situation as one in which violence is an appropriate response (Baron 1997; Kennedy and Baron 1993).

The only other variable to reach significance in our direct effect model is income. Contrary to expectation, youths who report greater amounts of legal income report higher aggravated assault totals. Nevertheless, these findings suggest that factors other than the perceived threat of formal sanctions appear to influence serious violent altercations. Further, they suggest that the effects of threatened sanctions appear to be different for violent offenses than for property offenses.

We again discover that the variables significantly related to perceptions of certainty and severity are not directly related to criminal behaviour. Homelessness, peer support, income, and job commitment have no direct effect on our aggravated assault measure. Unlike our property crime models, certainty and severity are not significant predictors of violent crime, suggesting that the indirect influence of homelessness, peer support, income, and job commitment will be somewhat muted.

Discussion

This research set out to explore the deterrent effect of formal sanctions on a population of "at risk" youths living on the margins of society, while at the same time trying to uncover how these perceptions of punishment were altered by various factors in these youths' lives. We discover that the perceived threat of formal sanctions (particularly severity) within this population is reasonably high, and we find that those with higher levels of certainty and severity have reduced levels of property crime. Alternatively, we find that those youths who perceive the threat of formal sanctions for property crime to be low are more likely to commit this type of behaviour. On the one hand, this suggests that deterrence does have an effect on those street youths who perceive sanctions to be certain and severe. But it also implies that the threat of punishment does not restrict the property crime of a small group of high rate offenders on the street.

In terms of violent offenses, we found that the perceived threat of punishments did not influence our respondents' behaviour one way or another. We might want to characterize the knife fights that take place on the street as guided more by impulse and the sway of emotion than by reflection, judgement, or premeditation. Zimring and Hawkins (1973) argue that carefully planned acts are probably more easily deterable than those that emerge from sudden emotional impulse. Decisions made quickly, as a reaction to a situation, may be less susceptible to threats because emotional arousal can eclipse thoughts of future consequences by focusing attention on the present situation. Further, it appears that third parties may fan this emotional fire escalating the seriousness of the battle, as youths on the street may be swayed more by the pressure of peers than the sanctions of the legal system. In sum, expressive crimes on the street may be less deterable than instrumental crimes despite the recognition of severe sanction. It may still be the case that we can predict the conditions under which aggression gets played out. Kennedy and Forde (1996) argue that we must fully explore the social context and situational aspects of disputes if we are going to limit violent transactions.

Our findings also reveal that perceptions of legal punishments can be influenced by a number of factors. For example, we discover that the attitudes of peers decreases perceptions of threat. Peers provide additional knowledge that help offenders more accurately gauge their chances of getting caught and can provide some context to the severity of the punishment. The positive support of peers may also sway calculations and reduce fear in spite of objective threats. Nevertheless, youths who come into contact with peers who approve of criminal behaviour have lower perceptions of the threat of formal punishment.

Like peers, heavy drug use also appears to reduce perceptions of threatened sanctions. The use of these substances may influence calculations and perceptions regardless of the objective odds of punishment. Inciardi et al. (1993; Inciardi and Russe 1977) note that drugs can make offenders feel omnipotent and allow them to undertake risky and dangerous offenses by eliminating the fear of apprehension and punishment.

Living on the margins of society can also impinge on people's perceptions of punishment. Youths who report minimal legal economic resources have a reduced perception of fear. Respondents with greater legal incomes have elevated perceptions of sanction severity. Thus, as Zimring and Hawkins (1973) argue, poor economic circumstances can undermine the effects of deterrence by reducing the perceptions of certainty and severity of punishment.

The above implies that one method of increasing the threat of formal sanctions is to reduce the influence of those factors that decrease perceptions of certainty and severity. Threats of punishment may be increased by providing minimal economic resources, drug rehabilitation, and integration into conventional peer groups.

We also discover that negative economic circumstances and substance abuse can increase the perceptions of threat.

Homelessness may increase perceptions of certainty, perhaps because youths characterized by these conditions spend a significant amount of time on the street corner where their exposure to, and contact with, police is magnified. Frequent interactions with police may create the impression that they are vulnerable to apprehension and punishment. It may also be the case that these youths believe their homelessness makes them attractive suspects to the police when a crime is reported or discovered. Heavy alcohol use also appears to increase the fear of legal sanctions. It may be that the depressant effect of this substance leads actors to be more pessimistic in their views of punishment.

What appears to be vital in the creation of fear of formal sanctions is the development of normative constraints against criminal behaviour and a moral commitment to conventional society. Those who felt certain behaviours to be morally wrong feared formal sanctions. Further, those who worried about jeopardizing future accomplishments by engaging in criminal behaviour feared formal sanctions. Those who have not developed moral constraints and conventional commitments, or those who have had these eroded by living on the street, are poor candidates for deterrence because these conditions are related to a reduced fear of sanctions. Again, this suggests one possible avenue for increasing the threat of formal sanctions is to increase these youths' bonds to conventional society through employment and other conventional activities.

The direct effects of our measures on criminal behaviour support the idea that values, experiences, and other factors including perceptions of threats are important in understanding criminal decisions (Schneider 1990). We discover that some street youths retain a psychological link to their parents where they fear their disapproval. Many of our street youths see little wrong with their criminal behaviour, and with the lack of internal controls comes an orientation that fails to restrict criminal actions. Here, individuals commit crimes free of guilt that their actions are wrong, making them extremely difficult to deter. Thus, not only do street youth lack the fear of formal sanctions but they suffer from an absence of informal controls that might restrict their criminal behaviour.

The threat of informal sanctions appears to be replaced by peers who are themselves heavily involved in criminal activities and who support these illegal behaviours. Thus, the direction of the informal sanction is reversed: criminal behaviour is approved of and rewarded. Further, these peers likely provide criminal partnership providing the assistance needed to undertake these activities successfully (Reiss and Farrington 1991).

The use of drugs also appears to be vital in explaining the criminal behaviour of street youth. Survey and ethnographic studies alike show that persistent offenders spend much of their criminal gains on alcohol and drugs (Shover and Honaker 1992). Walsh (1986) suggests that the proceeds of these offenders' crimes are used for "personal, nonessential consumption (e.g., nights out)" and "enjoying good times" rather than basic needs. This lifestyle is often enjoyed in the company of others who share the consumption of drugs and/or alcohol in bars, on street corners, and in other locations (Shover and Honaker 1992). In this lifestyle, the relationship between substance abuse and crime is a "most" general one (Inciardi et al. 1993). Both are required to participate in the subculture and to reap its rewards and satisfactions. Success in the subculture is defined by substance using and criminal activity (Faupel 1996). It is the commitment to this lifestyle more than addiction that is important in explaining either drug use or crime within this population. Within this lifestyle, crime is more than simply a method of getting substances. Crime finances and facilitates use, and use encourages more profit making crimes to support an ever growing pattern of use (Inciardi et al. 1993: 111; Austin and Lettieri 1976; Faupel 1996; Gandossy et al. 1980; Inciardi 1992; McBride and McCoy 1982; Weissman 1978). Within this way of life, crime is more than simply a means of getting drugs; its success affects usage and usage can affect crime by making risky and otherwise difficult offenses psychologically easier (Inciardi et al. 1993;

Goldstein 1985; Inciardi and Russe 1977). Thus, the diminished contact with conventional others and efforts to sustain substance consumption increasingly means contacts become limited to other street people, values become altered to fit behaviours, and crime becomes an accepted part of life (Faupel 1996; Inciardi et al. 1993; Shover and Honaker 1992).

While our findings reveal how poverty, homelessness, peer support, and conventional commitments influence perceptions of threatened formal sanctions, they do not exhibit any direct effects on crime. It may be the case that these conditions merely expose street youths to the street lifestyle and assist in isolating them from conventional attachments and institutions, increasing the likelihood that they will be drawn into this lifestyle. On the street they find the criminal peers and substances that may become central to their existence on the street.

Some may argue that these findings demonstrate the need to increase the threats of punishment to the point where even high rate "chronic offenders" view the punishments to be certain and severe. Our results suggest that the perceived severity of punishment in the sample is already quite high. The rates of certainty are somewhat lower, increasing with lengthy homelessness. Would an increase in certainty and severity deter these high rate serious offenders? To answer this, we must keep in mind that deterrence is based on perceptions of punishment, not objective conditions of punishment. This distinction is important because it means that actors may differentially interpret the threat of punishment and the variation in these interpretations may depend on a number of factors.

Our findings suggest that harsher penalties probably will not deter those most at risk for criminal behaviour, because they are involved in a lifestyle that reduces the perceptions of risk and provides them with an environment where criminal behaviour is required and rewarded. Harsher penalties will only clog up our penal institutions at great cost, while the positions vacated by the incarcerated are being filled by the next crop of youth fleeing to the streets in hope of something better (Currie 1985). If we follow our results and the findings that populate the work on more conventional samples, it would seem that a more positive option would be to provide routes for reincorporation into conventional society, by building up informal controls and normative constraints while at the same time establishing levels of economic support that create a stake in conformity. Elliott Currie (1985) suggests a number of different programs including those focused on family support, employment, and education. He argues that such programs may help to prevent youths from becoming immersed into the street lifestyle, and it may be through these programs that youths can come to gain a stake in conformity and become reattached to conventional society. Schneider's (1990) work on deterrence and adjudicated delinquents suggests that programs can be effective if they provide a tangible measure of success for the participants, increase remorse, and enhance people's sense of citizenship. This implies that successful intervention depends more on improving and strengthening individuals' capacities for success in law-abiding activities and commitment to conventional society than on sanctions that enhance perceptions of certainty and severity of punishment (Schneider 1990).

Future research would do well to continue to examine the role of various types of sanctions in the behaviour of those on the margins of society while exploring for other possible factors that influence the perceptions of these threatened sanctions. It should also explore more fully the differences between instrumental and expressive offenses. The lack of work on marginal populations has left us with a vacuum in our knowledge and has forced us to rely on research that focuses on conventional populations. While this work is important, it is insufficient and leaves speculation as the alternative.

Notes

1. Please address all correspondence to: Stephen W. Baron, Dept. of Sociology and Anthropology, University of Windsor, Windsor, Ontario, Canada. Funding for this research came from the Social Sciences and Humanities Research Council of Canada and the University of Windsor Research Board. The authors give thanks to Darrell Langevin and the Boyle Street Coop for their assistance and to the anonymous reviewers for their suggestions.
2. Both the researchers and their university's ethics committee concluded it was improper for a male researcher to ask female respondents questions of this nature. Methodologically, the nature of the data collection (relatively short, "one shot" interviews in a semi-public place) may have affected the validity and reliability of responses from female respondents to these questions. One potential solution was to eliminate these questions. However, past research suggested that these types of variables were particularly important in explaining the backgrounds and behaviours of both male and female street youth. Since the lack of financial support precluded hiring a female interviewer, and these questions could not be eliminated, the decision was made to restrict the sample to male street youth. Due to concerns raised in the ethics review about the sensitive nature of some of the questions bearing on physical and sexual victimization, as well as other issues raised in the interviews including substance abuse, a referral list of relevant social service agencies was a constant companion of the researcher. Despite the sensitivity of a number of the questions, the interviews proceeded without issue and the respondents seemed at ease in responding to the interview questions.
3. Upon assent, they were supplied with informed consent forms outlining study goals and apprising them of their rights within the interview situation. Subjects were notified that they were not obliged to respond to any of the questions and were provided the option to withdraw from the interview at any time. None of the youths exercised this power.
4. The fact that respondents may have been informed of some questions prior to the interview by their peers is not believed to have greatly influenced responses. The fact that the interview process took over 45 minutes, and contained a large number of questions in a number of areas beyond the present analysis makes it likely that prior respondents would be able to provide only general references to questions and would not consistently focus on one area of the interview. Further, part of the questionnaire contained a factorial design that provided a randomized scenario component prior to the "deterrence" questions that made interviews somewhat dissimilar that probably would have left "well prepared" respondents questioning the accuracy of their friends' reports.
5. The income variable was recoded to 1-394 = 1, 395-1000 = 2, over $1000 = 3. This division reflects the level of state support in Alberta for a single employable which in 1995 was $394.
6. This table is available from the authors upon request.

7. The variance inflation factor is a diagnostic that allows for the detection of collinear data and assesses the extent to which the collinearity has altered estimated parameters. Estimates are produced for the variance of each regression coefficient. As the variance inflation factor increases, so does the variance of the regression coefficient. If the tolerance level of a variable is small, its collinearity is close to a linear combination of the other independent variables (Norusis 1993).

References

Anderson, Elijah
1994 The code of the streets. The Atlantic Monthly. May: 81-94.

Anderson, Linda S., Theodore G. Chiricos, and Gordon P. Waldo
1977 Formal and informal sanctions: A comparison of deterrent effects. Social Problems 25: 103-114.

Austin, G.A. and D.J. Lettieri
1976 Drugs and Crime. Rockville, MD: National Institute of Drug Abuse.

Baron, Stephen W.
1997 Risky lifestyles and the link between offending and victimization. Studies on Crime and Crime Prevention, 6: 53-71.

Baron, Stephen W.
1995 Serious offenders. In James Creechan and Robert A. Silverman (eds.), Canadian Delinquency. Toronto: Prentice Hall.

Baron, Stephen W. and Timothy F. Hartnagel.
1996 'Lock em Up': Attitudes toward punishing juvenile offenders. Canadian Journal of Criminology 38 (2): 191-212.

Bishop, Donna M.
1984 Legal and extra legal barriers to delinquency. Criminology 22: 403-419.

Brennan, Tim, David Huizinga, and Delbert S. Elliott
1978 The Social Psychology of Runaways. Toronto: Lexington Books.

Burkett, Steven and William Carrithers
1980 Adolescent's drinking and perceptions of legal and informal sanctions. Journal of Studies on Alcohol 41: 839-853.

Burkett, Steven and Eric Jensen
1975 Conventional ties, peer influence, and the fear of apprehension: A study of adolescent marijuana use. The Sociological Quarterly 16: 522-533.

Burkett, Steven and David A. Ward
1993 A note on perceptual deterrence, religiously based moral condemnation, and social control. Criminology 31: 19-134.

Caputo, Tulio and C. Ryan
1991 The Police Response to Youth at Risk. Ottawa: Solicitor General.

Cook, Philip J.
1977 Punishment and crime: A critique of current findings concerning the preventive effects of punishment. Law and Contemporary Problems 41: 164-204.

Currie, Elliott
1985 Confronting Crime. New York: Pantheon.

Curtis, Lynn A.
1975 Violence, Race, and Culture. Lexington, Mass.: D.C. Heath.

Decker, Scott, Richard Wright, and Robert Logie
1993 Perceptual deterrence among active residential burglars: A research note. Criminology 31: 135-147.

Fagan, Jeffrey A. and Sally Jo Jones
1984 Towards an integrated model of violent delinquency. In Robert Mathias, Paul DeMuro, and Richard S. Allinson (eds.), An Anthology on Violent Juvenile Offenders. Newark: National Council on Crime and Delinquency.

Faupel, Charles. E.
1996 The drugs-crime connection among stable addicts. In Paul Cromwell (ed.), In Their Own Words. Los Angeles: Roxbury Pub. Co.

Felson, Richard B. and H.J. Steadman
1983 Situational factors in disputes leading to criminal violence. Criminology 21: 59-74.

Gandossy, Robert P., Jay R. Williams, Jo. Cohen, and Henrick J. Harwood
1980 Drugs and Crime: A Survey and Analysis of the Literature. Washington, D.C.: National Institute of Justice.

Geerken, Michael R. and Walter Gove
1975 Deterrence: Some theoretical considerations. Law and Society Review 9: 497-513.

Goldstein, Paul J.
1985 The drugs/violence nexus: A tripartite conceptual framework. Journal of Drug Issues 15: 493-506.

Grasmick, Harold G. and Lynn Appleton
1977 Legal punishment and social stigma: A comparison of two deterrence models. Social Science Quarterly 1: 15-28.

Grasmick, Harold G. and Donald E. Green
1981 Deterrence and the morally committed. Sociological Quarterly 22: 1-14.

Grasmick, Harold G. and Steven D. McLaughlin
1978 Deterrence and social control. American Sociological Review 43: 272-278.

Hagan, John and Bill McCarthy
1992 Streetlife and delinquency. British Journal of Sociology 42. 533-561.

Hamparian, Donna M., Richard L. Schuster, Simon Dinitz, and John P. Conrad
1978 The Violent Few: A Study of Dangerous Juvenile Offenders. Lexington, MA: Lexington Books.

Hartnagel, Timothy F. and Stephen W. Baron
1995 'It's time to get serious': Public attitudes toward juvenile justice in Canada. In James Creechan and Robert A. Silverman (eds), Canadian Delinquency. Toronto: Prentice-Hall.

Hindelang, Michael J.
1973 Causes of delinquency: A partial replication and extension. Social Problems 20: 471-487.

Hirschi, Travis
1969 Causes of Delinquency. Berkeley: University of California Press.

Huizinga, David, and Delbert S. Elliott
1986 Reassessing the reliability and validity of self-report delinquency measures. Journal of Quantitative Criminology 2: 293-327.

Inciardi, James A.
1992 The War on Drugs 2: The Continuing Epic of Heroin, Cocaine, Crack, Crime, AIDS, and Public Policy. Mountain View, CA: Mayfield.

Inciardi, James A. and Brian R. Russe
1977 Professional thieves and drugs. International Journal of the Addictions 12: 1087-1095.

Inciardi, James A., Ruth Horowitz, and Anne E. Pottieger
1993 Street Kids, Street Drugs, Street Crime. Belmont, Calif.: Wadsworth Pub. Co.

Jensen, Gary F., Maynard Erickson, and Jack P. Gibbs.
1978 Perceived risk of punishment and self-reported delinquency. Social Forces 57: 57-78.

Johnson, Bruce D., Paul J. Goldstein, Edward Preble, James Schmeidler, Douglas S. Lipton, Barry Spunt, and Thomas Miller
1985 Taking Care of Business: The Economics of Crime by Heroin Abusers. Lexington, MA: Lexington Books.

Kennedy, Leslie W. and Stephen W. Baron
1993 Routine activities and a subculture of violence: A study of violence on the street. Journal of Research in Crime and Delinquency 30: 88-113.

Kennedy, Leslie W. and David R. Forde
1996 Pathways to aggression: A factorial survey of 'routine' conflict. Journal of Quantitative Criminology 12: 417-438.

Krohn, Marvin D. and James L. Massey
1980 Social control and delinquent behavior: An examination of the elements of the social bond. Sociological Quarterly 21: 529-543.

Kufeldt, Kathleen and Margaret Nimmo
1987a Kids on the street they have something to say: Survey of runaway and homeless youth. Journal of Child Care 3: 53-61.

Kufeldt, Kathleen and Margaret Nimmo
1987b Youth on the street: Abuse and neglect in the eighties. Child Abuse and Neglect 11: 531-543.

McBride, Duane C. and Clyde B. McCoy
1982 Crime and drugs: The issues and literature. Journal of Drug Issues 12: 137-152.

McCarthy, Bill
1995 Not just 'for the thrill of it!': An instrumentalist elaboration of Katz's explanation of sneaky thrill property crimes. Criminology 33: 519-538.

McCarthy, Bill and John Hagan
1991 Homelessness: A criminogenic situation? British Journal of Criminology 31: 393-410.

McCarthy, Bill and John Hagan
1992 Mean streets: The theoretical significance of destitution and desperation among homeless youth. American Journal of Sociology 98: 597-627.

Meier, Robert and Weldon Johnson
1977 Deterrence as social control: The legal and extralegal production of conformity. American Sociological Review 42: 292-304.

Meier, Robert, Steven Burkett, and Carol Hickman
1984 Sanctions, peers and deviance: Preliminary models of a social control process. The Sociological Quarterly 25: 67-82.

Norusis, Marius J.
1993 SPSS for Windows: Base Systems User's Guide, Release 6.0. Chicago, Ill.: SPSS Inc.

Palenski, Joseph E.
1984 Kids Who Run Away. Saratoga Calif.: R & E Publishers.

Paternoster, Raymond
1987 The deterrent effect of the perceived certainty and severity of punishment: A review of evidence and issues. Justice Quarterly 4: 173-217.

Paternoster, Raymond
1988 Examining three-wave deterrence models: A question of temporal order and specification. Journal of Criminal Law and Criminology 79: 135-179.

Paternoster, Raymond
1989a Absolute and restrictive deterrence in a panel of youth: Explaining the onset, persistence/desistance, and frequency of delinquent offending." Social Problems 36: 289-309.

Paternoster, Raymond
1989b Decisions to participate in and desist from four types of delinquency: Deterrence and the rational choice perspective. Law and Society Review 23: 7-40.

Paternoster, Raymond, Linda E. Saltzman, Gordon P. Waldo, and Theodore G. Chiricos
1983 Perceived risk and social control: Do sanctions really deter? Law and Society Review 17: 457-479.

Paternoster, Raymond and Leeann Iovanni
1986 The deterrent effect of perceived severity: A reexamination. Social Forces 64: 751-777.

Radford, J.L., A.J.C. King, and W.K. Warren
1989 Street Youth and AIDS. Ottawa: Health and Welfare Canada.

Rankin, Joseph H. and L. Edward Wells
1982 The social context of deterrence. Sociology and Social Research 67: 19-39.

Reiss, Albert and David P. Farrington
1991 Advancing knowledge about co-offending: Results from a prospective longitudinal survey of London males. The Journal of Criminal Law and Criminology 82: 360-395.

Roberts, Julian V.
1992 Public opinion, crime, and criminal justice. In M. Tonry (ed.), Crime and Justice: A Review of Research. Chicago: University of Chicago Press.

Roshier, Robert
1989 Controlling Crime: The Classical Perspective in Criminology. Chicago: Lyceum Books.

Rothman, Jack
1991 Runaway and Homeless Youth. New York: Longman.

Sacco, Vincent F. and Holly Johnson
1990 Patterns of Criminal Victimization in Canada. Ottawa: Minister of Supply and Services Canada.

Schneider, Anne L.
1990 Deterrence and Juvenile Crime. Springer-Verlag: New York.

Sherman, Lawrence W.
1993 Defiance, deterrence, and irrelevance: A theory of criminal sanction. Journal of Research in Crime and Delinquency 30: 445-473.

Shover, Neal and David Honaker
1992 The socially bounded decision making of persistent property offenders. Howard Journal of Criminal Justice 31: 276-293.

Silberman, Matthew
1976 Toward a theory of criminal deterrence. American Sociological Review 41: 442-461.

Smart, R.G., E.M. Adlaf, K.M. Porterfield, and M.D. Canale
1990 Drugs, Youth and the Street. Toronto: Addictions Research Foundation.

Sorrells, James M.
1977 Kids who kill. Crime and Delinquency 23: 312-320.

Sprott, Jane B.
1996 Understanding public views of youth crime and the youth justice system. Canadian Journal of Criminology 38 (3): 271-290.

Stafford, Mark C. and Mark Warr
1993 A reconceptualization of general and specific deterrence. Journal of Research in Crime and Delinquency 30: 123-135.

Strasburg, Paul A.
1978 Violent Delinquents. New York: Monarch.

Tittle, Charles R. and A.R. Rowe
1973 Moral appeal, sanction threat, and deviance: An experimental test. Social Problems 20: 488-498.

Waldo, Gordon P. and Theodore G. Chiricos
1972 Perceived penal sanction and self-reported criminality: A neglected approach to deterrence research. Social Problems 19: 522-540.

Walsh, Dermott
1986 Heavy Business. London: Routledge and Kegan Paul.

Webber, Marlene
1991 Street Kids: The Tragedy of Canada's Runaways. Toronto: University of Toronto Press.

Weissman, James C.
1978 Understanding the drugs and crime connection: A systematic examination of drugs and crime relationships. Journal of Psychedelic Drugs 10: 171-192.

Williams, Kirk R. and Richard Hawkins
1986 Perceptual research on general deterrence: A critical review. Law and Society Review 20: 545-572.

Williams, Kirk R. and Richard Hawkins
1989 Controlling male aggression in intimate relationships. Law and Society Review 23: 591-612.

Wolfgang, Marvin E. and Franco Ferracuti
1967 The Subculture of Violence. London: Tavistock.

Wolfgang, Marvin, Robert Figlio, and Thorsten Sellin
1972 Delinquency in a Birth Cohort. Chicago: University of Chicago Press.

Zimring, Frank E. and G.J. Hawkins
1973 Deterrence: The Legal Threat in Crime Control. Chicago: University of Chicago Press.

CHAPTER TEN

The State Versus Squeegee Kids

Patricia O'Reilly
and ***Thomas Fleming***

REVISIONIST THEORIES OF MORAL PANIC HAVE PLACED THE MEDIA IN A central position vis-avis the creation of public fears and societal reactions to difference (Fleming, 1997) while extending our understanding of fundamental changes in the manufacture of what constitutes "news". Early theorists of moral panic were cogniscent of the centrality of the British media as both an interpreter and source of distortion in the production of panic. However, while moral panics were once the product of ordinary events which occurred infrequently but which were then amplified out of proportion to the original occurences through reactions by the media, government spokespersons and police sources, contemporary forms are often direct creations of news agencies themselves. The creation of moral panics has evolved into a well-established manner of dealing with ordinary events which may then serve to increase consumers of the print and electronic media. Increasing competition in the field of internet media and other forms of electronic delivery of news services has been created by the rapid proliferation of new media and media news forms.

One product of these developments has been increased pressure on news agencies to find stories which will attract viewers and readers. The exploitation of the sensational to attract consumers is increasingly more difficult in an age where both on television and on the internet, "sensational" has become commonplace. There are only a certain number of stories which compel consumers to return consistently to the subject matter, no matter the chosen vehicle, or which can provide a media outlet with a continuing range of stories stretching over an extended period of time. These factors have lead to a heightened sensitivity to potential behaviours which can be reconstituted into a moral panic through the news selection process. The strong appeal of "law and order" news stories has been demonstrated to be a powerful force, not only in attracting readers/viewers, but also in influencing voting behaviours (Fleming, 1985).

This chapter explores the manufacture of a moral panic in Canada's largest city, Toronto. Specifically, attention focuses upon the "squeegee kids problem" as it emerged and was selected as moral panic material by the media, municipal and provincial politicians, and police. Drawing upon post-critical (Fleming, 1997) forms of theorizing, it is argued that the case of societal reaction to squeegee kids provides an opportunity for examination of the process of the exploitation of a moral panic.

Consideration will be directed towards the effects upon those labelled intolerable or dangerous to society, and the various uses moral panics can provide to various institutions and agencies. Contrary to existing accounts of moral panics and their interpretation (Cohen, 1972), this episode in social control cannot be classified as either a clear success or failure. However, moral panics while ideally viewed by authorities as an opportunity to reinforce law and order policies are not correctly viewed as long term issues but rather momentary issues which can be used to further the political appeal of specific politicians. Since squeegee kids form part of a marginalized street culture which is viewed as "dangerous" by many citizens, they form a natural target for interventionist "get tough" policies which have an immediate appeal to citizens' generalized view of homeless persons as shiftless, lazy, degenerate, addicted, alcoholic or criminal (Fleming, 1993).

Moral panics are recognized as performing a maintenance function for moral boundaries suggested by Durkheim between the socially acceptable and the publically intolerable. It is no surprise given their almost non-existent political strength that squeegee kids, like Cohen's (1972) earlier mods and rockers were seized upon by both politicians and the media as a symbol of the creeping influence of the culture of narcissism and self-indulgence and its translation into annoying public nuisance behaviours. One need only reconsider the legal and political energy expended upon an earlier generation of youth during the hippie era of the late 1960s and early 1970s in Canada to be aware that there are a number of interests who recognize the political and media value of persecuting the weak. The squeegee kids saga is illustrative of the power of law and order campaigns to focus public attention away from important social issues towards more volatile and visible "created" social problems, that is, problems that are created rather than emerge from some form of self-momentum.

The Emergence of Squeegee Kids

Squeegee kids are relative newcomers to the streets of Toronto. Squeegeeing was, until recently associated with skid row men in New York city. Aggressive and unrelenting, they have been depicted in numerous films and television dramas as frightening and potentially dangerous individuals. However, under incumbent mayor Guiliani, strenuous efforts were made to remove squeegee "bums" from the city. This law-and-order campaign was consistent with the "broken windows" theory of urban decay developed by Gibson and Kelling in an influential 1982 article in *Atlantic Monthly* and popularized by William Bratton as Police Commissioner of New York. This theory argues that one broken window leads to more, and encourages a downward spiral of decay and crime. The hard line approach adopted in New York enjoyed a large measure of success in removing threatening squeegees from the street.

Squeegee kids emerged in significant numbers worthy of public notice in the summer of 1996. Their arrival can best be understood in the context of the growing homeless crisis which has continued to grow exponentially in Canada throughout the 1990s (Fleming, 1993; Layton, 2001). By 1993, large numbers of persons, men, women, children and families were homeless in Canada. Toronto, as Canada's largest urban centre is also

Canada's homeless capital. The homeless "crisis" has been further exacerbated by both federal and provincial government policies which have had a serious impact on the production of homelessness. In Ontario, provincial government cuts to welfare, the removal of rent controls, the gentrification of neighbourhoods, and restrictions on the redevelopment of rental units as sole living units have all added to the homeless problem. At the federal level, a lack of investment in the provision of affordable low income housing has proven to be a substantial factor in the disappearance of appropriate living units. In the fall of 1998, the City of Toronto Council voted to have homelessness declared a national disaster as cold weather descended on the city. City shelters reported having no further accomodation despite an ever-growing number of persons requesting shelter. Toronto residents have grown accustomed to homeless persons in all areas of the city as the sheer number of homeless have grown to the extent that the downtown core can no longer contain them. In 2001 proposals for homeless shelters have arisen in the city's east end as downtown area councillors complain about other areas not sharing the burden of homelessness.

In 1993 Fleming argued that homelessness had already reached crisis proportions and that given the influence of global economics upon the Canadian economy the crisis would continue to deepen government and public pacifity concerning the plight of the homeless and a lack of clear policies which attacked the root causes of homelessness lead to rapid growth in the number of homeless Canadians. During the 1990s the population diversified to include large numbers of young people with the average age of the homeless reaching 29 by 1993. Visible street homeless persons have become an unchanging feature of the urban interstices including teenaged beggars, panhandlers and squeegees. Within the group of women and men under the age of 30 there are limited opportunities to earn income independently rather than rely solely on welfare. In many cases the income earned at other activities provides a supplement to inadequate and declining welfare assistance.

Amongst homeless street youth, "employment" opportunities are often comprised of illegal and quasi-legal behaviours. These include prostitution, scalping event tickets, sales of non-medicinal and medicinal drugs, theft (Fleming, 1993) as well as break and entry. Given low levels of educational achievement and life skills deficits, full-time gainful employment capable of sustaining accommodation, food and other basic needs is a remote possibility. Research has demonstrated that many of the homeless are actually employed on a part-time or full-time basis but at wages insufficient to cover their basic needs (Fleming, 1993). For many street youth, the entrance to street life is motivated by the necessity to escape a combination of sexual, physical and/or psychological abuses in the parental home. For these youth, the street represents an escape from the control of adults and the routines of everyday life. Seeking a greater degree of personal freedom these young street dwellers literally "drop out" of society preferring the dangers and troubles of the street to the strictures and rules of society. Thus, attempts to secure full-time employment for youths who have recently come to the street are not common, since employment represents acquiescence to the social norms that they have left behind and a surrender of the "freedoms" they have found on the street.

Squeegeeing emerged as a response by street kids to a lack of non-criminal means of survival. While begging would not, at least on the surface appear to be a criminal act, it was, until recent amendments introduced by the Harris Tory government, an infraction of city by-laws regarding panhandling in public places. The charge for panhandling under this by-law was over $50 when the charges were upheld by the court. For street kids not wanting to prostitute themselves, become thieves or sell drugs, squeegeeing emerged as an outcropping of recent street grouping trends amongst homeless youth. Street life is well-documented as the site of frequent violent altercations (Fleming, 1993). The response of many street kids has been to seek a protective network of friends to increase personal safety. These loose groupings referred to as "street families" may contain from a handful to several dozen members.

Family members may provide back-up in case of attack, share money, drugs, food and alcohol. Networking also permits members a greater chance of finding temporary accommodation. "Piggybacking" that is, the practice of living in another person's apartment is common. Squatting in abandoned buildings by street families has become common in Toronto, as have "tent cities" located on abandoned industrial sites. They provide members with a greater degree of personal security and provide companionship in the hostile world of the street.

Squeegeeing emerged in Toronto during a period of positive tolerance of diversity on the street during the mayoralty of Barbara Hall. The smaller city of Toronto was amalgamated into the Greater Toronto Area (GTA) including surrounding suburbs under the new mayor Mel Lastman. Street families quickly realized the economic potential of squeegeeing and its "fit" with street family forms. Squeegeeing could be done either as a lone activity or in conjunction with a family grouping. Family groups allowed the coverage of all four corners of major street intersections as well as both the inside and outside lines of traffic. Persons not squeegeeing could provide support running for cigarettes, food, or drugs without individuals having to take a break from squeegeeing and risk forfeiting a "prime location" to others. Those who were not actively squeegeeing could also act as lookouts for the police, and provide backup against attacks by other street people and irate business owners.

Squeegeeing also appealed to young people since it required little in start-up expenses beyond a pail, some soap, a rag and a squeegee. Second, squeegee kids could retain their own sense of fashion style and personal appearance which would make them unemployable in all but a few businesses. The typical clothing style and personal appearance of squeegees at this time included multiple body and facial piercings, multiple tatoos, brightly dyed hair cut in unusual styles (most notably the extended mohawk), Doc Maarten hightop boots, ripped jeans and t shirts. Third, squeegeeing can best be done in groups as indicated above since coverage of every available lane can result in significantly greater earnings during the period of car window washing. Squeegeeing was largely confined to major intersections scattered throughout the downtown area where large volumes of rush hour traffic moves slowly through the intersections twice per day. Motorists who must stop due not only to light changes but also due to sheer traffic volume make conditions safer for squeegee kids, and allow for more profit in a shorter period of time. Less lucrative intersections are typically worked by individuals while large volume intersections are controlled by groups. In the latter category one could include the Spadina-Bloor, Bathurst-Bloor intersections, York, Bay and Yonge-Lakeshore crossroads. Church-Wellesley and Dundas-Yonge are secondary positions with a lower traffic volume or problems of frequent police intervention.

Squeegeeing can be viewed as offering legitimate employment opportunities to street youth. At a base level squeegeeing is a service offered to a potential customer who may accept or decline the offer. Motorists are free to determine what amount of money, if any, to give to the squeegee once they have agreed to have their automobile windshield cleaned. A payment of one dollar is the generally accepted renumeration. Customers are approached by the street person who holds the squeegee brush up to the side of their head while engaging the motorist's attention. The motorist either signals agreement to the squeegee's offer by nodding their head or speaking through the window. Refusal is similarly indicated by a nod of the head or a verbal response. If the motorist refuses service, the squeegee kid simply approaches the next car. The intent of the squeegee is to make as much money as possible in the shortest amount of time.

While squeegee kids do not report income for the purposes of taxation, it can be argued that they are engaging in constructive work rather than relying on welfare for their survival. While it is accurate to say that some squeegees "double dip" receiving welfare as well as this form of income there are other positive aspects to this practice. It is without doubt a far more positive economic activity than the commission of crimes of survival. As hardworking and industrious entrepreneurs, it might be expected that law enforcement and political forces would adopt a favourable response to squeegee kids. This was not, however, to be the response adopted by either group. Rather the response, as we shall discover, was to vilify the squeegee kids, engage in police campaigns and criminalize the activities of squeegees as well as homeless panhandlers.

The Squeegee Wars

The election of Mel Lastman to the position of mayor of the new "megacity" signalled a dramatic change in municipal political and law enforcement response to squeegee kids. Given previous academic inquiry into the clashes between deviant youth and social control agencies, an escalation of attempts to both curtail and outlaw squeegeeing could have been predicted (Cohen, 1972). The police were the first to publicly voice their displeasure with the lack of "effective" law which would permit them to deal effectively with squeegee kids. The police presented a reasoned case that they were hamstrung in their attempts to control this form of public behaviour since there were no existing criminal code provisions which outlawed the activity. The police were forced to fall back upon the provincial *Highway Traffic Act* in alleging that squeegees impeded the flow of traffic at intersections. However, simple observations of squeegee kids in action do not support the police contention since squeegees time their washing of car windows so as to avoid impeding traffic and to remove themselves from potential harm on the road.

The police calls to make squeegeeing a criminal act were based upon unreleased citizen complaints concerning the actions of squeegee kids. It was alleged that squeegee kids had perpetrated damage to motorists' cars and that some motorists had been threatened by the squeegee's appearance, words or actions. There is some merit in this argument. There is little doubt that many motorists find squeegee kids to be a nuisance. It is also reasonable to assume that they have little tolerance for being asked to even respond to a request by a strangely clad individual to wash their windshield. This is consistent with the generally held attitudes of intolerance that Canadians exhibit towards public displays of deviance, political protest, and interference in their passage either on foot or in cars through city streets and roads.

Squeegee kids' attempts to engage in their economic pursuit are often met with a barrage of derogatory language. Some motorists take the view that their personal space is being invaded when a squeegee kid approaches their car. They do not appreciate being interrupted on their cell phone, in conversation or when listening to the radio. They also feel a sense of vulnerability since their car cannot proceed while squeegees on the other hand are free to move around their car. Given recent epidemic volumes of so-called "road rage" it is evident that a significant percentage of motorists are not only under stress when commuting but view minor social conflicts as opportunities to vent their frustrations on others. Squeegees as politically powerless and "other" appearing individuals represent an easy target for frustrations associated with driving. It is also reasonable to assume that while squeegees are not, in fact impeding cars, anxious motorists may nonetheless view them as doing so since even anticipated delays which do not occur can increase stress levels. Squeegees are a much more visible and vulnerable target for complaint than a passing driver in another car. Motorists may also pay for the service when they would rather not, but afterward be resentful of yet another "urban toll". Single female drivers alone in their car have reported feeling intimidated by squeegees since there is literally no escape from them until a traffic light changes and there is a resumption of passage. One cannot discount a certain felt level of harassment particularly if squeegees represent for women some form of symbolic assailant.

While Alan Borovoy, the chief counsel for The Canadian Civil Liberties Association has defended the right of the squeegees to carry on their pursuits and had pointed to a lack of criminal behaviour in their activities, politicians took a decidedly different view. Mayor Lastman publicly referred to squeegees as "thugs" and "squeegee people" rather than "kids". The premier also adopted a dim view of their activities. Lastman refused to speak with a delegation of squeegee kids and instead concocted a plan to license squeegee kids to shine shoes. The plan flopped almost overnite as it became apparent that the majority of squeegee kids were not about to radically alter their appearance to fit in with the "straight" world and that there were already individuals making a living doing this in the downtown core who were well established in the business. A male-female couple, for example, carried on an informal street shoeshine business for many years on Yonge Street just south of College.

Throughout the summer of 1998 the squeegee kids were subjected to growing police harassment. The mayor vowed to remove all squeegee people from the street. This represented a declaration of war not only on squeegees but on any street person engaged in "aggressive panhandling".

Making Squeegee Kids into "Thugs"

The transformative process of turning automobile window washers into thugs armed with squeegees on poles must be understood in a framework which recognizes the symbolic as well as the hidden functions of deviance crusades. Previously, (Fleming, 1999; Fleming and Visano, 1983) it has been argued that the marginalization and attempted criminalization of target groups provides authorities with an opportunity to create what Gramsci termed "a web of ideas" that reinforce encroachments on specific civil liberties. In pursuing a course of action against homeless street youth, authorities acted in a manner consistent with previous efforts to reinforce hegemony and promote the repression of personal freedoms. Undoubtedly authorities recognized that marginalized persons should be unlikely to garner support for their position from a large segment of the population. As previously discussed, the personal style of squeegee kids immediately separates others from identifying with them. North Americans generally demonstrate little interest in homeless persons either not seeing them (so-called "invisibility" more correctly termed "selective invisibility") or viewing them as shiftless, lazy and flaunting social rules. Working persons or those enjoying leisure activities who have the benefit of a regular income often view the homeless as not wanting to work and contribute to society but rather choosing to live a parasitic existence. While more widespread understanding of homelessness has entered public consciousness, there is a great difference between sympathy expressed towards the plight of the homeless in conversation and the fears which arise when many are confronted by ever growing numbers of homeless on the street. Despite widely held fears and misconceptions which characterize the homeless generally as drug/alcohol dependent, suffering from mental disorder, potentially violent or abusive, most individuals experience the homeless merely as a regular nuisance or object of sporadic pity. While many Toronto motorists and commuters hold negative views of squeegee kids in particular, a greater number have little or no experience of this group other than that gained through second hand media accounts of squeegee activities, police warnings about the aggressive and violent nature of these individuals and political denouncements.

In building a moral panic, news sources tend to present a marginalized group in stereotypical fashion. News agencies build upon viewers' recipe knowledge of established deviant types, whether based upon reality or expedient invention. In this schema, squeegee kids translate as "squeegee swinging thugs" whose appearance and personal style are closely associated in the public mind with punk and skinhead culture. This presentation is not random, it is meant to elicit reader interest by playing to consumer fears concerning crime. There is clear evidence that persons' fears of crime tend to far exceed the reality of crime, even when crime is declining. News reporters in the construction of contemporary moral panics have recognized that panics may be drawn out over considerable periods of time and revisited as sources of news-entertainment. Much like a modern soap opera there is a sense of a continuing saga, a "good versus evil" morality play in which police are seen to be ridding the streets of unacceptable, dangerous, aggressive and "filthy" thugs. But such stories also present a very fragmented and one-sided view of the reality of street life. Squeegee kids have little or no access to the media to present their viewpoints in comparison to police sources upon whom crime reporters rely to construct their stories on a daily basis. However sophisticated readers are concerning the reality of deviance in their community, there are significant populations who relish the playing out of a law and order campaign in the media.

However, since the early 1980s attempts to mount moral panics may be characterized as having failed in their purpose because of a section of the public which is unwilling to accept "official" explanations of deviance. Similarly these individuals and groups have rejected the enforcement of rules or laws which are considered Draconian in nature (Flemingand Visano, 1983). In the next section of this chapter we examine the factors which resulted in the failure on a number of important levels of the war against squeegees in Toronto.

The Failure of a Moral Panic

The management of a moral crusade is essential to its success in achieving the ends of the "moral authorities" who either guide or feed into the campaign. It is important to note that crusades of this sort are rarely planned nor conspiratorial in nature. While come exceptions do exist (the 1981 Toronto bath house raids for example) most moral panics are initiated by the media and fed by politicians and law enforcement when there appears to be an initial positive response by the community to "action" being taken. Many readers on the subject of deviance are fascinated by the lifestyle of the street person while at the same time somewhat repulsed by their lack of integration into what they view as civil society. The process of the initiation and building of a moral panic in contemporary society is a complex and largely unpredictable series of events. Why do some groups become the subject of intense scrutiny and harassment while others are largely ignored?

Entering the millennium, Toronto is a diverse society with a growing tolerance of behaviours which were previously considered deviant. The influence of the internet which has made both tolerable and intolerable deviant behaviours available to Canadians has introduced them to a multitude of ways of living and behaving differently. The right to be different in our society has been reinforced by the Charter guarantees as well as legal challenges in the courts. Individuals have also banded together to form advocacy groups recognizing the political power which flows from voting and economic power. The campaign to eliminate squeegee kids through an artificial process of criminalization and the use of excessive authority failed on several levels which we will now attempt to outline.

First, the essential behaviour which squeegee kids engage in is not criminal. It may reasonably be argued that the act of squeegeeing is a freedom protected under the Charter. Specifically, squeegeeing can be viewed as a form of freedom of expression. Commercial activity in public places has been found by the Supreme Court to be an activity that is constitutionally protected. The provincial government of Ontario introduced the *Safe Streets Act* in 2000 as a measure designed to remove squeegees and "aggressive panhandlers" from the street. What constitutes "aggressive panhandling" is the subject of considerable debate. The overwhelming majority of beggars or panhandlers act in a civil manner and politely ask for money from those passing them by on the street. They have learned that a humble demeanour is a much more effective way to solicit change than aggressive or even assertive entreaties. However we can also understand that for many persons the homeless are frightening because they occupy the role of stranger. Public views of the homeless are also informed by misinformation and myths concerning the relative danger that the homeless pose. Certainly being asked for money in a bank lobby when one has just withdrawn money from an instant teller machine can be irritating and frightening depending upon the location of the machine, the time of day, whether there are other customers in the enclosed area, the appearance of the homeless person, and their demeanour. However, enacting laws which are based upon a few significant exceptions is contrary to the spirit of our law to respect the person regardless of their socio-economic circumstances. In January 2001, Ontario courts heard an appeal of the legality of the *Safe Streets Acts* and its provisions arguing the Charter protects the rights of individuals to ask for charity in a public place or engage in economic activity. If sufficient provision for the homeless is not set aside by society, then to criminalize and jail individuals for attempting to merely survive by asking for charity places them in a Catch-22 situation which is intolerable in a democratic society.

Second, it is apparent to us that squeegee activity does not conform to negative beliefs concerning the homeless which have been propagated in the media. Rather than being pushed into obscurity as invisible homeless who for generations have faded into the urban landscape, squeegee kids decided to flaunt their difference in a public forum. There own appreciation of the manner in which homeless persons are ignored, verbally and physically assaulted because of their condition, and relegated to parks, doorways, and under blankets hiding from the light of day has caused them to seek to break the cycle of society's disregard for the plight of the homeless. Much of the negative imagery associated with squeegees arises, we would argue, not from motorists, experience but rather from the complaints of business owners whose stores, restaurants or other businesses are directly adjacent to the corners where squeegees work. The extremely negative views held by many business owners concerning the homeless and squeegees has been well documented in both Canada and the United States (Fleming, 1993). Squeegees are viewed as blocking access to establishments, frightening potential customers (particularly female customers) and as creating a public nuisance through their activities. Such views, while held by business owners and employees who must watch squeegees outside their doors, are difficult to substantiate and more research is certainly needed on this phenomenon. Squeegees rarely lounge on the street for more than a few seconds between cars, since they are engaged in trying to earn money. Even if they were not, they have a right as Canadian citizens to stand in a public place unharassed even if we do not appreciate them being there. Whether it is public drunkenness or vagrancy, throughout the history of capitalist society there has been a demonstrated intolerance of public loitering and public displays of personal freedoms which many believe they should not be subjected to. Consider the Gay Pride Day parade in this context. Should gay persons not parade in public and exercise their rights to freedom of expression and enjoy the solidarity of others? Similarly, should squeegees just disappear and reappear as presentable shoe shine kids or should they exert their rights to security of the person and freedom of expression? Would you fight to retain your right to earn an income even if others were extremely upset with the manner in which you did so, and with your personal appearance? The answer is undoubtedly, both legally and morally, a resounding yes!

Finally, there is an increasing emphasis in contemporary legal practice toward dispute resolution through discussion and mediation. The refusal of the Mayor and other politicians to even listen to squeegee kids was dismissive and unreasonable in our view. Yielding to other political voices, the City of Toronto council voted in 2000 to provide $250,000 to initiate educational training efforts for squeegees to help them move off the street and into more gainful long term employment. While is too early to come to any conclusions about the results of this effort, it is a step in the right direction. Having charged the squeegees with numerous infractions under the *Safe Streets Act* and municipal by-laws, as well as engaging in "blitz" campaigns in the downtown area, squeegees were largely removed from city streets by the end of summer 2000.

However, having prevented them from working, authorities forced squeegees back onto welfare rolls, a position which squeegee spokespersons had argued against in conversations with the media and community groups.

Conclusions

In our new lean economy squeegee kids represent another disenfranchised group with few marketable skills and scant opportunities for meaningful employment over their life course. Unlike the children of the well-to-do they cannot take a year off school and travel the world. The only world they can reasonably travel to is that of the street, with its attractions and dangers viewed in the context of the realization of personal freedoms. Like the hippies before them they do not want to "settle down" and begin a life of expected employment drudgery, that, for many will come soon enough. But unlike the young people of the hippie era they are not rejecting opportunities in a thriving economy but rather reacting to a lack of employment in a world where those who have significant educational deficits are often left behind.

The squeegees of the summers of the late 1990s have now largely disappeared, some into the adult homeless shelters and street life, others escaping the street and beginning new lives. However, the partial victory of authorities is likely to be shortlived as more and more young homeless people, lacking opportunities look to the street for excitement, freedom and sustenance. One cardinal rule of crusades against deviance seems to have escaped officials; when you publicize deviant lifestyles you also attract many new recruits to it (Fleming and Visano, 1983).

References

Cohen, Stanley
1972 Mods and Rockers. London: Basil Blackwell.

Fleming, Thomas and L. Visano
1983 Deviant Designations: Crime, Law and Deviance in Canada. Toronto: Butterworths.

Fleming, Thomas
1985 The New Criminologies in Canada: Crime, State and Control. Toronto: Oxford University Press.

Fleming, Thomas
1993 Down and Out in Canada: Homeless Canadians. Toronto: Canadian Scholars Press.

Fleming, Thomas
1997 Post Critical Criminology. Toronto: Prentice-Hall.

Layton, Jack
2001 Homelessness:The Making and Unmaking of a Crisis. Toronto: Penguin.

PART THREE

Violence, Drug Use, and Injustice

CHAPTER ELEVEN

Is the "quality" of youth violence becoming more serious? [1]

Anthony N. Doob
and ***Jane B. Sprott***
Centre of Criminology
University of Toronto
Toronto, Ontario

IN THE PAST FEW YEARS, THERE HAVE BEEN A NUMBER OF PUBLIC statements about the change in the "quality" of youth violence. The argument is made that, although rates of violence in Canadian society may not have changed, the nature or quality of violent acts committed by young people has somehow become more serious. There have also been claims, of late, that female youth crime in particular is getting "more serious". For example, in describing a recent assault, an article on the front page of *The Globe and Mail* reported that: "[this assault] is yet another example of what law-enforcement officials and experts say is an alarming wave of violent crimes by girls across Canada" (Vincent 1998). In this article, these "experts" claim that there is "no doubt" that the number of violent crimes committed by females is increasing and that the nature of it appears to be worse. One police officer is quoted as saying, "I have seen assaults and robberies over the years, but I've never seen a torturing incident like this before" (Vincent 1998: A5). Similar types of statements have been made about youth crime generally.

The assertion that youth violence has become more violent is difficult to assess. We have no independent assessment of the seriousness or the quality of violent acts coming to the

Canadian Journal of Criminology/Revue canadienne de criminologie, April/avril 1998, pp. 185–194.

attention of the police over time. There are, however, some data that might be examined. Looking at crime generally, we know that homicide rates in Canada have been more or less stable over the past twenty years (Fedorowycz 1997). The number of youths charged with homicide offences in Canada has varied enormously from year to year, but it is hard, when looking either at the raw data (Doob, Marinos, and Varma 1995), or at the rates (Fedorowycz 1997), to find evidence of a sustained increase in the involvement of youths as suspects in homicides. Similarly, overall reported crime rates have stabilized (Kong 1997) and the rate in Canada of bringing cases to youth court has been relatively stable (Hendrick 1997). Victimization survey data too, have suggested that between 1988 and 1993 there was no substantial change in the rate at which Canadian adults have been victimized (Gartner and Doob 1994). Finally, the Canadian Centre for Justice Statistics recently concluded that the consistency of various indicators "enhances confidence" in the conclusion that crime is not increasing (Du Wors 1997).

Inferences about crime trends from reported crime rates and from charge rates are, however, very risky. As we demonstrated in an earlier paper, the rate of taking youth to court varies dramatically from province to province (Doob and Sprott 1996) in a manner that appears to relate more to the response of adult criminal justice officials to crime than it does to the behaviour of young offenders. The number of serious violent cases coming to youth court is not random, however, and the pattern of these cases can tell us something about the "quality" of the violence. It seems reasonable to suspect that the more serious the offence, the more likely it will be to be brought to court (See, for example, Doob and Chan 1982).

The *Criminal Code* has three levels of assault graded, roughly, by the severity of the harm. Unfortunately, the middle range of assaults – assault with a weapon or causing bodily harm (S. 267) includes a rather broad range of behaviours. Nevertheless, one might expect that, if the "quality" of violence really has worsened, there should be an increase in the number of cases coming to court for the most serious levels of assault. A careful examination of youth court records in the past five years, then, may give us an indication of whether the "quality" of violence really has changed. More serious violence should result in an increased number of serious violent offences (i.e., the highest of the three levels of assault). We have examined youth court data for Canada from 1991-1992 (the first year when all provinces contributed data) to 1995-1996 (Canadian Centre for Justice Statistics 1992; 1994; 1995; 1996; 1997). In all cases we used the principal charge (the most serious charge in a case as it enters the court process – Table 3) from the *Youth Court Statistics* published annually by the Canadian Centre for Justice Statistics, Statistics Canada.

Looking at Table 1, Column 1, we see that the number of cases has, if anything, decreased over the past five years. Expressed in terms of the number of cases per 1,000 youths, the rate shows a small decrease (Table 1, Column 2).

When we turn to violence, however, we see quite a different pattern. The number of cases involving violence has gone up 16.4% in this five year period (Table 1, Column 3). Corrected for population size changes (Table 1, Column 4), we still see an increase of 7.1%. Perhaps most relevant to the "crime is getting more violent" thesis is the finding that the proportion of youth court cases with a violence offence as the principal charge is also increasing (Table 1, Column 5).

Does this suggest that youths are getting more violent? Not necessarily. In recent years some policies have mandated that increased numbers of violence cases be brought to court (e.g., Ontario's policy of "zero tolerance" toward violence in schools). Such policies can be expected to result in increased numbers of minor cases of violence – these are the cases that are likely to have been ignored in the past. As expected, the increase over the years in the court processing of cases of minor assault cases is dramatic. During this five year period, the number of minor assault cases has increased by 31.3% (Table 2, Column 1). One can see, by comparing Table 2 Column 1 and Table 1 Column 3, that minor assaults constitute a

Table 1
Changes in the distribution of youth court cases (all cases and violence cases – Canada 1991-1996)

	Column 1 Number of cases to court	Column 2 Rate of cases per 100,000 YO age youth	Column 3 Number of cases with principal charge of violence	Column 4 Rate violence cases per 100,000 YO age youth	Column 5 % cases with principal charge of violence
1991-1992	116,397	5309	19,824	904	17.0%
1992-1993	115,187	4983	21,653	937	18.8%
1993-1994	115,949	4972	23,374	1002	20.2%
1994-1995	109,743	4650	23,010	975	21.0%
1995-6	111,027	4656	23,084	968	20.8%
Change	-5,370	-653	+3,260	+64	+3.8%
from 1991-2	-4.6%	-12.3%	+16.4%	+7.1%	
to 1995-6					

substantial portion of the violence cases coming to court in Canada.

Looking at the next level of assault (assault with a weapon or causing bodily harm S. 267), we see a smaller (7.7%) increase in the number of cases coming to court between 1991-2 and 1995-6 (Table 2, Column 2). Finally, there is an even smaller increase (1.3%) in the number of level 3 assault cases between 1991-2 and 1995-6 (Table 2, Column 3). Once these numbers are corrected for population size (rates per 100,000 young offender age youths), we see that the only increase (20.7%) is in minor assaults (Table 2, Column 4). In the second and third levels of assault, where we would expect to find an increase if violence were really getting "worse", we see a slight decrease, or more conservatively, no substantial change over the years (Table 2, Columns 5 and 6). If young people today really were violent and brutal in a way that was unheard of a few years ago, one would expect the increase to be larger in

Table 2
Changes in the distribution of youth court cases (three levels of assault — Canada 1991-1996)

	Column 1 Number of minor assault cases (level 1)	Column 2 Number of cases of assault with a weapon or causing bodily harm (level 2)	Column 3 Number aggravated assault cases (level 3)	Column 4 Cases of minor assault per 100,000 YO age youths (level 1)	Column 5 Cases of assault with a weapon or causing bodily harm per 100,000 YO age youths (level 2)	Column 6 Cases of aggravated assaults per 100,000 YO age youths (level 3)
1991-1992	8,594	3,431	308	392	156	14.0
1992-1993	9,717	3,685	311	420	159	13.5
1993-1994	10,854	3,836	309	465	165	13.3
1994-1995	10,906	3,745	317	462	159	13.4
1995-1996	11,280	3,695	312	473	155	13.1
Change	+2,686	+264	+4	+81	-1.0	-0.9
from 1991-2	+31.3%	+7.7%	+1.3%	+20.7%	-0.64%	-6.4%
to 1995-6						

the "high end" assaults — in particular, aggravated assault. The data provide no support for such a supposition.

Female Youth Crime. Concerns have been expressed not only about youth crime generally, but also, as the example quoted earlier in this paper shows, about the quality of violence committed by girls. Looking at only female violent youth crime, we see much the same trend as we saw for youths on the whole. Overall there is an increase in violence cases and, in particular, a very large increase in the number of minor assault cases (level 1) going to youth court. There is a proportionately smaller increase in the number of cases of assault with a weapon or causing bodily harm (level 2) cases going to court. And there is a slight decrease in the number of level three assault charges (Table 3, Columns 1, 2, 3 and 4).

Turning these numbers into rates per 100,000 young offender age girls, we see a similar pattern with the size of the increase being largest for the least serious forms of violence (Table 3, Columns 4 to 6).

The main difference between the data for girls and the data for all youths is that there is, for girls, an increase in the number and rate of the middle level assaults (Table 3, Columns 3 and 7). It would, however, be risky to assume that increase to be indicative of any real change in behaviour, since, as we have already noted, the second level of assault is an extremely broad category. For example, a minor injury, but something more than "transient or trifling in nature," can be an assault causing bodily harm and virtually anything can be a "weapon." One would, we believe, have more confidence that this increase reflected a change in girls' behaviour if it were to have shown up in the "most serious" category of assaults. When one does look at aggravated assaults, however, (Table 3, Columns 4 and 8) it is clear that the rate of charging girls has remained relatively low and stable since 1991-2.

Finally, on a slightly different, but related topic, there is evidence that the more serious the violent crime, the less likely it is that a girl will be accused of doing it. Table 4 presents data from the most recent year for which statistics are available

Table 3
Changes in the distribution of youth court cases (Girls only) (three levels of assault – Canada 1991-1996)

	Column 1 Number of cases with principal charge of violence	Column 2 Number of cases of minor assault (level 1)	Column 3 Number of cases of assault with a weapon or causing bodily harm (level 2)	Column 4 Number of cases of aggravated assault (level 3)	Column 5 Cases involving violence per 100,000 YO age girls	Column 6 Cases of minor assault per 100,000 YO age girls (level 1)	Column 7 Cases of assault with a weapon or causing bodily harm per 100,000 YO age girls (level 2)	Column 8 Cases of aggravated assault per 100,000 YO age girls (level 3)
1991-1992	3,547	2,354	532	44	332	220	49.8	4.12
1992-1993	3,947	2,774	573	41	350	246	50.9	3.64
1993-1994	4,688	3,277	706	48	412	288	62.1	4.22
1994-1995	4,484	3,127	659	43	390	272	57.3	3.74
1995-1996	4,684	3,272	658	35	403	281	56.6	3.01
Change	+1,137	+918	+126	-9	+71	+61	+6.8	-1.11
from 1991-2 to 1995-6	+32.1%	+39.0%	+23.7%	-20.5%	+21.4%	+27.7%	+13.7%	-26.9%

Table 4
Proportion of cases with girls as the accused as a function of the severity of the violence charged (Canada: 1995-1996)

Offence (principal charge)	Total cases	Cases with girl as the accused	Proportion of cases with girl as the accused
Murder, manslaughter	44	2	4.5%
Attempted murder	64	4	6.3%
Aggravated assault	312	35	11.2%
Assault w. weapon or causing bodily harm	3695	658	17.8%
Minor assault	11,280	3272	29.0%

(1995-6). Only 4.5% of the youths charged with a homicide offence are girls. At the other extreme – the lowest level of assault – 29% of the youths charged are girls. Thus, girls – who constitute 49% of young offender age youth – are underrepresented at all levels of assault, but particularly at the most serious levels.

The data presented in this paper are all published data, easily available to any interested person. Thus, this debate about the supposed change in the "quality" of violence did not need to happen. We have no doubt that in some province, for some set of offences, increases could be found. Small numbers are notoriously variable, especially when turned into percentage increases or decreases. The most obvious inference across Canada as a whole, however, is that there have been no changes in the rate of the most serious types of violent crime.

What is left of the hypothesis that the nature of youth violence is getting worse? The answer is simple: such a hypothesis is only a slight variant of the hypothesis that a few decades ago (where "few" depends largely on the age of the speaker) youths were better behaved. As one commentator put it, "The great increase in juvenile crime is certainly one of the most horrible features of our time" (Hulton 1939: 38). The fact that this was said almost 60 years ago should give us pause when we modify it only slightly to read, "The great increase in wantonly violent juvenile crime is certainly one of the most horrible features of our time." Youth crime is serious enough in Canadian society that we do not have to manufacture false trends.

Notes

1. The preparation of this paper was supported by a grant from the Social Sciences and Humanities Research Council of Canada to A.N. Doob.

References

Canadian Centre for Justice Statistics
1992 Youth Court Statistics 1991-1992. Ottawa: Statistics Canada.

Canadian Centre for Justice Statistics
1994 Youth Court Statistics 1992-1993 (Revised). Ottawa: Statistics Canada.

Canadian Centre for Justice Statistics
1995 Youth Court Statistics 1993-1994. Ottawa: Statistics Canada.

Canadian Centre for Justice Statistics
1996 Youth Court Statistics 1994-1995. Ottawa: Statistics Canada.

Canadian Centre for Justice Statistics
1997 Youth Court Statistics 1995-1996. Ottawa: Statistics Canada.

Doob, Anthony N. and Janet B.L. Chan
1982 Factors affecting police decisions to take cases to court. Canadian Journal of Criminology 24: 25-38.

Doob, Anthony, N., Voula Marinos, and Kimberly N. Varma
1995 Youth Crime and the Youth Justice System in Canada: A Research Perspective. Toronto: Centre of Criminology.

Doob, Anthony, N. and Jane B. Sprott
1996 Interprovincial variation in the use of the youth courts. Canadian Journal of Criminology 38(4): 401-412.

Du Wors, Richard
1997 The Justice Data Factfinder. Juristat. Vol 17(13). Ottawa: Canadian Centre for Justice Statistics.

Fedorowycz, Orest
1997 Homicide in Canada – 1996. Juristat. Vol 17 (9). Ottawa: Canadian Centre for Justice Statistics.

Gartner, Rosemary and Anthony N. Doob
1994 Trends in Criminal Victimization – 1988-1993. Juristat. Vol 14(3). Canadian Centre for Justice Statistics.

Hendrick, Dianne
1997 Youth Court Statistics 1995-96. Juristat. Vol 17(10). Ottawa: Canadian Centre for Justice Statistics.

Hulton, Edward
1939 Crime and punishment. Picture Post. 28 January 1939. Page 38.

Kong, Rebecca
1997 Canadian Crime Statistics – 1996. Juristat. Vol 17(8). Ottawa: Canadian Centre for Justice Statistics.

Vincent, Isabel
1998 Teen's torture again reveals girls' brutality. The Globe and Mail. 20 January 1998. Pages A1 and A5.

CHAPTER TWELVE

Factors affecting custodial dispositions under the Young Offenders Act[1]

Peter J. Carrington
University of Waterloo
Waterloo, Ontario
and **Sharon Moyer**
Moyer & Associates
Toronto, Ontario

> There is general agreement that the YOA is somewhat more "offence" oriented than was the JDA. (Doob and Meen 1993)[2]

BELIEF IN THE OFFENCE ORIENTATION OF THE YOA APPEARS TO HAVE arisen from three sources. One is the extensive legal analysis of the statute, particularly its Declaration of Principle (s. 3), but also the parts (ss. 20 to 26) concerning dispositions (e.g., Bala 1992; Beaulieu 1989, 1991; Leschied and Jaffe 1991; Markwart 1992; Trépanier 1989). A second source is the limited research that has been done on judges' attitudes to dispositions under the YOA. On the basis of a survey in 1987 of 67 Ontario youth court judges, Hanscomb concluded that "the focus is no longer on the offender but the offence... a more tariff-like approach has become established... [with an] emphasis on punishment or accountability... [and] deterrence" (cited in Corrado and Markwart 1992: 221). According to Gabor, Greene and McCormick (cited in Corrado and Markwart 1992; 221), their interviews in 1985 with Alberta youth court judges suggested a much less definite shift in dispositional philosophy: only six of thirteen judges said "they had changed their

Canadian Journal of Criminology/Revue canadienne de criminologie, April/avril 1995, pp. 127–162.

attitudes to place more emphasis on young offenders taking responsibility for their actions". Summarizing discussions among youth court judges at a seminar in late 1988, Doob (1989: 197-8) says:

> There is, apparently, some disagreement as to how "central" the offence is in the *YOA*. Some argue that there are "hints" enough to suggest that the *YOA* philosophy is "offence" in its orientation and that dispositions should be assessed largely in terms of offence seriousness and handed down in such a way that disposition severity is proportional to the seriousness of the offence... other commentators suggest that only in contrast with the *JDA* can the *YOA* be considered to be focusing on the offence rather than the offender... [and that it] should not be confused with what has come to be termed a "just deserts" orientation or... that dispositions be proportional to the seriousness of the harm done.

A third source of this belief in the offence orientation of the YOA is the accumulating evidence of a substantial increase in the use of custody under the YOA (Corrado and Markwart 1992; Doob 1992; Doob and Beaulieu 1992; Leschied and Jaffe 1988). Several authors have suggested that this apparent increase in the use of custody may have resulted from a supposed offence orientation of the YOA (Archambault 1991: x; Bala and Kirvan 1991: 98; Corrado and Markwart 1992; Leschied and Jaffe 1991; Markwart and Corrado 1989: 10). On the other hand, Bala (1992: 59) and Doob (1992) have pointed out that the apparent increase in the use of custody is so far not clearly established, and that even if it were, it could have many causes other than the orientation of the YOA: for example, more, or more violent youth crime, changes in police practices unrelated to the YOA, or the effect of a general societal "get tough" attitude.

On the one hand, we have an apparent increase in the use of custodial dispositions; on the other hand, a statute which contains at least "hints" of offence orientation. The question is, does the latter explain the former? As Bala has suggested (1992: 59, fn. 93), what is needed to answer this question is an empirical analysis relating offence characteristics to youth court dispositions.

Sentencing orientations

What, exactly, does "offence orientation" in sentencing – particularly in sentencing to custody – entail? Implicitly, it is contrasted with sentencing that is oriented to the characteristics of the offender. "Offence oriented" sentencing is based on the *seriousness of the offence*, which is not at all simple to ascertain, but is related to the culpability of the offender in, and the degree of harm caused by, the instant offence(s) – i.e., the offence(s) for which the offender is currently being sentenced (Canadian Sentencing Commission 1987: 133). These involve

> At a minimum... consideration of harm to the victim, malevolence of intent, degree of involvement, victim precipitation, prior relationship between the offender and the victim, premeditation, and many other factors... (Blumstein 1982)

Thus, "offence oriented" sentencing does not necessarily imply a simple relationship between the "type" of offence, as defined by the *Criminal Code*, and the type or quantum (amount) of the sentence. The existence of large disparities among sentences for similar offences, however, would suggest at least that sentencing is not entirely offence oriented (Corrado and Markwart 1992: 223).

Offender orientation in sentencing refers to the consideration of the characteristics of the offender. In (adult) criminal court, this is done with a view to evaluating dangerousness, likelihood of re-offending, and likelihood of rehabilitation. For example, an offender with a lengthy prior record of violent criminal activity might be judged as dangerous and incorrigible, and therefore given a punitive or incapacitative sentence, whereas a first offender might be given the benefit of the doubt with a noninterventionist or rehabilitative sentence (Nadin-Davis 1982: 67-83; Ruby 1994: 201-239). Although prior record is by far the most important offender characteristic in sentencing, many others may be taken into consideration (see Nadin-Davis 1982 and Ruby 1994 for lists and discussion of these).

Obviously, any systematic relationship between offender characteristics and sentences is *prima facie* evidence that sentencing is not entirely offence-oriented. Such a relationship may, in fact, be due to offence-oriented sentencing. For example, much research on sentencing in criminal court has found that female offenders tend to be sentenced more leniently than male offenders; but some further analysis has found that this is explained by the tendency of females to commit less serious offences than males, although this is by no means universally agreed (see Nagel and Hagan 1982 and Chesney-Lind 1987 for reviews of this issue).

Offence-oriented sentencing is consistent with the crime control and justice models of justice systems, but not with the welfare model.(3) Offender-oriented sentencing is consistent with the crime control and welfare models, but not with the justice model.

In the crime control model, the function of criminal justice is protection of society (Packer 1968). Sentencing is supposed to contribute through deterrence of crime and incapacitation(4) of criminals. Both objectives of sentencing are served by consideration of offence and offender characteristics. Under this model, sentences are proportional to the seriousness of offences in order that more serious crime be deterred more vigorously than less serious crime, and in order that the perpetrators of more serious crime be incapacitated more than the perpetrators of less serious crime. Sentences are also proportional to offender characteristics that are indicators of the likelihood of reoffending ("incorrigibility") and/or of likely seriousness of re-offending ("dangerousness") in order to incapacitate most efficiently. The main indicator available to the court is the criminal history of the offender.

The justice, or due process model, emphasizes protection of the rights of the individual (Packer 1968). Protection of the offender from arbitrary punishment implies sentencing according the "just deserts" philosophy, in which the severity of the sentence is proportionate to the seriousness of the offence, and to nothing else (Canadian Sentencing Commission 1987: 133; Reid-MacNevin 1991: 25). Proponents of desert-based sentencing generally agree that the seriousness of the offence is a function of the wrongfulness, or harmfulness, of the offence, and of the culpability of the offender. Although the concept of culpability has been thoroughly developed in the substantive criminal law, there is still disagreement among desert theorists on the meaning and measurement of the degree of wrongfulness of offences (von Hirsch 1985: chap. 6). This disagreement has serious implications for any empirical attempt to assess the proportionality of sentencing.

Desert theorists also disagree about what constitutes "the offence" whose seriousness is being gauged (von Hirsch 1993: 60n).[5] Some (e.g., Ashworth 1992; von Hirsch 1985, 1993; Wasik 1987) argue that the existence or length of a criminal history preceding the instant offence affects its seriousness, although the criminal history is less important in determining seriousness than the nature of the instant offence. In particular, there is a "first offender discount" on seriousness (von Hirsch 1985: 87), by which first offences are, *ceteris paribus*, less serious than second and later offences; and "progressive loss of mitigation" (Ashworth 1992), as an accumulating criminal record provides evidence of incorrigibility. Others (e.g., Fletcher 1978; Singer 1979) argue that criminal history is irrelevant to determining the wrongfulness of the present offence, and that consideration at sentencing of the offender's prior convictions implies the incorporation of principles in addition to desert – for example, of incapacitation, deterrence, or rehabilitation. This view of the rationale for considering the absence or length of a criminal history was pithily expressed by the English Court of Appeal in 1973 (cited in Ruby 1994: 202):

> The learned judge increased the sentences... because of his view, for which there was ample evidence, that these young men were enemies of society. But the Court has to bear in mind that in our system of jurisprudence there is no offence known as being an enemy of society... If [on the other hand] the evidence does establish that the accused are dangerous men, then it is no good their saying that they have no previous convictions...

In other words, the presence or absence of a criminal history speaks to the dangerousness of the offender, which is relevant to considerations of deterrence, incapacitation, or rehabilitation, not to desert.

In our opinion, the presence or absence of a criminal history is an attribute of the offender, not of the offence, and is irrelevant to gauging the seriousness of the offence. Von Hirsch appears to agree with this distinction, as he rejects assessment of the desert of the "criminal career" (1985: 81). He then proceeds to try to justify the "first-offender discount" on grounds of "tolerance". We disapprove less of first offenders, he says, because:

> ...some sympathy is due human beings for their fallibility... we know that even the self-control of those who ordinarily refrain from misconduct may fail... [the first offender's misconduct is] a misstep... atypical of his past conduct (1985: 82-85).

This argument illustrates the danger in shifting attention from the desert of the offence to the desert of the offender. To accept "typicality" as a criterion of desert is to accept that the seriousness of offences is related to the "type" of person committing them – those that are "typically" law-abiding ("who ordinarily refrain from misconduct") and those that are typically criminal. This distinction – so similar to that between "respectable" people and "the criminal element" – seems out of keeping with the tenor of desert-based sentencing.

In the welfare model, the offender is seen as being anti-social or "in trouble" as a result of environmental influences such as the family and peers. The court process is seen as an attempt to diagnose the offender's "needs", and the sentence is a prescription for rehabilitating the offender. "Comprehensive investigation of the whole youth", particularly as reported in the "social history" of the pre-disposition report, forms the basis for an individualized disposition (Reid and Reitsma-Street 1993). Thus, the disposition is related to the unique situation of the offender, including but not particularly emphasizing the prior record, and the nature of the current offence itself is almost irrelevant. Indeed, in the more extreme manifestations of the welfare model, guilt or innocence as charged are irrelevant, since charging the offender is merely an opportunity to introduce him/her to the (involuntary) diagnostic/treatment facilities of the court (Beaulieu 1991: 133).

The *Young Offenders Act*, like the adult criminal justice system, incorporates elements of all three models, although there is some disagreement as to the relative importance of each. The Declaration of Principle (s. 3) refers to young persons' "responsibility for... contraventions", suggesting the justice model and offence orientation; to "protection from illegal behaviour" and "prevent[ion of] criminal behaviour", suggesting the crime control model; and to the "special needs" and "require[ment for] guidance and assistance" of young persons, suggesting the welfare model. Reid and Reitsma-Street (1993) concluded from content analysis of the Declaration of Principle that all three models have "equal prominence", and noted the lack of guidance provided to judges by the YOA in choosing among these models. Other analyses have also noted the ambivalence of the YOA regarding the priority among principles to be assigned at disposition (Bala 1992; Doob and Beaulieu 1992; Trépanier 1989).

Thus, we might reasonably expect to find that youth court dispositions are related both to offence and to offender characteristics (Archambault 1991), including offender characteristics in the broadest sense, such as those features of the offender's "environment" that are typically considered in sentencing under the welfare model. The strength and consistency of the relationship between dispositions and offence characteristics would be indications of the adherence of judges at disposition to the justice or crime control models. A strong relationship between disposition and the prior record of the offender would suggest that priority is being given to incapacitation and deterrence – the crime control model. Relationships between disposition and personal or environmental characteristics of the offender, and a lack of consistency in dispositions, would suggest the operation of the welfare model.

Previous research on the determinants of youth court dispositions

Two empirical studies have been reported by Doob and colleagues, which have attempted to determine the sentencing orientations of youth court judges from their actual or hypothetical behaviour rather than from attitude surveys.

In the first study, performed in 1988, the researchers provided descriptions of four hypothetical youth court cases (involving two hypothetical incidents, with two accused in each) to 43 youth court judges from across Canada, and asked them to comment on the disposition they would assign, and other aspects of the cases (Doob and Beaulieu 1992). Although they did not ask judges specifically to compare offence and offender orientation, or justice, welfare, and crime control models, they did ask about the relative importance in each case of punishment, rehabilitation, and deterrence as goals of sentencing; and they asked judges to rank the importance in determining disposition of such factors as "offence seriousness", "level of involvement", "making him accountable", "protecting society", and "providing help" (Doob and Beaulieu 1992: Table 8). They found "substantial variation both in the dispositions... and in the priority of the goals that they were trying to achieve."

Re-analysis of their data on judges' rankings of the goals of sentencing (Doob and Beaulieu 1992: Table 3) suggests that judges rated deterrence as most important (46 percent), followed by rehabilitation (40 percent), punishment (15 percent), and incapacitation (0.5 percent). The low ranking give to incapacitation is particularly striking since two of the four cases arose from a hypothetical incident involving a serious violent offence: a "racially motivated" assault causing bodily harm, in which the victim "lost one tooth and had a badly cut lip requiring stitches". In ranking the importance of various case characteristics in determining disposition, judges made little distinction between offence and offender characteristics, ranking them all as important (Doob and Beaulieu 1992: Table 8).

These findings suggest that these judges' dispositions were both offence and offender oriented, and that they were operating under a combination of crime control (through deterrence) and welfare (through rehabilitation) models. Their stated lack of priority for punishment, and the substantial variation in their assigned dispositions, suggest that desert was not a major factor in their thinking. Of course, caution must be exercised in drawing conclusions from a study involving only 43 judges and four hypothetical cases, in which the judges knew that their "decisions" would have no consequences.

In the second study, Doob and Meen (1993) analyzed data from dockets for 370 cases heard during 1989 and 1990, and 427 cases heard during 1984 to 1986, in three Toronto youth courts, and compared them with a sample of cases heard under the JDA. For both periods under the YOA, they found that offence characteristics (most serious charge and number of charges at sentencing) were significant predictors of the type of disposition, and that offender characteristics (sex and age) were not; whereas, in the sample of JDA cases, this was not the case.

We agree with Doob and Meen that, for these samples, dispositions under the YOA were more offence oriented than under the JDA. It should not be concluded from their findings that dispositions under the YOA are especially offence oriented. First, the statistical relationship between offence type and type of disposition was not strong.[6] Second, since the prior record of the offender was not included in the analyses, it is possible that the reported correlations between disposition and offence characteristics were partly or entirely spurious, and were actually due to the prior record. In other words, judges might have been making the dispositional decision primarily on the basis of the prior record, but offenders with serious prior records might have been committing more serious and/or numerous current offences, thus creating an empirical correlation between disposition and offence seriousness. Third, as Doob and Meen pointed out, the sample of 370 cases from three Toronto courts might not be representative of Canadian youth courts in general.

Design of the current study

The present study uses a large, cross-sectional sample of youth court cases, and includes data on the offender's criminal history. The data, supplied by the Canadian Centre for Justice Statistics (CCJS) from the Youth Court Survey, comprise all youth court cases reaching disposition between April 1, 1990 and March 31, 1991 in eight provinces. Data were not available for Ontario or Nova Scotia. Cases heard in the Yukon and Northwest Territories were excluded because of the marked differences between juvenile crime in these two territories and the provinces. The unit of analysis was the "case", defined as a set of charges disposed of at the same hearing.[7] As defined, a case can involve multiple charges and multiple dispositions. The disposition analyzed for each case was the "most serious disposition", coded as "custodial" (including open and secure custody), versus "non-custodial".[8] The seriousness of the offence(s) in the case was indicated by the "most serious charge", using *Criminal Code* offence categories grouped into 25 categories, and also by the number of charges in the case on which there was a finding of guilt (a "conviction").[9] Other case characteristics included the offender's gender, age at commission of the offence, and, as indicators of the criminal history, the number of prior convictions under the YOA, and whether any prior disposition under the YOA was custodial.(10)

The strength of these data lies in their comprehensiveness: they include the large majority of cases disposed of in youth court in eight provinces in one year – 34,743 cases.(11) Their weakness is the skeletal nature of the data for each case: the number of guilty findings and a 25-category classification of the most serious charge in the case are only a crude representation of the rich information concerning the current offence that is available to the judge at disposition (although perhaps one should not exaggerate the "richness" of the information used in sentencing cases involving guilty pleas). The same is true of the indicators of the prior record. Therefore, a failure to find consistent relationships between case characteristics and dispositions could indicate inadequacy in our indicators as much as an actual lack of relationship; but positive findings – of consistent relationships between dispositions and current offence or prior record – can be regarded as probably conservative, that is, as likely to understate the strength of actual relationships.

The general approach to assessing the strength and consistency of the relationships between the likelihood of a custodial disposition and the characteristics of the case was to calculate the proportion of custodial dispositions received by cases classified by different offence and offender characteristics. The first set of classifications used information on the current offence (Tables 1, 2). Next, we considered indicators of prior record (Tables 3, 4). These were then combined (Table 5). Finally, indicators of the offender's personal characteristics were examined (Table 6). Where multiple case characteristics were examined simultaneously, multiple classification analysis, derived from analysis of variance, was used to assess the effects of one indicator while holding the other constant.

Analysis and results

Proportionality and the seriousness of the offence

Although there is no definitive ranking of the seriousness of types of offence, common approaches utilize a hierarchy of types of harm: either (a) offences against the person ("violent" offences), offences against property, then other offences, such as offences against the administration of justice, public order, drug and alcohol offences, all of which are generally "victimless"[(12)]; or (b) the *Criminal Code* hierarchy of indictable, "hybrid"[(13)], and summary offences.

The detailed offence typology shown in panel (a) of Table 1 groups and ranks the 25 categories of offence according to the two ranking schemes cited in the preceding paragraph. Since there is no obvious principle for ranking the offences within each group, they are ranked according to the proportion of custodial dispositions which each offence type received.

According to von Hirsch (1993: 18), the basic principle of desert-based sentencing – that the severity of the sentence should be proportionate to the seriousness of the offence – can be expressed by three sub-requirements:

- *parity*: offences of similar seriousness should receive sentences of similar severity. This does not necessarily mean that all offences in a given *Criminal Code* category should receive the same disposition, as there are significant variations of seriousness within most *Criminal Code* categories;[(14)]
- *rank-ordering*: if offence A is more serious than offence B, then the sentence for A should be more severe than the sentence for B;
- *spacing*: if offence A is much more serious than offence B, and B only slightly more serious than offence C, then the "space" between the sentences for A and B should be greater than that between the sentences for B and C; in practice, according to von Hirsch, "spacing" may be difficult to assess because of the

imprecision of our measurements of offence seriousness and sentence severity.

If we assume (unrealistically – see below) that in Table 1, panel (a), each of the 25 offence categories constituted cases of the same level of seriousness, then the degree of *parity* in these dispositions is indicated by the proportions of custodial dispositions. Perfect parity would be indicated if every proportion was either 0 percent or 100 percent: i.e., if each group of equally serious cases all received the same disposition. The degree of parity can be summarized by the eta statistics.[15] Eta would have its maximum value of 1.0 in the case of perfect parity. It would have its minimum value of 0.0 if the offence category made no difference to the likelihood of a custodial disposition; that is, if the cases in all offence categories received custodial dispositions in the same proportions (which would necessarily also be the overall proportion of custodial dispositions – 22 percent).

In fact, eta is 0.38, reflecting the fact that the degree of parity – if offence seriousness is correctly identified by this offence typology – is rather low. Few offence categories have a characteristic disposition; many have a proportion of custodial dispositions not far from the overall average (22 percent), which is the "worst case" from the point of view of parity.

Another way of assessing parity is to ask how many of the 34,743 dispositional decisions can be explained entirely by the type of offence. In other words, let us hypothesize that dispositions are made according to a determinate sentencing scheme, based entirely on the seriousness of the offence, as classified here. How many of the actual dispositions can be accounted for, or correctly "predicted" after the fact, by such a reconstructed sentencing model?

The best such hypothetical sentencing model is shown by the shaded cells in Table 1, panel (a): these identify categories of offences which would, according to the model, result in a custodial disposition, because over 50 percent of them actually did receive a custodial disposition.[16] This sentencing model accounts for 27,943, or 80.4 percent, of the actual dispositional decisions. This can be compared to a hypothetical baseline model – which ignores entirely the nature of the case and simply predicts that all cases resulted in non-custodial dispositions – which would be correct 78.1 percent of the time (27,136 cases). Thus, attributing the disposition to the offence category improves explanatory power by 807 cases, or 2.3 percent of the total, over a model in which dispositions are based on knowing nothing about the case. This is something, but not much. The problem is the lack of parity – the heterogeneity of dispositions for similar offences. For many offence categories, knowing the category of offence does not distinguish the case from any other case, as far as disposition goes.

The degree to which von Hirsch's second criterion of proportionality – *rank-ordering* – is fulfilled by these dispositions can also be assessed by panel (a) of Table 1. This criterion requires that more serious offences receive more severe penalties. Since there are only two levels of severity of disposition in the present data (custodial and non-custodial dispositions), the criterion of rank-ordering requires simply that more serious offences receive dispositions which are at least as severe as those of less serious cases. For example, in panel (a) of Table 1, 68 percent of cases of break and enter received non-custodial dispositions. These dispositions were less severe than the custodial dispositions given in numerous cases with less serious offences, and therefore in violation of the criterion of rank-ordering with respect to those less serious cases. On the other hand, the custodial dispositions given in 32 percent of cases of break and enter violated rank-ordering with respect to the numerous cases involving more serious offences (e.g., robbery) which received non-custodial dispositions.[17]

Complete fulfilment of the criterion of rank-ordering would require that all cases in all offence categories above a certain level of seriousness (call it the *cut-off point*) receive custodial dispositions, and all cases in offence categories below that level

Table 1
Proportion of custodial dispositions by the seriousness of the offence

(a) Detailed offence typology

Offence type	n	Proportion
Impaired driving	830	.02
Summary/hybrid drug	600	.08
Disorderly conduct	396	.05
Other administration of justice	352	.13
Misc. summary/ hybrid victimless	1641	.15
YOA	2809	.26
Escape custody/ unlawfully at large	1100	.84
Mischief under $1000	1825	.09
Theft under $1000	7120	.09
Other summary/ hybrid property	1333	.12
Possession under $1000	1303	.16
Assault	2254	.16
Other summary/ hybrid person	571	.18
Sexual assault	436	.29
Trafficking/ importing drugs	324	.28
Other indictable victimless	411	.29
Other indictable property	388	.19
Possession over $1000	909	.28
Theft over $1000	1453	.30
Break and enter	6666	.32
Other indictable person	1289	.28
Sexual assault: aggravated or weapon	34	.41
Aggravated assault	71	.52
Robbery	604	.53
Murder, manslaughter	24	.92
Total	34743	.22
Eta		.38
Gamma		.20
Correct predictions	27943	.804

(b) Aggregated offence typology

Offence type	n	Proportion
Summary/ hybrid drug & alcohol	1430	.04
Summary/ hybrid victimless, except YOA & escape/UAL	2389	.13
YOA	2809	.26
Escape/UAL	1100	.84
Summary/ hybrid property	11581	.10
Summary/ hybrid person	3261	.18
Indictable victimless	735	.29
Indictable property	9416	.30
Other indictable person	1289	.28
Violent indictable person	733	.54
Total	34743	.22
Eta		.37
Gamma		.21
Correct predictions	27935	.804

Note: Shaded categories of cases are "predicted" to receive custodial dispositions in the best hypothetical determinate sentencing model.

receive non-custodial dispositions. The degree of fulfilment of rank-ordering can be assessed by the gamma statistic. Gamma would have its maximum value of 1.0 if there were perfect rank-ordering. It would decrease in value for each case that violated this rule of rank-ordering: i.e., each case that involved an offence below the cut-off point in seriousness but received a custodial disposition, or that was at or above the cut-off point and received a non-custodial disposition. It would reach its minimum value of 0.0 if less serious offences were just as likely as more serious offences to receive a custodial disposition; i.e., if the proportions of custodial dispositions for all offence categories were equal.(18)

It is apparent from panel (a) of Table 1 that, if the ordering of the offence categories is correct, then the dispositions in many cases violated von Hirsch's principle of rank-ordering. This is borne out by the rather low value of gamma (0.20). For example, 47 percent of the cases of robbery, 48 percent of cases of aggravated assault, and 59 percent of cases of violent sexual assault did not result in custodial dispositions, although these offence categories are more serious than all others except homicide, if seriousness is assessed by current offence type alone. These cases violated rank-ordering vis-à-vis the numerous cases involving less serious offences that resulted in more severe – i.e., custodial – dispositions.

However, the most striking violations of the principle of rank-ordering were in the offence categories of "escape from custody/unlawfully at large", and offences under the YOA (almost all being "wilful failure to comply with a community disposition", mainly breaches of probation orders). Although escape/UAL offences are classified as hybrid by the *Criminal Code*, are victimless, and cause little or no identifiable harm,(19) they received a higher proportion of custodial dispositions (84 percent) than any other category except homicide. "Offences against the YOA" are victimless, summary offences, but attracted a higher proportion of custodial dispositions (26 percent) than any other summary or hybrid offence, including offences against persons and property, with the exception of sexual assault, which received about the same proportion of custodial dispositions.

The sentencing of these cases appears to be a substantial departure from the principle of punishment proportionate to seriousness of offence, whether the seriousness of the offence is gauged by the *Criminal Code* classification (summary/hybrid/ indictable) or by harm done. A plausible explanation is that, for these offences, judges were responding to concerns other than proportionate punishment. Some breaches of probation orders may be seen as indications that the offender requires a higher level of control (incapacitation) than probation provides. Similarly, escaping from, or not returning to, an open custody facility, may be seen as indicating the need for a more secure kind of custody: i.e., increased incapacitation. It is also plausible that, as Ruby (1994: 640) suggests in the sentencing of adult escapers:

> A primary consideration... is general deterrence aimed at preserving the integrity of the custodial system.

Thus, crime control principles of incapacitation and deterrence appear to predominate over the principle of proportionate punishment in these cases.

On the other hand, it is possible that sentencing of these cases, particularly cases of escape/UAL, is influenced more by the prior record than by the current offence.[20] An escape from custody implies a prior custodial disposition,[21] which suggests at least one prior conviction for a serious offence, or numerous less serious prior convictions; thus, the escaper has already established that s/he is a serious or persistent offender. Perhaps judges in these cases were responding to this (offender-oriented) consideration of the prior record more than to the escape itself. Once again, we see this as related to crime control motives of deterrence and incapacitation, rather than to offence-oriented proportionate punishment.

In summary, it is difficult to account for the dispositions in many of these cases in terms of the seriousness of the current offence alone – which we would argue is the criterion of offence-oriented desert-based sentencing. Apparently, there were numerous departures from the principles of parity and rank-ordering,[22] as shown by the rather low values of eta and gamma. Cases involving escape from custody/unlawfully at large and breaches of probation were the most striking such departures. It was not possible to reconstruct a determinate sentencing model based solely on the current offence, as the offence categories did not unambiguously determine the disposition of the case. All of this evidence suggests that either there was considerable indeterminacy dispositional decision-making, or that it was oriented toward offender characteristics, such as the criminal history, in addition to the current offence.

Because the cases in many of the offence categories in panel (a) of Table 1 had similar proportions of custodial dispositions, it was possible to simplify the offence typology by combining categories for further analysis. The revised ten-category offence typology is shown in panel (b) of Table 1. This typology fulfils von Hirsch's criteria of parity and rank-ordering practically as well as the detailed typology, and is practically as powerful as the detailed classification in predicting custodial dispositions: 27,935, or 80.4 percent of the dispositions could be accounted for by a determinate sentencing model based on current offences classified thus. Like the 25 offence categories of the detailed typology, these ten categories were nowhere near decisive in determining disposition: only the first and last categories were close to 0 percent or 100 percent custodial dispositions. Since this typology is conceptually simpler than the detailed typology, it was used in the rest of the analysis.

The number of current charges on which there was a guilty finding

Apart from the nature of the most serious charge, the seriousness of the offence may also be indicated by the number of charges on which there were guilty findings. Table 2 shows the proportion of custodial dispositions in cases cross-classified by the offence typology and the number of guilty findings. Cases involving a single guilty finding (column 1) made up almost two-thirds of the entire sample of disposed of cases, and usually resulted in non-custodial dispositions (the overall proportion of custodial dispositions for cases involving a single guilty finding was 14 percent), unless the charge was escape/UAL (the proportion of custodial dispositions was 85 percent) or a serious indictable person charge (39 percent). Generally, the likelihood of receiving a custodial disposition increased with the number of guilty findings: the value of gamma for the simple bivariate relationship between the number of guilty findings and the likelihood of a custodial disposition was 0.50.

Shaded categories in Table 2 had a proportion of custodial dispositions greater than 50 percent. In a hypothetical determinate sentencing model based on the most serious current conviction and the number of charges resulting in guilty findings, these categories of cases would be predicted to result in custodial dispositions. Including information about the number of guilty findings in the hypothetical sentencing model increases the precision of prediction: using this cross-classification, we can identify some types of cases involving less serious indictable offences, YOA offences, and even some summary or hybrid person offences as being more likely than not to result in a custodial disposition, if there were multiple guilty findings. Since there were actually rather few such cases, the improved model increases the accuracy of *post hoc* prediction only slightly: from 80.4 percent correct, based on the most serious charge alone, to 81.1 percent correct, based on the most serious charge and the number of guilty findings.

The pattern of proportions of custodial dispositions in Table 2 suggests that in determining disposition, judges considered the most serious charge and the number of guilty findings fairly independently of each other. Within most categories of offence type, the proportion of custodial dispositions increased with increases in the number of guilty findings; and within each number of guilty findings, the proportion of custodial dispositions generally increased with the seriousness of the offence.

Table 2
Proportion of custodial dispositions by offence type and number of findings of guilt

Offence type	Number of findings of guilt					Overall row proportion	Adjusted row proportion
	1	2	3	4	5		
Summary/hybrid drug & alcohol	.02 (1177)	.05 (169)	.13 (40)	.45 (22)	.45 (22)	.04 (1430)	.09
Summary/hybrid victimless, except YOA & escape/UAL	.08 (1805)	.20 (378)	.35 (117)	.38 (50)	.62 (39)	.13 (2389)	.17
YOA	.20 (2024)	.36 (512)	.48 (145)	.55 (65)	.68 (63)	.26 (2809)	.29
Escape/UAL	.85 (915)	.80 (120)	.68 (38)	.92 (12)	.93 (15)	.84 (1100)	.89
Summary/hybrid property	.06 (8093)	.16 (1959)	.21 (733)	.29 (326)	.35 (470)	.10 (11581)	.12
Summary/hybrid person	.10 (2060)	.21 (692)	.32 (211)	.44 (112)	.56 (186)	.18 (3261)	.18
Indictable victimless	.22 (468)	.29 (135)	.47 (57)	.57 (30)	.60 (45)	.29 (735)	.29
Indictable property	.17 (4323)	.31 (1945)	.41 (1049)	.48 (665)	.54 (1434)	.30 (9416)	.26
Other indictable person	.16 (752)	.34 (249)	.38 (111)	.55 (47)	.67 (130)	.28 (1289)	.26
Violent indictable person	.39 (352)	.53 (151)	.75 (81)	.70 (56)	.82 (93)	.54 (733)	.50
Overall column proportion	.14 (21969)	.26 (6310)	.36 (2582)	.45 (1385)	.53 (2497)	.22 (34743)	
Adjusted column proportion	.15	.26	.36	.44	.51		

Notes: The number of cases is in parentheses. Shaded categories of cases are "predicted" to receive custodial dispositions in the best hypothetical determinate sentencing model.

This impression is reinforced by the multiple classification analysis reported in the "adjusted proportions" column and row. The "adjusted proportion" for each category of offence and for each number of guilty findings is calculated by statistically "controlling" or "holding constant" the other factor. This answers such questions as, what would the proportion of custodial dispositions have been for escape/UAL cases, if these cases had involved an average number of guilty findings (whereas, in fact, escape/UAL cases involved fewer than average guilty findings, and most were single-charge cases)? In this example, the adjusted proportion is 89 percent, which is a little higher than the actual proportion (84 percent); in other words, the effect of the actual preponderance of single charge cases in the escape/UAL category was to reduce what would otherwise have been a very high rate (89 percent) of custodial dispositions. In contrast, the adjusted proportion of custodial dispositions (26 percent) for indictable property offences (of which the majority were break and enters), was lower than the actual proportion (30 percent), suggesting that the multiple guilty findings which were more common in these cases were seen as aggravating factors by judges.(23)

The prior record of the offender

In Table 3, the proportion of custodial dispositions is shown for a cross-classification of cases by two indicators of the offender's criminal history: the number of findings of guilt in previous cases, and whether or not s/he had received a custodial disposition in the past. The results are striking. Over half of the cases involved first offenders, who had a very low rate of custodial dispositions (9 percent). Less than 15 percent of the cases involved young offenders with a prior custodial disposition, and 66 percent of these received custodial dispositions in the current cases. This proportion of custodial dispositions did not vary greatly with the number of prior findings of guilt: the prior custodial disposition – or the prior convicted offences which resulted in that prior custodial disposition – were apparently the paramount consideration. In the remaining cases – those not involving a first offender or an offender with a prior custodial disposition – the proportion of custodial dispositions increased with the number of prior findings of guilt, but did not reach 50 percent, even for cases with 7 or more prior findings.

Using a hypothetical determinate sentencing model based on these two indicators of criminal history alone (i.e., with no reference to the seriousness of the current offence), it is

Table 3
Proportion of custodial dispositions by number of prior findings of guilt and prior custodial disposition

Number of prior findings of guilt	Prior custodial disposition?				Row total		Adjusted Row Proportion
	No		Yes				
	n	Proportion	n	Proportion	n	Proportion	
0	18506	.09			18506	.09	.14
1	3782	.13	204	.57	3986	.16	.18
2	2251	.19	248	.54	2499	.23	.24
3	1412	.25	328	.54	1740	.30	.29
4	943	.27	322	.52	1265	.33	.29
5	703	.32	306	.62	1009	.41	.36
6	494	.35	318	.61	812	.45	.38
7+	1892	.42	3034	.72	4926	.60	.46
Overall column proportion	29983	.15	4760	.66	34743	.22	
Adjusted column proportion		.18		.48			

Note: Shaded categories of cases are "predicted" to receive custodial dispositions in the best hypothetical determinate sentencing model

possible to account for 82.4 percent (28,627) of the actual dispositional decisions. This is better than prediction based on the two indicators of the current offence. Because of the large correlation between the two indicators of prior record,[24] and the lesser predictive importance of the *number* of prior findings of guilt, it is possible to combine the two indicators into one typology, without losing predictive power (Table 4).[25]

The seriousness of the current offence

To assess the relationship between custodial *versus* non-custodial disposition and current offence and prior record together, we repeated the analysis shown in Table 2, breaking the sample down into the three categories of prior record developed above. This analysis is summarized in table 5.

Table 4
Proportion of custodial dispositions by prior record typology

First offender	Recidivist		Total	Eta	Correct predictions
	No prior custodial disposition	Prior custodial disposition			
.09 (18506)	.24 (11477)	.66 (4760)	.22 (34743)	.46	.826 (28694)

Note: Shaded categories of cases are "predicted" to receive custodial dispositions in the best hypothetical determinate sentencing model.

Although all three case characteristics played a role in determining disposition, Table 5 suggests that the prior record took precedence. The sentencing model underlying Table 5 could be expressed as:

- **first offenders receive non-custodial dispositions, except:**
  - those found guilty of escape/UAL, and
  - those found guilty of a violent indictable person offence, with guilty findings on a total of at least 3 current charges;
- **offenders with a prior custodial disposition receive a custodial disposition, except:**
  - those found guilty of summary or hybrid drug offences or impaired driving, and
  - those found guilty of summary or hybrid victimless or property offences, if there was a guilty finding on only one current charge;
- **others (i.e., recidivists with no prior custodial disposition) receive a non-custodial disposition, except:**
  - those found guilty of summary or hybrid person offences, YOA offences, or indictable victimless or property offences, if there are guilty findings on at least four current charges,

Table 5
Proportion of custodial dispositions by offence type, number of findings of guilt, and prior record typology

<table>
<tr><th>Prior record typology</th><th colspan="5">Number of findings of guilt</th><th colspan="2">Total</th></tr>
<tr><th>Current offence</th><th>1</th><th>2</th><th>3</th><th>4</th><th>5+</th><th>n</th><th>Proportion</th></tr>
<tr><td colspan="8">First offenders</td></tr>
<tr><td>All except escape/UAL & violent indictable person offence</td><td colspan="5">less than .50</td><td>17942</td><td>.08</td></tr>
<tr><td>Escape/UAL</td><td colspan="5">more than .50</td><td>136</td><td>.76</td></tr>
<tr><td>Violent indictable person offence</td><td colspan="2">less than .50</td><td colspan="3">more than .50</td><td>428</td><td>.39</td></tr>
<tr><td>Subtotal</td><td>.05
(12505)</td><td>.11
(3032)</td><td>.17
(1188)</td><td>.21
(595)</td><td>.33
(1186)</td><td>18506</td><td>.09</td></tr>
<tr><td colspan="8">Recidivists, no prior custodial disposition</td></tr>
<tr><td>Summary/hybrid victimless offence, except YOA & escape/UAL; and summary/hybrid property offence</td><td colspan="5">less than .50</td><td>4897</td><td>.13</td></tr>
<tr><td>YOA, summary/hybrid person offence, indictable victimless & indictable property offence</td><td colspan="3">less than .50</td><td colspan="2">more than .50</td><td>5964</td><td>.30</td></tr>
<tr><td>Escape/UAL</td><td colspan="5">more than .50</td><td>113</td><td>.65</td></tr>
<tr><td>Indictable person offence, except violent offence</td><td colspan="2">less than .50</td><td colspan="3">more than .50</td><td>327</td><td>.41</td></tr>
<tr><td>Violent indictable person offence</td><td>< .50</td><td colspan="4">more than .50</td><td>176</td><td>.65</td></tr>
<tr><td>Subtotal</td><td>.13
(6805)</td><td>.27
(2320)</td><td>.40
(941)</td><td>.52
(529)</td><td>.63
(882)</td><td>11477</td><td>.24</td></tr>
</table>

Recidivists, prior custodial disposition

Summary/hybrid drug & alcohol offence	less than .50					103	.26
Summary/hybrid victimless offence except YOA & escape/UAL; & summary/hybrid property offence	< .50	more than .50				1185	.48
YOA, escape/UAL, summary/hybrid person offence ,& all indictable offences	more than .50					3472	.74
Subtotal	.59 (2659)	.69 (958)	.77 (453)	.86 (261)	.86 (429)	4760	.66

Notes: The number of cases is in parentheses. Shaded categories of cases are "predicted" to receive custodial dispositions in the best hypothetical determinate sentencing model.

those found guilty of (less serious) indictable person offences, if there are guilty findings on at least three current charges,

those found guilty of violent indictable person offences, if there are guilty findings on at least two current charges, and

those found guilty of escape/UAL.

However, most of the "exception" groups in this model comprised few actual cases, so making special predictions for them results in little improvement in the overall accuracy of prediction. This more elaborate model, incorporating more information on the seriousness of the offence, is correct for 83.5 percent of the cases (29,003) – an improvement of only 376 cases, or 1.4 percent of the total, over the previous model, based simply on the prior record of the offender.

To sum up, both the statistical analysis and our attempts to reconstruct hypothetical determinate sentencing models underlying actual dispositions suggest that these dispositions were influenced more by the offender's prior record than by the seriousness of the current offence. The "first offender discount" and "progressive loss of mitigation" (with growing criminal history) seem to explain many of these decisions without regard to the current offence. Only cases involving the most or least serious current offences provided systematic exceptions to these general rules, but even these were only partial exceptions; for example, over half of young offenders found guilty of serious offences against the person were first offenders, and over half of these received non-custodial dispositions. It was only in cases involving the residual category of prior record – recidivists with no prior custodial disposition – that the current offence seemed to play a substantial role in determining disposition. Few types of cases in this group were unambiguously characterized as to disposition: most types received about an average proportion (22 percent) of custodial dispositions. Thus, even in this group, where prior record did not determine disposition, the seriousness of the current offence was not a good predictor either.

Although imputations of sentencing rationales from statistical analysis of decisions must be somewhat tentative, it appears that judges were not sentencing primarily on the basis of a desert-based model – even the desert-based model of von Hirsch and other writers, which affords a *limited* role to the criminal record, and "primary emphasis... on the seriousness of the current crime" (von Hirsch 1985: 91). Rather, they seem to have been influenced more by crime control considerations of progressive incapacitation and deterrence, based more on the past criminal activity of the offender than the seriousness of the current offence.

Perhaps the weak relationship between offence seriousness and disposition was due partly to the crudity of our coding of the current offence into 25, then ten, categories. However, more detailed breakdowns of *Criminal Code* offence categories do not improve the relationship with the likelihood of a custodial disposition – see, for example, Table 8 of the most recent report of the Youth Court Survey (Canadian Centre for Justice Statistics 1993), which cross-classifies the disposition by 70 categories of current offence, with practically no improvement in prediction of custodial dispositions over our ten-category offence typology. *Criminal Code* offence categories do not give a complete picture of the culpability of the offender and the harm done to the victim or society in each case. It is possible that if more precise information on the nature of the current offence were incorporated into the analysis, its relationship with the disposition would become more apparent. This does not obviate the *relative* predictive power of the prior record: it predicted the disposition better than did the current offence, even when the prior record was recoded into only three categories (Tables 4 and 5).

Gender

Table 6 shows the actual proportions of custodial dispositions for cases broken down by offender's gender and age at commission of the offence, and the adjusted proportions when the two indicators of current offence and the combined indicator of prior record were controlled. The actual proportions show that cases involving female offenders (about 15 percent of the sample) received custodial dispositions in smaller proportions (11 percent) than those involving male offenders (24 percent; eta equals 0.11). However, the *adjusted* proportions are much less dissimilar (18 percent and 23 percent respectively; beta equals 0.04). This is due to the phenomenon mentioned in the introduction: the apparently more lenient treatment of females by the criminal justice system is often due to their current offences and prior record being less serious.

Comparison of the prior record and current offence of the male and female young offenders in this sample confirmed this (not shown in table form). Males were more likely than females to have committed (or, at least, to have been charged with and found guilty of) each of the four groups of indictable offences shown in panel (b) of Table 1; whereas, females were more likely than males to have been found guilty of the summary and hybrid offences. Males also had, on average,

Table 6
Proportion of custodial dispositions by gender and age at commission of offence

		Actual		Adjusted	
	n	Proportion	Eta	Proportion	Beta
Gender			.11		.04
Male	29445	.24		.23	
Female	5298	.11		.18	
Age			.08		.03
12	924	.09		.18	
13	2688	.14		.20	
14	5052	.20		.22	
15	6992	.22		.22	
16	9029	.24		.23	
17	10058	.24		.22	

Note: "Adjusted" proportions and beta incorporate controls for current offence type (ten category typology), number of current guilty findings, and prior record (three category typology).

slightly higher numbers of current and prior guilty findings, and were over twice as likely to have a prior custodial disposition. When all of these differences in case characteristics were controlled, a difference of 5 percent persisted between the "adjusted" proportions of custodial dispositions received in cases involving male and female young offenders (Table 6). This could be evidence of discrimination in favour of females, or it could indicate that cases involving males were more serious than those involving females, in ways that were not captured by our coding, and therefore could not be statistically controlled.

Age

The differences by age in the actual proportions of custodial dispositions were in the expected direction, but small (Table 6; eta equals 0.08). These differences almost entirely disappeared when the other case characteristics were controlled, suggesting that the actual differences by age were mainly due not to lenient treatment of younger offenders, but to a tendency for older offenders to have more serious cases. This was confirmed by analysis of case characteristics by age (not shown). Cases involving 14- to 17-year-olds (which made up about 90 percent of the sample) were more likely than those of 12- and 13-year-old offenders to include the more serious person offences, offences under the YOA, and escape/UAL – the three groups of offences for which custodial dispositions were most likely. The older group of offenders were also much more likely to have multiple prior findings of guilt and a prior custodial disposition; whereas 12- and 13-year-olds were more likely to be first offenders.

The fact that the adjusted proportions of custodial dispositions for 12- and 13-year-olds (18 percent and 20 percent respectively) were close to the overall average (22 percent) indicates that the main reason for their lower actual proportions of custodial dispositions was their less serious case characteristics: if their current offences and prior records had been as serious as those of the 14- to 17-year-olds, they apparently would have received custodial dispositions in almost the same proportions. This apparent absence of leniency accorded to 12- and 13-year-olds is surprising in view of the special provisions in s. 24 of the YOA concerning custodial dispositions for this group. When case characteristics were controlled, there was also no apparent "grading" of severity of disposition by age in the 14- to 17-year-old group: 14-year-olds were just as likely as 17-year-olds to receive a custodial disposition.

Summary and conclusions

Although some "offence orientation" was evident, the primary factor in deciding between custodial and non-custodial dispositions in this sample of youth court cases appeared to be the offender's prior record. First offenders were rarely given custodial dispositions, even when convicted of serious offences;

offenders who had already received a custodial disposition in the past were likely to receive another one, unless the current offence was very minor. The seriousness of the current offence did play some role in determining disposition, but it was decisive in only a few types of cases. The least serious offences, such as summary or hybrid property or other offences, particularly drug offences or impaired driving, received few custodial dispositions. The most serious types of indictable person ("violent") offences, such as homicide, robbery, and aggravated assault, were likely to receive a custodial disposition if there were guilty findings on multiple charges. Conviction on a charge of escaping custody or detention, or being unlawfully at large, had a strong likelihood of a custodial disposition, even for the few offenders with no prior record. For the great majority of cases, which did not involve either of these extremes, however, the seriousness of the current offence was not a good predictor of the disposition.

The personal characteristics of the offender on which information was available – age and gender – played little role in the decision as to custodial *versus* non-custodial disposition. Their apparent importance was inflated by the tendency for younger and female offenders to have less serious cases. Female offenders did appear to receive slightly more favourable treatment, as did 12- and 13-year-olds – but the leniency was slight in both cases.

All these findings concerning the decision as to a custodial *versus* a non-custodial disposition suggest a crime control orientation, emphasizing protection of society through incapacitation and/or deterrence, with a secondary orientation toward rehabilitation under the welfare model. The importance of the prior record, particularly a prior custodial disposition or being a first offender, suggests a concern with incapacitation: offenders who already have established themselves as serious or persistent offenders are prime candidates for escalation of control measures, while first offenders are eligible for rehabilitation or non-intervention. A control orientation is also suggested by the severity of the reaction to the relatively harmless (in themselves) offences of wilful failure to comply with a community disposition and escaping custody or detention: again, much more an escalation of control measures than a punishment for harm done. The small amount of leniency shown toward female and younger offenders suggests that dispositions were not oriented toward personal characteristics – at least, those for which data were available. The minimal influence of the justice model, with its emphasis on proportionate punishment and equity, is indicated by the relatively weak and secondary relationship between the indicators of offence seriousness and the likelihood of a custodial disposition. Although the YOA itself may be offence oriented, the actual choices made by youth court judges between custodial and non-custodial dispositions suggest that their main concern in this decision was protection of society through control or deterrence, with rehabilitation a secondary interest; and that these concerns were put into practice by orienting the decision primarily toward the offender's prior record.

In view of these findings, it is implausible that any increase in custodial dispositions under the YOA has been due to "offence orientation". If there has indeed been an increase in the use of custody, it is more likely that it reflects an escalation in control measures in response to increased recorded recidivism. This recidivism could have any number of causes: actual youth crime, police charging practices, screening practices, youth court processes leading up to adjudication... or, simply, better record-keeping.

Notes

1. Based partly on research performed under contract to the Department of Justice Canada (Moyer, Axon, and Carrington 1992). Preparation of this paper was supported by the Social Sciences and Humanities Research Council General research grant to the University of Waterloo. We gratefully acknowledge comments by Glen Doherty, Roy Jones, Bruno Marceau, Julian Roberts, and the *Journal*'s two anonymous referees on earlier versions of this paper.
2. In a sense, this "general agreement" is necessarily correct, because the *Juvenile Delinquents Act* (JDA) was so utterly non-offence-oriented.

The JDA recognized only one "offence" – that of "delinquency":

> Thus a young child who shoplifts a chocolate bar is not convicted of theft, and is not labelled a thief; one who commits murder is not a murderer. Both are guilty of the offence of "delinquency"... (Bala and Clarke 1981: 168)

Any of the dispositions provided for in the JDA could be applied to a "delinquent", regardless of the nature of the offence. The disposition was supposed to be determined only on the basis of "the child's own good and the best interests of the community" (JDA, R.S.C. 1970, c. J-3, s. 20(5), cited in Wilson 1982: 177). However, in spite of the great discretion allowed by the statute, the little research available on judicial practice suggests that dispositions under the JDA, at least in its latter years, had some relationship to legal variables such as the nature of the offence and the offender's prior record (Carrington and Moyer 1990; Kueneman and Linden 1983).

3. For discussions of these models, see Corrado 1992. These are ideal-typical models; real justice systems contain elements of all three models, in varying combinations.
4. "Incapacitation" does not necessarily mean total incapacitation; for example, in a high security prison. Rather, it refers generally to the exertion of varying degrees of control over the offender; thus, probation and open custody can serve incapacitative functions.
5. We are indebted to the Editor of the *Journal* and an anonymous referee for pointing this out.
6. In the 1989-90 sample, where the relationship was strongest, 24 percent of cases involving a "violent" offence received a custodial disposition (Table 5). Therefore, 76 percent of "violent" offenders received dispositions other than custody. Clearly, a "violent" offence did not determine a custodial disposition. Among cases involving only property, drug, or alcohol (i.e., "non-violent") offences, 7 percent received custodial dispositions, and the rest were spread evenly over the other three categories of dispositions. Thus, the absence of violence did not preclude a custodial disposition. The overall measure of association, Cramer's V, for the crosstabulation of type of disposition with type of offence had a value of 0.286, which is much less than the value of 1.0 which would indicate a perfect relationship. Similarly, in the multiple regression model predicting severity of disposition, the coefficients for the effect of the number and seriousness of the charges were 0.235 and 0.334, far from 1.0; and the R^2 for the model was only 0.191, indicating that only 19 percent of the variation in dispositions was explained by offence characteristics. As Doob and Meen concluded, these relationships were (statistically) "significant", but all that means is that they were greater than nil, not necessarily that they were strong.
7. This definition reproduces the "cases" upon which judges' dispositional decisions were based. In contrast, the Youth Court Survey publications of the Canadian Centre for Justice Statistics (CCJS) are based on cases defined as a set of charges first presented to the court on the same date (i.e., having the same date of first hearing). A set of charges first presented to the court as one case do not necessarily end up as a case

at disposition, since some may not reach disposition, some may become separated into another "case", and some may be merged with charges which began as a separate "case". Therefore, the numbers of cases reported here do not match the numbers reported in publications of the Youth Court Survey.

8. The small numbers of cases which were transferred to ordinary court and which resulted in a disposition of "detention for treatment" were omitted from this study.
9. "Most serious disposition" and "most serious charge" in this study correspond to "most significant disposition" and "most significant charge" in publications of the Youth Court Survey. See "Glossary" in Canadian Centre for Justice Statistics (1991) for definitions.
10. Prior record was coded by CCJS by searching for each offender that was disposed of in 1990-91 in the Youth Court Survey database for all previous years since the YOA came into force. Because of incomplete coverage in the early years of the YOA, and possible matching problems, prior record is probably slightly underestimated.
11. Canadian Centre for Justice Statistics (1991) warns: "The published information based on *these data must be interpreted as indicators of caseload and case characteristics rather than precise measures for several reasons*. It is not known to what extent undercoverage impacts on the data..." (emphasis in original).
12. If their commission had been combined with commission of an offence against person or property, the case would have been classified under the "more serious" person or property category, so these are pure "other" cases, the great majority of which involve only one charge.
13. These are offences which may be indictable or summary, at the option of the Crown.
14. Furthermore, von Hirsch assigns a role, albeit minor, to the (lack of a) criminal history as a possible mitigating factor; we reject this position (see "Sentencing orientations", above).
15. Eta is normally used with an interval dependent variable; however, it is appropriate here because the dependent variable – the type of disposition – has only two values (custodial or non-custodial), and is therefore equivalent to an interval variable.
16. For example, if the case involved homicide, the hypothetical model would predict a custodial disposition, since 92 percent of such cases received custodial dispositions, and would account for 92 percent of cases – a good result. If the most serious charge in the case resulting in a conviction was robbery, of which 53 percent received custodial dispositions, the model would predict a custodial disposition, and would account for only 53 percent of the cases. In cases of break and enter (which comprised 19 percent of all disposed-of cases), the model would predict a non-custodial disposition, and be correct only 68 percent of the time. In fact, the only categories of offence for which such a model would predict a custodial disposition are escape/UAL, homicide, robbery, and aggravated assault: a total of only 1799 cases, or 5 percent of all cases disposed of. In all other cases, it would predict a non-custodial disposition, and be wrong much, though not most, of the time.

17. This example illustrates that this principle can only be applied by *comparing* pairs of cases.
18. Gamma could have a negative value, if less serious cases had higher proportions of custodial dispositions than more serious cases.
19. Hackler (1991: 43) approvingly quotes a juvenile court judge in France as saying "Leaving a residence without permission is not a crime." Note that if the escape involved any harm to person or property, the case would be classified under the more serious person or property offence category; thus, "escape/UAL" cases are those involving escape/UAL and nothing worse.
20. We are indebted to an anonymous referee for suggesting this.
21. This offence includes escapes from police custody; however, as Table 5 (below) shows, few escapers did not have a prior custodial disposition.
22. Von Hirsch's third criterion – spacing – would normally be assessed statistically by assigning numerical seriousness scores to offence types and numerical severity scores to dispositions. We did not attempt to assess this, due to the difficulty of measuring seriousness and severity precisely.
23. The other evidence of the independence of the effects of offence type and the number of guilty findings comes from comparison of the values of eta and beta for each variable. The beta statistic summarizes the strength of the relationship between each variable and the likelihood of a custodial disposition, while controlling the other variable. If the two indicators of offence seriousness were highly correlated, and therefore they were mutually redundant as predictors of disposition, then at least one of the betas would be much smaller than the corresponding eta – because that variable would have a minimal effect on disposition if the other was held constant. In fact, there was very little difference between the value of eta and of beta for each indicator of offence seriousness: for the ten category classification of offence type, eta was 0.37 and beta was 0.35; for the number of findings of guilt, eta was 0.29 and beta was 0.28.
24. The majority of cases involved first offenders, who necessarily had the same value for both indicators: no prior findings of guilt and no prior custodial dispositions.
25. The utility of the distinction between first offenders and recidivists with no prior custodial disposition becomes apparent when this typology of prior record is combined with the indicators of the current offences (Table 5, discussed below).

References

Archambault, J.R. Omer

1991 Foreword. In Alan W. Leschied, Peter G. Jaffe, and Wayne Willis (eds.), The Young Offenders Act: A Revolution in Canadian Juvenile Justice. Toronto: University of Toronto Press.

Ashworth, Andrew

1992 Sentencing and Criminal Justice. London: Weidenfeld and Nicolson.

Bala, Nicholas
1992 The Young Offenders Act: The Legal Structure. In Raymond R. Corrado, Nicholas Bala, Rick Linden, and Marc LeBlanc (eds.), Juvenile Justice in Canada. Toronto: Butterworths.

Bala, Nicholas and Kenneth L. Clarke
1981 The Child and the Law. Toronto: McGraw-Hill Ryerson.

Bala, Nicholas and Mary-Anne Kirvan
1991 The statute: Its principles and provisions and their interpretation by the courts. In Alan W. Leschied, Peter G. Jaffe, and Wayne Willis (eds.), The Young Offenders Act: A Revolution in Canadian Juvenile Justice. Toronto: University of Toronto Press.

Beaulieu, Lucien (ed.)
1989 Young Offender Dispositions. Toronto: Wall and Thompson.

Beaulieu, Lucien
1991 A comparison of judicial roles under the JDA and YOA. In Alan W. Leschied, Peter G. Jaffe, and Wayne Willis (eds.), The Young Offenders Act: A Revolution in Canadian Juvenile Justice. Toronto: University of Toronto Press.

Blumstein, Alfred
1982 Research on sentencing. Justice System Journal 7: 307-30.

Canadian Centre for Justice Statistics
1991 Youth Court Statistics. 1990-91. Ottawa: Statistics Canada.

Canadian Centre for Justice Statistics
1993 Youth Court Statistics. 1992-93. Ottawa: Statistics Canada.

Canadian Sentencing Commission
1987 Sentencing Reform: A Canadian Approach. Ottawa: Ministry of Supply and Services Canada.

Carrington, Peter J. and Sharon Moyer
1990 The impact of legal representation on Canadian juvenile court dispositions. Presented at the Annual Meeting of the American Society of Criminology.

Chesney-Lind, Meda
1987 Female offenders: paternalism reexamined. In Laura L. Crites and Winifred L. Hepperle (eds.), Women, the Courts, and Equality. Beverly Hills: Sage.

Corrado, Raymond R.
1992 Introduction. In Raymond R. Corrado, Nicholas Bala, Rick Linden, and Marc LeBlanc (eds.), Juvenile Justice in Canada. Toronto: Butterworths.

Corrado, Raymond R. and Alan E. Markwart
1992 The evaluation and implementation of a new era of juvenile justice in Canada. In Raymond R. Corrado, Nicholas Bala, Rick Linden, and Marc LeBlanc (eds.), Juvenile Justice in Canada. Toronto: Butterworths.

CHAPTER THIRTEEN

Bad, sad, and rejected: The lives of aggressive children[1]

Jane B. Sprott
and ***Anthony N. Doob***
Centre of Criminology
University of Toronto
Toronto, Ontario

COUNTRIES VARY IN DEFINING THE AGE AT WHICH YOUNG CHILDREN SHOULD be held criminally responsible for their acts. For example, the minimum age of criminal responsibility in Sweden and Austria is 14 (Kangaspunta 1995). In England and Wales, the minimum age is 14 (or 10 if it can be proven that the child knows "right" from "wrong") while in the Netherlands the minimum age of criminal responsibility is 12 (Kangaspunta 1995). Within the United States, there is state to state variation in the minimum age of criminal responsibility. Some states have a minimum age of seven, while other states have a minimum age of 10 (Snyder and Sickmund 1995).

In Canada, the minimum age of criminal responsibility is 12, but there is pressure to lower the age to 10, especially when the child commits an act of violence (Standing Committee on Justice and Legal Affairs 1997). When the *Youth Criminal Justice Act* was introduced in March 1999, it was criticized because the age of criminal responsibility was not lowered to age 10. Indeed, on a broad level, there appears to be considerable public support for using the justice system to deal with very young children who commit acts of violence.

A public opinion poll carried out in early 1999 by the Department of Justice asked a representative sample of 1,200

Canadian Journal of Criminology/Revue canadienne de criminologie, April/avril 2000, pp. 123–133.

people across Canada for their views on the youth justice system. One question asked respondents to "[i]magine this situation: A ten-year-old boy has just committed a serious violent offence. How appropriate do you think it would be to have him charged with this offence and dealt with by the court? He then could be sentenced to serve a sentence in a prison for youth". Roughly 70% of respondents believed that charging the youth would be very, or somewhat appropriate. Thus, on this broad level, with no other option provided, there appears to be a great deal of public support for addressing violence by youth in the justice system. Respondents were then asked this follow-up question:

> Another option, instead of having the youth charged with the offence and taken to court, would be to have the ten-year-old boy dealt with by the mental health system or the child welfare system. He could immediately be sent for treatment in a locked facility to deal with the problems that led him to behave violently. Do you prefer or oppose this approach instead of having the youth dealt with by the courts?

Close to 77% of the people surveyed preferred this approach instead of charging the youth and dealing with him in the youth justice system. Put differently, support for a criminal justice approach to under-age offending fell from 70% to 23% when a choice of a criminal justice or a child welfare approach was provided. Even people who initially believed that charging the child would be "very appropriate" preferred the mental health choice when given the option. Table 1 shows the relationship between the responses to those two questions. Of the people who initially believed that it would be "very appropriate" to deal with the child in the justice system, 62.1% preferred the mental health approach when given the choice. Over 80% of the people who believed it would be "somewhat appropriate" or "inappropriate" to deal with the child in the justice system preferred the mental health approach when given the choice

Table 1
Relationship of initial support for a criminal justice approach to support for a mental health/child welfare approach (when choice was provided)

	Initial view of the appropriateness of charging the child		
Preference/Opposition to mental health approach	Very appropriate	Somewhat appropriate	Inappropriate
Prefer mental health approach	62.1%	80.2%	86.2%
Oppose mental health approach	37.9%	19.8%	13.8%
Total	100% (354)	100% (429)	100% (341)

Chi-square = 61.40, df = 2, p<.001

Thus, although on a broad level there appears to be widespread public support for dealing with violent young children in the youth justice system, that support diminishes substantially when people are given a choice of ways with which to deal with the child. Concern over the minimum age of criminal responsibility, in particular for violent acts, is not new, and will likely not disappear. While the majority of the public does not appear to support criminally charging young violent children, it would be useful to know something about the lives of the children who cause society so much concern. Traditionally, very young, very aggressive children have been seen as "disadvantaged" in a number of different ways (e.g., having dysfunctional families, unhappy home lives, low self-esteem, inadequate parenting, etc.) (Yoshikawa 1994). Recently, however, the notion that young violent children are "unhappy" or have "low self-esteem" has been challenged.

Baumeister, Boden, and Smart (1996: 8) recently argued that people of all ages who commit acts of violence have very high self-esteem.[(2)] Specifically, they hypothesized that "the major cause of violence is high self-esteem combined with an ego threat.... That is, people turn aggressive when they receive feedback that contradicts their favorable views of themselves and implies that they should adopt less favorable views. More to the point, it is mainly the people who refuse to lower their self-appraisals who become violent"

The supportive data related to youth cited by Baumeister *et al.* (1996) were, however, rather limited. For example, they cited work by Olweus (1994) which suggested that Norwegian school bullies (age 8 to age 16) were generally secure and free from anxiety. That characterization is, obviously, somewhat different from suggesting that they have high self-esteem. Furthermore, there is no clear evidence that school bullies are representative of generally aggressive children (see Farrington 1993 for a full review of the research on bullying). Baumeister *et al.* (1996) also cited the Glueck and Glueck (1950) finding that their "delinquent" sample of youth was less likely than their "non-delinquent" sample to suffer from feelings of helplessness, insecurity, and feelings of being unloved. Baumeister *et al.* (1996: 22) therefore concluded that "[v]iolent youths seem sincerely to believe that they are better than other people, but they frequently find themselves in circumstances that threaten or challenge these beliefs".

The characterization of violent youth as being self-satisfied could easily be used to support increasingly punitive criminal justice responses to these youth. The inference that violent youth are self-satisfied, however, is based on limited measures of specific samples of young people. The fact that this characterization has been cited in the criminological literature (e.g., Loeber and Hay 1997: 394) suggests that it should be examined more carefully. What is needed is a direct examination of children's feelings from their own self-reports. Such data are essential if one is going to argue that generally aggressive or "delinquent" young children have high self-esteem.

Using survey data from Statistics Canada, we tested the hypothesis that aggressive young children generally have high self-esteem. We used the first wave of data from the National Longitudinal Study of Children and Youth (NLSCY) which contained information on a random sample of children (from birth to age 11) across Canada. The NLSCY is, in fact, quite unusual in that it provides the perspectives of three key people: the children themselves, the adult in the household most knowledgeable about the child (the "Person Most Knowledgeable" (PMK) – typically the mother), and the child's school teacher.

We did not attempt to do a study on the causes of delinquency, nor did we draw any causal inferences from the data. Our point was to try to understand the view that very young aggressive children have of themselves and views that others hold of them. If high self-esteem is, in fact, related to aggressiveness in young children, then our sample of very aggressive children should be more likely than the less aggressive children to describe themselves in positive terms. For a measure of self-esteem we examine the children's self-reported feelings and social relationships. Children's broad feelings and social interactions are theoretically consistent with Baumeister *et al.*'s (1996) general definition of self-esteem.

Method

In this study, we focused on a "conduct disorder/physical aggression scale" created by Statistics Canada (1998). The scale ranged from 0 (no physical aggression) to 12 (high physical aggression). Most children (roughly 45%) were at 0. The scale was a composite of six questions such as: "Would you say that [Name of child] gets into many fights?"; "Would you say that [Name of child] physically attacks people?" and "Would you say that [Name of child] threatens people?" The questions were administered, with the appropriate wording changes to the PMK, the teacher, and the child.

In all of our analyses, we looked only at those children in the NLSCY who were 10 or 11 years old at the time of the first wave of data collection. They were the only children to be asked about their own behaviors, and, therefore, they were the only children whose behavior could be examined from their own and others' perspectives.

Since many 10- and 11-year-olds exhibit behavior that could be considered physically aggressive, we decided to examine those who were on the "worst" end of the continuum – presumably those with whom society is likely to have the most difficulty. Thus, we arbitrarily chose to try to understand the views and perceptions of the "worst" 10% (in terms of physical aggression) of the children compared to the "other" 90% of the children.(3)

The next issue was whose perspective to use – the child's self-report of aggressiveness, the PMK's, or the teacher's? There was some overlap between the different ratings of the child's behavior, but the relationship was not overwhelmingly strong. This was not surprising, nor, as the results demonstrate, was it important. There were also three different perspectives on the child's feelings and social relationships: the child's, the PMK's, and the teacher's. In all then, there were nine possible combinations of perspectives. Since we were interested in the child's self-reported feelings these are presented in this paper. In order to have a different perspective defining who was "very aggressive", we used the PMK's ratings of aggressiveness.

Results

Comparing the "worst" 10% of the children (in terms of physical aggression from the perspective of the PMK) to the "other" 90% resulted in a set of remarkably consistent findings. From all perspectives, regardless of gender, the "most aggressive" children were more likely to describe themselves in terms that simply made them sound unhappy when compared to the "other" children. Looking at Table 2, 54.4% of the "most aggressive" girls reported not feeling as happy as other children, whereas 32.8% of the "other" girls reported not feeling as happy as other children. The same trend held for boys as well. The "very aggressive" girls and boys were more likely than the "other" girls and boys to report feeling miserable, feeling left out of school, having trouble enjoying themselves, and having a negative self-image.(4)

Table 2
The relationship between children's self-reported feelings and aggressiveness

	PMK's identification of "aggressiveness"			
	Girls		Boys	
Child's self-report of feelings	Most aggressive	Other	Most aggressive	Other
I don't feel as happy as other children	54.4% (100)*	32.8% (1279)	35.0% (196)*	32.5% (1181)
I feel miserable	48.7% (98)*	36.0% (1275)	46.3% (191)*	34.0% (1176)
I feel left out at school	36.4% (102)*	17.0% (1284)	27.4% (198)*	14.8% (1186)
I have trouble enjoying myself	49.3% (97)*	29.0% (1272)	34.8% (189)*	25.1% (1190)
I have a "negative" self- image	51.9% (99)*	27.8% (1257)	48.6% (191)*	28.8% (1142)

* Significant (based on unweighted frequencies), $p<.05$
Percents based on weighted data. N's (in parentheses) presented in the table are the unweighted numbers on which the percents are based.

The same pattern of results emerged when we looked at the children's social relationships. As shown in Table 3, 47.6% of the "very aggressive" girls reported having negative relations with family whereas only 25.6% of the "other" girls reported having negative relations with family. Again, the same trend held for boys. The "very aggressive" children were more likely than the "other" children to report having negative relations with friends, and to perceive their parents as rejecting them and their teachers as being unfair. The "very aggressive" children were also more likely than the "other" children to report that children say mean things to them and bully them.[5]

As it turned out, this pattern held no matter whose perspectives were examined – the PMK's, the teacher's, or the child's. Examining ratings of aggressiveness from the child, the PMK and the teacher with the child's self-report, the PMK's perception and the teacher's perception of the child's feelings

Table 3
The relationship between children's self-reported social interactions and aggressiveness

	PMK's identification of "aggressiveness"			
Child's self-report of social relationships	Girls		Boys	
	Most aggressive	Other	Most aggressive	Other
negative relations with family	47.6% (101)*	25.6% (1269)	49.1% (211)*	25.6% (1172)
negative relations with friends	42.6% (104)*	22.9% (1308)	54.6% (219)*	28.9% (1219)
perception of parental rejection	47.5% (95)*	30.7% (1244)	47.2% (185)*	35.5% (1136)
perception of teacher being "fair"	51.2% (102)*	68.8% (1295)	56.1% (202)*	63.1% (1199)
other children say mean things to you	18.9% (101)*	8.7% (1285)	21.8% (200)*	7.7% (1189)
other children "bully" you	19.2% (99)*	7.5% (1274)	24.7% (197)*	12.4% (1189)

*Significant (based on unweighted frequencies), p<.05
Percents based on weighted data. N's (in parentheses) presented in the table are the unweighted numbers on which the percents are based.

and social relationships produced 102 comparisons between the "most aggressive" children and the "other" children. In 2 of the 102 comparisons there were "reversals" (where the "other" children were worse off then the "aggressive" children). There were no statistically significant reversals. The findings were overwhelmingly consistent: aggressive children were less happy with their lives than were other children.

Conclusion

The findings are clear: the most aggressive 10- and 11-year-olds (identified by their own reports, the reports of their PMK, or their school teacher) are unhappy children. The notion that they believe themselves to be "better than other people" or, in a more colloquial sense, are happy-go-lucky children who enjoy their aggressive lives is simply not supported by data from a representative sample of over 3,000 Canadian children.

Ultimately, the decision of whether to criminalize their aggressive behavior is likely to be a political one rather than one based on utilitarian principles. If politicians were to listen carefully to members of the public, they would hear that there is, in fact, very little support for a criminal justice intervention when alternatives are offered. Thus, from a political perspective, one reason not to criminalize the behaviour of 10- and 11-year-olds is that the public, when given a choice, prefers a welfare approach over a criminal justice approach.

The second reason not to criminalize the misbehaviour of 10- and 11-year-olds is that these are children who are much more likely than other children to indicate that they feel miserable, left out, rejected by parents, bullied by other children, etc. Presumably, were their misbehavior dealt with in a punishment oriented criminal justice system, they would add "the state" to the list of people or institutions that had rejected them as children.

Notes

1. The preparation of this paper was financially supported by the Applied Research Branch of Human Resources Development Canada in 1997-1998, and by a research grant from the Social Sciences and Humanities Research Council of Canada to Anthony N. Doob.
2. By "self-esteem" they mean "a favorable global evaluation of oneself" (pg. 5).
3. In fact, we examined what were "roughly" the "worst 10%" from each perspective. The cutoffs were not exactly at the 10% point because we were using 12 point scales and it was not always possible to create a cutoff at exactly the 10% point. It, in fact, did not matter how the conduct disorder scale was divided up. Whether we divided the scale up into thirds, or by a top 10% compared to the other 90%, the more aggressive the child, the more likely he or she was to report unhappy feelings and difficult social interactions.
4. These measures were all three or four point scales. For the measures of not feeling as happy as other children, feeling miserable and having trouble enjoying yourself, we used the proportion of children who "often" or "sometimes" reported feeling that way. For feeling left out of school, we used the proportion of children who "always", "most of the time", or "sometimes" reported feeling that way. "Self-image" was a

scale – we took the top third of the distribution to capture those children who, by their own perception, were most negative about themselves.

5. Negative relations with family, friends and parental rejection were all scales. We took the top third of the distribution reporting the highest level of negative relations and parental rejection. The other three measures were all four point scales. We used the proportion of children who reported that their teacher was fair "all the time"; the proportion of children who reported that other children "all of the time" or "most of the time" said mean things to them; the proportion of children who reported that they were bullied "always", "most of the time" or "sometimes".

References

Baumeister, Roy F., Joseph M. Boden, and Laura Smart
1996 Relation of threatened egotism to violence and aggression: The dark side of high self-esteem. Psychological Review 103(1): 5-33.

Farrington, David P.
1993 Understanding and preventing bullying. In Michael Tonry (ed.), Crime and Justice: A Review of the Research. Vol. 17. Chicago: University of Chicago Press.

Glueck, Sheldon and Eleanor T. Glueck
1950 Unraveling Juvenile Delinquency. Cambridge, MA: Harvard University Press.

Kangaspunta, Kristiina
1995 Profiles of Criminal Justice Systems in Europe and North America. Publication series #26. European Institute for Crime Prevention and Control. Helsinki, Finland: Tammer-Paino Oy.

Loeber, Rolf and Dale Hay
1997 Key issues in the development of aggression and violence from childhood to early adulthood. Annual Review of Psychology 48: 371-410.

Olweus, Dan
1984 Bullying at school time: Long-term outcomes for the victims and an effective school-based intervention program. In R. Huesmann (ed.), Aggressive Behavior: Current Perspectives. New York: Plenum Press.

Snyder, Howard N. and Melissa Sickmund
1995 Juvenile Offenders and Victims: A National Report. Washington, D.C.: Department of Justice, Office of Juvenile and Delinquency Prevention.

Statistics Canada
1998 National Longitudinal Survey of Children and Youth: Users Handbook and Microdata Guide. Cycle 1, Release 2. Ottawa: Human Resources Development Canada.

Standing Committee on Justice and Legal Affairs, (House of Commons, Canada).
1997 Thirteenth report: Renewing youth justice. Shaughnessy Cohen (Chair). Ottawa: Parliament of Canada.

Yoshikawa, Hirokazu
1994 Prevention as cumulative protection: Effects of early family support and education on chronic delinquency and its risks. Psychological Bulletin 115: 28-54.

CHAPTER FOURTEEN

Adolescent drug use and a general theory of crime: An analysis of a theoretical integration

Ann Marie Sorenson
Department of Sociology
University of Toronto
Toronto, Ontario
and ***David Brownfield***
Department of Sociology
Erindale College
University of Toronto
Toronto, Ontario

CRIMINOLOGISTS HAVE EXPRESSED CONSIDERABLE DISSATISFACTION WITH existing theories of crime and deviance. Textbook writers (see, for example, Nettler 1984; Jackson and Griffiths 1991) routinely present lengthy discussion of criticisms of crime and deviance theories. One of the principal criticisms of these theories is the lack of explanatory power provided by these ideas. Most researchers concede that nearly every theory, or certain propositions of nearly every theory, receives some level of empirical support. The level of empirical support is almost uniformly modest or weak.

One recent response to the dissatisfaction with current theories has been theoretical integration. Integration, following a dictionary definition, has been defined as efforts "to bring parts together into a unified whole" (Liska, Krohn, and Messner 1989: 1). The notion of a unified whole implies some ordering or establishing of relationships among parts. Thornberry (1989: 52) more systematically defines theoretical

Canadian Journal of Criminology/Revue canadienne de criminologie, January/janvier 1995, pp. 19–37.

integration as "the act of combining two or more sets of logically interrelated propositions into one larger set of interrelated propositions, in order to provide a more comprehensive explanation of a particular phenomenon".

Canadian criminologists have made significant contributions to integrated explanations that include control theory elements. For example, Linden and his colleagues (Linden and Hackler 1973; Linden and Fillmore 1981) combine social control theory with differential association to develop a more complete explanation than is provided by either theory by itself. Hagan's (1989) power-control theory combines structural factors based on occupational status and autonomy with social control theory variables. LeBlanc and his colleagues (see, e.g., Caplan and LeBlanc 1985) may have developed the most thorough integration of control theory by including elements of differential association, personality traits, and structural variables such as social status. American criminologists such as Elliott (Elliott, Huizinga, and Ageton 1985) have attempted to integrate control theory with social learning and strain theories.

Despite previous opposition to theoretical integration (see Hirschi 1979; 1989), Travis Hirschi (in a co-authored book with Michael Gottfredson (1990)) has joined the ranks of the integrationists by combining classical theory with the concept of "self-control" in a new general theory of crime. Hirschi (1989) and others may argue that this does not represent true integration of theories in that combining such perspectives merely combines cognate and perhaps identical theories.[1] Yet Gottfredson and Hirschi's general theory of crime is precisely the kind of theoretical effort that follows the definitions of integration set forth by Liska *et al.* and by Thornberry. These definitions require that a "unified whole" be created (or ordered relationships be established) and that the propositions of the constituent theories be logically interrelated.

Both classical theory and the self-control concept assume that individuals are self-seeking or pursue pleasure and avoid pain, and will attempt to maximize their individual well-being.

Under this model, individuals will refrain from crime and deviance only if constrained from such behavior. The assumption about the motivation to deviate is identical in both classical theory and the self-control concept: individuals are assumed to have a constant or invariant motivation to deviate.

In this paper, we will analyze the integration of classical theory and the concept of self-control in Gottfredson and Hirschi's (1990) general theory of crime. We will discuss classical theory and the self-control concept, noting the logical consistency of these constituent theories and describing the integration of these theories. In addition, we will empirically assess the utility of the general theory of crime as an explanation of adolescent drug use.

Classical theory and self-control

The classical theory of crime is usually consigned to a brief review in undergraduate criminology classes and texts, and then lectures and texts proceed to the currently important theories. Gottfredson and Hirschi (1990) imply that we may be shortchanging our students and our own understanding of crime and deviance by not devoting more attention to classical theory. Roshier (1989) provides an excellent discussion of classical theory and its potential relevance for contemporary criminological theory.

Among the classical theorists, Beccaria and Bentham were the two most influential writers in the late eighteenth and early nineteenth centuries. Beccaria and others of the classical perspective were particularly influential in stating ideas leading to reform of the criminal justice systems that were brutal, arbitrary, and excessive in the punishment inflicted on offenders. The notion of free will in classical theory implied grading punishment to the seriousness of the offense in a more refined way. Imprisonment substantially displaced capital punishment and grotesque forms of corporal punishment, as the classical theory principle that the threatened punishment must simply outweigh (and not overwhelm) the rewards of crime became more accepted.

Both Beccaria and Bentham shared a utilitarian conception of human behavior in which calculations of pleasure and pain guided the choices and actions of individuals. Subsequent neoclassical philosophers modified the absolute principles of the earlier classical school writers, allowing for mitigating circumstances in assigning punishment against, for example, the mentally ill. (Most social scientists do not share the free will approach, nor would many social control theorists accept the notion of completely unrestricted free will.)

Although some considered Bentham an ivory tower theorist, "untainted by human experience" (Jackson and Griffiths 1991: 177), his influence on criminology and criminal justice was enormous. Gottfredson and Hirschi (1990: 85-87) demonstrate this enduring influence by drawing on Bentham's classical theory. Gottfredson and Hirschi characterize classical theory as an underdeveloped form of social control theory given the emphasis on moral sanctions rather than legal punishment in Bentham's writings. While most criminologists have focused on the policy implications of classical theory, which has led to an emphasis on legal sanctions, Bentham and other classical theorists actually emphasized moral and social sanctions as more crucial than legal penalties (Gottfredson and Hirschi 1990: 85).

Classical theory fails to predict individual differences in the propensity to commit crimes that remain stable regardless of the circumstances or situation encountered. All individuals pursue the pleasure-pain principle according to classical theorists; offenders differ from nonoffenders only in their calculation of the costs and benefits of crime under this conception. Gottfredson and Hirschi (1990: 87) comment that classical theory thus fails to account for differences in what they label "self-control"; individual differences in self-control persist regardless of risk or the perception of risk of punishment.

Gottfredson and Hirschi assert that the classical theory and the concept of self-control are remarkably compatible. Classical theory focuses on the external control of behavior based on perceived costs of crime, which vary according to the individual's location or social bonds. The self-control concept focuses on the individual's internal control of behavior of the degree to which individuals may succumb to tempting situations. "Combining the two ideas thus merely recognizes the simultaneous existence of social and individual restraints on behavior" (Gottfredson and Hirschi 1990: 88).

Classical theory and the concept of self-control are both compatible with a free will or choice conceptualization of crime and deviance. Neither classical theory nor the self-control concept are deterministic since both recognize the possibility of individual decision making. The image of the individual pursuing pleasure and avoiding pain depicted by Bentham is also completely compatible with the self-control concept. Thus, Gottfredson and Hirschi integrate the propositions of classical theory and the concept of self-control.

Other control theorists have advanced similar theoretical combinations previously (cf. Akers 1991). For example, Reiss (1951) distinguishes between personal and social controls as barriers to delinquency. Reckless (1967) used the concepts of inner and outer containment as a similar distinction of internal and external restraints. Hirschi (1969) does not explicitly distinguish individual and social restraints in his earlier version of social control theory; however, the element of commitment is similar to the classical theory focus on stakes in conformity or a rational investment in conformity, while the element of attachment forms a portion of the new concept of self-control.

The concept of self-control includes attachment to others, but Gottfredson and Hirschi (1990: 89-91) incorporate many other dimensions of character in their description of this concept. For example, self-control refers to the ability to defer gratification. Criminals and drug users tend to pursue the immediate gratification of their desires. Individuals who lack self-control will pursue immediate pleasures that include not only drinking and drug use, but also gambling and illicit sex. Those lacking self-control are even predicted to be more likely to be involved in automobile accidents. The theory is "general" in the sense that it may explain diverse forms of crime, including burglary, drug use, violence, and white collar crime.

Self-control implies that individuals are diligent and persistent. In contrast, the offender cannot tolerate frustration and seeks to obtain things easily or effortlessly. Long term commitment to a conventional career and to relationships such as marriage and family tends to be lacking among those with little self-control. The notion of self-control is, therefore, inconsistent with the criminal career paradigm in that it asserts that crimes do not provide long term benefits; instead, crimes inhibit long term commitments to marriage, friends, and family.

Individuals who lack self-control neither possess nor value cognitive or academic skills. The skills required for most acts of deviant behavior such as drug use are minimal. Individuals with a high level of self-control tend to be cautious as well as cognitive. Offenders tend to be more inclined to be thrill seeking and adventuresome. The risk of an action such as taking cocaine or hallucinogens is attractive to the person lacking self-control. In a recent study of drinking and driving, Keane, Maxim, and Teevan (1993) conclude that measures of self-control or risk-taking behavior are significantly correlated with driving under the influence. Risk-taking behavior such as the failure to wear seat belts is linked to higher levels of blood alcohol concentration (Keane *et al.* 1993: 40).

Individuals who lack self-control are self-centered or egotistical, indifferent to the feelings and needs of others. Those lacking in self-control are indifferent to the harm created by their actions or to the trust that is broken by such actions.

Based on classical theory, Gottfredson and Hirschi (1990: 220) state that controls for opportunity to commit offenses should be considered independent of the characteristic of self-control. For example, individuals lacking self-control may still refrain from drug use if these substances are not available. Grasmick, Tittle, Bursik, and Arneklev (1993) report interactions between measures of opportunity and self-control that are significantly related to assault and fraud. Bachman, Johnston, and O'Malley (1990) find, however, that perceived availability of drugs such as marijuana and cocaine is not significantly related to recent declines in drug use.

Based on Gottfredson and Hirschi's general theory, we predict that measures derived from classical theory and the self-control concept will be significantly correlated with adolescent drug use. We predict that this integrated theory will provide a substantial increase in explained variance compared with previous theories. Finally, we hypothesize that the effects of general theory variables on drug use will remain significant controlling for the influence of other factors such as peer delinquency.

Data

The data used in the analysis in this paper are taken from interview and questionnaire responses in the Seattle Youth Study (Hindelang, Hirschi, and Weis 1981). More than eleven hundred (N = 1,119) male and female high school students completed interviews or questionnaires in this study.

Hindelang *et al.* (1981: 37) report a somewhat higher level of alcohol and marijuana use in the Seattle study than in previous self-report studies. For example, they note a prevalence rate of marijuana use of about seventy percent in the sample. This rate of marijuana use is also noted to be similar to the rates found in contemporary surveys of adolescents. Further, the prevalence rate of heroin use in the Seattle sample is also reported to be very similar (about one percent) to the prevalence rates in other contemporary studies.

The Seattle Youth Study contains several variables relevant to the measurement of the construct of self-control and for the measurement of constructs based on classical theory. In the Appendix, we provide a more complete description of the variables used in this study, including item wording and scoring of the variables.

Classical theorists focus on the calculation of risk by the individual in terms of the likelihood of punishment for engaging in criminal or deviant acts. Many prior studies (eg, Jensen, Erickson, Gibbs 1978; Klepper and Nagin 1989; Bachman *et al.* 1990; Keane *et al.* 1993) have used measures of perceived risk of punishment. In this paper, we will use the following measure of *perceived risk of punishment*: "People who break the law are almost always caught and punished" (CAUGHTP). We would prefer to have measures of perceived risk of punishment for drug offenses in particular, but no such variables are available in this study.

Classical theorists also emphasized the role of informal sanctions and deterrence. Gottfredson and Hirschi (1990: 97-105) further observe that self-control is developed in part by effective socialization within the family. Parents must not only recognize deviant behavior among their children but they must also be willing and able to punish or correct such behavior (cf. Patterson and Dishion 1985). In this study, we use the following measure of *parental supervision*: "As far as my father is concerned, I'm pretty much free to come and go as I please" (DADSUP).

As mentioned earlier, the "self-control" construct includes several aspects of individual character that provide restraints against deviant behavior. Among these are the individual's concern for the opinion of others, such as parents and teachers. *Parental attachment*, in accordance with Hirschi's (1969) operationalization, is measured by the following item: "Would you like to be the kind of person your father is?" (IDDAD). *Attachment to teachers* is measured by the following item: "Do you care what teachers think of you?" (CARTCH).

Self-control also refers to the tendency to be diligent and persistent in a course of action. Those who lack self-control tend to seek immediate gratification of their desires. One measure of diligence in the Seattle study asks respondents about their *academic effort* in the following item: "I try hard in school" (TRYHARD).

Much of Gottfredson and Hirschi's (1990) discussion of self-control revolved around academic issues. Some of this discussion focuses on the extent to which individuals value academic achievement and ability. The following item was selected to measure the respondent's *evaluation of academics*: "Such things as books, school, and education don't interest me very much" (INTELL). Gottfredson and Hirschi also stress actual effort and accomplishment in school as indicators of self-control. Respondent's *school performance* was measured by the following item: "Putting them all together, how would your grades average out?" (GRADES). *Time spent on homework* was measured by the question, "How many hours per week do you spend doing homework?" (HOMEWK). Self-control also refers to the individual's tendency to plan and engage in long term commitments. As an indicator of this tendency, the following measure of *educational expectations* will also be included in the analysis: "How much schooling do you actually expect to get eventually?" (EDEXP).

Several factors considered in prior research and theory are not incorporated in Gottfredson and Hirschi's general theory of crime. Most notably, the influence of peers is excluded as a causal factor from this theory. In stating a version of control theory, Gottfredson and Hirschi retain the assumption that the motivation to deviate is constant and therefore requires no explanation, such as the presence of peer influence. This assumption may be tested empirically by including measures of peer influence in our analysis to determine if the general theory constructs are sufficient to account for variations in drug use or if alternative explanations must also be considered. Bailey and Hubbard (1990) report that peer use and possession of alcohol and marijuana is significantly related to initiation of marijuana use among eighth and ninth grade students, but not among children in lower grades.

We include the following measures of *peer delinquency* and *attachment to peers* in our analysis: "How many of your best friends have been picked up by the police?" (POLFR); and, "Do you share your thoughts and feelings with your best friend?"

(FRSHAR). We would have preferred a measure of peer drug use in particular, but no such variables were available in the Seattle data. White, Pandina, and LaGrange (1987) report that measures of peer delinquency and peer drug use are comparably related to measures of self-reported drug use (including the use of alcohol, marijuana, hallucinogens, and cocaine).

Several studies (e.g., Higgins and Albrecht 1977; Burkett and Warren 1987; Marcos, Bahr, and Johnson 1986) have also found that religion has a significant effect on drug use. Based on the theoretical discussion of D'Antonio, Newman, and Wright (1982), which distinguishes the "social control" and "social support" functions of religion and the family, Brownfield and Sorenson (1991) construct an index of social support derived from measures of religious and family life. This index was found to have a significant effect on self-reported drug use among adolescents. The social support index includes measures of church attendance, religiosity, church affiliation, and communication with the father. Confirmatory latent variable analysis reveals that the same index may be constructed for male and female respondents. We will include this *social support index* (SUPPORT) along with the measures of peer influence as variables potentially necessary to account for drug use in addition to the general theory variables.

The measure of drug use employed in this study is based on a modified Guttman scale (Sorenson and Brownfield 1989). This modified Guttman scale is constructed from responses to the following five observed measures of drug use: (1) "Have you ever drunk beer or wine?"; (2) "Have you ever smoked marijuana (grass, pot)?"; (3) "Have you ever taken barbiturates (downers) or methedrine (speed or other uppers) without a prescription?"; (4) "Have you ever taken angel dust, LSD, or mescaline?"; (5) "Have you ever used cocaine?"

We found no significant differences between males and females in patterns of self-reported drug use. Latent variable analysis for male and female respondents produced a four category measure of drug use, with the percentage of the sample in each category noted in parentheses: (1) no drug use or alcohol use only (18.7%); (2) alcohol and marijuana use (36.9%); (3) alcohol, marijuana, and limited use of drugs such as barbiturates or cocaine (28.0%); and (4) use of the drugs described in all five observed measures (16.3%).

Findings

Our empirical analysis begins with an assessment of the bivariate relationships between drug use and the measures derived from classical theory elements of Gottfredson and Hirschi's general theory of crime. We find that both formal (*perceived risk of punishment*, CAUGHTP) and informal (*parental supervision*, DASUP) types of control seem to inhibit drug use. Those who believed that people who break the law (CAUGHTP) are caught and punished are slightly less likely to report extensive or serious drug use than those who believe that people may break the law with impunity (Somers's *d* = .08). Respondents who report a high level of informal control as measured by paternal supervision (DADSUP) are also less likely to be involved in drug use than those whose fathers are more lackadaisical in their supervision. In Table 1 we summarize the bivariate analyses of drug use by all of the independent variables included in this study.

Consistent with the general theory, we find that all of our measures of self-control are significantly correlated with adolescent drug use. For example, our measure of *academic effort* (TRYHARD) is significantly correlated with drug use. Students who claim to try hard in school are less likely to report extensive involvement in drugs than those who claim to be less diligent (Somers's *d* = .26). All of the remaining measures of self-control in Table 1 are significantly correlated with drug use in the predicted direction.

Consistent with previous research and Linden's integrated theory (Linden and Fillmore 1981), we find that *peer delinquency* (POLFR) is positively and strongly correlated with self-reported drug use (Somers's *d* = .40). We also find that *attachment to peers* (FRSHAR) is positively correlated with self-reported drug

Table 1
Summary of bivariate analyses of drug use by general theory measures, peer relationships, and social support

	Somers's d	Pearson's Chi-square
Independent variables		
General theory variables:		
Perceived risk of punishment (CAUGHTP)	.08	25.13*
Parental supervision (DADSUP)	–.11	32.51*
Parental attachment (IDDAD)	.18	46.12*
Attachment to teachers (CARTCH)	.22	67.08*
Academic effort (TRYHARD)	.26	119.04*
Evaluation of academics (INTELL)	–.21	81.98*
School performance (GRADES)	.25	137.20*
Time spent on homework (HOMEWK)	–.27	138.08*
Educational expectations (EDEXP)	–.24	109.01*
Variables excluded by the general theory:		
Peer delinquency (POLFR)	.40	202.98*
Attachment to peers (FRSHAR)	.12	17.73*
Social support index (SUPPORT)	.25	38.56*

* $p < .05$

use (Somers's *d* = .12). This is contrary to predictions based on Gottfredson and Hirschi's version (and other versions) of control theory. This finding is consistent with prior research on attachment to peers and deviant behavior (see, e.g., Massey and Krohn 1986). Finally, we find that the index of social support (SUPPORT), which includes measures of religious involvement and paternal communication, is significantly correlated with drug use. Those who were found to have a high level of social support are about half as likely (9.5%) to report use of all five drug types than those who were found to have a low level of social support (23.1%).

We next considered multivariate analyses of drug use and the variables based on Gottfredson and Hirschi's general theory of crime, including controls for peer relationships and the index of social support. It is possible that variables based on the general theory do not have a significant effect on drug use once we consider alternative factors such as peer influence. For example, *academic effort* (TRYHARD) may not be relevant to drug use if we control for the effects of *peer delinquency* (POLFR). To test for this possibility (and for the possibility that other general theory variables may be eliminated from consideration), we must use a multivariate statistical analysis. Here we treat the measure of drug use as a continuous variable and we use multiple regression. In Table 2, we present the results of our regression analysis.

Overall, we find that several of the general theory variables remain significantly related to drug use. As predicted by Gottfredson and Hirschi (1990), measures based on both classical theory and on the self-control concept appear to be important correlates of drug use. Both of the measures based on the classical theory component of the general theory, *perceived risk of punishment* (CAUGHTP) and *parental supervision* (DADSUP), remain significant predictors of drug use.

Some of the measures based on the self-control concept also remain significantly related to drug use. *Parental attachment* (IDDAD), *academic effort* (TRYHARD), and *school performance* (GRADES) are significantly correlated with drug use in the multivariate analysis. *Attachment to teachers* (CARTCH), *evaluation of academics* (INTELL), *time spent on homework* (HOMEWK), and *educational expectations* (EDEXP), however, become statistically insignificant in their effects on drug use. The effect of the *social support index* (SUPPORT) also is no longer statistically significant after controlling for the general theory variables and peer relationships measures. Both measures of peer relationships, *peer delinquency* (POLFR) and *attachment to peers* (FRSHAR), remain significantly associated with drug use.

The total amount of variance accounted for by all of the included variables ($R^2 = .21$) is consistent with the levels of variance accounted for in numerous other studies of deviance.

Table 2
Regression of drug use on general theory variables, peer relationships, and social support.

Independent variables	b	SE	B
General theory variables:			
Perceived risk of punishment (CAUGHTP)	.10	.04	.08*
Parental supervision (DADSUP)	–.11	.04	–.14*
Parental attachment (IDDAD)	.07	.04	.09*
Attachment to teachers (CARTCH)	–.05	.07	–.03
Academic effort (TRYHARD)	.14	.05	.12*
Evaluation of academics (INTELL)	–.02	.05	–.02
School performance (GRADES)	.07	.03	.11*
Time spent on homework (HOMEWK)	–.06	.05	–.06
Educational expectations (SCHEXP)	.02	.04	.02
Variables excluded by the general theory:			
Peer delinquency (POLFR)	.69	.10	.27*
Attachment to peers (FRSHAR)	.15	.05	.10*
Social support index (SUPPORT)	.01	.01	.01

Constant = 1.57, R^2 = .21
*$p < .05$

If we consider the amount of variance accounted for by only the general theory variables (R^2 = .13), we can tentatively conclude – contrary to our prediction – that the explanatory power of this new theoretical integration seems relatively modest.

Summary

In this paper, we have discussed the theoretical integration of classical theory and the self-control conceptualization in Gottfredson and Hirschi's (1990) general theory of crime. We have attempted to show that logically interrelated propositions of the constituent theories have been combined into a larger single set of interrelated principles. For example, both classical theory and the self-control conceptualization assume that human nature is self-seeking, with individuals striving to maximize pleasure and minimize pain. Both classical theory and the self-control conceptualization assume that individuals will refrain from crime and deviance only if they are constrained from such behavior. Both classical theory and the self-control conceptualization assume that there is a constant motivation to deviate; unlike learning theory, no provision of a motive to deviate is necessary. Both classical theory and the self-control conceptualization are compatible with a free will or choice perspective on crime and deviance; neither of the constituent theories is deterministic.

A key omission in classical theory, according to Gottfredson and Hirschi, is its inability to predict individual variation in capacity to resist temptation regardless of perceived risk of punishment. To overcome this limitation of classical theory, Gottfredson and Hirschi add the concept of self-control to produce a theory that includes external and internal restraints on behavior.

In our analysis we find that, indeed, both measures of self-control and external restraints (based on classical theory) must be included to account for variation in drug use. These measures based on Gottfredson and Hirschi's general theory of crime remain significantly correlated with drug use controlling for factors such as peer delinquency, peer attachment, and an index of social support that incorporates measures of religious participation. Consistent with prior research, we find that peer delinquency has the strongest effect on drug use of any single variable considered in this study.

In reference to theoretical integration, Liska *et al.* (1989: 18-19) argue that theoretical growth and development should be evaluated partly in terms of the logical coherence of ideas and in terms of inspiration of further research. Theoretical integrations may help overcome the perceived state of exhaustion in tests of traditional theories. Gottfredson and Hirschi have created a logically consistent integration of classical theory and the self-control concept that should inspire new theorizing and empirical research for years to come.

Nevertheless, Liska *et al.* (1989) observe that theoretical growth and development has often been evaluated primarily in terms of increasing empirical support. If we assess Gottfredson and Hirschi's general theory of crime on the basis of its ability to account for variation in drug use, then this analysis yields only moderate support for the theory. We find the level of variance accounted for by general theory measures to be comparable to or somewhat below levels of variance accounted for by existing theories of crime and deviance.

Some omissions of the current study should be explicitly acknowledged. These omissions may in part account for the modest level of explained variance in this study. First, there are no measures of the time orientation of individuals in the data set analyzed. Time orientation, or the ability to defer gratification, is a key aspect of the concept of self-control. Second, no measures of opportunity (Gottfredson and Hirschi 1990: 220) were included in this data set. For example, indicators of the actual availability of drugs (cf. Bachman, Johnston, and O'Malley 1990, who assess perceived availability of drugs) may be essential to provide a more complete test of the general theory of crime.

Finally, we have focused only on adolescent drug use in this paper. Future tests of Gottfredson and Hirschi's general theory should analyze a wide range of criminal and deviant acts.

Appendix

Variable names and description of variables

Perceived risk of punishment:

CAUGHTP. "People who break the law are almost always caught and punished". Strongly agree = 1, agree = 2, undecided = 3, disagree = 4, strongly disagree = 5.

Parental supervision:

DADSUP. "As far as my father is concerned, I'm pretty much free to come and go as I please". Strongly agree = 1, agree = 2, undecided = 3, disagree = 4, strongly disagree = 5.

Parental attachment:

IDDAD. "Would you like to be the kind of person your father is?" In every way = 1, in most ways = 2, in some ways = 3, in just a few ways = 4, not all = 5.

Attachment to teachers:

CARTCH. "Do you care what teachers think of you?" Care a lot = 1, care some = 2, don't care much = 3.

Academic effort:

TRYHARD. "I try hard in school". Strongly agree = 1, agree = 2, undecided = 3, disagree = 4, strongly disagree = 5.

Evaluation of academics:

INTELL. "Such things as books, school, and education don't interest me very much". Strongly agree = 1, agree = 2, undecided = 3, disagree = 4, strongly disagree = 5.

School performance:

GRADES. "Putting them all together, how would your grades average out?" A = 1, A– = 2, B+ = 3, B = 4, B– = 5, C+ = 6, C = 7, C– = 8, D or below = 9.

Time spent on homework:

HOMEWK. "How many hours per week do you spend doing homework?" 0 hours = 1, 1-3 hours = 2, 4-6 hours = 3, 7-10 hours = 4, 11-14 hours = 5, 15 or more hours = 6.

Educational expectations:

EDEXP. "How much schooling do you actually expect to get eventually?" Some high school = 1, high school graduation = 2, on the job apprenticeship = 3, trade or vocational school = 4, some college or junior college = 5, college graduation = 6.

Peer delinquency:

POLFR. "How many of your best friends have been picked up by the police?" None = 0, one or more = 1.

Attachment to peers:

FRSHAR. "Do you share your thoughts and feelings with your best friend?" Never = 1, sometimes = 2, often = 3.

Social support index:

SUPPORT. High = 1, low = 2.

Notes

1. Although compatible in several respects, social control theory and rational choice theory remain distinctive explanations that have not been integrated. For example, Hirschi (1986) observes that a key difference between the two theories is that rational choice theory tends to focus on the explanation of specific acts of crime or deviance while social control theory tends to assume that all such acts are manifestations of the single underlying trait of the absence of restraint.

References

Akers, Ronald
1991 Self-control as a general theory of crime. Journal of Quantitative Criminology 7: 201-211.

Bachman, Jerald, Lloyd Johnston, and Patrick O'Malley
1990 Explaining the recent decline in cocaine use among young adults. Journal of Health and Social Behavior 31: 173-184.

Bailey, Susan and Robert Hubbard
1990 Developmental variation in the context of marijuana initiation among adolescents. Journal of Health and Social Behavior 31: 58-70.

Brownfield, David and Ann Marie Sorenson
1991 Religion and drug use among adolescents. Deviant Behavior 12: 259-276.

Burkett, Steven and Bruce Warren
1987 Religiosity, peer associations, and adolescent marijuana use. Criminology 25: 109-131.

Caplan, Aaron and Marc LeBlanc
1985 A cross-cultural verification of a social control theory. International Journal of Comparative and Applied Criminal Justice 9: 123-138.

D'Antonio, William, William Newman, and Stuart Wright
1982 Religion and family life: How social scientists view the relationship. Journal for the Scientific Study of Religion 21: 218-225.

Elliott, Delbert, David Huizinga, and Suzanne Ageton
1985 Explaining Delinquency and Drug Use. Beverly Hills: Sage.

Gottfredson, Michael and Travis Hirschi
1990 A General Theory of Crime. Stanford: Stanford University Press.

Grasmick, Harold, Charles Tittle, Robert Bursik, Jr., and Bruce Arneklev
1993 Testing the core empirical implications of Gottfredson and Hirschi's general theory of crime. Journal of Research in Crime and Delinquency 30: 5-29.

Hagan, John
1989 Structural Criminology. New Brunswick, NJ: Rutgers University Press.

Higgins, Paul and Gary Albrecht
1977 Hellfire and delinquency revisited. Social Forces 55: 952-958.

Hindelang, Michael, Travis Hirschi, and Joseph Weis
1981 Measuring Delinquency. Beverly Hills: Sage.

Hirschi, Travis
1969 Causes of Delinquency. Berkeley: University of California Press.

Hirschi, Travis
1979 Separate and unequal is better. Journal of Research in Crime and Delinquency 10: 34-38.

Hirschi, Travis
1986 On the compatibility of rational choice and social control theories of crime. In Derek Cornish and Ronald Clarke (eds.), The Reasoning Criminal. New York: Springer-Verlag.

Hirschi, Travis
1989 Exploring alternatives to integrated theory. In Steven Messner, Marvin Krohn, and Allen Liska (eds.), Theoretical Integration in the Study of Deviance and Crime. Albany: SUNY Press.

Jackson, Margaret and Curt Griffiths
1991 Canadian Criminology. Toronto: Harcourt, Brace, Jovanovich.

Jensen, Gary, Maynard Erickson, and Jack Gibbs
1978 Perceived risk of punishment and self-reported delinquency. Social Forces 57: 57-78.

Keane, Carl, Paul Maxim, and James Teevan
1993 Drinking and driving, self-control, and gender: Testing a general theory of crime. Journal of Research in Crime and Delinquency 30: 30-46.

Klepper, Steven and Daniel Nagin
1989 The deterrent effect of perceived certainty and severity of punishment revisited. Criminology 27: 721-746.

Linden, Rick and Cathy Fillmore
1981 A comparative study of delinquency involvement. Canadian Review of Sociology and Anthropology 18: 343-361.

Linden, Eric and James Hackler
1973 Affective ties and delinquency. Pacific Sociological Review 16: 27-46.

Liska, Allen, Marvin Krohn, and Steven Messner
1989 Strategies and requisites for theoretical integration in the study of crime and deviance. In Steven Messner, Marvin Krohn, and Allen Liska (eds.), Theoretical Integration in the Study of Deviance and Crime. Albany: SUNY Press.

Marcos, Anastasios, Stephen Bahr, and Richard Johnson
1986 Test of a bonding association theory of adolescent drug use. Social Forccs 65: 135-161.

Massey, James and Marvin Krohn
1986 A longitudinal examination of an integrated social process model of deviant behavior. Social Forces 65: 106-134.

Nettler, Gwynn
1984 Explaining Crime. New York: McGraw-Hill.

Patterson, Gerald and Thomas Dishion
1985 Contributions of families and peers to delinquency. Criminology 23: 63-79.

Reckless, Walter
1967 The Crime Problem. New York: Appleton-Century-Crofts.

Reiss, Albert
1951 Delinquency as the failure of personal and social controls. American Sociological Review 16: 196-207.

Roshier, Bob
1989 Controlling Crime: The Classical Perspective in Criminology. Chicago: Lyceum.

Sorenson, Ann Marie and David Brownfield
1989 Patterns of adolescent drug use. Social Science Research 18: 271-290.

Thornberry, Terence
1989 Reflections on the advantages and disadvantages of theoretical integration. In Steven Messner, Marvin Krohn, and Allen Liska (eds.), Theoretical Integration in the Study of Deviance and Crime. Albany: SUNY Press.

White, Helene, Robert Pandina, and Randy LaGrange
1987 Longitudinal predictors of serious substance use and delinquency. Criminology 25: 715-740.

CHAPTER FIFTEEN

Justice for Canadian girls: A 1990's update

Marge Reitsma-Street[1]
Human and Social Development
University of Victoria
Victoria, B.C.

IN ITS MAY 1998 *STRATEGY FOR THE RENEWAL OF YOUTH JUSTICE*, the Canadian Department of Justice outlines crime prevention initiatives and the need for a new youth justice statute to replace the 1984 *Young Offenders Act*. But the Department of Justice is concerned about the lack of information on girls. On one hand, only 20 percent of all youth apprehended by the police are girls and yet, on the other hand, there seems to be an increase in the number of females charged, especially for personal injury offences. The Department concludes that there is a "clear need for more research in this area, so that appropriate programs for these young women can be developed" (1998: 8).

To help frame directions for research on girls, this article examines six critical issues. Each of the issues explores a contradiction that is problematic or that reveals a gap in practice. Smith (1987) calls these types of contradictions disjunctures and recommends looking for evidence, experiences, and perceptions to uncover them. By examining issues in which these types of contradictions are situated, it is hoped that taken-for-granted policies and practices are questioned. The questioning can prompt new research directions, previously unseen or unthinkable (Ristock and Pennell 1996).

Canadian Journal of Criminology/Revue canadienne de criminologie, July/juillet 1999, pp. 335–363.

It is also hoped that an examination of critical issues on girls in conflict with the law will encourage an interest in conducting a gender-based analysis of the proposed new youth justice statute for Canadian youth (Department of Justice Canada 1998). A gender-based analysis (Status of Women Canada 1996) would examine how the assumptions, procedures, and impact of a policy or proposed statute has used, or has not used research on the experiences and circumstances of girls, and how a policy or proposal could reflect a more equitable and just approach for girls. An examination of the following six critical issues demonstrates that the lives of girls have not been satisfactorily addressed in Canadian youth justice policy or practice. The research questions raised by each issue could assist in a gender-analysis of the proposed new youth justice statute and associated prevention initiatives.

The six issues are: (1) continuing inequities despite equality under the law; (2) the prosocial behaviours of girls despite their devalued status; (3) the conformity of girls despite the high socio-economic costs they pay for that conformity; (4) the high public fear of girl crime despite actual low rates; (5) the unjust variations in practice despite a national law; and (6) the profound, but invisible racism in justice for girls. The first three of the issues are examined in more detail, with illustrations drawn from published studies and an analysis of Canadian juvenile and youth court statistics.[2] The last three critical issues are emerging ones, and await further exploration.

Neither benign nor just

The first critical issue may be familiar, with a new variation. Research in the 1960's and 1970's found that juvenile justice laws, policies, and interventions for the most part were based on the experiences of boys. This minimalist approach was neither just, chivalrous, nor benign to girls. Under the old 1908 *Juvenile Delinquents Act*, few girls were charged, and those who were received a caution or a referral to community agencies.

Far more girls than boys were charged for offenses of sexual immorality, truancy, running away, or disobeying parents (Brenzel 1983; Parent 1986; Reitsma-Street 1993; West 1984). Those girls perceived by police and judges as not "respectable" or not tied to a parental or marital home faced longer and more restrictive judicial sanctions than boys convicted of similar offenses. Fewer than 40% of girls in Canadian correctional institutions, for example, were admitted for serious delinquencies. Girls often endured long stays, repeated gynaecological investigations, threats of abuse, and minimal training except in sex-typed, low paying work such as hairdressing, sewing, and housecleaning.

This gap between the pursuit of justice and problems of practice prompted thinking about the limits of paternalism and the need to change Canadian youth justice laws and practices. In the late 1970's, changes occurred: provinces repealed truancy laws, closed training school beds, and started legal services for youth (Leschied, Jaffe, and Willis 1991; Reitsma-Street 1989-1990; West 1984). The 1984 *Young Offenders Act* replaced the 1908 *Juvenile Delinquents Act.* Status offenses were decriminalized; indeterminate sentences for the broad offence of being in the state of juvenile delinquency were transformed into determinate ones for specific offences. Youth gained rights to lawyers and new community dispositions were legalized (Bala 1992).

Despite the improvements, however, injustices are resurfacing in new forms. For example, there is one pattern of charges that brings an increasing number of girls into the justice system, as shown in Table 1. One reason for the rise in the numbers (in Table 1) is that Ontario did not report its statistics to the federal agency until 1992. The apparent increase in violence among girls as an explanation for the rise in total charges is addressed later in the article. Another reason for the increase is that there are more girls in the Canadian population. Also, the maximum age under the jurisdiction of the youth courts changed from 16 before the *Young Offenders Act (YOA)* to 18 years after its introduction.

The increase in population and older age maximum, however, cannot adequately explain the increase as several populous provinces were charging 16- and 17-year-old girls (and sometimes boys) before the *YOA* made this 18-year maximum age limit mandatory across Canada in 1985, and the youth population has not increased dramatically in the past decade.

Table 1
Girls in Canadian youth courts for failure to comply and total charges, 1985-1996

Year	Failure to comply charges,[1] in all provinces except Ontario	Total charges	% of total charges
1985-86	549	9,072	6.1%
1986-87	1,316	10,791	12.2%
1987-88	2,395	11,459	20.9%
1988-89	2,333	11,615	20.1%
1989-90	2,866	13,361	21.5%
1990-91	3,491	14,619	23.9%
Year	**Failure to comply cases,[1] in all provinces including Ontario**	**Total cases**	**% of total cases**
1992-93	4,968	17,927	24.0%
1993-94	5,589	19,258	25.5%
1994-95	5,630	19,353	27.9%
1995-96	5,985	17,573	27.3%

Source: Canadian Centre for Justice Statistics (1987; 1989a; 1989b; 1989c; 1990; 1991; 1993; 1995; 1996; 1997) *Youth Court Statistics*.

1. Includes escape custody, failure to appear in court, 'Against the YOA' charges which include failure to comply with a disposition, failure to comply with an undertaking, and contempt against youth court.

There is another reason for the increase, and it is one that raises concerns about justice for girls. There is a striking increase in the number and rates of charges of failure to comply with judicial orders, from 6.1% of total charges against girls in 1985-86 to 27.3% of the total female cases in 1995-96. (Data on boys are available but not shown: 3.9% of their total charges are for failure to comply offences in 1985-86, increasing to 21.6% of the cases in 1995-96.) It appears the old status offences have been replaced by new 'status-like' failure to comply offences. Included in these non-compliance offences are the infrequent 'escape custody,' 'breach of recognizance', and 'failure to comply with an undertaking', and the more frequent 'failure to appear in court' and 'failure to comply with a disposition'.(3) The number of the girls charged with escaping custody or breaches of recognizance has remained low over the past decade. But the number charged under Section 26, 'the failure to comply with a disposition' is not low, and has increased over time. Section 26 was a new offence passed in a 1995 amendment to the *YOA*. Section 26 reads:

> A person who is subject to a disposition made... and who wilfully fails or refuses to comply with that order is guilty of an offense punishable on summary conviction.

Case law has upheld appeals of the use of Section 26 (Harris 1998). Appeals have been successful when the forms were not correctly completed or the parents and youth were not properly notified of the conditions. Court dispositions can have lawful enforceable conditions such as curfews, requirement to reside with parents and not associate with certain friends if the youth has signed the required forms indicating the conditions have been explained and the youth has accepted them. Parents can be involved in carrying out the sentence, and in initiating a breach. The *YOA* was amended again in 1995 (c. 19, Bill C-37) to give authorities even more discretion in responding to failure to comply offenses. Since then, either open or secure custody can be considered for any breach of a court's disposition, including Section 25.

Conway (1992) found that contrary to expectations, girls had been sentenced to custody if found guilty of failure to comply offences. Gagnon and Doherty (1993) found that *more* Canadian youth who had been found guilty of these non-compliance offences were sentenced to custody, than those found guilty of a violent offense: 47% compared to 38% in 1991-1992. This pattern of charging more Canadian youth for failure to comply with judicial orders is costly to the youth, to the family, and to the courts and society. When a girl is locked up for committing such an offence, the costs become more expensive in every way.

This pattern of charging more Canadian youth, especially girls, with the new 'status-like' non-compliance offences and the trend to locking girls up for these offences mirrors the American pattern. In the United States, amendments to the *American Juvenile Justice and Delinquency Prevention Act* in 1974 permitted judges to reclassify status offenders as delinquent if they violate a court order (Chesney-Lind and Sheldon 1998). Chesney-Lind (forthcoming) reports that in various states more girls than boys were cited for contempt violations; if convicted of contempt, they quadruple their chances of facing incarceration, and are more likely to face a custodial sentence than boys convicted of similar charges. Other researchers report an increase in "voluntary" referrals of delinquent girls to private facilities for rehabilitation (Shichor and Bartollas 1990).

As a new justice statute for Canadian youth is being considered, it is necessary to examine the possibly unintended, seemingly unjust consequences of the *YOA*, such as the heavy use of these new 'status offences' for over one-fourth of the charges heard in youth court against girls and one-fifth of those against boys. If the proposed new statute aims to reduce the use of custody for non-violent offenders and to increase cultural and gender-sensitive prevention and diversion services (Department of Justice 1998: 21), one place to begin is creating alternatives to the high use of these failure to comply types of charges.

Devalued, but still prosocial

The second critical issue is also familiar. Most approaches to explaining delinquency and to designing interventions have been developed by males about boys. One could ask why this male-centred scholarship developed and what are the consequences of making girls invisible. A most important concern now facing researchers and policy-makers, however, is that they are going into the 21st century with theories that do not adequately help explain the empirical and experiential data on girls.

Delinquency theories on youth predict that those most alienated, marginalized, and devalued by adults and societal institutions would be the most delinquent. Despite the gains of the women's movement, girls remain more marginalized and devalued than boys (Bourn, McCoy, and Smith 1998; Brown and Gilligan 1992; Holmes and Silverman 1992; Jiwani 1998; Lees 1997). The girls, therefore, should be more delinquent than boys. The reverse is true as Figure 1 clearly shows. In the early 1980's, only one in ten of charges laid in youth court was against a girl. Despite the increase in the total number of charges against girls since then, over 80% of charges laid in youth court in 1995-96 are against boys. If self-report studies are examined, it is not uncommon for girls to say they engaged in some antisocial behaviour in the last year. Girls and boys report relatively similar participation in shoplifting, using drugs, and leaving home without permission, but girls self-report far less serious or violent misbehaviour than do boys (Chesney-Lind and Sheldon 1998; Hagan, McCarthy, with Parker and Climenhage 1997; Reitsma-Street 1991).

Table 2 sets out a comparison of the *Criminal Code* charges brought against girls in Canadian youth courts in 1980 versus 1995/96. Although the overall number of charges laid has increased, the absolute numbers for *serious* charges like murder, arson, break and enter, fraud, robbery, major theft, and trafficking or possession of drugs are low and have remained constant. For example, in 1980, 1,152 break and enter charges were laid against girls under the old *Juvenile Delinquents Act* with its lower maximum age, while 1,087 charges for break and enter were laid against girls in youth courts in 1995/96 when the higher maximum age applied. There are notable increases however, in less serious charges.

Figure 1
Comparison of sex ratio of charges before Canadian youth court

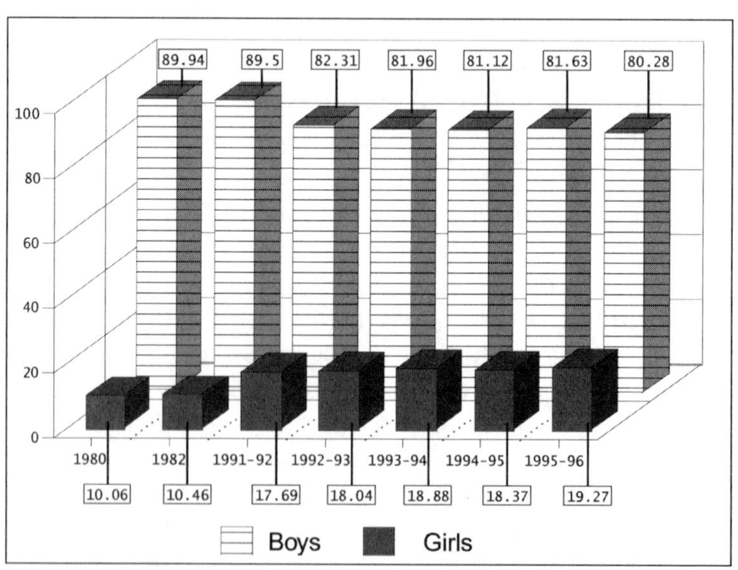

Sources: Canadian Centre for Justice Statistics (1981; 1983) Juvenile Delinquents. Canadian Centre for Justice Statistics (1992; 1993; 1995; 1996; 1997) *Youth Court Statistics.*

Petty theft charges doubled in the past 15 years while failure to comply offences increased by over 1,000%. Offences against the person have also increased dramatically, but for minor or moderate assault, not for the serious offences. Doob and Sprott (1998) also found very few Canadian girls were charged with violent crimes in the last five years: less than 300 girls per 100,000 population of Canadian girls between 12 and 18 years of age have been charged with minor assaults; less than 60 per 100,000 for assault with a weapon or causing bodily harm; and under 4 in 100,000 girls for aggravated assaults. In brief, in 1980, and 15 years later in 1995-96, four-fifths of the most significant charges heard in youth courts against girls are for property offences or offences of non-compliance.

Making visible the anomalous discrepancy between the theoretically expected delinquency rates and the observed

Table 2
Comparison of charges against girls in youth court for Criminal Code and federal statute offences in 1980 and 1995-96.

Most significant charge	1980 charges under the JDA (ages 7 to 15)[1]		1995-96 cases under YOA (ages 12 to 18)	
	N	%	N	%
Murder; attempt	9	.11	6	.03
Robbery	89	1.12	369	1.69
Arson	42	.53	53	.24
Against person[2]	710	8.97	4,434	20.25
Theft over/auto	504	6.36	525	2.40
Break & enter	1,152	14.55	1,087	4.96
Fraud	457	5.84	559	2.55
Theft under/ stolen goods	3,411	43.01	6,820	31.15
Trafficking/possession	265	3.35	573	2.62
Mischief	446	5.63	662	3.02
Nuisance/disorderly	240	3.03	171	.78
Immorality/vice/ soliciting	98	1.24	198	.90
Failure to comply[3]	450	5.68	5,985	27.33
Other/unknown	46	.58	456	2.08
Total	7,919	100.00	21,898	100.00

Sources: Canadian Centre for Justice Statistics. Special unpublished Table 12 "Nature of delinquency by sex and age of accused" for 1980 and Canadian Centre for Justice Statistics (1997) *Youth Court Statistics*, Table 3.

1. Sixteen and 17-year-old girls included in statistics from Manitoba and Québec.
2. Against person includes major assaults per year, minor assaults, intent to use weapons, possession of weapon, kidnapping, and impaired driving. In 1980, there were fewer than 25 major assaults (.32% of total charges), while in 1995/96, 693 (or 3.16%) of the cases involved aggravated assault or assault with a weapon.
3. Includes charges of escape custody, failure to comply with a disposition or to appear, and against the YOA.

prosocial behaviours has prompted a search to explain it. One new theoretical direction is to build sophisticated models of prediction, such as the gendered general strain theory of Broidy and Agnew (1997). The other theoretical direction that I draw on for this article does not compare girls to boys. It concentrates only on girls, preferring to understand and to see patterns in the barely visible worlds of girls, using quantitative and qualitative data (Reinharz 1992; Lees 1997).

Trying to understand the anomaly of the primarily prosocial behaviour of girls despite their devalued status, researchers have revealed the strong similarities in the everyday lives of girls, whether they are officially categorized as normal, at risk, delinquent, abused, drug abusers, anorexic, or as unwed teen mothers (Bowker and Klein 1983; Cain 1989; Comack 1996; Rains 1971). In an Ontario study of 26 delinquent and non-delinquent sisters close in age, Reitsma-Street and Offord (1991) found that the sisters learned that females, no matter what abuse or indifference they have encountered, had to learn to be nice, to look feminine, and to care for others, especially a boyfriend. These lessons in caring far outweighed their differences in delinquencies, temperament, school experiences, or aspirations. For example, one delinquent girl had loved fighting, but by late adolescence she had learned "from mom to hold it all in, and to cry like her." (p.16) Another had finished her time in training school, and learned "that if I stay at home, be good, all will be okay." (p. 16)

In a 1998 review of research on delinquent and non-delinquent girls, Reitsma-Street (1998) reaffirmed the finding that learning to look good, to be nice, and to perform caring labour, especially for boyfriends, fathers, or brothers were the strongest constants in the lives of girls. Whether in Ontario and British cities, whether in New York or Parisian gangs researchers found girls still feel they need to avoid being seen as a "slag" (Lees 1997: 19) so they could attract a boy as "boys are girls' destiny because boys are girls' livelihood" (Cain 1989: 9; Campbell 1984; Kostash 1987; Lagrée and Lew Fai 1989). In the 1990's, there is an additional pressure faced by girls, delinquent or not: girls now feel that they should want to find a job, earn money, and contribute to the family income, and still continue to look good, be nice, and do nurturing work (Baker 1985, Brown and Gilligan 1992, Holmes and Silverman 1992; Lees 1997; Sharpe 1994).

In brief, when researchers examine the lower delinquency rates of girls, they are challenged to explain why girls seem so prosocial, despite their devalued status. By seeking to understand the discrepancies between delinquency theories and the data from everyday life, researchers and policy-makers may create promising initiatives that build on the strong similarities in the daily lives of girls, delinquent or not, such as their interest in relationships, prosocial capacities and resilience (Artz and Riecken 1997; Duffy 1994; Henggeler and Borduin 1995; Leadbeater, Ross, and Way 1996; Peters and Russell 1996; Varpalotai 1996).

Not just socialized, but policed to care

As the third critical issue in the research on girls may be less familiar, this section is more developed. The problem to examine is why it is that, despite the high costs, hard work, personal sacrifices, and modest rewards associated with becoming a good girl, girls continue in their pursuit of this constrictive goodness occasionally using delinquent or violent means if necessary. Girls appear quite timid in their resistance and exploration of alternative paths to development. Two decades ago, McRobbie and McCabe (1981: 4) summed up the costs paid by British girls, some of whom were officially delinquent: "Growing up for girls is little more than preparation for growing old prematurely". In 1998, Reitsma-Street (1998: 97) concludes a review of Canadian girls:

> The costs of economic vulnerability and long working days for females of all backgrounds and races are rooted in a key conundrum. By caring for others more than for self in their early years, girls risk not being able to care for themselves or those they love in later years.

The constrictive goodness and high costs borne by girls are not inevitable. Nor is the prosocial behaviours the obvious outcomes of socialization by family, school, and peers. There is some research on the active struggles to regulate girls and to reinforce their nurturing behaviours (Bourne *et al.* 1998;

Brown and Gilligan 1992; Lees 1997; McRobbie 1991; Vanstone 1996). There is also interest in examining how girls attempt to resist this regulation and the stereotypes of what is expected of a girl (Leadbeater *et al.* 1996; Reitsma-Street 1998). If the proposed new youth justice statute in Canada is serious about encouraging community prevention, then the following aspects of policing need to be considered to make the ventures helpful to girls.

Donzelot (1979) speaks of policing as the "techniques of regulation." Policing means enforcing what is expected by those with the power to determine what is expected. If the expected behaviours, attitudes, and words of a good girl are not forthcoming, those who do the expecting monitor and punish the infractions. Shunning and slandering are the everyday policing acts that we all have the power to use to punish differences in delinquent or non-delinquent girls (Lees 1997). Words that destroy reputations include slag, fat, slut, dumb. In the 1990's, the adjectives of poor, lazy, and on welfare are also now used to slander and shame a girl (Adler and Baines 1996; Kostash 1987; McRobbie 1991). The worst name to call a boy is a girl or a bitch, an indication of how devalued girls are as a gender, and how fierce is the daily work of policing reputations. Advertisements, the teen magazines, the self-help columns, and popular music instruct girls to make themselves beautiful, desirable, and loving to males (McRobbie 1991; Wolf 1990). Alternative approaches to time management, body shape, sexuality, opinions, and dreams are silenced or sent underground (Bourne *et al.* 1998; Brown and Gilligan 1992). To avoid the names and the costs, a girl is pressured to become a loner or to keep a steady relationship with one boy. If perceived by others as nonconforming, a girl can risk losing her reputation, access to friends, excitement, legitimate sex, a boyfriend, and eventually a home and legitimate children.

The infliction of intermittent, but not infrequent violence is another way to keep girls in line. Most girls know the person who attacks them. This effective and inexpensive form of policing is carried out mostly by males through acts of incest and date rape, threats and physical assault, limiting movements and access to money, and refusal to wear a condom or to use clean needles (Jiwani 1998; Johnson and Sacco 1995; Galt 1997). Sometimes girls use physical violence themselves to defend themselves and their reputation, or to protect those they love (Appleby 1994; Artz 1998; Comack 1996). More often, girls restrict their daily behaviours, friendships, and future dreams in the hope of minimizing the risk of physical, emotional, sexual, and financial assault from those they most care about: family members and especially boyfriends (Brown and Gilligan 1992; Kostash 1987; Lees 1997; Sharpe 1994).

Besides the private daily judging and the intermittent violence that polices girls to continue bearing the costs of being good girls, there are public forms of policing. Social and justice policies regulate the arenas in which delinquent and non-delinquent girls can develop, especially if they live in poor families or are from a visible minority. Unemployment and poverty among youth are increasing in Canada at the same time as the entitlements of youth to public assistance, social services, higher education, and good jobs are being reduced, especially for girls (Evans and Wekerle 1998; Gadd 1998; National Council of Welfare 1997; Statistics Canada 1998). Independent living arrangements for youth under 18 years of age are very limited unless they can find a good job or a benefactor. The eligibility to social assistance has been severely curtailed in most provinces in the 1990's for girls under 18 years of age, and of "employable" young women over 18 years. The work of raising children, still mostly done by women, has been devalued further in the 1990's. For example, in the five most populous provinces, a parent, usually a young woman, is now considered employable when applying for welfare if her youngest child is older than six months in Alberta, or 3 years in Ontario, or 7 years in British Columbia. Two years ago young women in these provinces did not have to seek paid work to remain eligible for welfare until their youngest child was 18 years old or out of school (Freiler and Cerny 1998: 67).

If a girl does not live in a family with adequate income; if she does not abide by the rules of her family; if she does not find a good job; or if she does not attach herself to a person who has adequate regular income, she then risks losing even those few options open to "good" girls. She may face the terrors and crimes of the street or the systematic invasion of privacy by the public authorities and neighbours (Lundy and Totten 1997; Hagan *et al.* 1997). The policing that comes with public surveillance of poor people has intensified in the 1990's with, for example, Ontario's welfare snitch lines and penalties of $15,000 or six months in prison for persons who "knowingly aid or abet another person" to obtain assistance prohibited by the Ontario Works Act (Statutes of Ontario, 1997, Sec. 59). To remain eligible for social assistance or social housing in all provinces, girls must submit to an exhaustive investigation of their financial and social relationships and an array of obligatory programs that pushes them from welfare into the low wage world of work.

The final strategy used to regulate the prosocial behaviours of girls despite costs is the youth justice system. On one hand, alternative measures and special services for youth are encouraged in the *YOA* and community dispositions of probation and service remain the most common sentences for Canadian girls for the past 25 years, as presented in Table 3. On the other hand, alternative measures are not mandatory in the law, and the least intrusive types of sentence after a finding of guilt has steadily decreased over the years. Contrary to the intent of the *YOA,* the use of minimal sanctions went down for girls, while the use of custody increased. In 1982, 32.4% of all dispositions for girls were minimal, including for example suspended sentences. By 1995/96, the rate of minimal sanctions such as the absolute discharge plunged to 4.2 % of total dispositions.

So too has the use of custody increased since 1962. The data in Table 3 summarizes research on girls up to age 19 before and after the introduction of the *YOA*. Custody as a percent of all dispositions for girls (ages 16 to 19 years old) was 17.4% in 1962 dipping to a low of 7.8% of girls 12 to 17 years old in 1982, as provinces anticipated the changes to the justice

Table 3
25-year comparison of most serious disposition for principal charge against girls in Canadian youth courts (Figures in percentages)

Disposition	1962	1972	1982	1992-93	1995-96
Custody	17.4	12.3	7.8	18.9	23.4
Probation	45.2	33.7	27.9	45.8	55.8
Fine or restitution	15.3	39.3	25.6	6.8	5.4
Community service order	0.0	0.0	0.0	16.7	9.1
Minimal sanction (e.g. suspended sentence, absolute discharge)	17.7	13.0	32.4	6.6	4.2
Other/unknown	4.0	1.7	7.3	5.2	2.1
Total	100.0	100.0	100.0	100.0	100.0

Sources: 1962 population is 645 16 to 19 year old girls and 1972 population is 1,733 16- to 19-year-old girls (Biron and Gauvreau 1984: 94); 1982 population is 6,150 girls age 12 to 17 found guilty in Canadian youth courts by most significant decision (Reitmsa-Street 1993: 447); 1992-93 populations 12,628 female cases (ages 12 to 17) found guilty in Canadian youth courts by most significant decision (Canadian Centre for Justice Statistics 1993; *Youth Court Statistics, 1992-93*, Table 5); 1995-96 population is 13,229 female cases age 12 to 17 found guilty (Canadian Centre for Justice Statistics 1997; *Youth Court Statistics, 1995-96*, Table 5).

system. Custody rates climbed back up to 23.4% by 1995-96 for 12- to 17-year-old girls. In the early years after the *YOA* was introduced, custody dispositions had not increased in length (Doob 1992). Sentence length, however, and the number of girls in custody at any time are expected to increase as the *YOA* has been amended several times to permit longer sentences; as of 1995 the maximum is 10 years for murder. Custodial dispositions and the number of girls in custody are expected to increase even more, if the recommendations that adult sentences *must* be considered by youth courts for youth 14 years and older for serious violent personal crimes is adopted in the proposed youth justice statute (Department of Justice 1998: 25).

As Canadians debate the direction of the proposed new youth justice statute, the impact of the heavy private and public policing strategies used to regulate girls needs close examination. Making girls pay such high costs to remain "good" is not the only option open to policy-makers or practitioners. Developing alternatives that promote the prosocial behaviours of girls with fewer socio-economic costs to all is timely.

Emerging critical issues

In brief, directions for research on girls and alternative justice policies are suggested by examining the contradictions in three issues: discriminatory practices despite equality under the law; the infrequent delinquent behaviours of girls despite their devalued status; and the conformity of girls despite the high costs they pay for that conformity in terms of socio-economic status and security. The information presented to illustrate the contradictions suggests that justice for Canadian girls in the 1990's remains elusive.

There are other contradictions that need research and policy attention as we debate a proposed new youth justice statute in 1999. This section raises three emerging ones about which our current understanding is but a beginning: the gap between the actual low rate of girl crime and the disproportionately high public fear that girls are out of control; the unjust variations in practice despite a common federal *YOA*; and the profound, but nearly invisible racism in justice for girls.

Low actual rates but high public fear of violence. In the 1998 *Strategy for the Renewal of Youth Justice,* the federal government expressed its concern about the increase in personal injury offences committed by girls and their participation in violent, gang-related activities such as the repeated beatings and murder of Reena Virk by seven 'violent' girls and one boy (Department of Justice 1998: 8; News Group Report on Youth Violence 1997). The facts do not support these concerns. In the previous discussion of Table 2 and in the research of Doob and Sprott (1998), it is clear that the increase in personal injury charges is not for serious violent crime. Table 4 proves conclusively that charges for murder and attempted murder by girls are infrequent and constant for the past 20 years.

Table 4
Number of murders, attempts, and manslaughter by Canadian girls

Charges under the JDA (ages 7 to 15 in all provinces; up to 18 in Québec & Manitoba)	
1978	10
1979	6
1980	9
1981	8
1982	5
1983	9
Cases under the Y0A (ages 12 to 18)	
1992-93	13
1993-94	9
1994-95	8
1995-96	6

Source: Canadian Centre for Justice Statistics. Special unpublished tables for 1978, 1979, 1980, 1981, 1982, 1983 "Nature of delinquency by sex and age of the accused" provided by the Centre. Canadian Centre for Justice Statistics (1993; 1995; 1996; 1997) *Youth Court Statistics*, Table 3.

One wonders then about the discrepancy between these "facts" and the public fear of violence in girls and the need to "go to war against youth crime" (Appleby 1994; Callahan and Callahan 1997; McIlroy 1998a). It is possible that the focus on the apparent increase in violence deflects attention away from other ills, such as a rise in poverty and despair among girls and the fragmented, inadequate public support for the educational, social, and economic development of girls (Evans and Wekerle 1998; Schissel 1997). A group of British researchers (Hall, Critcher, Jefferson, Clarke, and Roberts 1978) unravel how one horrible mugging by a group of black youth in Birmingham was turned into a national "mugging crisis." They traced how the problems of inner city poverty and racism in Britain were transformed into problems of mugging and youth gangs. This reframing of the problems of racism and poverty into that of youth violence then justified more public expenditures on police and longer custody sentences without additional entitlements to educational, employment, or social services.

To avoid emphasizing the violence of a few Canadian girls at the expense of ignoring broader problems affecting many girls, more understanding is needed to understand the discrepancy between fact and fear. Research is also urgently needed to test the innovative budget recommendations regarding prevention and community alternatives made by Parliament's all party Standing Committee on Justice and Legal Affairs in its report *Renewing Youth Justice* (1997). Would public fears of violence decrease and would the well-being of youth and society increase if Recommendations 4 and 6 of the Standing Committee were implemented? Recommendation 4 states that there should be a statutory allocation of between 1.5% and 5% of police, court, and correction budgets for prevention efforts, and Recommendation 6 states that 80% of federal-provincial justice costs should be allocated for non-custodial programs.

Practice variations despite common policy. This issue is not new. One of the reasons for changing the 1908 *Juvenile Delinquents Act* was the wide variations in provincial implementation (Reitsma-Street 1993). Girls up to age 18 in Manitoba and Quebec, and in Alberta before 1971 appeared in juvenile courts, while girls of the same age in other provinces appeared in adult courts and, if found guilty, were subjected to adult sentences. To minimize some of the geographical injustices, the *YOA* proclaimed a maximum upper age of 18 for all Canadian girls, as well as access to lawyers and to appeal procedures.

Despite the significant provisions in the *YOA* that promote equality before the law irrespective of where a girl lives in Canada, there remain troubling variations in youth justice practices (Carrington and Moyer, 1994). Doob and Sprott (1996) found considerable interprovincial variations in the numbers of youth brought to youth court and sentenced to custody, especially for minor offences. The variations could not be explained by provincial differences in youth behaviours.

Returning to the data on the new 'status-like' charges of failure to comply with judicial orders, it is clear that the numbers of girl cases brought to youth courts varies significantly by province as presented in Table 5. Quebec has nearly the same population of girls as does Ontario, and far more girls than do either Alberta or British Columbia. Yet, in each of the last five years, fewer than 100 girl cases were brought to Quebec courts for these non-compliance offences but over 2,000 were brought to Ontario courts.

Table 5
Provincial variation in number of female cases heard by youth courts for failure to comply charges

Year	Quebec	Ontario	Alberta	B.C.
1992-93	56	2,055	1,149	365
1993-94	66	2,357	1,280	418
1994-95	75	2,190	1,397	421
1995-96	90	2,398	1,268	496

Source: Canadian Centre for Justice Statistics (1993; 1995; 1996; 1997) *Youth Court Statistics.*

As the administration of youth justice is a provincial responsibility, and as the *YOA* and the proposed new statute are under federal jurisdiction, variations in policies and practices may be expected (Hackler 1991). Quebec has a clear policy of minimal judicial intervention towards youth that began well before implementation of the *YOA* (Trépanier 1986). If the proposals for a new youth justice statute are serious about "jailing fewer youths" (McIlroy 1998b; Department of Justice 1998), then examination of those approaches that keep girls out of the court system merit attention. What has Quebec learned about approaches and policies that help youth courts keep girls out of custody for minor property offences and non-compliance charges? It is not variety, flexibility, or innovation themselves that are problematic. Provincial and regional variations that are unjust, ineffective, or harmful need closer scrutiny, as do those variations that appear to best promote justice and the development of girls.

Profound, but nearly invisible systemic racism. This last critical issue is most problematic. Until recently, the race of those charged and convicted has been virtually invisible in Canada (Mosher 1996; Wortley 1996). We are just beginning to acknowledge that girls of all races are not treated equally in Canadian society and in the youth justice system. There is, and there has been since Confederation, a disproportionate number of First Nations girls and females of colour in the justice system (Chunn 1998, Bourne *et al.* 1998; Canadian Association of Elizabeth Fry Societies and Correction of Services Canada 1990; Leah 1995; LaPrairie 1995). That pervasive injustice exists in Canada and that systemic racism is reinforced by Canadian laws and judicial institutions are key findings in recent reports such as *Aboriginal Peoples and the Justice System (1993)* written for the Royal Commission on Aboriginal Peoples.

What is even more difficult to see is how white ideas of justice are themselves rooted in contradictory values, including on one hand impartial fairness to all, and on the other hand an oppressive notion that there is but one just approach to justice. The *YOA* is premised on the idea that to promote order and to minimize disorder, there must be universal standards of prosocial behaviour. If a youth misbehaves, she (or he) must acknowledge individual guilt and be coerced in a helpful way to behave in the future.

There are other ideas, experiences, histories, and values that are not premised on these white notions of uniform standards, individual guilt, and the necessity of punishment to enforce order. Restorative justice for instance, does not concentrate on individual guilt, accountability, protection of society, and the administration of a 'just' punishment. Rather, it seeks to restore harmony in the lives of the offenders, victims, and society at large through healing, teaching, respect, honesty, and resources for self-determination.

Understanding the lives of girls of colour, challenging the structural inequalities, resisting the stereotypes, and building a new Canadian youth justice statute that begins with a premise of restorative justice are not just challenges, but opportunities as we enter the 21st century (Leadbeater *et al.* 1996; Faith 1995; Ross 1992).

Concluding comments

Mohawk writer, mother, wife, and law professor Patricia Monture-OKanee said to the Royal Commission on Aboriginal Peoples that, until the contradictions of colonialism, racism, and sexism are uncovered and expressed, the oppression will continue, hurting youth of all races (1993: 118). Expressing the contradictions helps to challenge "the philosophies and beliefs of the mainstream" and is the only way that "meaningful and substantive long-term change can be secured." (1993: 110).

The challenge of proposing a strategy for renewal of youth justice in Canada (Department of Justice 1998) is to make it new. Starting with girls, and examining the alternative ideas that are freed when critical issues and contradictions are not ignored are steps towards meeting this challenge. Canadian national and local youth justice policies could take up the alternative possibilities prompted by facing the contradictions discussed above: the new forms of discrimination despite equality under the law; the reasons for prosocial behaviours of girls despite their devaluation by adults; the policing needed to ensure conformity despite its high socio-economic costs to girls caused by this conformity; the creation in the public of fear of youth crime despite actual low crime rates; the geographical injustices despite a common national law; and the invisible racism despite its profound, systemic presence. The old ways are not inevitable. Nor can current crime rates and justice practices be explained primarily by, or blamed on, what girls do. There are better ways to address delinquency and to promote society's well-being.

Notes

1. For further information, write to Dr. M. Reitsma-Street, Associate Professor with the Multidisciplinary Master's Program, Faculty of Human and Social Development, University of Victoria, P.O. Box 1700, Victoria, B.C., V8W 2Y2, e-mail mreitsma@hsd.uvic.ca. A draft of this paper was presented to the Western Association of Sociology and Anthropology, Vancouver, May 1998. The author thanks Barbara Egan, and Harry Street for help in preparing the text.
2. Although the source for all the youth court statistics is the Canadian Centre for Justice Statistics of Statistics Canada, the numbers are found in a variety of unpublished, preliminary, and published tables and documents. Details on specific charges broken down by sex of the accused in 1978, 1979, and 1980 were made available to me upon specific request to the Canadian Centre for Justice Statistics with funds awarded by Nipissing University College in North Bay, Ontario. The documents that include the preliminary and revised tables for the early years following the introduction of the *YOA* are listed in full in the references as are the publications of the 1990's. The author thanks the SSHRC for a grant to Laurentian University, Sudbury, Ontario, and Pat Kavanaugh and Angela Mione for preparing the data for the tables.
3. Statistics on specific types of charges in the broad category of "against the administration" are not shown but are available from the author. In *Youth Court Statistics*, failure to comply with a disposition is recorded under "against the *YOA*" charges.

References

Adler, C. and M. Baines
1996 ... And When She Was Bad? Working with Young Women in Juvenile Justice and Related Areas. Hobart, Tasmania: National Clearinghouse for Youth Studies.

Appleby, Timothy
1994 Crime rate falls again, except among teen girls. The Globe and Mail July 23, p. A1.

Artz, S.
1998 Sex, Power and The Violent School Girl. Toronto: Trifolium Books.

Artz, Sibylle and Ted Riecken
1997 What, so what, then what?: The gender gap in school-based violence and its implications for child and youth care practice. Child and Youth Care Forum 26(4): 291-303.

Baker, M.
1985 What Will Tomorrow Bring? A Study of the Aspirations of Adolescent Women. Ottawa: Canadian Advisory Council on the Status of Women.

Bala, Nicholas
1992 The Young Offenders Act: The legal structure. In Raymond R. Corrado, N. Bala, R. Linden, and M. LeBlanc (eds.), Juvenile

Justice in Canada: A Theoretical and Analytical Assessment. Toronto: Butterworths.

Biron, L. and D. Gauvreau
1984 Portrait of Youth Crime. Report A84.4. Ottawa: Secretary of State, Policy-Coordination Analysis and Management Systems Branch.

Bourne, Paula, Liza McCoy, and Dorothy Smith
1998 Girls and schooling: Their own critique. Resources for Feminist Research 26 (1 & 2): 55-68.

Bowker, Lee H. and Melanie W. Klein
1983 The etiology of female juvenile delinquency and gang membership: A test of psychological and social structure explanations. Adolescence 18 (Winter): 739-751.

Brenzel, B.
1983 Daughters of the State: A Social Portrait of the First Reform School for Girls in North America 1856-1905. Cambridge, Mass.: The MIT press.

Broidy, L. and R. Agnew
1997 Gender and crime: A general strain theory perspective. Journal of Research in Crime and Delinquency 34(3): 275-306.

Brown, L.M. and C. Gilligan
1992 Meeting at the Crossroads: Women's Psychology and Girls' Development. New York: Ballantine.

Cain, M. (ed.)
1989 Growing Up Good: Policing the Behaviour of Girls in Europe. London, Newbury Park, New Delhi: Sage.

Callahan, M. and K. Callahan
1997 Victims and villains: Scandals, the press and policy making in child welfare. In Gordon Ternowetsky and Jane Pulkingham (eds.), Child and Family Policies. Halifax: Fernwood.

Campbell, A.
1984 Girls in the Gang: A Report from New York City. Oxford: Basil Blackwell.

Canadian Association of Elizabeth Fry Societies and Correctional Services Canada
1990 Creating Choices: The Report of the Task Force on Federally Sentenced Women. Ottawa: Correctional Services Canada.

Canadian Centre for Justice Statistics
1981 Juvenile Delinquents, 1980. Ottawa: Ministry of Supply and Services.

Canadian Centre for Justice Statistics
1983 Juvenile Delinquents, 1982. Ottawa: Ministry of Supply and Services.

Canadian Centre for Justice Statistics
1987 Youth Court Statistics, Preliminary 1985-86. Ottawa: Youth Justice Program, Can. Centre for Justice Statistics. Revised July.

Canadian Centre for Justice Statistics
1989a Youth Court Statistics, Preliminary 1986-87. Ottawa: Youth Justice Program, Can. Centre for Justice Statistics. Revised April.

Canadian Centre for Justice Statistics
1989b Youth Court Statistics, Preliminary 1986-87. Ottawa: Youth Justice Program, Can. Centre for Justice Statistics. Revised April.

Canadian Centre for Justice Statistics
1989c Youth Court Statistics, Preliminary 1988-89. Ottawa: Youth Justice Program, Can. Centre for Justice Statistics. Revised August.

Canadian Centre for Justice Statistics
1990 Youth Court Statistics, Preliminary 1989-90. Ottawa: Youth Justice Program, Can. Centre for Justice Statistics, September.

Canadian Centre for Justice Statistics
1991 Youth Court Statistics, Preliminary 1990-91. Ottawa: Youth Justice Program, Can. Centre for Justice Statistics, September.

Canadian Centre for Justice Statistics
1992 Youth Court Statistics, 1991-92. Ottawa: Youth Justice Program, Can. Centre for Justice Statistics, September.

Canadian Centre for Justice Statistics
1993 Youth Court Statistics, 1992-93. Ottawa: Youth Justice Program, Can. Centre for Justice Statistics, December.

Canadian Centre for Justice Statistics
1995 Youth Court Statistics, 1993-94. Ottawa: Minister for Statistics Canada and Industry, Science and Technology, January.

Canadian Centre for Justice Statistics
1996 Youth Court Statistics, 1994-95. Ottawa: Minister for Statistics Canada and Industry, Science and Technology, March.

Canadian Centre for Justice Statistics
1997 Youth Court Statistics, 1995-96. Ottawa: Minister for Statistics Canada and Industry, Science and Technology, October.

Carrington, Peter J. and Sharon Moyer
1994 Interprovincial variations in the use of custody for young offenders: A funnel analysis. Canadian Journal of Criminology 36(3): 271-290.

Chesney-Lind, M. and R. Sheldon
1998 Girls, Delinquency and Juvenile Justice (2nd edition). Belmont, CA: Wadsworth.

Chesney-Lind, M.
Forthcoming What about girls: Challenging the invisibility of young women in the juvenile justice system. Manuscript prepared for The American Annals of Political and Social Science. Special Issue edited by Ira Schwartz.

Chunn, Dorothy
1998 Whiter than white: sexual offences, law, and social purity in Canada, 1885-1940. Paper presented at the Western Association of Sociology and Anthropology, Vancouver, May 15.

Comack, E.
1996 Women in Trouble. Halifax: Fernwood.

Conway, Joan
1992 Female young offenders, 1990-1991. Juristat Service Bulletin. Canadian Centre for Justice Statistics. May 12(11).

Department of Justice Canada
1998 A Strategy for the Renewal of Youth Justice. Ottawa: Department of Justice Canada.

Donzelot, J.
1979 The Policing of Families (Robert Hurley Trans.) New York: Pantheon Books.

Doob, A.N.
1992 Trends in the use of custodial dispositions for young offenders. Canadian Journal of Criminology 34(1): 75-84.

Doob, A.N. and J.B. Sprott
1996 Interprovincial variation in the use of the youth courts. Canadian Journal of Criminology 38(4): 401-412.

Doob, A.N. and J.B. Sprott
1998 Is the "quality" of youth violence becoming more serious? Canadian Journal of Criminology 40(2): 185-194.

Duffy, M.A.
1994 Linden lore: Images of a new educational model for young women. Resources for Feminist Research 23(3): 32-36.

Evans, Patricia M. and Gerda R. Wekerle (eds.)
1998 Women and the Canadian Welfare State. Toronto: University of Toronto Press.

Faith, Karlene
1995 Aboriginal women's healing lodge: Challenge to penal correctionalism. The Journal of Human Justice 6(2): 79-104.

Freiler, C. and J. Cerny
1998 Benefiting Canada's Children: Perspectives on Gender and Social Responsibility. Ottawa: Status of Women Canada.

Gadd, Jane
1998 Connections still key to landing job, survey finds. The Globe and Mail, May 26.

Gagnon, M. and C. Doherty
1993 Offences Against the Administration of Youth Justice in Canada. Ottawa: Canadian Centre for Justice Statistics.

Galt, V.
1997 U.S. Study cites teens; need for parental involvement. The Globe and Mail, September 10, p. A1.

Hackler, Jim
1991 Good people, dirty system: The *Young Offenders Act* and organizational failure. In A. Leschied, Peter G. Jaffe, and Wayne Willis (eds.), The Young Offenders Act: A Revolution in Canadian Juvenile Justice. Toronto: University of Toronto Press.

Hagan, J., B. McCarthy, (with Patricia Parker and Jo-Anne Climenhage)
1997 Mean Streets: Youth Crime and Homelessness. Cambridge, New York: Cambridge University Press.

Hall, Stuart, Chas Critcher, Tony Jefferson, John Clarke, and Brian Roberts
1978 Policing the Crisis: Mugging, the State and Law and Order. London: The MacMillan Press.

Harris, Peter J.
1998 Young Offenders Act Manual. Aurora, Ontario: Canada Law Book, Inc.

Henggeler, S.W. and C.M. Borduin
1995 Multisystemic treatment of serious juvenile offenders and their families. In Ira. M. Schwartz and Philip AuClaire (eds.), Home-Based Services for Troubled Children. Lincoln & London: University of Nebraska Press.

Holmes, J. and E.L. Silverman
1992 We're Here, Listen To Us! A Survey of Young Women in Canada. Ottawa: Canadian Advisory Council on the Status of Women.

Jiwani, Yasmin
1998 Violence and the girl child: Out of the public purse. Kinesis, November, 17-18.

Johnson, H. and V. Sacco
1995 Researching violence against women: Statistics Canada's national survey. Canadian Journal of Criminology 37(3): 281-304.

Kostash, Myrna
1987 No Kidding: Inside the World of Teenage Girls. Toronto: McClelland and Stewart.

Lagrée, Jean-Charles and Paula Lew Fai
1989 Girls in street gangs in the suburbs of Paris. In Maureen Cain (ed.), Growing Up Good: Policing the Behaviour of Girls in Europe. London: Sage.

LaPraire, Carol
1995 Seen but not heard: Native people in four Canadian inner cities. The Journal of Human Justice 6(2): 30-45.

Leadbeater, B., J. Ross, and N. Way, (eds.)
1996 Urban Girls: Resisting Stereotypes, Creating Identities. New York: New York University Press.

Leah, Ronnie
1995 Aboriginal women and everyday racism in Alberta. The Journal of Human Justice 6(2): 10-29.

Lees, Sue
1997 Ruling Passions: Sexual Violence, Reputation and the Law. Buckingham: Open University Press.

Leschied, Alan, Peter G. Jaffe and Wayne Willis (eds.)
1991 The *Young Offenders Act*: A Revolution in Canadian Juvenile Justice. Toronto: University of Toronto Press.

Lundy, C. and M. Totten
1997 Youth on the fault line. The Social Worker. 65(3): 98-106.

McIlroy, Anne
1998a War on crime to target young. The Globe and Mail, June 1, p. 1.

McIlroy, Anne
1998b Plan aims to jail fewer youths. Globe and Mail, May 12, p. 1.

McRobbie, Angela
1991 Feminism and Youth Culture: From 'Jackie' to 'Just Seventeen'. London: Macmillan Education.

McRobbie, Angela and R. McCabe (eds.)
1981 Feminism For Girls. London: Routledge & Kegan Paul.

Monture-OKanee, Patricia A.
1993 Reclaiming justice: Aboriginal women and justice initiatives in the 1990's. In Aboriginal Peoples and the Justice System of the Royal Commission on Aboriginal Peoples. Ottawa: Canada Communications Group.

Mosher, Clayton
1996 Minorities and misdemeanours: The treatment of black public order offenders in Ontario's criminal justice system – 1892-1930. Canadian Journal of Criminology 38(4): 413-438.

National Council of Welfare
1997 Poverty Profile 1995. Ottawa: National Council of Welfare.

News Group Report on Youth Violence
1997 Reaching out on teen violence: Understanding the problem, finding a solution. Victoria News, Dec. 17, 1997. Supplement 17 pages. Victoria, B.C.

Parent, C.
1986 Actualités and bibliographies: La protection chevaleresque ou les réprésentations masculines du traitement des femmes dans la justice pénale. Déviance et Société 10(2): 147-175.

Peters, R. and C. Russell
1996 Promoting development and preventing disorder: The Better Beginning: Better Futures Project. In R. de Vos Peters and R.J. McMahon (eds.), Preventing Childhood Disorders, Substance Abuse and Delinquency. Thousand Oaks, CA: Sage.

Rains, Prudence M.
1971 Becoming An Unwed Mother: A Sociological Account. Aldine: Atherton.

Reinharz, S.
1992 Feminist Methods in Social Research. New York: Oxford.

Reitsma-Street, M.
1989-1990 More control than care: A critique of historical and contemporary laws for delinquency and neglect of children in Ontario. Canadian Journal of Women and the Law 3(2): 510-530.

Reitsma-Street, M.
1991 A review of female delinquency. In Alan Leschied, Peter G. Jaffe, and Wayne Willis (eds.), The *Young Offenders Act*: A Revolution in Canadian Juvenile Justice. Toronto: University of Toronto Press.

Reitsma-Street, M.
1993 Canadian youth court charges and dispositions for females before and after implementation of the *Young Offenders Act*. Canadian Journal of Criminology 35(4): 437-458.

Reitsma-Street, M.
1998 Still girls learn to care; girls policed to care. In Carol Baines, Pat Evans, and Sheila Neysmith (eds), Women's Caring: Feminist Perspectives on Social Welfare. Revised Edition. Toronto: Oxford University Press.

Reitsma-Street, M. and D.R. Offord
1991 Girl delinquents and their sister. Canadian Review of Social Work 8(1): 11-27.

Ristock, J.L. and J. Pennell
1996 Community Research As Empowerment: Feminist Links, Postmodern Interruptions. Toronto: Oxford University Press.

Ross, Rupert
1992 Dancing with a ghost: Exploring Indian reality. Markham: Octopus Books.

Royal Commission on Aboriginal Peoples
1993 Aboriginal Peoples and the Justice System. Ottawa: Canada Communications Group.

Schissell, Bernard
1997 Youth crime, moral panics, and the news: The conspiracy against the marginalized in Canada. Social Justice 21(2). 165-184.

Sharpe, S.
1994 Just Like A Girl. Harmondsworth: Penguin.

Shichor, David and Clemens Bartollas
1990 Private and public juvenile placements: Is there a difference? Crime and Delinquency 36(2): 286-299.

Smith, Dorothy
1987 The Everyday World As Problematic: A Feminist Sociology. Toronto: University of Toronto Press.

Standing Committee on Justice and Legal Affairs, Canada, Parliament. House of Commons
1997 Renewing Youth Justice. 13th Report. Ottawa: Queen's Printer.

Status of Women Canada
1996 Gender-based analysis: A guide for policy-making. Ottawa: Status of Women Canada.

Statutes of Ontario
1997 Ontario Works Act (Bill 142) 1st session, 36th Legislature, Ontario 46 Elizabeth II. Toronto: Legislative Assembly.

Statistics Canada
1998 Labour Force and Participation Rates. CANSIM, Matrix 3472. May 27. statcan.ca/English/Pgdb/People/Labour/labour 20a. htm

Trépanier, Jean
1986 La justice des mineurs au Québec: 25 ans de transformations (1960-1985). Criminologie XIX (1): 189-214.

Vanstone, S.
1996 Young women and feminism in Northern Ontario. In Marg Kechnie and Marge Reitsma-Street (eds.), Changing Lives: Women in Northern Ontario. Toronto: Dundurn Press.

Varpalotai, A.
1994 Women only and proud of it: The politicization of the Girl Guides of Canada. Resources for Feminist Research 23(1/2): 14-23.

West, G.W.
1984 Young Offenders and the State: A Canadian Perspective on Delinquency. Toronto: Butterworths.

Wolf, Naomi
1990 The Beauty Myth. Toronto: Vintage Books.

Wortley, Scot
1996 Justice for all? Race and perceptions of bias in the Ontario criminal justice system – A Toronto survey. Canadian Journal of Criminology 38(4): 439-468.

CHAPTER SIXTEEN

Factors affecting the referral of young offenders for medical and psychological assessment under the Young Offenders Act[1]

Lindsey A. Jack
and **James R.P. Ogloff**
Simon Fraser University
Burnaby, B.C.

ALTHOUGH THE *YOUNG OFFENDERS ACT* (YOA), INTRODUCED IN 1984, was designed to improve the balance between the young person's rights and the protection of society (Corrado 1992), the Act has proven to be controversial (Leschied and Gendreau 1994). Researchers have commented extensively on the YOA, focussing on a number of central issues – for example, the lack of stated priority in the principles of the YOA, procedural problems relating to the clarity of guidelines within the Act, and the resulting discretion afforded to juvenile justice decision-makers (Doob and Beaulieu 1992; Parker, Casburn and Turnbull 1981; Reid and Reitsma-Street 1984). Other critics have suggested that the YOA undermines the objectives of rehabilitation, treatment, and the individual needs of the young person (e.g., Leschied and Gendreau 1986). In a similar vein, Archambault (1991: ix) commented that

> ...while the Act was intended to provide a better balance between the protection and interest of society and the rights and needs of young persons, it strikes me, on the one hand, that the "justice" and "legal" objectives of the Act are being

Canadian Journal of Criminology/Revue canadienne de criminologie, July/juillet 1997, pp. 247–273.

effectively realized while, on the other hand, the "needs" and "treatment" aspects thereof leave much to be desired.

In fact, a minor portion of the YOA directly addresses the needs of the young offender. Only section 13, for example, deals with the medical and psychological assessment of young offenders. Section 13 assessments may be ordered: (a) to consider an application to transfer a youth to ordinary court; (b) to determine whether a young person is suffering from a mental disorder and is unfit to stand trial; or (c) to make or review a disposition under the Act (see s. (2)(a) to s. (2)(e)). The latter reason most commonly precipitates an order for assessment (Awad 1991).

Since section 13 is, for young offenders, an important point of access between the legal and mental health systems, the decision process at this juncture is especially critical. Legal decision-makers must differentiate among young offenders and determine which individuals should be referred for a mental health assessment. This process is complicated by the imprecise language and lack of guidance of the YOA. Section 13 will be described below.

Section 13: Medical and psychological reports

Under section 13(1) of the YOA, a youth court judge has the power to order the medical and psychological examination of a young person who is before the courts. This subsection states:

13. (1) A youth court may, at any stage of proceedings against a young person
    - (a) with the consent of the young person and the prosecutor, or
    - (b) on its own motion or on application of the young person or the prosecutor, where the court has reasonable grounds to believe that the young person may be suffering from a physical or mental illness or disorder, a psychological disorder, an emotional disturbance, a learning disability or mental retardation

> and the court believes a medical, psychological or psychiatric report in respect of the young person is necessary for a purpose mentioned in paragraphs (2)(a) to (e), by order require that the young person be assessed by a qualified person and require the person who conducts the examination to report the results thereof in writing to the court.

As the above section shows, only a vague description of the circumstances under which a youth court should order a medical and psychological assessment of a young offender is provided (i.e., "reasonable grounds" to suspect physical or mental illness, a learning disability or mental retardation). It neither defines these problems, nor does it offer guidelines as to what would constitute "reasonable grounds" for suspecting their existence. As a result, it is currently unknown which factors juvenile justice personnel consider when making the decision to refer a young offender for medical and psychological assessment.

Section 13 was amended when Bill C-37 was proclaimed on December 1, 1995. In addition to the guidelines described above, the amended section 13 includes two specific criteria (the young person's criminal record and the nature of the current offence) that the youth court may consider when deciding whether to refer a young offender for mental health assessment. Although these changes suggest that legal decision-makers considered section 13 inadequate, neither the reasons behind the decision to revise section 13 nor the rationale for the specific amendments are clear.

Bill C-37 was designed to alter a few specific sections of the YOA to fulfil Liberal Party election promises (Canada, House of Commons 1994). Some specific issues dealt with by the Bill include: increased sentences for young offenders convicted of specific offences; amendments to the transfer provisions; and "proposals to encourage rehabilitation and treatment of young offenders" (Canada, House of Commons 1994: 5387). This latter issue may be the pretence for the changes to section 13;

however, there was no explicit statement of any actual relationship between "rehabilitation and treatment" and mental health referral (Canada, House of Commons 1994). To address properly the changes to section 13 and the possible implications of these changes for young offenders, it is important to have information about the referral process under section 13. For example, as previously stated, little is known about the factors which influence the decision to refer young offenders for mental health assessment.

Implementation of section 13

Overall, fewer referrals for mental health assessments have been made under the YOA than under the Juvenile Delinquents Act (JDA) (Leschied and Gendreau 1986; Leschied and Jaffe 1986). In Ontario, the decrease in the number of referrals has been particularly apparent. Between April and November 1983, for example, 12% of youths charged under the JDA were referred for mental health assessments; whereas, between April and November 1985, only 5% of youths charged under the YOA were referred (Leschied and Jaffe 1986). In addition to the changes in referral rate over this time period, judges' most common reasons for referral also changed. Under the JDA, family problems were cited as the most common reason for referral; however, under the YOA, judges seemed to emphasize possible emotional disorders among young offenders. This shift in focus may have contributed to the reduced number of referrals under the YOA.

As there is no evidence that the number of juveniles in real need of mental health assessment has changed, the reduced referral rate has been attributed to the legalistic focus of the YOA itself (Awad 1991). Furthermore, Awad suggests that judges are less likely to order assessments under the YOA and tend to wait for the Crown or defence counsel to request mental health reports. Both Crown and defence counsel, however, may choose not to request such an assessment.

The extent to which these different sources of referral contribute to the reduced rate of referral for medical and psychological assessment under the YOA is unknown. Because the percentage of section 13 referrals made by each of these groups would vary across jurisdictions and within regions, a clear trend may not emerge from the overall section 13 referral rate.

Young offender characteristics and mental health referral

Few studies have compared the forensic (i.e., criminal record, age at first arrest, type of index offence) and demographic characteristics of referred and non-referred young offenders, notwithstanding the important policy implications of such work. If, for example, decision-makers consistently refer youths who recidivate at a high rate but evidence low amenability to treatment, available mental health resources may be ineffectively utilized. Additionally, the documentation of differences between the referred and non-referred juveniles may indicate that certain "types" of juveniles (e.g., psychiatric diagnoses, gender differences) are disproportionately represented in one of the two groups. Finally, to utilize mental health services in the most effective and appropriate manner, it is necessary to assess the degree to which the needs of referred juveniles match available services, as well as the relationship between group membership and subsequent disposition and recidivism.

Previous research in the area of juvenile mental health referral has been primarily descriptive, focussing upon the mental health consultation programs associated with juvenile or family court (e.g., juvenile court clinics, Chamberlain and Awad 1975; Pabon 1980; crisis assessment programs, Kelley 1978), rather than on the characteristics of the juveniles themselves. Prior studies provide insights on a limited range of juvenile clinical characteristics and/or crime variables and report conflicting estimates of the "usefulness" of clinic recommendations to the court (Kelley 1978). Furthermore, little research directly relevant to Canadian juvenile justice under the YOA is available.

Canadian research that focussed on medical and psychological assessment under the *Young Offenders' Act* was conducted in Ontario (Jaffe, Leschied, Sas, and Austin 1985). Intake information was collected on 616 juveniles referred by the court, between 1974 and 1981, to the London Family Clinic; however, a comparison group of non-referred youths was not included. The judges' primary referral concerns included: placement (32.5%); violence (13.5%); education (11.8%); family (31.6%); and emotional state (10.6%). The authors concluded that there was a "tendency ... to refer to the Clinic only the most troubled individuals – those charged with serious offences or who have chronic histories of emotional difficulty and delinquent behaviour" (Jaffe *et al.* 1985: 57).

The remainder of relevant psychological studies have been conducted in the United States. Because of the inconsistency in management of juvenile offenders across the different States, as well as the differences between the U.S. and Canadian systems, these studies may have limited applicability in Canada. Due to the dearth of psychological research in this area, however, several U.S. studies will be reviewed.

Lewis, Balla, Sacks, and Jekel (1973) collected data on both referred and non-referred juveniles. Although referred and non-referred youths did not differ significantly with respect to socioeconomic status, gender distribution, or occurrence of treated parental psychopathology, the referred youths tended to have committed a greater number of prior offences that were more serious in nature (offences against person), and were younger at the time of their first offence. Additionally, the juveniles referred for psychiatric evaluation had experienced significantly more physical trauma (including child abuse and head injuries), and were more likely to have parents who had received state-sponsored psychiatric care (Lewis, Balla, Shanok, and Snell 1976; Lewis and Shanok 1979).

Using a sample of non-referred and referred youths (Boston Court Clinic) Barnum, Famularo, Bunshaft, Fenton, and Bolduc (1989) found that neither the nature of the index charges nor the youth's previous delinquency record contributed significantly to the decision to refer a juvenile for mental health assessment. However, explicit probation officer impressions of the adolescent and his/her family and several demographic factors were associated with referral. The authors profiled a referred youth as a "young adolescent from a poor family with significant school, conduct, and family problems, involved in court for a relatively minor delinquency charge, the specific nature of which is relatively unimportant" (Barnum *et al.* 1989: 342).

As the above literature indicates, juvenile demographic and criminal characteristics likely influence the decision to refer a youth for medical and psychological assessment. Relatively few studies which delineate the characteristics of youths referred for mental health assessment are available; only one has dealt with a Canadian population (Jaffe *et al.* 1985). Other studies, relevant to juvenile mental health assessment, have been criticized on a number of fronts: (a) tendency to focus on mental health programs rather than on characteristics of referred juveniles; (b) investigation of a narrow range of juvenile clinical characteristics and crime variables; and (c) failure to include a comparison group of arraigned non-referred youths. The factors that affect decision-making under section 13 of the YOA have important policy implications and must be delineated.

The present study

The present study is an investigation of the young offenders referred under section 13 of the YOA. The study attempts to identify the forensic (i.e., criminal record, age at first arrest, type of index offence) and demographic characteristics that differentiate non–referred youths from those who are referred under section 13 of the YOA. Referred and non-referred youths are contrasted on the basis of the criminal case variables and demographic information available within official records (obtained from the British Columbia Provincial Court in Vancouver).

It was hypothesized that on demographic variables youths referred under section 13 would not significantly differ from youths who receive an immediate disposition. By contrast, on criminal case variables, it was expected that youths referred under section 13 would significantly differ from non-referred youths. Specifically, it was hypothesized that referred youths would differ in terms of nature of the alleged current offence (e.g., greater violence, injury to victim, greater number of sexual offences); and previous criminal behaviour (i.e., a greater number of previous convictions and court appearances).

To examine how the amendments to section 13 may affect the referral rate, the new criteria for referral (i.e., prior record and nature of current offence) were applied to the present sample of both referred and non-referred youths and the base-rate for referral, under these conditions, was calculated. It was hypothesized that the cases which would be referred using the amendments to section 13 would include a significant percentage of "non-referred" youths.

Method

The sample

Youth court records were obtained from the Vancouver, British Columbia Provincial Family and Youth Court. The records of all 4679 young persons, 12 to 18 years of age, arraigned on delinquency matters between May 1992 and July 1994 were examined. Only 101 (2.16%) youths were referred for an assessment under section 13. Of the referred cases, one file was unavailable and could not be coded, and four files contained sealed section 13 reports. Therefore, only demographic and criminal case variables were available for these youths. For 38 young offenders (9 referred, and 29 non-referred) court history details (i.e., prior record, and age at first arrest) were not available in the youth court records; therefore, this information was obtained from the Provincial Case File database (Ministry of the Attorney General).

The amount of file information available about offender characteristics varied depending upon whether or not the youth was referred. Information on juvenile clinical characteristics (e.g., alcohol and substance abuse, DSM-IV diagnoses), for example, are only available for the referred youths. The files of referred and non-referred youths, therefore, may only be compared on criminal case variables and demographic variables. Because official records for youths referred under section 13 contain considerably more information on juvenile clinical characteristics, more extensive descriptive information will be provided for the sample of referred youths.

Procedure

Permission was granted by the Vancouver Youth and Family Court to access the records of all 4679 young persons, 12 to 18 years of age, arraigned on delinquency matters between May 1992 and July 1994. Two types of records were contrasted: (a) youths referred under section 13 (n = 95) (80 boys, 15 girls); and (b) non-referred youths (n = 95) (77 boys, 18 girls). As noted above, the referred sample consisted of the 95 most recent cases (referred under Section 13) available. Each of the non-referred cases sampled had docket numbers that immediately followed each referred record. This selection process was chosen to control for any time period effect. The cases chosen were restricted to those administered by the Vancouver Youth and Family Court.

In addition to objective variables (i.e., demographic and forensic characteristics previously described), subjective ratings of the file information were collected. To determine whether the offences alleged to have been committed by referred youths were rated as more bizarre, two independent raters were presented with descriptive information about each offence. Specifically, each rater was provided with a paragraph that described the circumstances surrounding the offence (e.g., events leading up to the incident), the age and sex of the offender and, if applicable, the relationship of the offender to the victim and the degree of victim injury. "Bizarre" was operationally defined as criminal behaviour which is "outside the realm of ordinary" and/or "odd or strange" behaviour (Compact Edition of the Oxford English Dictionary 1971). A three-point scale (1 = bizarre, 2 = questionable, 3 = not bizarre) was used to rate each offence.

In addition to rating the "bizarreness" of the offences, raters were asked to determine whether they felt each offence was "intuitively associated with psychological aberration" (e.g., exhibitionism, fire-setting, or behaviour associated with drug or alcohol use, Melton, Petrila, Poythress, and Slobogin 1987: 187). Again, a three-point scale was used (1 = associated with psychological aberration, 2 = questionable, 3 = not associated with psychological aberration). Using the operational definitions (as discussed above) for "bizarre" and "psychological", two independent raters made judgements (using the three point scales) for each offence. The Kappa values for the bizarre and psychological ratings were .67 and .59, respectively. After their independent evaluation of each offence, the raters discussed the offences upon which they disagreed. In each of the cases, the raters reached an agreement, and the revised ratings were used to test the association between the judgements about the bizarre and psychological nature of each offence and referral status.

Results

Characteristics of the referred sample

The predominant legal reason for referral was "to make or review a disposition" (n = 89, 88%); however, four youths were referred for fitness to stand trial assessments, and two for "NCRMD" (Not Criminally Responsible on account of a Mental Disorder) assessments. All four individuals were found fit and one of the two youths remanded for NCRMD assessments was found NCRMD. Additionally, five young persons were referred for assessments related to transfer proceedings (section 16), however, these cases were removed from any further analyses because the assessment reports were missing. Referral took place, for most of these youths, after a guilty plea but before disposition (n = 71, 75%). Fifteen youths were referred before trial and nine were referred after a trial and a finding of guilt.

Most of the referrals were made by the presiding judge (n = 85, 89%). Only four youths were referred by their probation officers and one by defence counsel; two were self-referred. For three cases the referral sources were not delineated. Consent to the referral was given by 87 (92%) of the referred youths, and 63 (66%) assessments were conducted on an in-patient basis.

As shown in Table 1, referral concerns focus on legal issues such as placement (i.e., type of custody), the type of offence (e.g., violent offences against person, sexual offences), and non-compliance with previous orders (e.g., consistent breach of probation). Emotional state (including treatment issues), however, was cited as a referral concern in 21% of the cases. For some youths, more than one referral concern was delineated.

Although most youths (81%) had not been referred previously under section 13, 44% had been assessed previously by a mental health professional (e.g., Vancouver General Hospital Adolescent Unit, psychiatric assessment, community mental health centres). Almost 65% of these youths had been adjudicated prior to the current charges.

Table 2 shows that problems with school attendance, achievement, and behaviour were prevalent in the referred sample. Furthermore, 50% or greater had prior contact with the Ministry of Social Services (M.S.S.) as temporary or permanent wards, and/or had been placed in a group home. Drug use was noted in the section 13 report as a significant problem in 56 cases (62%) although only four youths were diagnosed with substance abuse disorder.

Information on psychopathology was available for 87 of the 95 referred youths, and is presented in Table 3. Sixty youths (69%) received a Diagnostic and Statistical Manual for Mental

Table 1
Intake information on referrals to youth court services, 1992–1994

Intake variables	Total (n = 91)[a]	
	n	%
Referral concern		
placement	38	42
violence/index offence	32	35
non-compliance	21	23
emotional state	19	21
family	4	4
education	1	1
Residence at referral		
family home	47	52
group home	19	21
no fixed address	9	10
foster home	7	8
detention	6	7
extended family	3	3
Prior adjudication		
no	32	36
once	16	18
two or more	43	47
Prior referral (s. 13)		
no	74	81
once	16	18
two or more	1	1
Prior assessment		
no	51	56
once	24	26
two or more times	16	18

[a] Four referred cases were excluded as the assessment reports were missing

Disorders, 4th Edition (DSM-IV, American Psychiatric Association 1994) diagnosis; 36 (60%) youths were diagnosed with one disorder, 23 (38%) youths received two diagnoses, and one youth (2%) received three diagnoses. Three categories were found (learning disability, *n* = 4, Fetal Alcohol Syndrome, *n* = 5 (FAS), or Fetal Narcotic Syndrome, *n* = 1, (FNS)), either in conjunction with a DSM-IV diagnosis or alone, to describe ten of the young offenders (see Table 3). Only the youths who received a DSM-IV diagnosis in addition to a designation of

Table 2
Assessment information on referrals to youth court services, 1992–1994

Social history and clinical variables	Total (n = 91)[a]	
	n	%
Academic/School problems		
School achievement problems	88	97
School attendance problems	85	93
School behaviour problems	83	91
Previously suspended or expelled	47	54
Residency problems		
Parental separation before 16 years	66	79
Previous M.S.S. contact, other	61	67
Previous group home	51	56
Previous M.S.S. ward	45	50
Psychiatric/Mental health		
Previous counselling	58	64
Previous residential treatment	32	35
Self-harm	27	33
Substance use		
Alcohol use	57	63
Drug use	56	62
History of abuse		
Physical abuse	48	58
Emotional abuse	46	55
Sexual abuse	24	29
Family of origin problems		
Alcoholism or substance abuse	46	55
Criminality	14	17
Psychiatric history	13	16
Other		
Prostitution	12	13
Number of different agency contacts		
0	11	12
1	11	12
2	12	13
3 or more	57	63
Gang involvement	8	10
Head injury	8	10

[a] Four referred cases were excluded as the assessment reports were missing

either learning disability, FAS or FNS, were coded as having received a diagnosis.

Table 3
Types and prevalence of diagnoses for referrals to youth court services, 1992–1994

DSM-IV category	Total (n = 60)	
	n	%
Axis I		
Conduct disorder	33	38
ADHD and conduct disorder	12	14
Attention deficit/hyperactivity disorder (ADHD)	7	8
Substance abuse	4	5
Major depression	3	3
Pedophilia[a]	3	3
Adjustment disorder	2	2
Psychosis NOS	2	2
Schizophrenia[b]	2	2
Attachment disorder	1	1
Communication disorders[c]	1	1
Tic disorders[d]	1	1
Axis II		
Mental retardation	3	3
Borderline personality disorder	2	2

Note: Some youths received more than one diagnosis, therefore, the total number of disorders present in this sample is greater than the number of youths counted as having received a diagnosis (n = 60).
[a] Homosexual pedophilia (n = 1), the other cases were not specified
[b] Disorganized, acute (n = 1), prodromal phase of the disorder (n = 1)
[c] Stuttering
[d] Tic disorder NOS

Conduct disorder and attention deficit hyperactivity disorder (ADHD) were the most common diagnoses. Disorders not classified as disorders of childhood and adolescence (e.g., depression) were relatively rare. Not surprisingly, the two youths who received diagnoses of schizophrenia were referred for fitness and/or NCRMD assessments. Both individuals were found fit, although the youth diagnosed with disorganized schizophrenia (with current delusions and hallucinations) ultimately was found NCRMD. All of the remaining youths who were referred for fitness or NCRMD assessments received diagnoses which differentiated them from the majority of youths who were diagnosed with a mental disorder (e.g., mental retardation, borderline personality disorder, adjustment disorder).

Comparison of referred and non-referred youths

Ethnicity and age at first arrest were the only demographic variables associated with a section 13 referral. White youths were referred at a higher rate than Native youths ($x^2(1, N = 142) = 4.08, p < .05$), and referred youths ($M = 14.4$, $SD = 1.4$) were significantly younger at first arrest than non-referred youths ($M = 14.9$, $SD = 1.6$), $t(181) = 2.38, p < .05$). Associations between criminal case variables and referral, however, were more numerous. For example, youths charged with an offence against persons were more likely to be referred ($x^2(2, N = 129) = 8.82, p < .01$). Additionally, referred youths were remanded to a detention centre at a higher rate than non-referred youths ($x^2(1, N = 189) = 29.99, p < .001$). Those charged with a sexual offence also were more likely to be referred ($x^2(1, N = 190) = 11.68, p < .001$). In fact, none of the charges against non-referred youths was sexual in nature, whereas, 11 of those referred were charged with sexual crimes. Referred youths ($M = 2.1$, $SD = 1.3$) had more charges pending at the time of referral than non–referred youths ($M = 1.7$, $SD = 1.0$), $t(188) = -2.29, p < .05$). There were no significant differences between groups, however, on current age, number of prior court appearances and number of prior convictions.

A logistic regression using backward elimination with the likelihood criterion was used to determine which demographic and criminal case variables were the best predictors of referral decisions. A logistic regression equation that included the number of current charges, whether or not the youth was charged with a sexual offence, and the youth's age at first arrest correctly predicted the referral decisions in 63.5% of the cases. This model predicted true negatives (73%) more often than true positives (54%).

Among the non-referred youths, 51 individuals received a community disposition, and 31 youths were sentenced to either open or closed custody. In 13 cases, an absolute discharge occurred. Among the referred youths, 43 individuals received a community disposition, 47 received a custodial sentence, and one youth was sentenced to an inpatient mental health setting. Four cases were excluded because the court disposition was missing. Chi-square analysis indicated that type of disposition was associated with referral status ($x^2(2, N = 185) = 16.83$, $p < 0.001$). An additional analysis, which excluded the youths that received an absolute discharge, however, was not significant ($x^2(1, N = 172) = 3.60$).

Finally, chi-square analyses indicated that independent raters' judgements about the bizarre and/or psychological qualities of each offence were associated with referral status. The offences committed by referred youths were more often judged as bizarre ($x^2(2, N = 190) = 21.90$, $p < 0.001$), and psychological ($x^2(2, N = 190) = 25.50$, $p < 0.001$), than those offences committed by non-referred youths.

Descriptive information for referred and non-referred youths

Table 4 shows that, for the total sample, assault, robbery, and uttering threats were the most common offences against persons. Both breach (i.e., breach of probation, escaping custody) and property offences (i.e., breaking and entering, theft, and possession of stolen property) were also fairly common. As noted, sexual charges were only found in the referred sample. The percentages of youths charged with robbery and breach also were higher for the referred group. A higher percentage of non-referred youths, however, were charged with drug related offences. A similar pattern between group differences occurred for prior convictions.

Amendments to section 13

About 48% of the total sample (i.e., referred and non-referred youths) had no prior convictions; 11% had committed ten or more offences. The effect of the new criterion "repeated findings of guilt under the Act" on referrals depends, of course, on the threshold value used to define "repeated" offence. If

Table 4
Frequency and type of index charges for total sample, referred youths, and non-referred youths

	Total (*n* = 370)		Referred (*n* = 211)		Non-referred (*n* = 159)	
Index charges	*n*	%	*n*	%	*n*	%
Against property						
Theft	46	12	26	12	20	13
Possession of stolen property	39	11	23	11	16	10
Break and enter	26	7	12	6	14	9
Possession of weapon or imitation	19	5	7	3	12	8
Mischief	18	5	7	3	11	7
Possession b/e instruments	11	3	6	3	5	3
Causing explosion	1	0	1	0	0	--
Against person						
Assault	38	10	18	9	20	13
Robbery	30	8	24	11	6	4
Uttering threats	20	5	10	5	10	6
Assault with weapon	16	4	10	5	6	4
Sexual assault	12	3	12	6	0	--
Arson – endanger life	4	1	4	2	0	--
Offences relating to a peace officer	4	1	3	1	1	1
Incest	3	1	3	1	0	--
Aggravated assault	2	0	2	1	0	--
Confinement	1	0	1	0	0	--
Indecent act	1	0	1	0	0	--
Breach						
Breach	35	9	25	12	10	6
Escape custody	5	1	3	1	2	1
Miscellaneous						
Dangerous operation of a vehicle	12	3	5	2	7	4
Possession of narcotics	7	2	2	1	5	3
Trafficking in narcotics	7	2	1	0	6	4
Offence in relation to prostitution	5	1	1	0	4	3
Carry a concealed weapon	3	1	3	1	0	--
Loitering	3	1	0	--	3	2
Failure to pay transit fare	2	1	1	0	1	1

this were to be set at three or more, 30 new referrals would be generated from the present sample. If it were set to five or more prior convictions, 20 new referrals would result (excluding two youths who committed serious personal injury offences, and would therefore certainly be referred under a different criterion anyway): if ten, eight: and if 15, five (excluding one youth counted in the serious personal injury category).

Including "serious personal injury" offenders with the above "repeat" offenders would result in six new referrals from the present sample (these youths were convicted of assault with a weapon or assault causing bodily harm). Thus, depending on which criteria are used to define "repeated findings of guilt," the amendments to section 13 may potentially generate between 11 and 36 new referrals out of 95, presently non–referred, youths (or 12-38% of the non-referred sample).

Of the youths referred under the current law, 37 (39%) had no prior convictions, 39 had at least three, 24 had at least five (excluding three youths in the serious personal injury group), 11 had at least ten (excluding two of the previous three), and four had at least 15 (one repeat offender still excluded). Seventy-five of the referred youths were not charged with an offence causing serious personal injury. If sexual assaults are not included as serious personal injury offences, then 86 out of 95 youths would not be charged with "serious personal injury."

Discussion

The present findings highlight two significant issues. First, not surprisingly, referred youths suffer from a number of emotional and behavioural problems. Identification of this group's difficulties should be given a high priority, as it could guide the development of treatment programs. Second, there are a number of differences between referred and non-referred youths. Factors which emerge as important for referral decisions include the type and number of index offences, as well as ethnicity and age at first arrest. This apparent emphasis on criminal behaviour and ethnicity (white youths are especially likely to be referred) is disconcerting, given that referral under section 13 is one of the few ways a young offender can gain access to medical and psychological evaluation and, possibly, treatment. Closer examination of the characteristics of the referred youths may reveal other factors which affect referral decisions.

Characteristics of referred sample

For the majority of youths undergoing a medical and psychological assessment, the legal reason for referral is to "make or review a disposition" (Awad 1991); this also was true for the current sample. The presiding judge was the referral source for over 92% of the youths in this sample, a result similar to that reported by Jaffe *et al.* (1985). This suggests that neither the lawyers nor the young offenders themselves consider mental health assessment desirable, or alternatively, that the judge simply refers the youth before any other parties have a chance to make the request. File information does not, however, permit discrimination between these alternatives, nor does it indicate whether the judges received input from other interested parties (e.g., youth's family, or social worker).

Questions surrounding placement of the young offender (either in the community or in custody) and the nature of the index offence (e.g., violence, sexual offence) were the most frequently cited referral concerns. These results (i.e., the focus on placement and non-compliance in the community) suggest that judges are placing greater emphasis on type of crime, and protection of society. This increased emphasis on the protection of society is consistent with the amendments to the YOA which were enacted under Bill C-12 (1991). Moreover, judgements which consider the protection of society paramount are in line with the views expressed by certain members of the community and the media (Bala 1992).

The referred youths presented with numerous behavioural (e.g., difficulties at school, self-injurious behaviour, and substance use) and familial problems (e.g., child abuse, family substance use, and parental separation before age 16 years).

About 69% of the present sample received at least one DSM-IV diagnosis. Conduct disorder was the most prevalent; diagnoses of schizophrenia and other major mental illnesses were relatively rare. Since Canadian research on the prevalence of mental disorder among young offenders is not available (Webster, Rogers, Cochrane, and Stylianos 1991), it is difficult to determine whether this result reflects rates of mental disorder in the population as a whole.

A recent survey of 75 studies generated estimates of co-morbidity rates of mental health problems and juvenile delinquency (Wierson, Forehand, and Frame 1992). Due to the overlap between the DSM-III criteria for conduct disorder and delinquent behaviour, the prevalence of conduct disorder among juvenile delinquents is extremely high (Wierson *et al.* 1992). One study, for example, reported that 90% of the youths in their sample met the DSM-III criteria for conduct disorder (McManus, Alessi, Grapentine, and Brickman 1984). The relationship between ADHD and delinquency is less clear; co-diagnosis of conduct disorder and ADHD, however, may be most predictive of juvenile delinquency. Forehand, Wierson, Frame, Kempton, and Armistead (in press, as cited in Wierson *et al.* 1992) found that incarcerated youths with a diagnosis of both conduct disorder and ADHD had more total arrests, and were first arrested at a younger age, than incarcerated youths diagnosed with conduct disorder only.

Personality, affective, and substance abuse disorders and mental retardation also seem to occur frequently among juvenile delinquents (Lefkowitz and Tesiny 1985; Mezzich, Coffman, and Mezzich 1991; Yates, Beutler, and Crago 1983; for a review see, Wierson *et al.* 1992). Conclusions regarding the relationship between mental disorders and juvenile delinquency are, however, tentative due to methodological weaknesses in much of the available research (e.g., failure to differentiate youths by sex, use of nonstandard assessment methods, and use of specific groups of young offenders, Wierson *et al.* 1992).

Identification of mentally disordered youths has major implications for treatment and recidivism (lack of mental health treatment may result in higher rates of recidivism) (McManus *et al.* 1984). Accurate information about referred youths would expedite the creation of programs appropriate to their needs. A functional example, within the current system, involves the referral of young offenders convicted of sexual crimes to the outpatient sex offender treatment program at Youth Court Services (YCS). In these situations, the youth's behaviour (i.e., type of crime) facilitates the referral decision and allows access to treatment. After referral, the diagnosis also may directly affect the youth's access to treatment. For example, each of the four youths who were diagnosed with substance abuse were given drug and alcohol treatment as a condition of their dispositions, whereas only one referred youth without that diagnosis received drug and alcohol treatment as a condition of probation. Furthermore, even though alcohol and/ or drug use was identified as a significant concern for over 50% of the referred youths, drug and alcohol treatment was only enacted by the court in 7% of the cases.

The high prevalence of conduct disorder within the referred sample also has implications for treatment and disposition decisions. Frick, O'Brien, Wootton, and McBurnett (1994) reviewed some of the psychological research on conduct disorder and concluded that this diagnosis is related to poorer treatment prognosis. In particular, children who do not show elevated levels of anxiety under stressful conditions are more aggressive, have more conflict with social systems, and respond more poorly to treatment. Future research involving larger samples should investigate the relationship between diagnoses of conduct disorder and judges' disposition decisions.

Comparison of non-referred and referred youths

Overall, the modal individual who tends to be referred for assessment is a white youth, currently charged with several offences, at least one of which is a crime against person. Furthermore, the referred youths became involved with the court at a younger age than non-referred youths, and were more likely to be held in a detention centre prior to adjudication.

Frequency of sexual charges strongly distinguished the referred from the non-referred youths. Judges may perceive sexual offenders as individuals who are, by definition, in need of mental health intervention. As Melton *et al.* (1987) have suggested, certain offences are more likely to be associated with psychological aberration. In fact, the existence of an outpatient treatment program for youthful sex offenders at YCS in British Columbia may influence the referral decisions and confirm any hypotheses regarding sexual offenders' need for treatment. Additionally, logistic regression analyses indicated that the presence of sexual charges was an important predictor of referral decisions. Sexual charges, when considered in conjunction with number of current charges and age at first arrest, correctly predicted referral decisions in 63.5% of the cases.

Contrary to predictions, referred and non-referred youths did not significantly differ in either the number of prior convictions or number of prior court appearances. Only about half of the youths had any prior criminal record; differences between these groups might not be evident in a sample of this size.

As anticipated, independent raters judged the offences committed by the referred youths as more bizarre and more psychological (i.e., "intuitively associated with psychological aberration" Melton *et al.* 1987: 187) than the offences committed by the non–referred youths. Although this result supports the contention that a small percentage of the referred cases are clearly identifiable as bizarre (9%) and/or psychological (22%) (Awad 1991; Melton *et al.* 1987), the majority of the offences did not meet these criteria and were referred for other reasons.

Policy implications and future research

A number of policy implications emerge in light of both current results and the proposed changes to section 13. In the present sample, about two percent of the cases examined were referred under s. 13; this is unquestionably lower than the rates reported in Ontario in the early and mid-1980s (Leschied and Jaffe 1986). Due to the dearth of research in this area, comparisons with more recent data are not possible; however, the trend in the data suggests that s. 13 referrals have continued to decrease since the inception of the YOA. This is surprising given the breadth of the criteria for referral and the wide discretion afforded to judges making referral decisions.

Some researchers have suggested that the "widening of the net" with respect to referral decisions may result in arbitrary decisions and misuse of the mental health system (Awad 1991; Mulvey 1989). The amendments to s. 13 do, in fact, introduce more restrictive referral criteria. The usefulness of these criteria for determining which youths should be referred is questionable, however. The focus on past criminal record and seriousness of current offence seems to suggest that youths who are perceived as high risk for recidivism should be referred. These same criteria also are used when determining whether to transfer a youth to ordinary court (s. 16). The amended s. 13 may serve to "widen the net" even further. The application of the new criteria to the current sample could potentially generate between 11 and 36 new referrals. These additional cases would require substantially more personnel resources, and also may require placement at an inpatient assessment unit. Clearly, the system could become overloaded.

In light of the amendments to s. 13, as well as the current findings, several avenues for future research should be pursued. First, an examination of the match between the available treatment programs and the needs of the referred youths would provide direction for the development of new programs and, potentially, the reform of current programs. Future research in this area also should include qualitative information which would allow an examination of the effects of informal discussions and court personnel characteristics on referral decisions. Informal discussions between court personnel (i.e., the youth court judge, defence attorney, Crown counsel, and probation officer), for example, may result in plea-bargains which substantially influence referral decisions. Unfortunately, the essence of these informal agreements is not generally recorded in official records, and, therefore, could not be measured in the present study. Finally, results consistently suggest that in addition to official records, ecological, economic, and decision-maker attitudes and background variables must be measured (Hogarth 1977). Although studies of this type are costly and suffer from high attrition, future research should investigate the contextual and intra-decision-maker characteristics that affect referral decisions.

Conclusion

The shift from the JDA's child welfare model of juvenile justice to the more legalistic YOA model was intended to better balance protection of society against the rights and needs of young offenders (Corrado 1992). Section 13, however, is one of the few sections of the YOA which addresses the needs of young offenders. Moreover, compared to those sections of the YOA directly relevant to the protection of society (e.g., transfer to ordinary court, Balla and Lilles 1989; disposition decisions, Doob and Beaulieu 1992), section 13 has been vastly under-emphasized and under-researched.

Ideally, section 13 should be utilized for youths most in need of mental health services. Arbitrary referral decisions or those based upon extraneous variables, however, may result in misuse of available mental health services. For example, referred youths who do not need intervention may be harmed; young offenders who would benefit from medical and psychological assessment may be overlooked.

The present study serves as a first step towards the identification of factors which affect such referral decisions. Although several variables distinguished referred from non-referred youths, future research should explore the influence of situational and decision-maker characteristics. Better understanding of the referral process under section 13 would permit more rigorous assessment of the appropriateness of such decisions, and would point the way to better agreement between clinicians and legal decision-makers. Consequently, the effectiveness of the treatment programs themselves could not help but improve.

Note

1. A version of this paper was presented at the 1996 Biennial Conference of the American Psychology–Law Society, Hilton Head, SC. The authors are grateful to Judge J. Auxier for granting access to the youth court files; without her support, this project would not have been possible. The authors also would like to thank Stephen Hart, Christopher Webster, and Raymond Corrado for their helpful comments on an earlier version of this manuscript. Correspondence may be addressed to James Ogloff, Department of Psychology, Simon Fraser University, Burnaby, British Columbia, Canada V5A 1S6. Email: jogloff@arts.sfu.ca.

References

American Psychiatric Association
1994 Diagnostic and Statistical Manual of Mental Disorders (4th ed.). Washington: American Psychiatric Association.

Archambault, J.R. Omer
1991 Foreword. In Alan W. Leschied, Peter G. Jaffe, and Wayne Willis (eds.), The Young Offenders Act: A Revolution in Canadian Juvenile Justice. Toronto: University of Toronto Press.

Awad, George A.
1991 Assessing the needs of young offenders. In Alan W. Leschied, Peter G. Jaffe, and Wayne Willis (eds.), The Young Offenders Act: A Revolution in Canadian Juvenile Justice. Toronto: University of Toronto Press.

Bala, Nicholas
1992 The Young Offenders Act: The legal structure. In Raymond R. Corrado, Nicholas Bala, Rick Linden, and Marc LeBlanc (eds.), Juvenile Justice in Canada: A Theoretical and Analytical Assessment. Vancouver: Butterworths Canada Ltd.

Bala, Nicholas and Heino Lilles
1989 Transfer to adult court: The most serious disposition. In L.A. Beaulieu (ed.), Young Offender Dispositions: Perspectives and Practice. Toronto: Wall and Thompson.

Barnum, Richard, Richard Famularo, Doris Bunshaft, Terrence Fenton, and Suzanne Bolduc
1989 Clinical evaluation of juvenile delinquents: Who gets court referred? Bulletin of the American Academy of Psychiatry and Law 17: 335-344.

Canada, House of Commons
1994 Minutes of the Proceedings and Evidence of the Standing Committee on Justice and Legal Affairs – Bill C-37 (35th Parliament, 1rst Sess: 38). Ottawa: House of Commons.

Chamberlain, Clive and George Awad
1975 Psychiatric service to the juvenile court: A model. Canadian Psychiatric Association Journal 20: 599-605.

Compact Edition of the Oxford English Dictionary
1971 New York: Oxford University Press.

Corrado, Raymond R.
1992 Introduction. In Raymond R. Corrado, Nicholas Bala, Rick Linden, and Marc LeBlanc (eds.), Juvenile Justice in Canada: A Theoretical and Analytical Assessment. Vancouver: Butterworths Canada Ltd.

Doob, Anthony N. and Lucien A. Beaulieu
1992 Variation in the exercise of judicial discretion with young offenders. Canadian Journal of Criminology 34(1): 35-50.

Frick, Paul J., Bridget S. O'Brien, J.M. Wootton, and Keith McBurnett
1994 Psychopathy and conduct problems in children. Journal of Abnormal Psychology 103(4): 700-707.

Hogarth, John
1977 Sentencing as a Human Process. Toronto, Ont: University of Toronto Press.

Jaffe, Peter G., Alan W. Leschied, Louise Sas, and Gary Austin
1985 A model for the provision of clinical assessments and service brokerage for young offenders: The London Family Court Clinic. Canadian Psychology 26(1): 54-61.

Kelley, Thomas M.
1978 Clinical assessment and the detention, disposition, and treatment of emotionally disturbed delinquent youths. Journal of Criminal Justice 6: 315-327.

Lefkowitz, Monroe M. and Edward P. Tesiny
1985 Depression in children: Parent, teacher, and child perspectives. Journal of Consulting and Clinical Psychology 52: 915-916.

Leschied, Alan W. and Paul G. Gendreau
1994 Doing justice in Canada: YOA policies that can promote community safety. Canadian Journal of Criminology 36(3): 291-303.

Leschied, Alan W. and Paul G. Gendreau
1986 The declining role of rehabilitation in Canadian juvenile justice: Implications of underlying theory in the Young Offenders Act. Canadian Journal of Criminology 28(3): 315-322.

Leschied, Alan W. and Peter G. Jaffe
1986 Implications of the consent to treatment section of the Young Offenders Act: A case study. Canadian Psychology 27(3): 312-313.

Lewis, Dorothy O., David A. Balla, H.L. Sacks, and J.F. Jekel
1973 Psychotic symptomatology in a juvenile court clinic population. Journal of the American Academy of Child Psychiatry 12: 660-674.

Lewis, Dorothy O., David A. Balla, Shelley S. Shanok, and Laura Snell
1976 Delinquency, parental psychopathology, and parental criminality: Clinical and epidemiological findings. Journal of the American Academy of Child Psychiatry 15: 665-678.

Lewis, Dorothy O. and Shelley S. Shanok
1979 Medical histories of psychiatrically referred delinquent children: An epidemiologic study. American Journal of Psychiatry 136: 231-233.

McManus, Michael, Norman E. Alessi, W.L. Grapentine, and Arthur Brickman
1984 Psychiatric disturbance in serious delinquents. Journal of the American Academy of Child Psychiatry 23: 602-615.

Melton, Gary B., John Petrila, Norman B. Poythress, and Christopher Slobogin
1987 Psychological evaluations for the courts: A handbook for mental health professionals and lawyers. NY: The Guilford Press.

Mezzich, Ada C., Gerald Coffman, and Juan E. Mezzich
1991 A typology of violent delinquent adolescents. The Journal of Psychiatry and Law: 63-78.

Mulvey, Edward P.
1989 Scenes from a marriage: How can juvenile justice and mental health go together? Forensic Reports 2(1): 9-24.

Pabon, Edward
1980 Mental health services in the juvenile court: An overview. Juvenile and Family Court Journal 31: 23-34.

Parker, H., M. Casburn, and D. Turnbull
1981 Receiving Juvenile Justice: Adolescents and State Care and Control. Oxford: Basil Blackwell.

Reid, S.A. and Marge Reitsma-Street
1984 Assumptions and implications of the new Canadian legislation for young offenders. Canadian Criminology Forum 7: 1-19.

Webster, Christopher D., Joy M. Rogers, Jeanette J. Cochrane, and Stanley Stylianos
1991 Assessment and treatment of mentally disordered young offenders. In Alan W. Leschied, Peter G. Jaffe, and Wayne Willis (eds.), The Young Offenders Act: A Revolution in Canadian Juvenile Justice. Toronto: University of Toronto Press.

Wierson, Michelle, Rex L. Forehand, and Cynthia L. Frame
1992 Epidemiology and treatment of mental health problems in juvenile delinquents. Advances in Behavioral Research Theory 14: 93-120.

Yates, Alayne, Larry E. Beutler, and Marjorie Crago
1983 Characteristics of young, violent offenders. The Journal of Psychiatry and Law 11(2): 137-149.

PART FOUR

Young Persons and the Courts

CHAPTER SEVENTEEN

Out of the carceral straightjacket: Under twelves and the law

Barry M. Clark[1]
Executive Director
John Howard Society of Windsor-Essex
and Professor of Criminology
University of Windsor
Windsor, Ontario
and **Thomas O'Reilly-Fleming**
Criminology Programme
Department of Sociology and Anthropology
University of Windsor
Windsor, Ontario

A DECADE HAS PASSED SINCE THE REPEAL OF THE 1908 Juvenile Delinquents Act (JDA), Canada's former federal youth legislation. In 1984, amid a clamour of opposition by concerned opponents and critics, the *Young Offenders Act* (YOA) came into effect as the JDA replacement. Even then, police, child protection agencies, visible minority groups, educators, and mental health representatives, among others, pointed to fundamental and critical deficiencies in the new legislation (O'Reilly-Fleming and Clark 1993; Leschied, Jaffe and Willis 1991, Hudson, Hornick, and Burrows 1988). Despite a decade of amendments to the legislation, which have partially addressed critical deficiencies, many defects remain. Still of major concern to critics of the YOA are issues relating to consent to treatment, equitable access to interim judicial release and alternative measures, waivers to ordinary court, appeals and reviews of dispositions, admissibility of evidence, disclosure of names, split jurisdiction, (over)use of custody,

Canadian Journal of Criminology/Revue canadienne de criminologie, July/juillet 1994, pp. 305–327.

absence of youth justice committees, inter-provincial sentencing disparities (the need for sentencing guidelines), and both the established upper and lower age limits. Because provincial and territorial interpretation and implementation of the YOA are differential and dynamic, this paper will focus on Ontario's response and, in particular, the provincial/federal child welfare arrangement as it relates to the 'under twelve' age group.

Fundamental issues

The adjustments of the upper and lower age limits in Ontario have had a substantive and, we believe, dual impact on the province's perception of and willingness to address age related issues. At the upper age limit, for instance, the Province of Ontario faces a numerically larger adjustment, through the inclusion of the sixteen- and seventeen-year-olds, than any other Canadian province. Quebec, with the nation's second largest youth population, had already established the maximum age for young offenders prior to YOA implementation, along with Manitoba, at eighteen years of age. The sixteen- and seventeen-year-olds typically account for a substantial amount of all youth crime, especially reported crime of a violent nature.

During the period of April 1, 1991, through March 31, 1992, Canada's youth courts dealt with 116,397 accused. Of this group, which involved 213,437 charges, 82% were males, and 52% were 16-17-year-olds (i.e., 60,242 16-17-year-olds and 52,718 12-15-year-olds). Ontario's youth courts, during the same period, dealt with 48,854 accused, of which 24,197 were 16-17-year-olds, and 22,569 were 12 through 15 years of age. Violent offenses during 1991/92 totalled 19,824 (16,277 male and 3,547 female), with 16-17-year-olds being charged with approximately 52% of youthful violent offenses (Canadian Centre for Justice Statistics 1992a; Department of Justice Canada 1993).

The absorption into the young offender system of this formidably criminal group, the sixteen- and seventeen-year-olds, attracted considerable attention and alarm. Indeed, the post-YOA increase in youth crime, especially violent crime, in Ontario can largely be explained by this statistical shift.

Since 16-17-year-old youth generate over 50% of young offender charges in Ontario, a rate which reflects the nation's, the Ontario public has been understandably alarmed by this sudden statistical but legislatively induced doubling of youth crime. To add to this obfuscation, a 1986 amendment to the YOA, which was proclaimed in December 1988, made 'failure to comply with a disposition" a new and separately punishable offense. Previously, such matters of non-compliance were addressed, rather reticently, by way of review of the original disposition. By further inflating the YOA offense count, this has provided generous fodder for the media and special interest groups who generate and benefit from exaggerated depictions of youth crime and, in particular, violent crime without reference to the source of these phenomena.

Public and professional reaction to what has been occurring with "under twelves", has been negligible when compared with the older, more industrious offenders. Weaknesses in child welfare legislation as they relate to "under twelves", as well as the lack of appropriate, accessible services for this group, create a situation in the Province of Ontario that is, in our opinion, conducive to the creation of persistent young offenders.

Under twelves: Highlights of uniform crime reporting

The Uniform Crime Reporting Survey has been operated since 1962 by the Canadian Centre for Justice Statistics. Only recently, however, has it begun to yield quantitatively informative and differential age data which permit a preliminary but important comparison of offense characteristics of the "under 12" and the 12-17 age categories. This dataset, gathered from 1988 to 1992, represents a total of 971,000 incidents and involves 4,757 accused persons under the age of twelve collected from 27 police forces across Canada. The data, while limited, allows for preliminary interpretation and inference relating to offense characteristics, offender typology, and differential programme prevention, intervention, and postvention.

In order to aid the discussion at hand, this dataset can be contextualized within the broader offense distribution in Canada. The accused child under the age of twelve, for instance, constitutes roughly 2% of total national offenses, while young offenders (age 12 through 17) represent 21% of that total. The remaining 78% are adult offenders. The 'under twelves' represent a comparatively minute offender population. This group, however, should be of special interest to crime prevention practitioners and to all concerned members of the community. Left unattended, the potentially cumulative impact of the 'under twelves' on the young offender system would be sufficiently significant to warrant a complete and serious reversal of traditional ways of responding to children in conflict with society. Children under 12 form a very small number of all those accused of a serious crime. There are, however, some areas of concern: sexual assault, assault with a weapon, common assault, arson, break and enter, theft under, and mischief.

The following are highlights of the Uniform Crime Report, 'Crimes Committed by Children Under 12' from the Canadian Centre for Justice Statistics (1992b):

- Of the 4757 accused children under 12 in the dataset a very small proportion commit 'serious' police-reported crime: one percent are alleged to have sexually assaulted someone, one percent are accused of using weapons in an assault, five percent of accused are linked to common assaults, and three percent are considered to have committed arson. These children are more prone to committing other offenses such as break and enter (19%), theft under (23%), and mischief (42%).
- The most common crimes among this group are mischief (in homes), theft under (shoplifting) and break and enter.

- The proportion of accused children who committed violent crimes is 8% (364): of these 62% were assault level 1 (common assault).
- Seventy-four percent of most serious 'weapons' used were physical force.
- The number of accused increases very rapidly with increased age.
- At all ages about 90% are males.
- About one-half of their victims of violent crime receive minor injuries, while 5% receive more serious injuries.
- The majority (82%) of assault victims were casual acquaintances of the children who attacked them. Only 4% were family members. This is in sharp contrast to adult assault victims.
- Alcohol and drugs do not appear to be a major factor among these children.

Exploring the highlights

The above highlights, from a crime prevention perspective, are instructive, particularly when analyzed in terms of age, gender, offense type, and offense location as well as the seriousness and frequency of offense patterns.

Males constitute the great majority of 'under 12' offenders, roughly 90% of the total. The majority of 'under twelves' in the sample, approximately 70% of males and females, fall within the 10 and 11 year age category with a further 27% being 8- and 9-year-olds. The balance of the accused, or 13%, are 7 years of age and under.

As indicated in Table 1, sexual and physical assaults represent a relatively small amount of the total offenses, as little as 7%.

A closer examination of assault frequencies, when measured as a separate category of offenses, reveals that the majority of physical assaults committed by "under twelves" were common assaults (level 1), constituting 75% of all violent offenses committed by the sample. More serious or aggravated

Table 1
Children under 12 by offense

Offense	Percentage
Sexual assault	1
Assault- Level 1	1
Assault- Level 2	5
Arson	3
Break & enter	19
Theft over	1
Theft under	23
Mischief	41
Other	6

Based on a total of 4,757 children under 12 implicated, for the years 1988-1992, and a sample of 27 cities.

assaults (level 3), causing physical damage or requiring hospitalization, were minimal, about 1% of total assaults by "under twelves". Eighty-two percent of the victims of violent crime by "under twelves" were casual acquaintances, followed by strangers (12%), family (4%), and friends (2%). In the commission of assaults the great majority of 'under twelves', or 74% did not use weapons; however, 8% used knives, 7% utilized a club or stick as a weapon, and 1% used a firearm.

Table 2 illustrates where property offenses occurred and suggests appropriate directions for anti-vandalism initiatives as well as potential, community-based programme collaboration and funding. With 62% of 'under 12' mischief occurring in homes, parking lots, streets and roads, one would presume a willingness on the part of real estate, insurance and car companies to sponsor school based anti-vandalism initiatives.

Table 3 and 4 provide important information on the nature of peer groups and older accomplices in under 12 crime. Clearly, either organized or spontaneous peer involvement in crime,

Table 2
Locations of mischief by children under 12

Location	Percentage
Homes	42
Parking lots	21
Commercial/Corporate	12
Streets/Roads	8
Open areas	7
Schools	6
Public institutions	4

Based on 1,886 children under 12 implicated in mischief for the years 1988-1992, and a sample of 27 cities.

of a youth group or "gang' nature, is negligible. However, collective participation in offenses involving older accomplices reveal the significant influence of immediately older accomplices, specifically 12- and 13-year-olds, who constitute roughly 70% of the total older accomplice group spanning 12 to 67 years of age.

The preceding data suggest directions for strategic crime prevention initiatives for "under twelves". Virtually 90% of the accused, for instance, are male. While this distinctive gender distribution may, in fact, be a partial artifact of socio-cultural response to, as well police discretion in the handling of males, this stark disproportion strongly suggests a need for detailed research. Self-report surveys, for instance, suggest a much more equitable gender distribution of offenses, particularly offenses of a non-violent nature (Gomme 1985).

Lessons from research

Before discussing some strategic options for expanding to "under twelves" involved in crime, it is useful to review some of the relevant research. In this brief review, we touch on alternative responses to anti-social behaviour, the importance

Table 3
Peer group involvement in crime: Number of children under 12 in each incident

Number in incident	Percentage
One	63
Two	26
Three	8
Four	2
Five to eight	1

Based on 3,111 incidents involving one or more children under 12 for the years 1988-1992. and a sample of 27 cities.

Table 4
Incidents involving children under 12 with an older accomplice — Frequency older accomplices by age

Age of older accomplice	Frequency of accomplices
12 years	585
13 years	301
14 years	181
15 years	102
16 years	57
17 years	15
18 years	9
19 years	6
20 years	2
21 years	20
22 to 67 years	26

Based on 1,305 older accomplices for the years 1988-1992, and for a sample of 27 cities.

of risk/need assessment, and some of the challenges facing youth today. History has emphatically demonstrated that narrow correctional interventions, especially formal and institutional processes, yield unfavourable and frequently counter-productive results. This is particularly evident when interventions are offense reactive, deterrence oriented, and denunciatory, and when they are applied to adolescents without consideration of or recourse to less punitive, community-based responses. In an applied sense, a social development (Waller and Weiler 1985) model that systemically addresses three primary social modalities, family, peers, and school, should act as templates for strategic action. Assessment of risk/need should be early, thorough and uncompromisingly individual, and should ensure that children not requiring intervention are not further enmeshed in the carceral network. An accurate description will best dictate the appropriate prescription for action (Levin 1991). A diagnostically sensitive, need-focused strategy will naturally and consequentially reduce risk. After all, risk factors are dialectically related and sensitive to need. Certain needs, in turn, are characteristically and abundantly evident in the "under 12" population. Leschied and Wilson (1988), in a study spanning the decade 1974-1984, focused on latency age children (7 to 11) who had been referred to the London Family Court Clinic, and followed them beyond their twelfth birthday. The study revealed that these "7-11's" possessed characteristics which warranted considerable intervention: chronic familial difficulties, spousal violence, parental separation and divorce, child abuse, and major difficulties at school. Another study found that dangerous clinical rating scores of adolescent offenders were associated with parental abuse, multiple placements outside their homes, as well as school and peer relation problems (Sas, Jaffe, and Reddon 1985).

Similarly, West and Farrington (1973), in Britain, found consistent covariates for early development of delinquency: poor family income, large family size, criminality of father, inadequacy of parenting, lower intelligence, and troublesomeness. Troublesomeness, as rated by teachers and peers at 8-10 years, was the best single predictor. This relationship between early troublesomeness at school and later delinquency should give rise to considerable concern, especially considering the high prevalence rate of conduct disorders in children. One study found 93,500 Ontario children and adolescents with conduct disorders (Offord, Boyle, and Racine 1988; Thompson 1988). Hawkins, Jenson, and Catalano (1988) cite a list of shared factors that appear to lead to serious, persistent delinquency and continual drug use in adolescence: early antisocial behaviour, parent/sibling substance abuse and criminality, inadequate parenting, poverty, maladjustment in early elementary grades, lack of commitment to school, negative peers, early rebelliousness, lack of stability, and neurophysiological and cognitive factors. Antecedents of substance abuse, not surprisingly, are closely associated with criminal risk (Bailey 1989; Allison 1989; Empey 1982; Watts and Wright 1990; Thornton and Voigt 1992). In addition, a variety of studies have underscored the significance of family rupture and parental deviance in increasing childhood vulnerability to delinquency and antisocial behaviours in youth (Rae-Grant 1979; Lewis, Lovely, Yaeger, Ferguson, Friedman, Sloane, Friedman, and Pincus 1988; Rogeness, Amrung, Macedo, Harris, and Fisher 1986; McManus, Alessi, Grapentine, and Brickman 1984; Loeber 1991; Raychaba 1987; West and Farrington 1973; 1977; Tremblay, Zhou, Gagnon, Vitaro, and Boileau 1991; Patterson, Debanyshe, and Ramsey 1989; Buikhuisen 1989; Rutter 1987; Hamparian, Schuster, Dinitz, and Conrad 1978).

Exacerbating childhood risk/need factors are the broader social and economic realities of the 1990s. In Canada, more than a million children, and over twenty percent of children below the age of six, are growing up in poverty. About 50,000 Canadian children are in the care of child welfare systems, half come from single parent families, and at least forty percent have experienced abuse or neglect. In that being on welfare provides one of the strongest predictors of psychiatric disorders and chronic health problems among children, it is significant to note that, in Ontario alone, 433,000 children receive social assistance (Canadian Child Welfare Association 1988). The situation is even worse for Canada's Native people (Warry 1991). Particularly vulnerable to poverty are single parent families, which are on the increase. Over one half of these families subsist below the poverty line. The ranks of the "working poor" are also on the rise and now comprise some thirty percent of food bank clients, including an increasing number of children (O'Reilly-Fleming 1993). Compounding the problem, social service areas such as welfare, health care, housing, recreation, mental health, and education have been affected by governmental fiscal belt-tightening and cutbacks. In looking at one aspect of state spending, Chambliss (1991) has cynically observed that surgical cuts in education suspiciously parallel "deep-end" increases in correctional spending. It may also be pointed out that, as a result of Ontario's recently negotiated social contract, provincial institutions are curtailing library services and, in some instances, formal schooling to provincial inmates. This move is particularly ironic when one considers that sixty-five percent of new offenders in Canada recently tested below grade eight level in mathematics and language on standardized tests. The educational picture for youth is further bleakened by national dropout rates over 30%, over 80% on some Native reserves (Sullivan 1988; Karp 1988). Not distinct from the above issue, job prospects for Canadian young persons have been diminishing at a rate that parallels waning government commitment to job strategy programmes for youth. This may be seen through the pre-recession decline in Ontario youth employment, from 1989 to 1991, which amounted to 144,000 lost jobs (John Howard Society of Ontario 1993). In June 1993, the jobless rate for the Province of Ontario was 21.6 percent for persons between the ages of 15 and 24, twice the provincial average.

Towards strategic action

The critical need for well-considered primary and compensatory strategies for children and youth is unarguable. Gendreau and Ross (1987) and Arbuthnot and Gordon (1988a; 1988b) have found that three ingredients are essential for effective prevention programmes: 1) that they begin early; 2) include the family; and 3) involve cognitive /behavioural, problem solving skills.

The national dataset gathered for accused "under twelves", supplemented by research findings on children in conflict with the law, argue compellingly against application of a traditional, correctional paradigm. Response should be less formal and offense-reactive and should focus, rather, on more informal, risk/need proactive strategies. The great preponderance of "under 12" offenses are non-violent (92%) and the majority of all offenses are committed by 10-11-year-olds.

The "under 12" offense data, notwithstanding their admittedly incomplete form, strongly suggest the appropriateness of a defined programme strategy both in terms of content and age application. Within the current federal/ provincial arrangement for children under the age of twelve, the following age differentiated service model can be conjectured: 5 years and under, ages 6-9, and 10-11-year-olds.

Offense characteristics and involvement would suggest that, for the 5 years and under group, early preventative measures should reflect a primary commitment to health and social promotion. As Boyle (1991) correctly points out, children's mental health or psycho-social well-being must be the superordinate concept in determining children's service provision and policy development. Examples include:

- effective prevention programmes
- infant stimulation programmes
- domestic support services
- pre-school "head start" initiatives

While the numbers of accused under the age of five reflected in the dataset are relatively small, constituting less than one half of one percent of overall cohort ages 0-11, their statistical insignificance understates the potential significance for early prevention. A general goal of early prevention is, through appropriate and effective assessment, to curtail what for some children appears to be a fairly consistent maladaptive sequence — early troublesomeness, conduct disorder, peer relationship difficulties, domestic dysfunction, lack of parental/school attachment resulting in deviant/criminal coping mechanisms. Diagnostically sensitive measures, holistically encompassing and longitudinally committed to the integrity of the child in his/her environment (Brofenbrenner 1979; Bateson 1972; Garbarino 1982), must effectively reach the troubled and endangered child before he/she becomes troublesome and dangerous.

Early interventions of a direct, non-correctionalist nature should occur in the 6-9 age group, which constitutes approximately 20% of the 0-11 age group. Classroom-based programmes should address issues such as break and enter (28% of offenses), theft under (32% of offenses), and shoplifting (58% of thefts), as well as mischief/vandalism (15% of offenses), and violence. One of Canada's most effective prevention programmes was the early Waterloo-Wellington Attendance Centre model, originated in Kitchener-Waterloo in 1979 (Clark and O'Reilly-Fleming 1993a; 1993b).

For the 10-11 age group, a strategically greater shift to an early-postvention model appears warranted. This upper age group is responsible for 70% of the total offenses of the under-12 accused cohort. More direct referrals from the police to more intensive and comprehensive services is warranted. Police provide the nation's only 24-hour social service response network for children, and police/child welfare collaboration is absolutely essential to the efficacy of a non-correctionalist prevention strategy for children. We recommend further cognitive/behaviourial programmes and services in the areas of gender/racial sensibilities, victim mediation, positive peer influences, peer mentoring, school and career planning, as well as an individual "buddy/mentoring" system by positive role models from the 12-13 age group. The negative influence of 12-13-year-old youth on the "under twelves" is statistically clear and provides compelling evidence of the susceptibility of "under twelves" to destructive peer influence. The importance of attachment to peers and its relationship to delinquent behaviour has been underscored by recent Canadian research (Brownfield and Thompson 1991).

Twelve- and thirteen-year-old youths, we noted, constituted nearly 70% of older accomplices in the commission of offenses by "under twelves". While drugs and alcohol appear to play a negligible role in "under 12" law-breaking activity, this paucity of involvement should be viewed as a "teachable moment" in prevention rather than an excuse to do nothing. An immersion curriculum on healthy lifestyles should be continued from earlier grades. Increasingly, with "under twelves" a repertoire of realistic, age and situation appropriate avoidance and denial strategies must be inculcated as part of the formal curriculum, as well as through collateral or extra-curricular services. Anti-drug, anti-violence, anti-crime scenarios should be discussed, role-played, and naturally incorporated in the pro-social and pro-health coping arsenal of "under twelves". Greater emphasis upon dialogue and interactive learning about violence, racism, sexism, and age discrimination are essential as the "under twelves" develop their cognitive/reasoning skills and they exercise their burgeoning powers of moral reasoning (Gendreau and Ross 1987; Piaget 1965; Kohlberg 1969).

Assaultive behaviour constitutes 8% of the total "under 12" offenses and, of this number, 82% are against acquaintances. This statistic would seem to underscore the need for a broad access to problem-solving, communications, conflict resolution, and anger management programmes. Specific initiatives such as "Panther's Paws/Pause to Prevent Violence", Princess Elizabeth Senior Public School, London, Ontario, "Conflict Busters", Lansdowne School, Sarnia, Ontario, 1992, "Peacemaking Skills for Little Kids" (Schmidt and Friedman 1993), Prevention of Violence in the School (Department of Community Health, Montreal General Hospital 1989), "Second

Step" (Committee for Children 1992), or the "New Leaf Programme" (Clark, Blyth, Groulx, and Srebro 1992), and "Safe Schools" (Auty 1992) provide encouraging examples for future programme development. An ecologically sensitive "risk/need" barometer would no doubt further suggest the advisability of expanded domestic violence programmes for abusive parents and their children, since parental violence begets violence (Jaffe 1987; Dutton 1982; Wolfe, Jaffe, Wilson and Zak 1985; Jaffe. Wolfe. and Wilson 1990). One Ontario study, for instance, found that children are present during 80% of acts of family violence (Jenson 1989). While assaults with weapons are relatively rare for "under twelves", this aspect of violence should be specifically and proactively addressed.

Educators in Ontario and other provinces have observed an increase in the use or presence of weapons on school property (Ontario Secondary School Teachers' Association 1992; Board of Education for the City of London 1992). While this reported increase may well be a measure of society's unwillingness to accept violence, the potential for increased school violence is certainly present. School programmes and policies on violence should be given priority. Failure to act preemptively will only increase the danger for teachers and students, not to mention the liability of school boards. Violent crimes of a sexual nature among "under twelves" constitute some 1% of offenses. Statistics convincingly reveal the need for early, preventative measures. Given the accessibility of sexually violent and degrading material and the fact that adolescents are the primary consumer group, this is a problem not likely to disappear in the foreseeable future. The importance of primary education and early assessment of deviant and sexually sadistic ideation in children is critical, especially as some would argue that such ideation is progressive. Knopf (1982) argues that sexually assaultive incidents by male youth are drastically underreported with deviant arousal occurring for many at 12 years of age or younger (Groth, Longo, and McFadin 1982). Again, effective prevention and intervention must transcend the limits of formal curriculum. Parental behaviour, cultural and societal norms, as well as media responsibility must be addressed in a comprehensive programme embracing issues of gender, power, and control.

While the preceding offense analysis and programme recommendations may appear overly idealistic, we would argue that, with a well-reasoned, principled, and concerted policy shift, these measures are neither monolithic nor impracticable.

Policy implications

The strategy that arises from the reviews of preliminary data and research for "under twelves" underscores the need for a commitment to an early, proactive, social development paradigm. Early risk/need, as our argument indicates, reflects a constellation of childhood problems and vulnerabilities. These factors are not, as yet, habituated or stylized as "criminogenic needs" (Andrews, Bonta, and Hoge 1988; Andrews, Zinger, and Hoge 1989). Certain factors, however, seem to predispose under 12" children to, or at least increase their susceptibility towards, pro-criminal attitudes and behaviour, perhaps in a sequential, cumulative, or even exponential manner.

The focus of early prevention/intervention should be on the psycho-social well-being of the child, not on an as yet undeveloped, characterological set of criminogenic needs. However, subsequent, more crime-specific intervention/postvention, particularly for 10-11-year-olds, would appear to warrant a detailed, initial assessment of burgeoning criminogenic needs, based upon the currently available and recommended measurements (Andrews, Leschied, and Hoge 1992).

We recommend an approach which is community-based, phasic, and appropriately scaled to risk/need with a suitable matching of client need(s) to client service(s). This paradigm should reflect the spirit and principles of child and youth legislation (Clark and O'Reilly-Fleming 1993a; 1993b) and the conceptual model of the prevention policy framework promulgated by the Ministry of Community and Social Services in Ontario (Ontario Prevention Clearinghouse 1990). This model proposes an "optimal continuum" of interventions, moving from the least restrictive to the most intrusive interventions, theoretically prioritizing a minimalist approach. With "under twelves", strategic, non-correctionalist alternatives present the most appropriate option and most sensibly reflect current legislative principles and policies. As we have argued elsewhere (O'Reilly-Fleming and Clark 1993), there is a profound dichotomy in Ontario between principles and practice, as well as between policies and programmes.

This strategy is ecological and, as such, reflects and indeed requires a diagnostic and service collaboration which cuts across traditional, sectoral lines. It reflects an inclusive, cooperative approach by education, mental health, health and welfare, housing, employment, and culture. Traditional corrections and juvenile justice should be excluded from this endeavour. The simplicity and availability of this paradigm is elusive since these hybrid but complementary systems are now artificially divided and sustained by bureaucratic and ministerial compartmentalization. Individual needs always and inherently transcend artificially imposed boundaries.

It is not the intent of this paper to focus, in detail, on precise policy recommendations. These have been advanced already, with considerable thought and penetration (Johnson and Barnhorst 1991; Advisory Committee on Children's Services 1990). We have recommended before, as have others (Advisory Committee on Children's Services 1990), that a new Ministry for Children and Youth and a Child Ombudsperson, such as Norway first initiated in 1981 in its Commissioner for Children Act (Allen 1993), be established in Ontario. We continue to feel that such strong and immediate measures are the only way that a hopelessly fragmented children's service network can be consolidated and coordinated into a functional system that will serve the totality of needs, interests, and entitlements of children. Substantial changes in practice will result only from substantive policy shifts and these, in turn, must be effected and orchestrated by a newly independent Ministry for Children and Youth.

Concern over "deep end" or reactive programme spending has been well documented (Markwart and Corrado 1989; Koenig 1991; O'Reilly-Fleming and Clark 1993; Clark 1985; John Howard Society of Ontario 1993; Chambliss 1991). As early as 1982 at a seminar entitled "Children's Services Past, Present and Future" held in Kitchener-Waterloo, Ontario, the Associate Deputy Minister of the Ontario Ministry of Community and Social Services, George Thomson, lamented that 94% of their children's services budget was spent on residential and institutional services. Obviously, meaningful changes in children's services must be accompanied by a dramatic reversal of current ideological and fiscal commitments. At present, Canada's imprisonment rate of adults and juveniles (112.7 per 100,000) is exceeded only by the United States, and is followed closely by the United Kingdom. A balanced and comprehensive shift from correctionalist deterrence and punishment, to proactive, multi-disciplinary health promotion and intervention, is necessary to curtail the symbiotic "cycle of disadvantage" (Schorr 1988) and "cycle of delinquency" (Bernard 1992). An undue reliance on residential and institutional responses has resulted in resounding failure in Canada (Polonosli 1980), in the United States (Conrad 1985; Miller 1991) and in the United Kingdom (Graef 1993; Vanstone 1993). Frances Allen (1974) puts this irony rather nicely: "It is important, first, to recognize that when, in an authoritative setting, we attempt to do something for a child, "because of what he is and needs," we are also doing something to him".

Conclusion

The Uniform Crime Report, "Crimes Committed by Children Under 12", provides a sufficiently large and geographically diverse dataset to make some initial assumptions about the nature of "under 12" crime. Complemented by a definitive body of interdisciplinary research on youth at-risk, empirically-based strategic planning and interventions are recommended.

The specific nature, degree, and location of "under 12" offenses each invite reasonable and particular responses. The primacy of a continuum of least restrictive/compensatory intervention is warranted, which must proceed logically from targeted health promotion and social development for the 5 years and under group, to multiple offense-specific interventions for the 10-11-year-old youths.

While this paper has focussed on the "under twelves", we contend that an ecological approach defies arbitrary age categories. The emphasis upon an early, collaborative and community-based paradigm must surely continue into the young offender system, involving youths 12-16 years old. Sensitive risk/need assessment and a correspondingly sensible matching of young persons and adults to a balanced service continuum is a promising approach (Andrews, Leschied, and Hoge 1992; Bonta and Motluk 1990). Ideally, effective and early prevention will deflect many children from later involvement in the young offender system. With unprecedented political will and integrity, young offender dollars and energies could be liberated and more appropriately and dually re-allocated to early prevention as well as to high risk/need offenders who are most apt to benefit from intensive, structured intervention/postvention. Child welfare and youth corrections must learn to co-exist as an integrated and complementary system.

In a decade of increasing financial restraint, there is, perhaps, cause to be cautiously optimistic that fundamental, ameliorative change must and will occur. A prodigious meta-analysis of psycho-correctional literature, supplemented by new directions in substance abuse and crime prevention, are indeed promising. The critical challenge, at this juncture in the traditional cycle of corrections, is to move from an academically rich thesis to a clinically informed praxis.

Notes

1. Barry Clark is Executive Director of the John Howard Society of Windsor-Essex and teaches Criminology at the University of Windsor. He is a Ph.D. candidate at the University of Stirling, Scotland, U.K.

Dr. Thomas O'Reilly-Fleming is a professor and chair of the Criminology Programme, Department of Sociology and Anthropology, University of Windsor and Director of the University's Criminological and Socio-Legal Research Unit.

The writers would like to acknowledge the kind assistance of The Canadian Centre for Justice Statistics, Ottawa, especially Roy Jones, Holly Johnson, and Richard DuWors. Also a note of appreciation to the Board of Directors of the John Howard Society of Windsor-Essex, to Lisa Colwill (M.A. Candidate) and Danielle Hebert for typing the manuscript, and to the anonymous referees for reviewing the article.

References

Advisory Committee on Children's Services
1990 Children First: Report of the Advisory Committee on Children's Services. Toronto: Queen's Printer.

Allen, R.
1993 Responding to youth crime in Norway: Suggestions for England and Wales. Howard Journal of Criminal Justice 32(3): 99-114.

Allen, F.
1974 Borderland of Criminal Justice: Essays in Law and Criminology. Chicago, Ill: University of Chicago Press.

Allison, K.
1989 Implications of the Ontario Student Drug Survey for School-Based Prevention Programmes. Toronto: Addiction Research Foundation.

Andrews, D., I. Zinger, and R. Hoge
1989 Does Correctional Treatment Work? A Clinically Relevant and Psychologically Informed Meta-Analysis. Ottawa: Carleton University.

Andrews, D., A. Leschied, and R. Hoge
1992 Review of the Profile, Classification and Treatment Literature with Young Offenders: A Social-Psychological Approach. Ottawa: Carleton University.

Andrews, D., J. Bonta, and R. Hoge
1988 Classification For Effective Rehabilitation: Rediscovering Psychology. Ottawa: Carleton University.

Arbuthnot, J. and D. Gordon
1988a Crime and cognition: community applications of sociomoral reasoning. Criminal Justice and Behavior 15(3): 379-393.

Arbuthnot, J. and D. Gordon
1988b The use of paraprofessionals to deliver home-based family therapy to juvenile delinquents. Criminal Justice and Behavior 15(3): 364-378.

Auty, S.
1992 The Safe School Task Force: Resource Kit. Toronto: OSSTF.

Bailey, G.
1989 Current perspectives on substance abuse in youth. Journal of the American Academy of Child and Adolescent Psychiatry 28: 151-162.

Bateson, Gregory
1972 Steps to an Ecology of Mind. San Francisco: Chandler Publishing Co.

Bernard, T.
1992 The Cycle of Juvenile Justice. New York, New York: Oxford University Press. Board of Education for the City of London
1992 A Curricular Resource Document for Violence Prevention. London: Board of Education for the City of London.

Bonta, J. and L. Motiuk
1990 Classification to halfway houses: A quasi-experimental evaluation. Criminology 28(3): 497-506.

Boyle, M.
1991 Children's mental health issues. In L. Johnson and D. Bamhorst (eds.), Children, Families and Public Policy in the 90's. Toronto: Thompson Educational Publishing.

Bronfenbrenner, V.
1979 The Ecology of Human Development: Experiments by Nature and Design. Cambridge: Harvard University Press.

Brownfield, D. and K. Thompson
1991 Attachment to peers and delinquent behaviour. Canadian Journal of Criminology 33(1): 45-60.

Buikhuisen, W.
1989 Juvenile delinquency: A multi-disciplinary theory. International Journal of Offender Therapy and Comparative Criminology 33(3): 185-195.

Canadian Centre for Justice Statistics
1992a Youth Court Statistics 1991-92. Ottawa Information and Client Services, Statistics Canada. Canadian Centre for Justice Statistics
1992b Crimes Committed by Children Under 12. Ottawa: Canadian Centre for Justice Statistics, Statistics Canada.

Canadian Child Welfare Association
1988 A Choice of Futures: Canada's Commitment to its Children. Ottawa: Department of National Health and Welfare.

Chambliss, W.
1991 Trading Textbooks for Prison Cells. Alexandria, Virginia: National Centre on Institutions and Alternatives.

Clark, Barry and Thomas O'Reilly-Fleming
1993a From care to punishment: Rehabilitating young offender programming in Ontario. In Barry Clark and Thomas O'Reilly Fleming (eds.), Youth Injustice: Canadian Perspectives. Toronto: Canadian Scholars' Press.

Clark, Barry and Thomas O'Reilly-Fleming
1993b Implementing the Young Offenders Act in Ontario: Issues of principles, programmes and power. Journal of Criminal Justice 32(2): 113-126.

Clark, Barry
1985 Community Corrections: In Search of a Less Restrictive Alternative. Paper presented at the Kids not Cons Conference (A Problem in Search of a Policy: Children Under 12 in Conflict with the Law). Toronto: Metro Children's Advisory Group.

Clark, B., K. Blyth, T. Groulx, and 1. Srebro
1992 New Leaf Anger Management Manual. Windsor, Ontario: John Howard Society. Committee for Children
1992 Second Step: Skill Training Curricula to Prevent Youth Violence. Seattle, Wash.

Conrad, J.
1985 The Dangerous and the Endangered. Toronto: Lexington.

Department of Community Health, Montreal General Hospital
1989 Prevention of Violence in the School: Teachers' Manual and Student's Workbook. Montreal: National Library of Quebec.

Department of Justice Canada
1993 Toward Safer Communities: Violent and Repeat Offending by Young People. Ottawa: Young Offenders Project, Department of Justice Canada.

Dutton, D.
1982 Proceedings and Evidence of the Standing Committee on Health and Welfare and Social Affairs: Inquiry into Violence in the Family 25(6)

Empey, L.
1982 American Delinquency: Its Meaning and Construction, Homewood, Ill.: Dorsey Press.

Garbarino, James
1982 Children and Families in the Social Environment. New York, New York: Aldine Publishing Co.

Gendreau, P. and R. Ross
1987 Revivification of rehabilitation: Evidence from the 1980s. Justice Quarterly 4: 349-407.

Gomme, I.
1985 Predictors of status and criminal offenses among male and female adolescents in an Ontario community. Canadian Journal of Criminology 27(2): 147-161

Graef, R.
1993 Living Dangerously: Young Offenders in their own Words. London, U.K.: Harper Collins Publishers.

Groth, A., R. Longo, and J. McFadin
1982 Undetected recidivism among rapists and child molesters. Crime and Delinquency 28(3): 450-458.

Hamparian, D., R. Schuster, S. Dinitz, and J.Conrad
1978 The Violent Few. Toronto: Lexington.

Hawkins, J., J. Jenson, and R. Catalano
1988 Delinquency and drug abuse implications for social services. Social Service Review 62(5): 258-284.

Hudson, J., J. Hornick, and B. Burrows (eds.)
1988 Justice and the Young Offender in Canada. Toronto: Wall and Thompson.

Jaffe, P.
1987 Annual Report. London, Ontario: London Family Court Clinic.

Jaffe, P., D. Wolfe, and S.K. Wilson
1990 Children of Battered Women. Newbury Park: Sage

Jenson, P.
1989 Spousal Abuse in Metropolitan Toronto: Research Report on the Response of the Criminal Justice System. Toronto: Metro Toronto Advisory Committee on Spousal Abuse.

John Howard Society of Ontario
1993 J.H.S.O. Fact Sheet, Toronto

Johnson, L. and D. Barnhorst
1991 Children, Families and Public Policy in the 90's. Toronto: Thompson.

Karp, E.
1988 The Drop-Out Phenomenon in Ontario Secondary Schools. Toronto, Ontario: MGS Publications Services.

Knopf, F.
1982 Remedial Intervention in Adolescent Sex Offenses: Nine Program Descriptions. New York, New York: Safer Society Press.

Koenig, D.
1991 Do Police Cause Crime? Police Activity, Police Strength and Crime Rates. Ottawa: Minister of Supply and Services Canada.

Kohlberg, L.
1969 Stage and sequency: The cognitive developmental approach to socialization. In D. Goslin (ed.), Handbook of Socialization. Chicago, Ill.: Rand McNally.

Leschied, A., P. Jaffe, and W. Willis
1991 The Young Offenders Act: A Revolution in Canadian Juvenile Justice. Toronto: University of Toronto Press.

Leschied, Allan D.W. and Susan Kaye Wilson
1988 Criminal liability of children under twelve: A problem for child welfare, juvenile justice or both? Canadian Journal of Criminology 30(1): 17-29.

Levin, M.
1991 Paper presented at Winds of Change, Conference on Learning Disabilities, MOLD, Chicago, Ill.

Lewis, D., R. Lovely, C. Yaeger, G. Ferguson, M. Friedman, G. Sloane, H. Friedman, and J. Pincus
1988 Intrinsic and environmental characteristics of juvenile murderers. Journal of the American Academy of Child and Adolescent Psychiatry 27(5): 582-587.

Loeber, R.
1991 Risk factors and the development of disruptive and antisocial behaviour in children. Forum On Corrections Research, Correctional Service Canada 3(3): 22-28.

Markwart, A. and R. Corrado
1989 Is the Young Offenders Act more punitive? In L.A. Beaulieu (ed.), Young Offender Disposition: Perspectives on Principles and Practice. Toronto: Wall and Thompson.

McManus, M., N. Alessi, W. Grapentine, and A. Brickman
1984 Psychiatric disturbance in serious delinquents. Journal of the American Academy of Child Psychiatry 23(5): 602-615.

Miller, J.
1991 The Last One Over the Wall: The Massachusetts Experiment in Closing Reform Schools. Columbus, Ohio: Ohio State University Press.

O'Reilly-Fleming, Thomas
1993 Down and Out in Canada: Homeless Canadians. Toronto: Canadian Scholar's Press.

O'Reilly-Fleming, Thomas and Barry Clark (eds.)
1993 Youth Injustice: Canadian Perspectives. Toronto: Canadian Scholars' Press.

Offord, D., M. Boyle, and Y. Racine
1988 The Epidemiology of Antisocial Behaviour in Childhood and Adolescence. Paper presented at the Earlscourt Symposium on Childhood Aggression. Toronto, Ontario.

Ontario Prevention Clearinghouse
1990 Newsletter 2(7).

Ontario Secondary School Teachers' Association
1992 The Safe School Task Force: Resource Kit. Toronto: OSSTF.

Patterson, G., B. Debanyshe, and E. Ramsey
1989 A developmental perspective on antisocial behaviour. American Psychologist 44(2): 329-335.

Piaget, J.
1965 Moral Judgement of the Child. New York, New York: Free Press.

Polonoski, M.
1980 Chronic Young Offenders, Ministry of Correctional Services, Toronto: Queen's Printer.

Rae-Grant, N.
1979 The State of the Art: A Background paper on Prevention. Toronto: Ministry of Community and Social Services, Children's Services Division.

Raychaba, B.
1987 Leaving Care — Where? Paper presented at the Canadian Conference to Observe the International Year of Shelter for the Homeless, Ottawa, Ontario.

Rogeness, G., S. Amrung, C. Macedo, W. Harris, and C. Fisher
1986 Psychopathology in abused or neglected children. Journal of the American Academy of Child Psychiatry 25(5): 659-665.

Rutter, M.
1987 Psychosocial resilience and protective mechanisms. American Journal of Orthopsychiatry 57(3): 316-331.

Sas, L., P. Jaffe, and J. Reddon
1985 Unravelling the needs of dangerous young offenders: A clinical-rational and empirical approach to classification. Canadian Journal of Criminology 27(1): 83-96.

Schmidt, F. and A. Friedman
1993 Peacemaking Skills for Little Kids. Miami Beach, Fl.: Grace Contrino Abrams Peace Education Foundation.

Schorr, L.
1988 Within Our Reach: Breaking the Cycle of Disadvantage. New York: Anchor Press.

Sullivan, M.
1988 A Comparative Analysis of Drop-outs and Non Drop-Outs in Ontario Secondary Schools. Toronto, Ontario: MGS Publications Services.

Thompson, A.
1988 Young offender, child welfare, and mental health caseload commonalities. Canadian Journal of Criminology 30(2): 135-144.

Thornton, W. and D. Voigt
1992 Delinquency and Justice. New York, New York: McGraw Hill.

Tremblay, R., R. Zhou, C. Gagnon, F. Vitaro, and H. Boileau
1991 Violent boys: Development and prevention. Forum On Corrections Research. Correctional Service Canada 3(3): 29-35.

Vanstone, M.
1993 A "missed" opportunity re-assessed: The influence of the day training centre experiment on the criminal justice system and probation policy and practice. The British Journal of Social Work 23(3): 213-229.

Waller, I. and D. Weiler
1985 Crime Prevention Through Social Development. Ottawa: Canadian Council on Social Development.

Warry, W.
1991 Ontario's First People. In L. Johnson and D. Barnhorst (eds.), Children, Families and Public Policy in the 90's. Toronto: Thompson Educational.

Watts, W. and L. Wright
1990 The relationship of alcohol, tobacco, marijuana, and other illegal drug use to delinquency among Mexican American, Black and White adolescent males. Adolescence XXV(Spring): 171-181.

West, D. and D. Farrington
1973 Who Becomes Delinquent? London: Heinemann.

West, D. and D. Farrington
1977 The Delinquent Way of Life. London: Heinemann.

Wolfe, D., P. Jaffe, S.K. Wilson, and L. Zak.
1985 Children of battered women: The relation of child behaviour to family violence and maternal stress. Journal of Consulting and Clinical Psychology 53: 657-665.

CHAPTER EIGHTEEN

"Lock 'em up": Attitudes toward punishing juvenile offenders[1]

Stephen W. Baron
Department of Sociology and Anthropology
University of Windsor
Windsor, Ontario
and **Timothy F. Hartnagel**
Department of Sociology
University of Alberta
Edmonton, Alberta

CONTROVERSY HAS FREQUENTLY CHARACTERIZED THE SUBJECT OF society's response to youth crime (Hylton 1994). The Canadian *Juvenile Delinquents Act* of 1908, with its broad definition of delinquency, and its non-adversarial, welfare approach certainly had its critics (Lovekin 1961; McGrath 1962; West 1984). Among other things, they pointed to its lack of due process rights for juveniles, the disparities in sentencing resulting from the informality and wide discretion of the courts and child welfare authorities, its lenient financial penalties, lack of uniform implementation across the country, and insufficient attention to punishment and the protection of society (Hylton 1994).

The *Young Offenders Act* proclaimed in 1984 replaced the *Juvenile Delinquents Act* with a new philosophy of responding to youthful offenders (Griffiths and Verdun-Jones 1989; Hylton 1994). But it took several proposed drafts of the Act through 17 years before it was passed by Parliament in 1982. A major reason for this delay was the disagreement and lobbying amongst interested groups over the conflicting models or

Canadian Journal of Criminology/Revue canadienne de criminologie, April/avril 1996, pp. 191–212.

philosophies of welfare, crime control, and due process (Bala 1994; Coflin 1988; Griffiths and Verdun-Jones 1989). Opposition to the legislative changes came from several quarters, with the police concerned about legal restrictions on them while social workers and criminologists argued for the primacy of professional definition of treatment needs (West 1991). In the view of a number of commentators, the final draft, while containing references to all three models, emphasized justice and due process at the expense of the welfare and rehabilitation of youthful offenders (Griffiths and Verdun-Jones 1989; Leschied and Gendreau 1986; 1994; Leschied and Jaffe 1991; Reid and Reitsma-Street 1984). More recently, Judge Archambault claimed that the *Young Offenders Act* gives undue attention to public protection over the needs and treatment of young offenders (Archambault 1991). Corroborating his opinion is the evidence of an increase in custodial dispositions under the new Act (Doob 1992; Leschied and Gendreau 1994; Leschied and Jaffe 1987; 1991).

Several amendments to the *Young Offenders Act* were passed in 1986 and in 1992, including several changes to tighten procedures and enhance crime control and public protection. These changes were also accompanied by considerable controversy (Bennett 1985; Bala and Kirvan 1991; Hylton 1994). More recently, often in reaction to a sensational case, considerable public criticism and political concern has been focused upon certain aspects of the Act. In particular, the perceived inadequacy of the maximum sentence for homicide and difficulties in transferring youth to adult court have been singled out (Bala and Kirvan 1991; Hylton 1994). Political figures and newspaper editorials have called for additional changes to the Act to hold youth more accountable and responsible for their behaviour and to protect the public from violent youthful offenders. Similarly, there have been numerous newspaper articles and letters to the editor concerned with youth crime and the *Young Offenders Act*. So although many were initially critical of the *Young Offenders Act* for its perceived harshness and emphasis upon holding youthful offenders responsible for their crimes, today there is increased concern that in certain respects the Act is too lenient (Corrado and Markwart 1994; Hylton 1994). As of this writing, Parliament has passed additional amendments that further emphasize punishment for young offenders and the protection of society.

Criminologists have become more interested in various aspects of public opinion regarding crime and criminal justice, at least partly due to the relationship between public opinion and criminal justice policy (Zimmerman, Van Alstyne, and Dunn 1988). In his recent review article, Roberts (1992) claims that it is clear that public officials' beliefs about public opinion influence criminal justice policy, so understanding public opinion will aid in understanding the origins of recent criminal justice policy changes. There have been a number of studies and review articles in recent years of public preferences for criminal justice penalties and policies (Cullen, Clark, Cullen, and Mathers 1985; Cullen, Clark, and Wozniak 1985; Roberts 1992). Perhaps surprisingly, however, there has been little research on public opinion regarding juvenile justice issues. A few survey results have been published in the United States (Schwartz, Guo and Kerbs 1993), but we are not aware of any recent Canadian research on public attitudes toward juvenile justice issues. So the current Canadian public policy debate in this area is proceeding in the absence of any systematic analysis of public attitudes.

The current research was designed to contribute to this area by testing a model predicting public attitudes toward juvenile justice. More specifically, we will specify and test a model to predict public support for a juvenile curfew, for moving juvenile court cases to adult court, and public opinion concerning youth court sentencing severity. The predictor variables are drawn primarily from the research literature concerned with adult criminal justice topics, and include such variables as fear of crime, conservative values, victimization experience, as well as demographic predictors. The data derive from the 1993 Winnipeg Area Study, an amalgam survey using telephone interviewing to obtain a representative sample of the adult population of Winnipeg, Manitoba.

Literature review

The few surveys of public opinion in the United States concerning juvenile justice have tended to focus on such topics as support for the juvenile death penalty, moving juvenile cases to adult court, the sentencing of juveniles compared to adults convicted of the same offense, and the incarceration of juveniles in adult prisons. There have also been a few attempts to examine the influence of demographic and attitudinal variables in explaining public opinions on these juvenile justice issues.

There is consistent evidence of fairly strong opposition to the juvenile death penalty (Gallup 1972; Skovron, Scott, and Cullen 1989). There is some evidence that males are more supportive of the juvenile death penalty, but attitudinal variables such as perceived effectiveness of rehabilitation and support for rehabilitative penal policies are more significantly and consistently related to views on the death penalty for juveniles than are demographic variables (Skovron *et al.* 1989).

While there appears to be the same widespread view that juvenile courts are too lenient in their handling of serious offenders (Opinion Research Corporation 1982) as there is with respect to the sentencing of adults (Blumstein and Cohen 1980; Sacco and Johnson 1990), a majority of respondents in several studies did not favour giving juveniles the same sentences as adults (Schwartz, Abbey, and Barton 1990; Schwartz, Guo, and Kerbs 1992; 1993; Steinhart 1988). Males again appear to be more punitive than females in this regard (Schwartz, Abbey, and Barton 1990; Schwartz, Guo, and Kerbs 1992; 1993). A majority of respondents appear to favour trying juveniles for serious crimes in adult courts, while there is little support for incarcerating convicted juvenile offenders in adult prisons (Schwartz, Abbey, and Barton 1990; Schwartz, Guo, and Kerbs 1992, Steinhart 1988). Schwartz, Guo, and Kerbs (1992), using a logistical regression model, reported that those with more education were less punitive on juvenile justice issues, while males, older respondents, and those more fearful of victimization held more punitive attitudes. Analyzing the same national data set, Schwartz, Guo, and Kerbs (1993) focused specifically upon the impact of age, ethnicity, and parental status. The results suggested that, net of other predictors, adults with children are less punitive toward juveniles than adults without children, but only with respect to giving juveniles the same sentence as adults. While ethnicity was not a significant net predictor, African-American parents were significantly more punitive than parents of other racial/ethnic groups. These authors also reported a curvilinear relationship between age and punitive attitudes: punitive attitudes toward juveniles decreased up to around fifty years of age, and then increased.

This small body of research suggests that public opinion distinguishes between the legal processing of juvenile offenders accused of serious crimes and the types of dispositions and correctional interventions juveniles should receive (Schwartz, Guo, and Kerbs 1993). More specifically, while the public favours having juveniles accused of serious crimes tried in adult courts, they do not favour giving juveniles the same sentences as adults nor sentencing them to adult prisons. Schwartz, Guo, and Kerbs (1993) interpret these findings as a willingness to move away from the ***parens patriae*** model of juvenile justice, but without a willingness to abandon systems of youth correction and rehabilitation. Furthermore, education, gender, age, and fear of victimization appear to be significant predictors of such attitudes, along with the possible impact of parental status. These results from U.S. research may not apply directly to Canadian public opinion.

Theoretical framework

Efforts to account for the increasingly punitive attitudes toward adult offenders found in United States public opinion research have tended to focus upon two theories with respect to how such attitudes arise (Langworthy and Whitehead 1986). One argument traces these punitive attitudes to increased levels of fear of crime, which in turn is attributable to personal or vicarious victimization, political exploitation of criminal justice issues, and media treatment of crime "news" (Sheley 1985). "Thus, fear of crime leads to punitive attitudes and to pressure on legislators to adopt punitive measures, restrict civil liberties, and ease due process safe guards (Langworthy and Whitehead 1986: 576)." The second theoretical argument links punitive attitudes to an individual's values, particularly the dimension of liberalism-conservatism (Scheingold 1984). Conservatives are more punitive because they believe criminals choose to commit crimes and deserve to be punished or that the costs of crime need to be increased through more consistent punishments in order to deter crime. Liberals, on the other hand, are more positivistic in their beliefs about crime and criminals and are therefore less punitive since they regard social programs as the primary solution to the crime problem (Langworthy and Whitehead 1986). Scheingold (1984: 56) also seems to suggest that the attitudinal response to fear of crime depends upon these basic values: "...whether we respond punitively or nonpunitively to our fears is culturally determined - attributable, that is, to the values and emotions which we bring to our thinking about crime...." In other words, in addition to whatever direct impact values may have on punitiveness, these values may also interact with fear to affect an individual's attitudinal response to crime.

The research evidence on the relationship between fear and punitiveness is mixed. While some research (Stinchcombe, Adams, Heimer, Scheppele, Smith, Taylor 1980; Taylor, Scheppele, and Stinchcombe 1979) has not found a consistent, strong relationship between fear of crime and punitiveness, other research (Langworthy and Whitehead 1986; Thomas and Foster 1975) has reported that fear is an important determinant of punitive attitudes. There is stronger support, however, for the role of values in shaping attitudes toward punishment. For example, Taylor *et al.* (1979) found that conservatives were more punitive, independent of fear or victimization, while Stinchcombe *et al.* (1980) reported that a liberal political orientation was somewhat related to leniency of attitude toward punishment. Similar results were reported by Langworthy and Whitehead (1986). Cullen *et al.* (1985a) found that those who had a more positivistic orientation toward crime – viewing it as determined – were less punitive and more in favour of rehabilitation.

The present research analyzes a model predicting punitiveness toward young offenders based upon this theoretical framework and previous research. We will test predictions that both fear of crime and underlying values affect punitive attitudes. More specifically, we expect a direct, positive effect of fear of crime on punitive attitudes, net of other predictors. Similarly, conservative values should have a direct, positive net effect on punitiveness. Furthermore, we include in the model a set of demographic variables related to punitiveness toward juvenile offenders, including parental status, and expect to find both direct and indirect effects of such background variables through the fear of crime and basic values (Langworthy and Whitehead 1986). The model also includes victimization, which we expect will only have indirect effects on punitiveness through fear of crime. Figure 1 presents this model and summarizes our predictions.

In addition to testing this model, we will explore the suggestion from Scheingold (1984) of possible interaction between fear of crime and basic values in predicting punitiveness.

Figure 1
Theoretical model predicting punitiveness

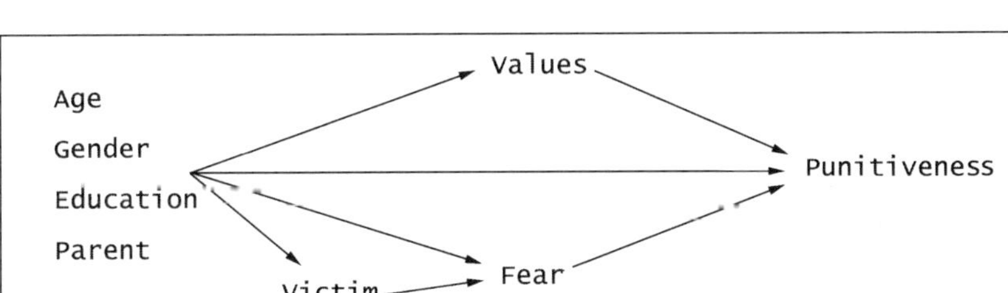

Data and methods

The data for this research come from the 1993 Winnipeg Area Study, an amalgam telephone survey of Winnipeg, Manitoba, households with telephone numbers in 1992 conducted from February 26th to May 1st, 1993. A random sample of 3000 telephone numbers was generated, with household as the primary sampling unit and gender, age, and residency in the household the selection criteria used to choose a respondent within each of the households. A random predesignation of each household as either male or female was recorded on the front of the interview form; an eligible respondent was also someone 18 years of age or older, and who resided at that address. Ten professional interviewers conducted the telephone interviews and they were instructed to phone a number at least ten times before listing it as a non-contact (N = 214). Respondents were replaced in 140 cases, primarily due to illness, deafness, or functional disability (N = 88) or limited/ no knowledge of English (N = 35). An analysis of types of contact, based on the 3-digit telephone prefix, showed no significant differences between the numbers where interviews were obtained and other types of contact. A sample of households was called by the field coordinator to ensure that interviews were being conducted professionally and no problems were reported. Interviews were completed in 499 households for a completion rate of 76% of eligible households. Comparisons, where possible with the 1986 Census of Winnipeg, indicate that this telephone sample is a reasonably accurate representation of the Winnipeg population for such characteristics as sex, age, household size, and home ownership.

Three separate indicators for the dependent variable of punitiveness toward young offenders were included in the interview schedule. Respondents were asked to agree or disagree on a seven point scale with the following statements: A curfew for children under 16 is a good idea; Young offenders who commit a second offence should be tried in adult courts; Youth courts have become too lenient with young offenders.

Table 1 displays the response frequencies for each of these indicators.

Table 1
Percentage Distributions for dependent variables

		Curfew for children under 16	Youth 2nd offense adult court	Youth courts too lenient
Strongly disagree	1	11.0%	4.8%	2.2%
	2	6.0%	4.8%	3.2%
	3	5.4%	7.6%	3.4%
	4	9.2%	10.4%	7.8%
	5	11.4%	13.8%	12.6%
	6	12.8%	16.4%	16.2%
Strongly agree	7	43.3%	36.7%	49.5%
	Total	100.0% (N = 495) X = 5.174	100.0% (N = 472) X = 5.322	100.0% (N = 474) X = 5.865

Each of these measures is fairly skewed toward the more punitive end of the scale, with fewer than 25% of respondents disagreeing with each statement.

The background variables of age, gender, and education were measured in standard ways. In addition, respondents were asked how many people under 18 presently live in the household. Sixty-two percent had no children, with a mean of .699. Victimization was measured by asking whether the respondent or any member of the household had been the victim of a crime in the last year, with response categories of yes (22%) or no. Fear of crime was indicated by responses on a four-point scale to the question: How safe do you feel or would you feel walking along in your neighbourhood after dark. Twenty percent indicated they feel somewhat unsafe, with 13% stating they feel very unsafe.

In measuring basic values, we distinguished among several aspects, each based upon Scheingold's (1984) argument that the dimension of liberalism-conservatism is significant in predicting punitiveness. For each item, respondents were asked to disagree-agree on a seven-point scale. Political liberalism was measured by the single item indicator "People who want to overthrow the government by revolution should be allowed to hold public meetings to express their views". Social liberalism was measured by an index constructed from the following three items: "Obedience and respect of authority are the most important virtues children should learn"; "People who come to Canada should change their ways of life to be more like everyone else"; "More women working outside the home has led to more unhappy marriages" (Alpha = .518). Finally, following Scheingold's (1984) linking of liberalism with a positivistic view of crime and conservatism with an emphasis upon retribution and deterrence, we also measured liberalism with respect to the purposes of punishment by two items: "Rehabilitating a young offender is more important than making the young offender pay for the crime"; and "Sending young offenders to jail will not stop them from committing crimes". Table 2 summarizes the distribution of responses to each of these four indicators of basic, liberal-conservative values.

Results

We used ordinary least squares regression to obtain path coefficients to test the model for each of the three measures of the dependent variable. Table 3 displays the total direct, and total indirect effects of the predictor variables for support for a curfew. Support for a juvenile curfew is not affected by the respondents' fear of crime, net of the other predictors. But those who are more conservative on the index of social values are significantly more likely to support a curfew for juveniles. This is the strongest net direct effect of the several predictors. But contrary to our initial expectations, those favouring rehabilitation are also in favour of a curfew. Of the four background variables only education has a significant and, as predicted, negative effect.

But close to half of the total effect of education is indirect and mediated primarily by the index of social values: respondents with more education are more liberal on social values and, therefore, less favorable toward a curfew. Also as expected, victimization does not have any significant direct effect, but its indirect effect via fear is also trivial.

Table 2
Frequency distributions for value measures

Political (Overthrow) Conservative (%)		Social (Index) Liberal (%)		Rehabilitation Conservative (%)		Deterrence Conservative (%)	
1	44.7	1	.2	1	4.5	1	15.8
1	44.7	1	.2	1	4.5	1	15.8
2	11.1	1.33	1.3	2	6.4	2	9.9
3	8.6	1.67	1.7	3	4.9	3	11.9
4	13.9	2	4.4	4	14.3	4	13.0
5	8.4	2.33	3.2	5	16.0	5	15.2
6	4.7	2.67	4.8	6	17.0	6	15.4
7	8.6	3	9.3	7	36.9	7	18.7
Liberal		3.33	6.3	Liberal		Liberal	
N = 488		3.67	8.2	N = 488		N = 486	
X = 2.79				X = 5.30		X = 4.23	
		4	7.2				
		4.33	8.0				
		4.67	4.8				
		5	13.1				
		5.33	5.5				
		5.67	7.8				
		6	4.2				
		6.33	3.4				
		6.67	2.3				
		7	4.4				
		Conservative					
		N = 475					
		X = 4.30					

Table 3
Curfew for children under age 16

Independent variables	Total indirect effects	Direct effect	Total effect
Age	.183	.073	.112
Gender	.006	.049	.056
Education	-.095	-.102*	-.196
Parent	.029	.068	.097
Victim	-.006	-.005	-.010
Fear	—	.083	.082
Rehabilitation	—	.116*	.116
Deterrence	—	-.019	-.019
Political	—	-.036	-.036
Social	—	.380****	.380

R2 = .189   * sig .05   *** sig .001
N = 429/499   ** sig .01   **** sig .0001

Turning to support for moving juvenile cases to adult court, Table 4 shows that, again, there is no significant net direct effect of fear of crime, while the more conservative respondents on the social values index are more likely to support moving young second offenders to adult court. Those who favour rehabilitation are significantly more likely to oppose this greater punitiveness toward young offenders. There are no significant direct effects from the background variables nor, as expected, from victimization, and its indirect effects via fear are again trivial. But, overall, the model fails to explain much of the variation in support for this criminal justice measure (R2 = .087).

For the general attitude that youth courts are too lenient the results in Table 5 indicate that fear again fails to have a significant impact, while conservative social values are the strongest net predictors of greater punitiveness. Those who are also more conservative politically are also more punitive,

Table 4
Youth committing a second offense tried in adult court

Independent variables	Total indirect effects	Direct effect	Total effect
Age	.073	.034	.106
Gender	–.049	.091	.042
Education	–.042	–.047	–.088
Parent	.032	–.040	–.007
Victim	.003	–.053	–.050
Fear	—	–.048	–.048
Rehabilitation	—	–.147**	–.147
Deterrence	—	–.066	–.066
Political	—	.004	.004
Social	—	.198***	.198

R2 = .087 * sig .05 *** sig .001
N = 418/499 ** sig .01 **** sig .0001

Table 5
Youth courts are too lenient

Independent variables	Total indirect effects	Direct effect	Total effect
Age	.117	.007	.124
Gender	–.040	.051	.010
Education	–.048	.016	–.032
Parent	.036	.015	.051
Victim	.000	–.074	–.074
Fear	—	–.001	–.001
Rehabilitation	—	–.087	–.087
Deterrence	—	–.120**	–.120
Political	—	–.134**	–.134
Social	—	.262****	.262

R2 = .149 * sig .05 *** sig .001
N = 415/499 ** sig .01 **** sig .0001

as are those who support the philosophy of deterrence. Again, there are no direct or indirect effects of victimization, nor are any of the background variables significant net predictors. Age appears to have an indirect effect through the social values index: older respondents hold more conservative social values which in turn predict greater punitiveness. Since analysis of the residuals revealed seven outliers, we repeated the regression with these cases dropped. The results remained essentially unchanged, except that those favoring rehabilitation now are significantly opposed to greater punitiveness and the variance explained is increased ($R2$ = .20).

We also explored the possible interactions between fear of crime and the value measures. Only one of the twelve interactions was statistically significant and the mean differences were small.

Discussion

We were surprised by the high degree of support for such punitive responses to delinquency as establishing a curfew for youth under 16 years of age and moving young offenders who have committed a second offense to adult court. Along with these punitive responses, most respondents also felt that youth courts have become too lenient. While the latter finding is similar to the public's perception of lenient sentencing in adult courts (Sacco and Johnson 1990), even here our respondents were more punitive in their attitude. Sacco and Johnson report that 62% of Canadians felt that sentences were not severe enough, while 78% of our respondents agreed that youth courts have become too lenient.

This high level of punitiveness toward young offenders is not based upon experiences of actual victimization. Overall, the level of recent victimization is only 22%. Furthermore, victimization has no significant net effect on any of our three measures of punitiveness. Similarly, although a third of the respondents express a fear of crime, the regression results fail to reveal the expected effect of fear on punitiveness.

The theoretical model receives only partial support in these results. Contrary to the model, neither fear nor the background variables have consistent net effects on punitiveness. As predicted, respondents holding more conservative social values are consistently more punitive in their attitudes toward juveniles. This result is similar to the recent American work of Grasmick and McGill (1994) linking conservative religious beliefs to greater punitiveness toward juvenile offenders through the intervening mechanism of a dispositional attribution style. Further, our results suggest that it is important to distinguish various aspects or dimensions of liberal-conservative value positions. Social values appear to be particularly significant predictors of punitiveness, much more so than political values. There is also some suggestion that underlying beliefs about the causes of crime and the purposes of punishment influence the degree of punitiveness, although the results here are not consistent across the three dependent variables. Yet this does provide some additional support for the view that attributional style is related to degree of punitiveness (Cullen *et al.* 1985a; Grasmick and McGill 1994). So, when background variables, fear, and values are all included in the same regression analysis, only the latter appear to predict punitive attitudes toward juveniles. Other variables clearly need to be included in the model to improve predictive accuracy, though the R2 values here are generally comparable to those found in previous research. The model needs to be expanded to consider additional sources of punitiveness.

It may be that the unexpectedly high degree of punitiveness toward young offenders observed here is related to the recent high profile given to issues related to the *Young Offenders Act* in the media, among certain politicians, and other special interest groups. Past research reveals that there is a degree of imbalance in the news reporting of crime (Muncie 1984; Doob and Roberts 1983). The press search for the most sensational, unexpected, and dramatic aspects of youth behavior, amplifying the phenomenon being reported. The reporting is rarely related to an actual increase in the incidents of such crimes (Muncie 1984). Since most respondents have little if any direct experience of the criminal justice system, the news media become their major source of information on these topics. The media tend to simplify complex criminal justice issues, providing, for example, only very brief reports of sentencing without much detail (Canadian Sentencing Commission 1987). It seems likely, then, that opinions concerning criminal justice issues are significantly influenced by how they are presented in the media. Roberts and Doob (1990) have demonstrated such media influence on attitudes toward sentencing. Subjects who were randomly assigned to read a news media account of a sentencing decision were much more likely to feel the sentence was too lenient than were those who read a summary of the actual court document on the case.

The media may play an important role in constructing youth crime into a social issue by articulating or bringing to awareness latent public fears. The reactions of the media, and of politicians, interest groups, and the general public are typically exaggerated and out of proportion to the real danger posed to society (Goode and Ben-Yehuda 1994). Hatt (n.d.) has argued that recent concern about youth violence in Canada is almost certainly a "moral panic" (Cohen 1972) generated by activities of special interest groups in concert with the media during a period of more general public anxiety. Such concern is disproportionate to the actual amount of youth crime (Doob, Marinos, and Varma 1995; Hatt, n.d.). Hatt claims that the media have given extensive and repetitive publicity to a few violent incidents, along with coverage of the comments and opinions of politicians, especially in electoral campaigns. The media in turn exploit the moral panics they have orchestrated to mobilize public moral indignation and give genesis to public crusades. Thus, the moral panic can become the first link in a spiral of events leading to increased maintenance of law and exercises in authority (Muncie 1984).

A focus on youth crime and comments by politicians from various parties concerning the alleged leniency of the *Young*

Offenders Act and the need to amend it were given prominent play in the media in the run-up to the 1993 federal election. For example, the then-Federal Solicitor General, Doug Lewis, was quoted as stating that "I'm told by police officials as I move around the country that they have trouble with repeat offenders who are laughing at the act and giving it a bad name" (*Edmonton Journal* 1992). Lewis went on to suggest that repeat offenders should automatically be tried in adult court.

A review of the Winnipeg *Free Press* coverage of crime and related stories during the first four months of 1993 revealed the expected pattern of a fairly frequent presentation of stories and articles dealing with juvenile crime, with a tripling of such coverage in April of 1993. There were 11 young offender stories in January (114 column inches), 7 in February (56 column inches), 10 in March (45.5 column inches), and 30 in April (357 column inches). Much of the increased attention to young offenders in April was focused on public concern regarding rising youth crime, gangs, violence in the schools, swamped youth courts, and the call to transfer more young offenders to adult court. Several of these stories received considerable space and/or front page treatment. While most of the coverage from January through April of 1993 was devoted to local area stories, there were some significant exceptions, including a series of stories in late February and early March reporting on the Liverpool U.K. abduction and murder of a toddler by several boys. So, while a more systematic analysis of the media over a longer time period would be required to draw firmer conclusions, at least, tentatively, it appears that a significant amount of attention was devoted to the subject of young offenders during the period of our data collection.

So, the media attention to youth crime and the *Young Offenders Act* and to the comments thereon of politicians and others may have contributed to the punitive attitudes expressed by most of our respondents. A majority (57%) certainly felt that the media paid too much attention to stories about crime and the criminal justice system. Rather than stimulating greater fear of crime leading to increased punitiveness on the part of the public, the media may have a more direct effect on attitudes toward punishment. As the major source of crime and criminal justice information, the media may increase the salience of such topics in the minds of the public and help shape public attitudes and opinions by defining the issues in an oversimplified and punitively oriented fashion. Future work in this area would do well, then, to include various dimensions of the media treatment of young offender "news" directly in the theoretical model.

It is possible that our results overstate the degree of punitiveness in public opinion regarding young offenders. Most (62%) of our respondents did not think that sending young offenders to jail would stop them from committing crimes; 70% responded that rehabilitating a young offender is more important than making the young offender pay for the crime. These results suggest, at least, that the public's attitude toward young offenders and the youth justice system is more complex than might first seem to be the case.

Public opinion surveys also often oversimplify the issues and fail to provide respondents with sufficient information (Roberts, 1992). Some research (Doob and Roberts 1983; Ellsworth 1978) has shown that, when more information is provided respondents, they become less punitive. Cullen *et al.* (1985a), in a study of causal attributions, reported that respondents who were positivistic in their explanations of criminal behaviour were less punitive in their attitudes toward offenders. More information about youth court cases in survey questions and systematic attempts to vary the meanings and motives attributable to young offenders might reveal somewhat more complex and less punitive attitudes. Conclusions from research such as the present study, then, need to be qualified by a recognition that single item measures lacking in contextual information do not adequately capture the complexities of public attitudes toward juvenile justice. In addition to more research on the topic of attitudes toward young offenders and youth courts, this additional research should expand the range or scope of the measurement of the dependent variables by, for example, providing case scenarios that systematically vary characteristics of the young offender and relevant facts about the offense.

In a related vein, measurement of the fear of crime should perhaps be more specifically directed toward the fear of young offenders. This measurement could be based upon specific examples or scenarios involving youth and could vary the characteristics of the offender(s) as well as the circumstances. This more specific measurement of the fear of youth crime might prove more predictive of punitiveness toward young offenders, as contrasted with the more general measure of how safe people feel walking in their neighbourhood after dark. Future research in this area, then, needs to move beyond reliance upon a few relatively simple measures in an amalgam-type survey to much more focused and detailed measurement of public attitudes toward youth crime, young offenders, and public policy.

Note

1. Revised version of a paper presented to the American Society of Criminology, Phoenix, October 1993. We wish to acknowledge the assistance of David Forde and the staff of the Winnipeg Area Study, as well as Cliff Kinzel, Harvey Krahn, and the Population Research Laboratory at the University of Alberta. Cora Voyageur provided some research assistance. Financial assistance was provided by Solicitor General Canada through the contributions grant to the Centre for Criminological Research, Department of Sociology, University of Alberta.

References

Archambault, J.R.O.
1991 Forward. In A.W. Leschied, P.G. Jaffe, and W. Willis (eds.), The Young Offender's Act: A Revolution in Canadian Juvenile Justice. Toronto: University of Toronto Press.

Bala, N.
1994 What's wrong with YOA bashing? What's wrong with the YOA? Recognizing the limits of the law. Canadian Journal of Criminology 36: 247-270.

Bala, N and M. Kirvan
1991 The Statute: Its principles and provisions and their interpretation by the courts. In A.W. Leschied, P.G. Jaffe, and W. Willis (eds.), The Young Offender's Act: A Revolution

in Canadian Juvenile Justice. Toronto: University of Toronto Press.

Bennett, J.F.
1985 Concerns about the Young Offender's Act. Provincial Judges Journal 8: 17-18.

Blumstein, A. and J. Cohen
1980 Sentencing of convicted offenders: An analysis of the public's view. Law and Society Review 14: 223-261.

Canadian Sentencing Commission
1987 Sentencing Reform: A Canadian Approach. Ottawa: Ministry of Supply and Services Canada.

Coflin, J.
1988 The Federal Government's role in implementing the Young Offender's Act. In J. Hudson, J.P. Hornick, and B.A. Burrows (eds.), Justice and the Young Offender in Canada. Toronto: Wall and Thompson.

Cohen, Stan
1972 Folk Devils and Moral Panics. London: MacGibbon and Kee.

Corrado, R.R. and A. Markwart
1994 The need to reform the YOA in response to violent young offenders. Canadian Journal of Criminology 36: 343-378.

Cullen, F.T., G.A. Clark, J.B. Cullen, and R.A. Mathers
1985 Attribution, salience, and attitudes toward criminal sanctioning. Criminal Justice and Behavior 12(3): 305-331.

Cullen, F.T., G.A Clark, and J.F. Wozniak
1985 Explaining the get tough movement. Federal Probation 49: 16-24.

Doob, A.N.
1992. Trends in the use of custodial dispositions for young offenders. Canadian Journal of Criminology 34: 35-50.

Doob, A.N. and J.V. Roberts
1983 An Analysis of the Public's View of Sentencing. Ottawa: Department of Justice Canada.

Doob, A.N., V. Marinos, and K. Varma
1995 Youth Crime and the Youth Justice System in Canada: A Research Perspective. Toronto: Centre of Criminology, University of Toronto.

Edmonton Journal
1992 Tougher teen crime law urged. Edmonton Journal 29 December.

Ellsworth, P.
1978 Attitudes toward capital punishment. Paper presented to the Society for Experimental Social Psychology, Princeton, New Jersey.

Gallup, George H.
1972 The Gallup Poll: Public Opinion 1935-1971. New York: Random House.

Goode, Erich and Nachman Ben-Yehuda
1994 Moral panics: culture, politics, and social construction. Annual Review of Sociology 20: 149-71.

Grasmick, H.G. and A.L. McGill
1994 Religion, attribution style, and punitiveness toward juvenile offenders. Criminology 32: 23-46.

Griffiths, Curt T. and Simon Verdun-Jones
1989. Canadian Criminal Justice. Toronto: Butterworths.

Hatt, Ken
n.d. The moral panic over youth violence. Unpublished paper, Department of Sociology and Anthropology, Carleton University.

Hylton, John H.
1994. Get tough or get smart? Options for Canada's youth justice system in the twenty-first century. Canadian Journal of Criminology 36: 229-246.

Langworthy, R.H. and J.T. Whitehead
1986. Liberalism and fear as explanations of punitiveness. Criminology 24: 575-591.

Leschied, A.W. and P. Gendreau
1986 The declining role of rehabilitation in Canadian juvenile justice. Canadian Journal of Criminology 28: 315-322.

Leschied, A.W. and P. Gendreau
1994 Doing justice in Canada. Canadian Journal of Criminology 36: 291-303.

Leschied, A.W. and P.G. Jaffe
1987 Impact of the *Young Offender's Act* on court dispositions. Canadian Journal of Criminology 29: 421-430.

Leschied, A.W. and P.G. Jaffe
1991 Dispositions as indicators of conflicting social purposes under the Juvenile Delinquent's Act and the Young Offender's Act. In A.W. Leschied, P.G. Jaffe, and W. Willis (eds.), The Young Offender's Act: A Revolution in Canadian Juvenile Justice. Toronto: University of Toronto Press.

Lovekin, E.R.
1961 Editorial: Truculent Juveniles. Criminal Law Quarterly 2: 413-414.

McGrath, W.T.
1962 Some suggested amendments to Canada's Juvenile Delinquents Act. Criminal Law Quarterly 4: 259-264.

Muncie, J.
1984 The Trouble with Kids Today. Dover, N.H.: Hutchinson.

Opinion Research Corporation
1982 National Public Opinion Survey: Public Attitudes Toward Youth Crime. Minnesota: H. Humphrey Institute of Public Affairs, University of Minnesota.

Reid, S.A. and M. Reitsma-Street
1984 Assumptions and implications of new Canadian legislation for young offenders. Canadian Criminology Forum 7: 1-19 .

Roberts, J.V.
1992 Public opinion, crime, and criminal justice. In M. Tonry (ed.), Crime and Justice: A Review of Research. Chicago: University of Chicago Press.

Roberts, J.V. and A.N. Doob
1990 News media influences on public views of sentencing. Law and Human Behavior 14: 451-468.

Sacco, Vincent F. and Holly Johnson
1990 Patterns of Criminal Victimization in Canada. Ottawa: Minister of Supply and Services Canada.

Scheingold, S.A.
1984. The Politics of Law and Order. New York: Longman.

Schwartz, I.M., J.M. Abbey, and W.H. Barton
1990 The Perception and Reality of Juvenile Crime in Michigan. Ann Arbor: Center for the Study of Youth Policy.

Schwartz, I.M., S. Guo, and J.J. Kerbs
1993 The impact of demographic variables on public opinion regarding juvenile justice: Implications for public policy. Crime and Delinquency 39(1): 5-28.

Schwartz, I.M., S. Guo, and J.J. Kerbs
1992 Public attitudes toward juvenile crime and juvenile justice: Implications for public policy. Hamline Journal of Public Law and Policy. 13(2): 241-251.

Sheley, J.F.
1985 America's Crime Problem. Belmont: Wadsworth.

Skovron, S.E., J.E. Scott, and F.T. Cullen
1989 The death penalty for juveniles. Crime and Delinquency 35: 546-561.

Steinhart, D.
1988 N.C.C.D. Focus – California Opinion Poll: Public Attitudes on Youth Crime. San Francisco: National Council on Crime and Delinquency.

Stinchcombe, A.L., R. Adams, C.A. Heimer, K.L. Scheppele, T.W. Smith, and D.G. Taylor
1980 Crime and Punishment – Changing Attitudes in America. San Francisco: Jossey-Bass.

Taylor, D.G., K.L. Scheppele, and A.L. Stinchcombe
1979 Salience of crime and support for harsher criminal sanctions. Social Problems 26: 413-424.

Thomas, C.W. and S.C. Foster
1975 A sociological perspective on support for capital punishment. American Journal of Orthopsychiatry 45: 641-57.

West, W. Gordon
1984 Young Offenders and the State. Toronto: Butterworths.

West, W. Gordon
1991 Towards a more socially informed understanding of Canadian delinquency legislation. In A.W. Leschied, P.G. Jaffe, and W. Willis (eds.), The Young Offender's Act: A Revolution in Canadian Juvenile Justice. Toronto: University of Toronto Press.

Zimmerman, S.E., D.J. Van Alstyne, and C.S. Dunn
1988 The national punishment survey and public policy consequences. Journal of Research in Crime and Delinquency 25(2): 120-149.

CHAPTER NINETEEN

Young people's knowledge of the Young Offenders Act and the youth justice system

Michele Peterson-Badali[1]
Department of Human Development and Applied Psychology, Ontario Institute for Studies in Education, University of Toronto Toronto, Ontario
and **Christopher J. Koegl**
Centre of Criminology University of Toronto Toronto, Ontario

THE *YOUNG OFFENDERS ACT (YOA)* HAS COME UNDER INCREASING FIRE over the last several years for failing to respond adequately to youth crime in Canada. Recent public opinion polls (e.g., Gallup 1994; Reid 1994) found that Canadians "favour a stricter *Young Offenders Act*", including provisions to increase penalties for offences, lower the age boundaries of the Act, and further facilitate the transfer of youths to adult court for trial. Furthermore, there is evidence (Gallup 1994) that public attitudes towards the *YOA* have harshened over the last five years.

Underlying these attitudes is a public perception, fostered by the media, that young people possess a sophisticated knowledge of the youth justice system that has allowed them to begin an escalating pattern of criminal activity without any serious penalty. Recent examples of this image include the portrayal in a CBC movie of an under-12 "offender" who

Canadian Journal of Criminology/Revue canadienne de criminologie, April/avril 1998, pp. 127–152.

repeatedly taunted the police with their inability to do anything about his activities (Savath 1996). This untested assumption is dangerous to the extent that it (1) contributes to legislative or policy change that harshens the *Act* (which has occurred several times since its proclamation over a decade ago), or (2) undermines the recognition of the importance of accurate public information about the youth justice system. Indeed, the implicit message being delivered as part of this image of the "savvy" young criminal is that youth knowledge of the *YOA* and the youth justice system is a "bad thing".

The provision of accurate knowledge about the *YOA* in an understandable way is important for several reasons. Saunders (1981: 712-713) notes that U.S. public legal education programs "operate on one or more of the following premises: (1) the law is important to every individual, (2) the vast majority of people lack sufficient knowledge of the law and its processes, and (3) many people are estranged from the law under which they live". For example, a young person's capacity to participate meaningfully in the youth justice system is compromised to the extent that he or she does not have basic information about how the system works. Indeed, previous research (Lawrence 1983) has indicated that defence lawyers overestimate their young clients' knowledge of the legal system, as do young people themselves. Therefore, they may not be routinely providing basic information that young people need in order to make effective decisions. It can also be argued that a youth's contact with the legal system is more likely to have a meaningful impact if he or she has some understanding of key roles, procedures, etc. At a more general level, with respect to both youth and adults, accurate knowledge about the *YOA* might have a positive effect on public confidence in the youth justice system, for example by increasing people's sense of the system as fair and just. This relationship has been discussed by others (e.g., Saunders 1981), and was examined empirically by Covell and Howe (1996) in a study of students' attitudes towards sentencing under the *YOA*. In this study, the authors found that subjects' age and the presence vs. absence of background information about a young offender were significant predictors of subjects' ratings of the leniency and appropriateness of youth court sentences described in several vignettes. Knowledge of the *YOA* did not predict subjects' ratings. It should be noted, however, that knowledge was measured by a brief (12 question) questionnaire that relied on a true/false format, and that attitudes were defined fairly narrowly, in terms of 'fairness' ratings of several youth court dispositions.

Despite these concerns, there is virtually no information about what young people actually know about the *YOA*. Two studies conducted after the *YOA* was proclaimed indicated that a majority of young people are ignorant of the age boundaries entailed in the *Act*. Peterson (1988) found that, of a sample of 144 middle-class Ontario school children ages 10-14, only 16% correctly suggested 12 as the minimum age of the *YOA*, although 36% correctly identified age 18 as marking the transition to adulthood in legal terms. Jaffe, Leschied, and Farthing (1987) reported similar figures, with 22% and 23% of their 12-18-year-old participants correctly identifying the minimum and maximum ages, respectively, for the *YOA*. Jaffe *et al.* (1987: 313) also asked youths about the maximum penalties for convicted young offenders, what happens to youth court records, whether treatment can be ordered, and whether parents are allowed in the courtroom. Overall, they concluded that "In the majority of areas investigated by the questions on the *YOA*, close to 75% of the respondents did not have accurate information". This ignorance of specific aspects of statutes is not restricted to young people, however. In a questionnaire study, Ribordy (1986: 29) assessed adults' knowledge of specific legal 'facts' from a number of Canadian statutes, and concluded that "most statutes are unknown to the majority of the population".

Given the dearth of information about young people's knowledge of the *YOA*, the present study sought to examine the knowledge of 10 - 17-year-old and young adult students from several cities across Canada. Through a questionnaire and a brief semi-structured interview, the present study assessed students' knowledge of a number of "black letter law" facts about the *YOA* relating to such issues as age boundaries, dispositions, procedures, youth court records, transfer to adult court, roles of legal personnel, etc.

While the primary purpose of the present study was to explore the knowledge of "regular" Canadian youth, data were also collected on a group of young offenders from an open custody facility in Toronto. As mentioned previously, one rationale for studying youth knowledge is that the principles and procedures of the youth justice system will be more meaningful to young people if they possess at least a basic understanding of how they work. This argument is particularly salient for young people who are directly involved with the system. Information about young offenders' knowledge of the *YOA* and the youth justice system is also necessary in order to examine the assumption, discussed earlier, that they possess an accurate and sophisticated understanding of the system. Indeed, in contrast to the image of the "savvy" young offender described earlier, the little research that exists on young offenders' knowledge of the legal system suggests that they may show poorer understanding than "regular" young people (e.g., Cashmore and Bussey 1993). It was of interest, therefore, to examine knowledge of the *YOA* and the youth justice system in young offenders. Because the young offender group was made up of a relatively small number of participants from one custody facility, they cannot be considered representative of Canadian young offenders generally, and were not compared statistically to the national sample of students.

Method

Participants

Participants were 730 students from Edmonton, Toronto, Ottawa, Montreal, Sherbrooke, and Charlottetown.[2] All were students in elementary, middle, secondary schools, or Board operated Adult Learning Centres. Participants were divided into five age groups: 10/11-year-olds, 12/13-year-olds, 14/15-year-olds, 16/17-year-olds, and 18 years and over). Overall, the age of the participants ranged from 10 to 49 years (mean = 15.09) with 90% of the participants from the oldest age group being 25 years of age or younger (mean = 20.56). The majority of participants in all samples were born in Canada. The Montreal, and Toronto student samples were more ethnically diverse than students from the other cities, as measured by parents' country of birth and language spoken at home. In these samples, the majority of participants had at least one parent born outside Canada (Montreal - 80%; Toronto - 69%). The socioeconomic status (SES) of the samples also varied somewhat, although most spanned lower middle to middle class.

Thirty young offenders from an open custody facility in Toronto (mean age = 15.6 years; range 12-18) were also studied. This sample was ethnically diverse: 53% of the participants were White, 27% were Black, 10% were Asian, and 10% were of other ethnic backgrounds. This sample was characterized primarily by low socioeconomic status (e.g., many of the participants' parents were receiving some form of social assistance).

Procedure and materials

Participants' knowledge was assessed by a questionnaire consisting of 16 questions aimed at a number of aspects of "black letter law" related to the *YOA*. It began with the following brief vignette:

> This is a story about a 14-year-old boy named Dale. One day Dale went to the mall to do some shopping. On his way out, he went into The Bay to look around and saw a CD that he wanted. He quietly slipped the CD into his knapsack without paying for it. Just as he walked out of the store, the security guard grabbed him and told him that he was calling the police. The police came and took Dale to the station and read him his rights. After the police read Dale his rights, he was charged with Theft.

A number of questions were asked in the context of this vignette (e.g., knowledge of the right to counsel, post-charge procedures, possible dispositions for shoplifting, and knowledge of the youth court record). Participants then answered several questions dealing with age boundaries under the *YOA*, the difference between youth and adult court, and factors considered by a judge in sentencing a young offender. Two multiple-choice question formats were used for the preceding questions: Some questions had one correct answer and three incorrect "distractor" items plus a "don't know" option, while others contained a number of choices, more than one of which was correct. Students' knowledge of the roles of various people within the youth justice system was assessed by creating a list of "key players" (defence counsel, crown, judge, police) and a list of roles, and having participants match the person to his or her correct role. Several incorrect role descriptions were also included as distractor items so that participants could not answer questions correctly through a simple process of elimination. Finally, participants were asked to give their opinion of the appropriateness of youth dispositions in general (on a 5-point scale ranging from "almost always too harsh" to "almost always too easy". Participants aged 13 and above responded to several additional questions that addressed their perceptions of youth crime more generally, for example rates of violent crime among youth and rates of custody dispositions for particular offences; (see Peterson-Badali (1996) for a report of these findings).

In the student sample, questionnaires were distributed to groups of approximately 30 students. A subset of the sample also participated in a brief interview which followed up in more detail several areas assessed in the questionnaire (e.g., knowledge of what the *YOA* is, what happens to youth court records, etc.). The young offender sample responded to the questionnaire as part of a larger individual interview about their knowledge and experience of the youth justice system.

Results

Data analyses

Much of the data in the present study are categorical in nature. These data were analyzed either using chi square or log linear technique, which is an extension of chi square for tables with more than two variables. Three sets of chi squares were performed on the student data set: by age, by gender, and by city. There were very few significant effects of gender in the chi square analyses so log linear analyses included only age and city as predictor variables. Each level of the age variable was compared to the average of subsequent levels (e.g., 10/11-year-olds would be compared to the average of the 12/13-, 14/15-, 16/17- and 18+-year-old students). Each city was compared to the average of all other cities. The statistic reported for these log linear analyses is the z score. Because of the large number of statistical tests performed, .01 was chosen as the cutoff for significance.

What is the Young Offenders Act, *anyway?*

When a subset of students was asked a general, open-ended question about what they thought the *YOA* was, a majority mentioned the relevance of age in their definition (64%). Age was mentioned in terms of the procedural differences between the youth and adult justice systems, in terms of differences in consequences for crimes, as well as in the context of vague explanations (e.g., "it's for kids under 18"). Overall, 40% of students explicitly defined the *YOA* as a law (e.g., "its a special law for children who commit a crime"), and 35% mentioned aspects of its underlying philosophy (e.g., "its when you're under age and you commit a crime, you're treated differently – you go to a different court and don't get as severe punishments"). Students age 16 and over were more likely than in younger students to mention philosophical aspects of the *YOA* ($x^2(4) = 23.2$, $p = .0001$), and a similar trend for law approached significance ($x^2(4) = 10.3$, $p = .03$).

Students also responded to multiple choice questions addressing their knowledge of specific aspects of the *YOA*. In one question students were asked "what is the difference between youth and adult court?", with the target distinction being that the dispositions might not be as harsh in the former. As shown in Panel A of Table 1, a substantial majority of students correctly identified the targeted difference. Compared to the older students, somewhat fewer of the 10-11-year-olds and 12-13-year-olds chose the correct response.

In contrast, knowledge of the age boundaries of the *YOA* was quite poor. As shown in Panel A of Table 1, when participants were asked "what is the youngest age at which a person can be charged under the *Young Offenders Act*?", less than half of the students chose the correct response (12 years). An even smaller percentage of students correctly identified 17 as the oldest age at which a youth is typically charged with a crime under the YOA.(3) Compared to older students, the 10/11-year-olds, 12/13-year-olds and 14/15-year-olds were less likely to choose the correct response. The most common incorrect response chosen was age 18, which was chosen by half of the youngest participants and by almost 40% of the 12 to 17-year-olds. It is possible that this choice reflects students' belief about when an individual becomes an "adult" from a criminal justice point of view. Only 15% of students were able to correctly identify 14 as the youngest age at which a youth can be transferred to adult court for trial. In fact, almost half of the students (41%) believed that a youth cannot be transferred before the age of 16.

Knowledge of roles in the youth justice system

Panel B of Table 1 displays the percentage of participants who correctly matched several "key players" in the youth justice system with their functions. Overall, a majority of students correctly identified the role of defence counsel ("tries to defend you"). Given the straightforward relationship between the term and the correct response (both of which used variants of the word "defend"), it is surprising that more participants did not choose the correct answer. This appears to be accounted for by the misconception, held by a substantial minority of students,

Table 1 - Panel A
Percentage of participants correctly answering YOA knowledge questions

	Age						
	10/11 (n = 127-128)	12/13 (n=129-130)	14/15 (n=177)	16/17 (n=174-175)	18+ (n=118-119)	Total students (n=726-728)	Young offenders (n=30)
Difference between youth court and adult court	76**	79*	87	87	90	84	90
Minimum age	52	48	43	53	51	49	90
Maximum age	18**	30**	41**	54	64	42	33
Minimum age for transfer to adult court	9	15	19	13	18	15	3

**Significant at .001 or greater; *significant at .01.

Table 1 - Panel B
Percentage of participants identifying the correct roles of youth justice system personnel

	Age						
	10/11 (n=114-127)	12/13 (n=116-130)	14/15 (n=166-177)	16/17 (n=170-175)	18+ (n=116-118)	Total students (n=682-724)	Young offenders (n=29)
Defence counsel	72	62	67	64	68	66	83
Meaning of right to counsel	35**	48**	67	75	72	61	69
Crown counsel	54**	66**	74**	91	86	76	90
Police	94	98	98	99	98	98	100
Judge	72	84	86	93	93	86	90

** Significant at .001 or greater; * significant at .01.

that a lawyer's job is to prove his or her client's innocence: almost a third of students (30%) chose the distractor "tries to prove that you are innocent of the crime".

Related to the role of defence counsel, students also answered a multiple choice question that required them to identify the correct definition of "the right to retain and instruct counsel". A majority of participants answered the question correctly, but there was also a significant effect of age. Only a third of the 10/11-year-olds and half of the 12/13-year-olds correctly answered the question, while a majority of the 14/15, 16/17, and 18+-year-old students responded correctly (see Panel B of Table 1). The most common incorrect answer chosen (by 17% of students) was the distractor item which stated that the accused "can choose to talk to a counsellor about his problems". These results suggest that children under 14 do not understand the right to counsel well, even when understanding is very liberally defined in terms of *recognition* of a correct response in a multiple choice question.

Three-quarters of students correctly identified the role of Crown counsel ("tries to prove you are guilty of the crime"). Compared to older adolescents and young adults, significantly fewer 10/11-year-olds, 12/13-year-olds and 14/15-year-olds chose the correct response.

Virtually all of the participants correctly identified the role of the police ("tries to catch people who break the law"). A substantial majority of students also correctly identified the role of the judge ("decides whether you are guilty or not guilty of committing the crime"). The 10/11-year-olds were less likely to choose the correct response than the older students.

Knowledge of police and youth court procedures

Post-charge police procedures

After hearing the shoplifting vignette described in the Method section, participants responded to a question that briefly examined their knowledge of discretionary police procedures following a criminal charge ("what can happen to Dale now"?).

Participants were instructed to choose as many answers as they thought were correct. Of five options, three were correct: "the police can send the accused home with his parents", "the police can keep the accused in custody overnight", and "the police can release the accused on a "promise to appear" in court". Two options were not correct: "the police can keep the accused in jail until his trial", and "the police can release the accused if he pays a fine". In general, the less severe options were chosen by greater numbers of students. Sixty-eight percent of students chose sending the accused home with parents, 57% checked off releasing the accused on a promise to appear, and 58% chose releasing the accused if he paid a fine. The substantial number of students who indicated that the police could release the accused if he paid a fine and returned the stolen CD indicates that many confuse the role of police and judge. Forty-five percent of students indicated that the police could keep the accused in custody overnight, and 17% believed that he could be held in custody until his trial. It should be noted that although the latter option is not correct as presented in the question (i.e., the police do not have the discretion to keep a youth in custody until trial), the distinction in who has authority to hold a youth in custody was not made highly explicit in the questionnaire (which was worded in terms of what the police "can" do). It is possible that participants did not recognize the distinction between police and other authority figures in "the system" (e.g., the judge), and interpreted the question in a more general sense.

Youth court records

Participants were also asked two questions about procedures concerning access to, and disposition of, youth court records. With respect to the question of who has access to youth court records, participants were instructed to choose as many responses as they thought correct. Of six possible choices (court, police, parents, school, employer, media) the first three were correct. Students' knowledge was relatively good, overall. Ninety one percent of students indicated that the court has access to the record, and 90% stated that police can see a youth's record. Fewer participants (60%) were aware that parents have access to their son or daughter's youth court record. A minority of participants indicated that a youth's school (30%) or employer (32%) has access to the record, and virtually none of the participants indicated that it was available to the media. There was only one significant age difference with respect to this question: more 14/15-year-old students than those in other age groups erroneously believed that employers have access to a young offender's record (42% vs. 24-31%; $x^2(4) = 14.8$, $p < .01$). It is possible that the younger children did not hold this belief because most would not yet be concerned with the employment ramifications of a criminal conviction, but that at age 14 and 15 youths are beginning to think in these terms, though they hold an inaccurate belief.

When students responded to a multiple choice question about whether a young offender's record gets destroyed when he or she becomes an adult, the results were divided. Basically, the record exists for five years from the date of a youth's conviction (for summary offences) or the completion of the youth's disposition (for indictable offences), providing there are no new convictions during the five year period. Thirty-seven percent of students stated that it was destroyed, and 33% thought that it did not get destroyed, 20% (correctly) answered that it depends and 10% stated that they did not know. Explanations for the "depends" response fell into several categories. The first was severity of the offence (mentioned by 28% of the subset of students who stated "depends"). This category was mentioned more frequently as age increased (from 10% in the 10/11-year-old sample to 43% in the 16/17-year-old group; $x^2(4) = 15.5$, $p < .01$). Overall, 22% of the students who stated that what happens to the youth court record "depends" mentioned the youth's subsequent behaviour as a criterion (e.g., "if you stay clean for a certain amount of time, it gets erased"). This response most closely approximates a correct response to this rather complicated question, although severity of offence is also relevant. Only 3% of participants (incorrectly) mentioned age as a relevant factor (e.g., "if you're older when you commit the crime then they keep the record when you're an adult").

Knowledge and opinion regarding dispositions

Students were also asked to choose from a list to identify all possible dispositions that would be available to the judge when the accused was convicted of the shoplifting offence (see Table 2). The most popular choices were a fine, community service, restitution, and probation. Only a quarter of the students thought that the judge could give the young offender a week in custody, and even fewer thought that he could receive a month in custody. In addition, only a quarter of participants overall indicated that the judge could order the young offender to attend school or adhere to a curfew.

There were significant age differences with respect to most of the disposition options but, as Table 2 shows, the actual pattern of age differences varied. The probation and one week's custody options suggested similar patterns, but in the opposite direction. Probation was recognized by fewer under 12 participants than those between 12 and 15 years of age and this disposition was recognized by even more 16/17-year-olds and young adults. Conversely, more under-12 participants than those between 12 and 15 years of age thought that the judge could sentence the young offender to a week in custody, and the 12-15-year-olds chose this disposition more frequently than the 16/17-year-olds and young adults. With respect to other dispositions, the young adults appeared different from the rest of the sample (e.g., they were less likely to recognize restitution as a possibility), while in another case the over-16 students responded differently than the younger participants (more frequently choosing an order to attend school).

Students were also asked to choose as many responses as they thought were correct from a list of factors that a judge would consider when deciding on a disposition. Of 10 choices, 7 were correct (at least in theory, a judge would not base a disposition on a youth's race, gender, or how he or she is

Table 2
Percentage of participants identifying possible dispositions for shoplifting (Theft under $1000)

Disposition	Age						
	10/11 (n=129)	12/13 (n=130)	14/15 (n=177)	16/17 (n=174)	18+ (n=118)	Total students (n=728)	Young offenders (n=30)
Fine	88	90	89	87	85	88	70
Community service	61	76	89	94	90	83	90
Restitution	74	77	73	81	62	74	33
Probation	47	63	66	73	83	67	93
Attend school	18	16	21	31	31	24	80
Curfew	21	21	29	33	38	29	70
Week custody	38	27	28	20	14	26	83
Month custody	19	11	14	8	15	13	67
Absolute discharge	8	3	15	27	24	16	30

dressed). The factors most frequently chosen were the crime itself and the young offender's previous contact with the law (both by 96% of students), followed by the harm to the victim (by 86% of students), the young offender's age (72%), and whether the crime was planned or unplanned (72%). Thus, students consider factors related both to the offence and to the offender. There were a number of offender factors that were chosen by very few students: gender, race, and clothing worn. Two offender factors – family background and employment/ school attendance status – were chosen by roughly a third of students. Only two significant effects of age emerged on the frequency with which students selected the factors: the under-12 participants were less likely to suggest age as a relevant factor in sentencing than the older respondents (57% vs. 68-80%, respectively; $x^2(4) = 24.5$, $p < .0001$)), and both the 10/11-year-old (73%) and 12/13-year-old (78%) groups were less likely than the older participants (88-94%) to recognize harm to the victim as a relevant sentencing factor ($x^2(4) = 37.2$, $p < .00001$). Thus, overall, students were good at selecting relevant sentencing variables.

Finally, students were asked to rate, in general, the harshness of dispositions given to young offenders on a 5-point scale ranging from "almost always too harsh" to "almost always too easy". Virtually none of the students endorsed items at the "too harsh" end of the scale. Thirty-seven percent of students felt that dispositions were "about right", the same number stated that they were "often too easy", and a further 20% felt that dispositions were "almost always too easy". Results revealed that on average, the 10/11-year-olds (M = 3.3), 12/13-year-olds (M = 3.5) and 14/15-year-olds (M = 3.6) viewed dispositions as "about right", while 16/17-year-olds (M = 3.9) and young adults (M = 4.1) viewed them as "often too easy" ($F(4,644)=22.6$, $p < .001$).

Regional differences in knowledge of the YOA

Regional differences were apparent in some of the questions, and the most striking finding was the distinction between the cities in Quebec (Montreal and Sherbrooke) and the rest of the cities sampled. Differences emerged with respect to knowledge of possible dispositions; knowledge of the difference between youth and adult court and recognition that parents have access to the youth court record (Sherbrooke only); and knowledge of the right to counsel and of post-charge police procedures (Montreal only). In all cases, fewer participants from Quebec than from the other cities selected the correct responses. Differences also emerged with respect to opinions about the *YOA*. For example, more students from Quebec rated youth dispositions as "about right" in general, while those from other cities tended to think that they were "often too easy".

Knowledge of young offenders

As with the student sample, the knowledge of the young offender group varied depending on the particular issue addressed. For example, the young offenders demonstrated good knowledge of the basic distinction between youth and adult court, and almost all correctly identified 12 years as the minimum age boundary of the *Act* (see Table 1, Panel A). Young offenders were also very successful at matching the names of various "players" in the youth justice system with their respective roles (see Panel B of Table 1). Indeed, with respect to the role of defence counsel, the young offender group was actually less susceptible than their "regular" age mates to the misconception that a lawyer's job is to prove his or her client's innocence (17% vs. 30% for young offenders and students, respectively).

Their knowledge of other aspects of the *Act* was extremely poor, most notably with respect to the typical maximum age of the *YOA*, and the minimum age for transfer to adult court (see Panel B of Table 1). With respect to the maximum age, a full third of participants indicated that 18 was the upper boundary of the *YOA*, while another 30% chose age 16. Two-thirds of the young offender group suggested that age 16 was also the minimum age of transfer to adult court (although it seems possible that at least some of these participants may have confused the concept of youth transfer to adult court with actually being considered an adult, in legal terms).

Knowledge of many of the other aspects of the youth justice system was mixed. For example, participants demonstrated reasonable levels of knowledge of a number of possible youth court dispositions for shoplifting: probation, community service, and fine (see Table 2). As Table 2 indicates, compared to the student sample, the young offender group was more aware of probation as a possible disposition, as well as the attend school and curfew provisions that often form part of a probation order. Young offenders were also much more likely to choose a week's custody as a possible disposition, and two-thirds indicated that a youth could be given a month in custody for shoplifting. Relatively few young offenders indicated two of the less punitive options: absolute discharge (24%) and restitution (33%). Overall the results suggest that, compared to the broader sample of students, these young offenders perceive the more punitive dispositions as more likely consequences for shoplifting than some of the less punitive ones. Interestingly, almost half of the young offenders (43%) rated youth court dispositions as "about right" and only 17% thought that they were "too easy". This finding stands in marked contrast to the student sample, 57% of whom rated youth dispositions as either "somewhat" or "much" too easy.

Knowledge of procedures concerning release post-charge and youth court records was also mixed. Seventy percent of participants indicated that police could call parents once a youth had been charged, and 90% stated that the accused could be held in custody overnight, or could be released on a "promise to appear". A majority of the young offender group (53%) also endorsed the misconceptions that an accused could be held in custody until trial, or could be released by the police upon payment of a fine.

With respect to knowledge about youth court records, all young offenders understood that the court has access to records, but only 70% realized that the police can see them and even fewer (63%) knew that parents would have access.

Young offenders appeared to be less susceptible to the misconception that schools and employers are entitled to see an offender's record: only 17% of participants chose either of these options. Fully half the sample erroneously indicated that a youth court record is "destroyed" when a young offender becomes an adult, while only 30% stated that it depends on the circumstances.

Discussion

As previous studies of youth knowledge of the legal system have found (e.g., Peterson-Badali and Abramovitch 1992; Saywitz 1989; Warren-Leubecker, Tate, Hinton, and Ozbek 1989), students' knowledge of the *YOA* and the youth justice system was variable depending on the particular issue addressed. For example, overall, students showed good knowledge of the difference between youth court and adult court, who has access to the youth court record, and were successful at matching the names "crown", "judge", and "police", with their respective roles. Students showed poor knowledge of what happens to the youth court record when a young offender turns 18, a number of participants appeared confused about the role of defence counsel, and relatively few participants showed a conceptual understanding of what the *YOA* is, though most understood that age was a relevant variable. Knowledge of critical age boundaries was also quite poor, with less than half of participants recognizing the correct minimum and maximum ages in multiple choice questions and only 15% correctly identifying the minimum age of transfer to adult court. When these results are compared with studies carried out shortly after the *YOA* came into force (Peterson 1988; Jaffe, Leschied, and Farthing 1987), there does appear to be some improvement in knowledge of minimum and maximum ages. It must be noted, however, that the previous studies used an open-ended question format in contrast to the multiple choice format used in the present study, and this may also have contributed to performance differences between the groups.

Age differences emerged with respect to many, but not all, of the issues addressed. For example, a greater percentage of older students than younger students knew the meaning of the right to instruct counsel, identified possible youth court dispositions, knew that youth court records are not automatically destroyed at 18, correctly matched the names "crown counsel" and "judge" with their appropriate roles, and correctly identified the maximum age of the *YOA*. Older students were also more likely to define the *YOA* in a conceptual way than younger participants, whose descriptions were very concrete. This result is consistent with the ability to think more abstractly that develops in adolescence, but could also be related to increased exposure to information about the *YOA* and the youth justice system in adolescence (e.g., in school curricula, media). Even so, less than half of students over 16 defined the *Act* in this way. They, along with younger students, were more likely to focus on concrete procedural or consequence elements of the *Act*.

Even where overall age differences were evident, the pattern of age trends varied by question. For example, in some cases the 10/11-year-old children were different from the rest of the sample (e.g., in terms of knowledge of post-charge police procedures, and recognition of age as a relevant sentencing factor). In a number of cases, the 10/11-year-olds and 12/13-year-olds both performed more poorly than the older students (e.g., in their knowledge of available dispositions, factors influencing sentencing, the difference between youth and adult court, the job of the crown attorney, and of the meaning of the right to counsel).

In several cases, significant age differences occurred between the under- and over-16 participants (e.g., in defining the *Young Offenders Act*, knowledge of the maximum age). In most cases the 16- and 17-year-old students exhibited knowledge levels that were comparable to young adults. It is possible, however, that sampling issues may have at least partially accounted for this result. While 18- and 19-year-old students in Ontario are part of the regular high school stream of students, high school in other regions of Canada ends sooner, so that young adult students are less common and may not represent young adults generally (e.g., if they have remained in school longer than usual due to failure to pass courses, complete academic programs, etc.). Further, students in the Montreal sample were taken from an adult learning centre that is run by a Montreal school board. These students would likely not be representative of the population of young adults in Montreal. In future studies, it would be interesting to compare the knowledge of a representative sample of older adolescents and young adults.

A number of regional differences also emerged in students' knowledge of the *YOA*, as well as in their perception of youth court dispositions. These differences cannot be attributed to language issues, since the Montreal sample was anglophone or allophone, and responded to questions in English. An interesting possibility is that the findings reflect differences in the underlying philosophy toward youth justice and/or procedures for administering justice between Quebec and other regions of Canada. It is possible, for example, that students from Quebec did not know "less" about the *YOA* than those from other regions in Canada, as smaller percentage correct scores on the questionnaire might suggest, but that their responses reflect their experience of the youth justice system in that province. Similarly, the administration of youth justice in Quebec may have resulted in differences in perceptions of youth dispositions between Quebec students and those from other regions in Canada.

Overall, the findings suggest a different picture of young offenders' understanding of the youth justice system than has been reported, either by the media, or in the results of earlier studies (e.g., Cashmore and Bussey 1993; Ferguson and Douglas 1970; Grisso 1981). On the one hand, previous research findings indicating that young offenders were disadvantaged in their understanding of aspects of the legal system relative to "regular" adolescents were not replicated here. Young offenders' knowledge with respect to many aspects of the youth justice system paralleled that of the student sample. At times, however, their specific pattern of knowledge was different from the students, and appeared to reflect young offenders' direct experience with the legal system. For example, compared to the students, young offenders were more likely to identify possible dispositions relating to probation, likely because a majority have received probation orders themselves. They were also less susceptible to certain misconceptions held by a significant minority of students (e.g., with respect to the role of defence counsel, who can have access to the youth court record). On the other hand, despite their direct experience with the legal system, the young offenders (like students) showed poor knowledge of a number of important aspects of the *YOA* and the youth justice system, including the maximum age, the minimum age for transfer to adult court, and the disposition of the youth court record. These findings do not support the increasingly common portrayal of young offenders as a "savvy" group of criminals who manipulate their sophisticated knowledge of the youth justice system in order to "get away with murder", either literally or figuratively. While acknowledging that the present sample of young offenders is not representative of the population of young offenders across Canada, there is no reason to believe that the present sample would be significantly less knowledgeable about the system than the general population of offenders. Indeed, the average age (almost 16) and the fact that the vast majority of participants had a youth court record prior to serving their current open-custody disposition, suggests that they would be at least as knowledgeable about the system as a representative sample.

Of particular interest is the pattern of findings that suggests that the young offender group perceive the system as more punitive than do students. This group was more likely than the student sample to choose the more punitive of post-charge options as possibilities: remaining in custody overnight and remaining in custody until trial, and a greater percentage chose custodial options as possible dispositions for shoplifting. They were also substantially less likely than students to view youth court dispositions as too lenient. Again, it is likely that the young offenders' direct experience with the legal system is responsible for these differences, as they have likely encountered youths who have been given custodial dispositions for shoplifting offences or denied bail and held in custody until trial, or even experienced these events themselves. Indeed, the results of the present study suggest that students' perception of youth court dispositions as "too lenient" may be accounted for at least partly by their lack of awareness of the fact that harsh penalties, such as custody, can be given for relatively minor crimes such as shoplifting. For example, criminal justice statistics indicate that in 1994-95, 19% of young offenders whose most significant charge was Theft Under $1000 were given some type of custodial disposition (open custody - 13%, closed custody - 6%) (CCJS 1994-95). Without direct experience with the youth justice system, young people's knowledge and perceptions are likely influenced by public (especially media) characterizations of youth dispositions as overly lenient. In fact, as they get older, children and adolescents likely get increased exposure to media "information" and public attitudes about youth crime and dispositions, which could account for the current finding that, with age, participants were increasingly likely to view dispositions as too lenient.

The results of this study can be used in several ways. On one hand, there appears to be a commonly held notion among politicians, policymakers, and practitioners with a strong 'law and order' approach to crime that knowledge of potential consequences can act as a general deterrent, an argument which is often used to justify more punitive responses such as custody, transfer to adult court, etc. If one accepts this notion (despite its lack of empirical support) then students' ignorance about aspects of the system such as minimum and maximum ages, minimum age for transfer to adult court, and being held in custody has particular implications for legal education.

It is our contention that reasonable levels of knowledge about the youth justice system benefit young people, as well as Canadian society as a whole, not because this knowledge will function to prevent crime, but because the system will be perceived in a more meaningful, and perhaps more reasonable, light than it currently is. If this assumption holds, a clear implication is that legislators should direct their energy toward improving public knowledge about the *Young Offenders Act* and the youth justice system rather than changing the *Act* itself in response to public dissatisfaction. This assumption needs to be addressed empirically in a systematic exploration of the relationship between knowledge, perceptions, and a sense of 'belonging' or 'ownership' in relation to the *YOA* and the youth justice system that includes samples of young people and adults. While some studies have begun to address this issue, the domains addressed (e.g., Covell and Howe 1996) and the procedures used (e.g., Saunders 1981) have been limited.

For practical purposes, information regarding absolute levels of knowledge can assist educators and curriculum planners to determine where young people show good basic knowledge, and can benefit from more fine-tuned, specific, or complex information, or (perhaps more importantly) where they show gaps in knowledge or misconceptions about the system that need to be addressed. Similarly, the results can be used in the context of developing empirically-based training programs that inform lawyers about what their clients need to be taught in order to optimize their capacity to participate meaningfully in legal proceedings.

Information about age differences in knowledge can be useful in gearing education efforts in a developmentally appropriate way. Younger children have less direct experience with the system, and have been exposed to fewer sources of information (and at times misinformation) about it (e.g., peers, media, school curricula) and, not surprisingly, show lower levels of knowledge with respect to many of the issues addressed. Good educational programs already take into account developmental differences in children's and adolescents' knowledge and thinking processes, and the present study findings can add to these efforts in terms of pinpointing specific areas where younger and older students differ in terms of their understanding. Similarly, information about regional differences may be useful in tailoring education programs for the specific communities sampled.

It is important to note that the "knowledge" that participants demonstrate is a function in part of the methods used to ask the questions. Simplified questions, and those which require students to choose a correct response from a series of choices, can generate either very high or very low levels of performance depending on how the questions are constructed. Many of the issues addressed in this study are not simple and the likely reality is that students have some knowledge about an issue but that knowledge may be quite basic and unelaborated, or the student may also possess misconceptions alongside correct information. Clearly, the present study is not exhaustive, either in terms of the methods used to elicit participants' knowledge or in terms of the issues addressed, but can serve as a starting point for future research. Subsequent studies should further explore young people's understanding of the "black-letter law" provisions of the *YOA*, but in addition, it will be important to study systematically youths' understanding of some of the more philosophical issues underlying the legislation, as well as their perceptions of how the *Act* fits into a larger legislative and social context. A focus on young people's understanding the more conceptual aspects of the youth justice system is particularly important if, as suggested above, one of the critical reasons for wanting to enhance legal knowledge is to increase a sense of ownership of or belonging to that system.

In addition, future research needs to address systematically the relationship between knowledge about the youth justice system and attitudes toward the *YOA*.

Notes

1. The present study was made possible by a contract from the Department of Justice, Canada. The authors would like to thank Steve Dunne, Kara Griffin, Tanya Herbert, Stephanie Rich, and Michele Venet for their assistance in conducting the study, and Shelley Trevethan for her advice and support throughout the project. We are also grateful to

the school board personnel, research directors, school principals, staff, and students who made this study possible by giving their time and effort. Requests for reprints should be sent to Michele Peterson-Badali at the Department of Human Development and Applied Psychology, Ontario Institute for Studies in Education of the University of Toronto, 252 Bloor Street West, Toronto, Ontario, Canada, M5S 1V6.

2. The Montreal students were recruited through the Protestant School Board of Greater Montreal. Ethnically, this sample was quite diverse, non-francophone, and thus demographically quite different from the rest of the population of Quebec. The Sherbrooke sample would be more typical of the Quebec population.
3. A person can be charged with a crime under the YOA at *any* age over 12 when the crime was committed between the ages of 12 and 17. For the purposes of the study, we wanted to find out how many students recognized the upper age boundary of the YOA and this seemed the least complicated way to find out.

References

Canadian Centre for Justice Statistics (CCJS)
1994-
1995 Youth Court Statistics. Ottawa: CCJS, Statistics Canada.

Cashmore, J. and Kay Bussey
1993 Children's perceptions of lawyers in children's criminal cases. Unpublished manuscript.

Covell, K. and R.B. Howe
1996 Public attitudes and juvenile justice in Canada. The International Journal of Children's Rights. 4: 345-355.

Ferguson, A.B. and A.C. Douglas
1970 A study of juvenile waiver. San Diego Law Review 7: 39-54.

Gallup Canada.
1994 The Gallup Poll: Canadians favour a stricter *Young Offenders Act*. June 23, 1994.

Grisso, T.
1981 Juveniles' Waiver of Rights: Legal and Psychological Competence. New York: Plenum

Jaffe, P., A. Leschied, and J. Farthing
1987 Youth's knowledge and attitudes about the *Young Offenders Act*: Does anyone care what they think? Canadian Journal of Criminology 29: 309-316.

Lawrence, R.A.
1983 The role of legal counsel in juveniles' understanding of their rights. Juvenile and Family Court Journal 34: 49-58.

Peterson, M.
1988 Children's understanding of the juvenile justice system: A cognitive-developmental perspective. Canadian Journal of Criminology 30: 381-395.

Peterson-Badali, M.
1996 Students' knowledge and perceptions of the *Young Offenders Act*. Ottawa: Department of Justice. Canada.

Peterson-Badali, M. and R. Abramovitch
1992 Children's knowledge of the legal system: Are they competent to instruct legal counsel? Canadian Journal of Criminology 34: 139-160.

Reid Report
1994 Canadians' views of the criminal justice system. Reid Report 9:18-23.

Ribordy, F.X.
1986 Legal education and information: An exploratory study. Ottawa: Department of Justice.

Saunders, L.
1981 Ignorance of the law among teenagers: Is it a barrier to the exertion of their rights as citizens? Adolescence 16: 711-726.

Savath, P. (Executive Producer).
1996, June 21 Little Criminals. Canadian Broadcasting Corporation.

Saywitz, K.
1989 Children's conceptions of the legal system: "Court is a place to play basketball". In S.J. Ceci, D.F. Ross, and M.P. Toglia (eds.), Perspectives on Children's Testimony. New York: Springer Verlag

Warren-Leubecker, A., C. Tate, I. Hinton, and N. Ozbek
1989 What do children know about the legal system and when do they know it? In S.J. Ceci, D.F. Ross, and M.P. Toglia (eds.), Perspectives on Children's Testimony. New York: Springer Verlag

Young Offenders Act. (1984).

CHAPTER TWENTY

The incarceration of female young offenders: Protection for whom?[1]

Raymond R. Corrado
Candice Odgers
Irwin M. Cohen
School of Criminology
Simon Fraser University
Burnaby, British Columbia

FEMALE YOUTH WHO COME INTO CONFLICT WITH THE LAW HAVE RECENTLY received a large amount of attention from the media, academics, and policy-makers. While the media portray a stereotype of the "new violent girl", academics argue over how we should study, research, and conceptualize young female offenders (Hoyt and Scherer 1998). Concurrently, policy-makers and practitioners also struggle to accommodate the increasing number of young females who come into the care of the youth justice system, a system allegedly designed by and for males (Reitsma-Street 1991). In the end, we are left with the media's depiction of the violent girl (Chisholm 1997), academics' concern for the neglected and victimized female youth within a patriarchal system (Chesney-Lind and Sheldon 1998; Reitsma-Street 1993; Sheldon 1998), and the frustration of policy-makers over the lack of detailed and accurate information on young females (Reitsma-Street 1999).

One of the common problems cited by researchers and policy-makers attempting to address the "girl problem" in Canadian youth justice is that there is very little known about female offending. Traditionally, research included young women only as a subset or as a minor variation of male

Canadian Journal of Criminology/Revue canadienne de criminologie, April/avril 2000, pp. 189–207.

delinquency (Figueria-McDonough 1992). Currently, however, research that focuses exclusively on females is becoming increasingly important in addressing policy issues. In particular, in order to respond to the perceived increase in violent offending among young females (Shaw and Dubois 1995), and their steadily rising rates of incarceration (Reitsma-Street 1999), it is crucial that we begin to explore the special needs of female youth and the factors that affect their treatment within the youth justice system.

The literature contains two dominant themes relating to female youth in conflict with the law. First, there is considerable debate surrounding the issue of whether violent crime among young females is actually increasing. The question of whether young women are becoming more violent has been controversial since Freda Alder's seminal publication *Sisters in Crime* in the 1970's, and it has recently been intensified by a wave of highly publicized violent crimes involving young women. The current media-drawn image of the extremely violent and uncontrollable female offender has emerged primarily because of several sensationalized murders and "gang" beatings instigated by young women. The most notorious occurred in Victoria, B.C. in 1997, when a large group of predominately female youths brutally assaulted Reena Virk, and, then, two youths from this group, including a young man, proceeded to severely beat her further and finally drown her. In the same year, a 17-year-old female was charged with the vicious and unprovoked murder of her grandmother in Boucherville, Quebec; and, in 1995, three teenage girls conspired to seduce, ambush, beat, and drown their pimp in Burnaby, British Columbia. The 1998 statement of the president of Safe Schools in Vancouver illustrates the climate and emerging discourse around the new female offender:

> You don't have to look at the numbers to know that young women are becoming more violent... I don't think that there is any question about it.... The intensity of the violence that girls are getting involved in is as intense as the male violence (*Vancouver Sun*, July 23: A2).

The second prominent theme that emerges from the literature is the debate concerning how young female offenders are being processed by the youth criminal justice system in Canada. The main issue is whether young females are being discriminated against under the *Young Offenders Act* (1982) given the fair procedure focus of this law. The abuses and discriminatory processing that occurred under the *Juvenile Delinquents Act* (1908) are well documented (Bala 1997; Reitsma-Street 1991). There is, therefore, a general consensus that, historically, under the welfare-based youth laws (Corrado 1992), female youths have been discriminated against by being disproportionately punished for status offences, such as immorality, incorrigibility, and promiscuity (Bala 1997; Chesney-Lind 1973; Chesney-Lind 1986; Reitsma-Street 1991; Sheldon 1998).

Despite the rights-based principles of the YOA and the abolition of status offences, one perspective is that the treatment of young females has not changed or improved (Duffy 1996; Reitsma-Street 1993). The reliance on custodial dispositions for nonviolent and nonserious offences committed by female youth is cited as evidence demonstrating that females continue to receive paternalistic and punitive forms of justice. Reitsma-Street (1991) argues that the Canadian judicial system continues to patrol the sexual and moral boundaries of female youth through the imposition of status-type offences. These offences consist of violations of administration conditions, most typically, breaches of probation. These administrative offences allow for a new charge to be laid. In effect, youth who are found to be in violation of their probation order conditions (such as failing to attend treatment, obey curfew, abstain from drugs and alcohol, and/or obey no-go and non-association orders) can be charged with a new offence. Typically, the response of the youth criminal justice system to these violations is a more punitive sentence, ultimately incarceration.

Reitsma-Street claims that the principle of least possible interference has not been realized for young women under the YOA due to patriarchal discrimination, whereby deviations from the traditional normative boundaries of femininity result in both neglect and extensive punishment. She asserts that judicial practices under the YOA "remain indifferent, inadequate, and discriminatory for female youths" (Reitsma-Street 1991: 439). In addition, numerous researchers contend that the youth justice system views girls to be in greater need of protection than their male counterparts, and has employed discretionary powers to reinforce traditional sex roles and patrol female sexuality as a result of this need (Grimes 1983). In effect, Chesney-Lind (1978), Reitsma-Street (1993), and others argue that these practitioners appear to be more concerned with the protection of the sexual status quo than with the protection of these young women (Sarri 1983). Patriarchal discrimination, therefore, is explicitly tied to control over the sexuality of female young offenders. It is our contention, however, that the sentencing recommendations made by youth justice personnel are primarily based on the desire to protect female youth from high-risk environments and street-entrenched lifestyles. Moreover, it does not appear that the pre-occupation with female sexuality that has historically plagued the youth justice system's response to female youth is continuing to govern the actions of key decision-makers within the system.

This latter explanation is based partly on the inability of community-based programs to protect certain female youth, the difficulties that these programs have in getting young female offenders to participate in rehabilitation programs, such as drug and alcohol rehabilitation, when they are not incarcerated, and the presence of some, albeit usually inadequate, treatment resources in custodial institutions. As well, cost-effectiveness issues concerning the provision of intervention programs for females engaged in minor offences must also be considered.

Since the inception of the YOA, the use of custodial dispositions for young females has not decreased as expected. In particular, there has been an increase in the use of custodial sentences for females engaged in minor or status-type offences (Reitsma-Street 1993). As mentioned above, there is the assertion that patriarchal discrimination, that is inexplicitly tied to female sexuality, underlies the higher incarceration rates for females (Edwards 1989; Grimes 1983; Reitsma-Street 1993), while alternatively, we maintain that the protection of young female offenders, including the immediate objective of saving the lives of certain particularly vulnerable offenders, is a more tenable explanation for this increase.

The proposed vulnerability of the young females that are filling our custodial institutions is based on the growing body of Canadian and American research that identifies a consistent multi-problem profile of the female young offender. This profile consists of: (1) extremely high rates of both physical and sexual abuse (Chesney-Lind and Sheldon 1998; Crawford 1988; Dembo 1989); (2) severe drug addiction (Crawford 1988); (3) increasing high-school drop out rates and low levels of academic and employment achievement (Figueria-McDonough 1993); and (4) chronic family dysfunction and abuse (Artz 1998; Lowman 1987). The youth criminal justice system, therefore, appears to be processing young women with a substantial number of needs/risk factors. It is not surprising, therefore, that there is considerable concern expressed by key decision-makers, particularly probation officers(2), concerning protection needs and issues.

Historically, most of the analysis on patriarchally-based discrimination focused on the excessive and inadequate "treatment" interventions forced on imprisoned female youths. Equally important, the punitive punishments for female youths were directed against those who had engaged in status offences; these offences were both unique to juvenile offenders and were disproportionately applied to young women. In order to address this hypothesis in the current historical period, we are exploring the youth justice system's response to female young offenders in the greater Vancouver metropolitan region. More specifically, we have gathered data concerning the offending and social profiles of young women in jail, and have obtained information that can assist in explaining the complex dynamics associated with the sentencing of female young offenders.[3]

It was hypothesized that: (1) overall, the offending and re-offending patterns among females would be characterized by high levels of administrative offences, (2) the majority of time that females spend in custodial institutions would be attributable to administrative charges, and (3) the explicit rationale behind the recommendation for a custodial disposition from criminal justice actors would be related directly to the treatment and physical/emotional protection of the youth, as opposed to alternative sentencing rationale, such as punishment, deterrence, or protection of society.

Method

A female-only research design was employed to explore the dynamics associated with the youth justice system's response to female youth. The rationale for this approach was twofold. First, this methodology was adopted in response to the criticism that males have continuously been used as the norm in delinquency research. Second, in order to capture an accurate and holistic picture of the special needs and complex dynamics relating to this group of female youth, it was essential to develop an understanding of them first in isolation, thereby eventually allowing for a comprehensive appreciation of both the between-gender differences and similarities.

A total of 67 incarcerated young females were interviewed over an eighteen month period between April 1998 and October 1999. Participants were drawn from one closed custody and one open custody location in Vancouver, British Columbia. The response rate was 94%. The two main reasons why an offender refused to participate in the research were that the interview interfered with an institutional program or with a previously scheduled visit. All of the participants were serving a custodial disposition at the time of the interview. Each youth participated in a one on-one semi-structured interview that lasted approximately 2 hours. The participants responded to questions on a myriad of issues including: the perceived fairness of their sentence, deterrence, attitudes toward past and future recidivism, self-identity, special needs, criminal history, social history, peers, mental disorders and illnesses, physical and sexual abuse, drug and alcohol dependency, and responses to institutional life.

In addition to participation in the interview, the subjects were tracked during a one year follow up period in order to record official re-offending. Prior to each interview, the provincial case file of the youth was reviewed and coded. For our subjects, provincial case files generally included predisposition reports, institutional assessments, psychological reports, a record of prior offences and dispositions, and other collateral file information.

Participants

The demographic summary of the sample relied on self report data, while prior and current offence information was coded from provincial case files. The average age of the females was 16 years old. A disproportionate percentage of the youth belonged to an ethnic minority group (47.9%), with Aboriginal youths comprising 42.3% of the entire sample. As shown in Table 1, the youth in this sample had experienced extremely high levels of abuse, immediate family dysfunction, and early home separation.

In addition, 68.8% of the subjects reported that a member of their immediate or extended family had a criminal record, while 64.6 % of the sample indicated that a member of their immediate or extended family had a drug abuse problem.

Measures of family conflict and early home separation (see Table 1) indicated that the vast majority of the young women either left home by their own volition (87.8%), or were kicked out of their homes (57.4%) at a relatively early age (12 years old). Interestingly, 58.1% of the sample was either living on their own or was in the care of the state at the time that they committed the offence that resulted in their incarceration. In addition, the average number of places lived, other than at

Table 1
Sample demographics and family history (n= 67)

	Percentage	Average
Age		16 years
Ethnicity		
Caucasian	52.1	
Aboriginal	42.3	
Asian	4.2	
Other	1.4	
Enrolled in school	49.3	
Last grade competed		Grade 8
Family history		
Criminality	68.8	
Mental illness	32.3	
Drug abuse	64.6	
Living at time of offence		
Immediate family	37.1	
Extended family	4.8	
Independent	24.2	
Ward of the state	33.9	
Kicked out of home		
Earliest Age		13 years
# of times		5 times
Left Home	87.8	
Earliest Age		12 years
# of times		10 times
# of places lived other than home		11.4

home, was 11. Clearly, there was very little residential stability found within this sample.

The majority of the participants were serving time for relatively minor offences. Breaches of court orders comprised 44.8% of all current charges, while property offences comprised an additional 23.8% of the current charges. Approximately one-quarter (27%) of the sample was serving a period of incarceration for a violent offence. Provincial case file data revealed relatively high rates of previous contact with the youth justice system. On average, the youths in our sample had been previously sentenced 3.6 times, served approximately three months in a custodial institution (93.7 days), and been under the supervision of a probation order for a total of 18 months.

The previous criminal history of each youth was gathered at the time of the original interview. This information was restricted to provincial case file information and offences documented in predisposition reports. Every previous offence that the youth had received a disposition for, such as custody, probation, community work service, or restitution, was recorded along with the date and length of each disposition. Recidivism data were collected through CORNET, the provincial file information system. All official charges, court dates, transfers, and sentences are captured by this system.

Table 2
Offence characteristics

	Percentage	Frequency
Current offence		
Breaches	44.8	30
Property offences	23.8	16
Assaults	19.4	13
Drug offences	4.5	3
Robbery	4.5	3
Murder	3.0	2
Totals	100	67

Results

i. Offending patterns

An analysis of prior offence data reveals the non-serious nature of the majority of these young women's criminal histories. Based on the disposition data, the most serious offence on a given disposition date was coded according to Uniform Crime Reporting criteria. Next, the offences were collapsed into the following three categories; violent, serious nonviolent, and administrative (status-type) offences. The majority of charges that resulted in a period of incarceration in the sample were relatively minor. Interestingly, status type offences comprised

69% of the entire charges for the sample, while only 6% of all previous charges were violent in nature.

Within the one year follow-up period, 55.2% (37) of the females were charged with a nonviolent offence and 13.4% (9) were charged with a violent offence. Thus, the majority of the youth who recidivated within the one year follow up period committed a nonviolent crime (80.4%). Within the nonviolent category, there was a total of 122 new charges, comprised of 102 breaches, 18 minor thefts, and 2 miscellaneous charges. Of the 13.4% of the youth that re-offended violently, there were 13 charges of assault (Level 1) and 2 charges of robbery. A substantial number of youths did not officially recidivate during the data collection period since 31.3% of the females had not received a subsequent official charge. It must be kept in mind that these results only indicate official recidivism based on formally laid charges.

For the purposes of the present analysis, the most interesting relationship is the association between the length of time between release from custody and nonviolent re-offending charges, since 74.5% of the new charges in our sample were for administrative offences. The majority of the females (78.3%) who were charged with a nonviolent offence, most commonly a breach, were charged within three months of their release from custody.

ii. Custodial time

An analysis of the official criminal histories of our sample revealed that, on average, the total amount of time that females had spent in custody for substantive offences, 59 days, was greater than the average total amount of time spent in custody for administrative offences, 47 days, (t = 5.593, df = 64, p = .000). When the number and type of offences were controlled for, however, females were spending longer amounts of time in custody, on average, for administrative offences, 26 days, than they were, on average, for substantive offences, 18 days (t = 5.053, df = 45, p = .000). In this case, a substantive offence was coded as any offence listed in the *Criminal Code*, while an offence against the administration of youth justice included breach of YOA and breach of probation. It is important to note that it is extremely common for a youth to receive one sentence for multiple offences, therefore, in order to minimize Type I errors, the most serious offence was coded.

iii. Multi-problem profiles

It is evident from this brief overview of the social histories of these young women that there are several distinctive needs/ risk factors that must be considered to explain the significantly greater amounts of time that they spend in custody for relatively minor offences, particularly for administrative offences.

As stated previously, this group of young women virtually all had histories of severe family dysfunction. In addition, 67% of participants had been the victim of physical abuse at some point in their lives, while 52% of the young women reported being a victim of sexual abuse. The levels of drug use also were extremely high, with 55% reporting crack use, 49% reporting heroin use, and 65.7% indicating cocaine use. The average age of the onset of drug use was 12 years old.

The probable impact of the rates of drug use were explored further in terms of the relationship between street needs/ lifestyle behavior and the type of re-offending. In addition to the type of drugs used, the young females were asked about the frequency of drug use, which was scored on a scale of 1-6, anchored by daily and rarely. Using the chi square exact test procedure, a significant relationship was found between the frequency of crack cocaine use and nonviolent reoffending ($x^2 = 18.9$, df = 8, $p = .012$). Of those girls who had recidivated nonviolently (n = 37), 76.5% reported using crack daily, 17.6 % reported that they used the drug twice a week, and the remaining 5.9% reported a frequency rate of once a week. It, therefore, appears that the frequency of crack use is important in whether or not a female was subsequently charged with an administrative offence. There was no relationship found between other types of drugs (marijuana, heroin, cocaine, acid, and downers) and re-offending.

The relationship between administrative offending and various lifestyle/risk variables was also examincd. The number of times the youth had been charged with an administrative offence was correlated with the number of places they reported living ($r = .372$, $p = .01$), the age that they were kicked out of home ($r = .637$, $p = .01$), the number of times that they changed schools ($r = .377$, $p = .05$), and how many sexual partners they reported having ($r = .336$, $p = .05$), which served as an indication of professional sex trade membership.

iv. Qualitative analysis

Qualitative or personal statements made during the interviews with these youths offered considerable insights into the youth justice system's handling of administrative offences. For example, many of the young women (72%) explained that "safe time" and a chance to "dry out" were the primary reasons that they believed they were serving time in custody. A typical example of such motivations was the statement by a fourteen year old heroin addict "I'm here because of drugs... that is it, the judge wants me off the streets". Other females similarly commented that: "Clean time... drugs are the only reason that I am here", and "drugs – that is why I would go out and do crime... he [judge] thinks that I am a danger to myself".

In order to understand the motivations of probation officers' recommendations of custodial time for violations of administrative conditions, a content analysis of predisposition reports was conducted with regard to sentencing recommendations involving administrative charges. The majority of probation officers (75%) made statements that were scored as protective responses. Recommendations were coded as protective if a probation officer cited an immediate physical and emotional danger to the young women, or expressed concern about their safety at home or on the streets as a basis for the decision to incarcerate. A typical example of the "protective" concerns raised by probation officers for a judge's consideration in sentencing are reflected in the following excerpt:

> ...short of a custodial disposition, which is not desirable at this point, the writer is at a loss as to how to control or assist this defiant young girl in the community ... her history reflects a continuous cycle of refusal to co-operate with treatment attempts and running away... It is the fear of this writer that this youth is in grave danger of further victimization and self harm if no action is taken.

In the above example, the youth received a custodial disposition of 45 days for two charges of breach of probation, despite the fact that it was "not desirable" to incarcerate her at that point. Interestingly, there were only three cases (4.5%) from the entire sample where the probation officer recommended a custodial sentence based on the need to protect society from the youth.

Discussion

There is considerable support for the first hypothesis relating to the high levels of administrative offences among the offending and reoffending patterns of the young women, given that 69.0% of the previous charges were administrative in nature. In addition, 74% of the females who re-offended within the one-year follow-up period were charged with an administrative offence.

The second hypothesis, concerning the length of time that females are spending in custodial institutions for administrative charges, also received considerable support. The analysis of prior dispositions revealed that young females are spending significantly longer amounts of time in custody for administrative offences, on average, as compared to the amount of time that they are serving in custody for substantive offences. An obvious explanation for this relationship involves the cumulative nature of sentencing, whereby a youths' prior offence history likely has a more significant role in the disposition for an administrative offence than it does for a substantive offence. This argument is based on the assertion that judges give harsher sentences for each subsequent breach due to a youth's history of noncompliance. A comparison of the breach dispositions using a one-way ANOVA revealed no significant differences based on prior offence history. It appears as though the standard disposition for a youth charged with an administrative offence is 30 days in custody, regardless of prior offence history.

Our third hypothesis concerning protection and treatment as the basis for the recommendation of a custodial disposition for female youth received a substantial degree of support. Of the variables examined, frequency of crack cocaine use was the most strongly associated with nonviolent re-offending. This finding coincides with the themes that arose from the analysis of probation officers' sentencing recommendations, namely the strong emphasis that was placed on the need to protect these young women from external risk factors and high risk environments, as opposed to the need to protect society from the "new wave of violent female offenders". Moreover, the predominant perception among the youth was that personal safety concerns, in particular drug use, play a substantial role in the decision-making process of some actors in the criminal justice system, namely judges and probation officers. It appears, therefore, that female offenders recognize that negative personal histories and treatment issues are paramount to whether they receive a custodial disposition.

Given the extremely high levels of hard drug use, and its high correlation with "breaching", it would follow that youth custody institutions should, at the very least, be equipped to deal adequately with drug addiction. A substantial body of research indicates, however, that youth custody institutions are not properly equipped to deal with the special needs of female youth, in particular, the severe drug addiction from which the majority of these young women suffer (Chesney-Lind and Sheldon 1998; Jackson and Glackman 1995).

With respect to the benefits received from custodial dispositions, one of the young women, a 16-year-old offender who uses crack, heroin, and cocaine everyday, and who had been both physically and sexually abused throughout her life, stated that: "Sentences don't mean anything, just do your time and leave – get back to how things were". Thus, although the intentions of the key decision-makers in many of these cases may be "in the best interests of the child", the lack of resources in custodial settings may not be producing the intended effects of the sentence. A 15-year-old Aboriginal female serving time for first degree murder, who claimed that "I have basically been raised by the system... been in and out of here since I was 12", summarizes the often fruitless cycle of incarceration with this statement: "we come in here and meet people and hook up on the outs, selling asses, getting crack... it repeats and repeats".

In addition, virtually, all of the young women in the sample scored high on measures of abuse, family dysfunction, drug abuse, and other high risk variables associated with delinquency, indicating the multi-problem composition of this group of young offenders. Unfortunately, key variables, such as involvement in prostitution and suicide attempts, could not be coded reliably. Additional data gathering is being conducted to include these variables in future analyses.

With respect to the rationale behind the use of custody for female youth, it appears as though traces of paternalism still remain. The paternalism that exists appears to be manifesting itself in a fundamentally different form than previous versions. It is not evident from our analysis of sentencing recommendations, or from the testimonies of the female youths, that the decisions made by probation officers and judges, many of whom were female, were based on traditional notions of paternalism that relied on unfettered moralistic judgments and/or sex role stereotypes. For example, a typical response from the probation officers, when discussing their rationale for breaching, is illustrated in the following statement by a probation officer:

> ... I breach her for her safety... she is threatening to leave to the US [Latino prostitution ring] if we try and make her a permanent ward of the state... her probation runs out in September and we are worried that she will become street

> entrenched... what else can we do? ...she won't leave the streets, and she is in some very real and immediate danger.

Interestingly, the current responses of youth justice personnel illustrate a desire to protect female youth from external deviant factors that may influence them (drugs, street-life, physical and sexual abuse), as opposed to illustrating the need to protect society from the "new violent girl".

Equally important, the responses of the incarcerated female youth indicate that they do not perceive their sentences as being punitive. Instead, many girls state that they recognize that their sentences are meant to help them get off and stay off drugs, reduce the control and authority that "pimps" may have on them, and/or remove them temporarily from abusive environments. While we are not suggesting that incarceration is an effective approach for these multi-problem youth, the inability of current community-based programs to assist many of these youths frequently leaves judges and probation officers with few, if any, alternatives.

The high levels of risk, in terms of physical harm and drug abuse, that accompanies street life is a very real concern for probation officers in charge of these young women. All too often, the brutal and sexualized discourse that dominates academic debates regarding the lives of these youth is a literal description of their lives. For example, a 15-year-old youth, who has been involved in prostitution since the age of 12, states that: "you know... you get the beats [from johns], but its just part of the gig... you get used to it after awhile". Another youth describes an instance were she was taken hostage by two "dates" for three days and was forced to perform sexual acts while the men: "just started pissing and shitting all over me... I don't really remember much. I think when they [the police] found me I was half dead, or fucked up anyway... shit happens! [laugh]".

There is a need to develop strategies that mirror the realities of these young women's lives. It is evident among this incarcerated group of young women that: (1) there are 12-year-olds on the streets selling their bodies to support heroin and crack cocaine addictions; (2) that the majority of young women receiving a custodial sentence are serving time for minor violations; (3) a substantial number of young women are returning to custody within three months of their release (43%); and (4) that there are very few effective non-custodial policy initiatives that are available for this group of young women. While it appears obvious that interventions are needed, it is not clear how programs can be available to these young women outside of custodial settings. Forced treatment options raises the specter of the traditional paternalistic abuses allowed during certain historical periods of the *Juvenile Delinquents Act.* Voluntary treatment options, however, are not very likely to be selected by these women.

It is also apparent from the testimonies of these young women, and those who work with them, that non-moralistic, paternalistic decision-making practices occur under the justice-based *Young Offenders Act.* Young women who are most likely to be a risk to themselves, as opposed to others, are continuing to be incarcerated. The majority of the young women interviewed expressed traditional personal goals centered on family and material goods. The multi-problem realities of the young women's lifestyles and immediate priorities, however, explains the tremendous pull that the street life has on them and why they constitute enormous obstacles to any effective means of non-custodial treatment and protection. Innovative community options are required. These programs would have to include interventions that would mitigate the intense attraction of street life and drug addiction. In short, a criminal justice system approach has not been effective beyond providing short-term protection.

If the assertion that custodial sentences are being used primarily for protection and, to a lesser extent, treatment, is accepted, then there is an immediate need for future research in the development of effective community corrections alternatives. With some exceptions for the most extreme violent young women, it appears that there is a consensus among researchers and policy-makers that incarceration is morally wrong and not a very effective use of already under-funded resources for young women.

Notes

1. This research was supported by a grant from the Social Science and Humanities Research Council of Canada (R-410-98-1246) to Raymond Corrado.
2. Typically, it is the probation officer's role to both gather information concerning a young offender's needs/risk profile and to write the predisposition report that youth court judges reflect on in their sentencing decisions.
3. The offending and social profiles of male offenders (n=300) was also collected, however, our preliminary analysis revealed that administrative offences were not as prevalent as they were with the female sample, and the desire to protect the male youth from high risk environments was not evident from the file review. A forthcoming analysis will address these between-gender differences.

References

Alder, Freda
1975 Sisters in Crime. New York: McGraw Hill.

Artz, Sibylle
1998 Sex, Power, and the Violent School Girl. Toronto: Trifolium Books Inc.

Bala, Nicholas
1997 Young Offenders and the Law. Toronto: Irwin Law.

Chesney-Lind, Meda
1973 Judicial enforcement of the female sex role. Issues in Criminology 8: 51-70.

Chesney-Lind, Meda
1978 Young women in the arms of the law. In L.H. Bowker (ed.), Women, Crime, and the Criminal Justice System. Massachusetts: Lexington Books.

Chesney-Lind, Meda
1986 Women and crime: The female offender. Signs 12: 78-96.

Chesney-Lind, Meda and Randall Sheldon
1998 Girls, Delinquency, and Juvenile Justice. Pacific Grove, CA: Brooks/Cole.

Chisholm, Patricia
1997 Bad girls. Macleans, December 8: 13-15.

Corrado, Raymond
1992 Introduction. In R. Corrado, N. Bala, R. Linden, and M. LeBlanc (eds.), Juvenile Justice in Canada: A Theoretical and Analytical Assessment. Markham: Butterworths Canada Ltd.

Crawford, J.
1988 Tabulation of a Nationwide Survey of Female Inmates. Arizona: Research Advisory Services.

Dembo, Richard
1989 Physical abuse, sexual victimization, and illicit drug use: Replication of structure analysis among high risk adolescents. Violence and Victims 4: 121-138.

Duffy, Ann
1996 Bad girls in hard times: Canadian female juvenile offenders. In Gary O'Bireck (ed.), Not a Kid Anymore. Scarborough: Nelson Canada Publishing.

Edwards, Anne
1989 Sex/gender, sexism and criminal justice: Some theoretical considerations. International Journal of the Sociology of Law 17: 165-184.

Figueria-McDonough, Josefina
1992 Community structure and female delinquency rates. Youth and Society 24: 3-30.

Figueria-McDonough, Josefina
1993 Residence, dropping out, and delinquency rates. Deviant Behavior: An Interdisciplinary Journal 14: 109-132.

Grimes, C.
1983 Girls and the Law. Washington, DC: Institute for Educational Leadership.

Hoyt, Stephanie and David Scherer
1998 Female juvenile delinquency: Misunderstood by the juvenile justice system, neglected by social science. Law and Human Behavior 22: 81-107.

Jackson, Margaret and Bill Glackman
1995 Corrections Branch Programming for Female Young Offenders: Perspectives and Visions. Burnaby, B.C.: Criminology Research Centre, Simon Fraser University.

Lowman, John
1987 Taking young prostitutes seriously. Canadian Review of Sociology and Anthropology 24: 99-166.

Reitsma-Street, Marge
1991 A Review of Female Delinquency. In A. Leshied, P. Jaffe, and W. Willis (eds.), The Young Offenders Act: A Revolution in Canadian Juvenile Justice. Toronto: University of Toronto Press.

Reitsma-Street, Marge
1993 Canadian youth court charges and dispositions for females before and after the implementation of the Young Offenders Act. Canadian Journal of Criminology 35: 437-458.

Reitsma-Street, Marge
1999 Justice for Canadian girls: A 1990's update. Canadian Journal of Criminology 41: 335-364.

Sarri, Rosemary
1983 Gender issues in juvenile justice. Crime and Delinquency 29: 381-397.

Shaw, Margaret and Sheryl Dubois
1995 Understanding Violence By Women: A Review of the Literature. http://198.103.98.138/crd/fsw/fsw.23/fsw23e.htm (March 3, 1999).

Sheldon, Randall
1998 Confronting the ghost of Mary Ann Crouse: Gender bias in the juvenile justice system. Juvenile and Family Court Journal 49: 11-26.

Vancouver Sun
1998 Violent crime by females on the increase. Canadian Press, July 23: A1-A2.

CHAPTER TWENTY-ONE

Understanding public views of youth crime and the youth justice system[1]

Jane B. Sprott
Centre of Criminology
University of Toronto
Toronto, Ontario

PUBLIC VIEWS AND MEDIA COVERAGE OF THE YOUTH JUSTICE SYSTEM have not been examined to the same degree as has the adult justice system (Doob, Marinos, and Varma 1995). Public opinion of the youth justice system is important, however, because it can affect the policy agenda. For example, the 1993 Liberal political agenda for young offenders appeared in some cases to be informed more by public concerns than by identifiable problems in the way in which adolescents are processed by the youth justice system. In the Liberal Party's 1993 policy document, the party listed as a problem the "clearing" of a youth's record after he or she turned 18 (Liberal Party of Canada 1993: 4). It incorrectly implied that all young people with a youth court record for violence could present themselves as first offenders if they were to appear in adult court at age 18[2]. Because public concern may have an impact on the reform process, it is important to understand the public image of youth crime, and to understand the public's main source of information about youth crime – the mass media.

Not only do the news media shape people's understanding of the world, but they also shape the nature of our society. Although the news media play a paramount role in constructing the reality of social phenomena for the public, the reality constructed by the news media discourse may not necessarily

Canadian Journal of Criminology/Revue canadienne de criminologie, July/juillet 1996, pp. 271–290.

reflect other images of reality. By virtue of the need to sell newspapers, journalists reporting news must interpret reality and tell stories as opposed to simply reflecting reality or gathering facts. Therefore, a reporter chooses, and then shapes and defines, events to make useful news media presentations (Ericson, Baranek, and Chan 1987).

Through the act of choosing to report particular events and then constructing those events in journalistic terms, information is presented in one particular way, thereby precluding other avenues of interpretation. The result is not a straightforward presentation of the facts, but the facts modified to the style of the particular news outlet. This has the potential to shape news-media discourse in two ways. First, an unrepresentative, but "newsworthy", selection of stories is presented. Second, and more subtly, a reporter's focus in the story determines which facts are conveyed, and how those facts are depicted.

Range of cases

The reporter, or others in the media organization, must first select which stories to report because it is not possible to present all types of stories in the media. This is one way in which the purposive focus of reporting provides a particular view of society. In an examination of criminal offenses reported in Canadian newspapers, Doob (1985) found that most of the offenses reported were crimes of violence. Indeed, compared to police statistics, the newspapers over-represented serious violent crimes.

The unrepresentative range of crimes reported in the media may contribute to public misperceptions of crime. People may realize that the media will only cover unusual or important news, but they do not weigh this adequately in their judgement of the frequency of crimes in society. The public overestimates the amount of serious crime and perceives crime to be increasing (Doob and Roberts 1988). For example, homicide rates were relatively high in the mid 1970's, but since the abolition of capital punishment in 1976, homicide rates have stayed the same, or declined slightly (Fedorowycz 1994; Figure 1). However, the majority of the public believed, in the mid-1980's, that murders had increased since the abolition of capital punishment (Doob and Roberts 1988).

Focus of story

The focus of a story – which facts are reported and emphasized – is also important. If the media focus on the criminal act, other important facts such as characteristics of the offender, the charge, and the disposition eventually imposed may be omitted. These ignored facts may be important if the public is to understand the event in its entirety and be able to evaluate whether the case was properly handled by the justice system.

Research has demonstrated that media reports of crimes exclude relevant information. In a series of studies (Doob and Roberts 1983), people were asked to read either a newspaper account of a sentencing decision, or a summary of court documents related to the disposition (e.g., a transcript of the sentencing hearing). Compared to those who read the summary of court documents, those who read the newspaper account rated the disposition as being too lenient. Moreover, the ratings varied depending upon which newspaper was read. The "facts" from one newspaper made the disposition appear more lenient than the "facts" from another newspaper, even though all the "facts" may have been accurately reported. It may be that the focus of the media discourse excludes information that people use to assess the fairness of a disposition. A systematic content analysis of newspaper coverage of sentencing stories conducted by the Canadian Sentencing Commission (1987) indicated that few details beyond the offence and the sentence were ever reported. Absent from many of the news reports were reasons for the sentence and the judicial logic underlying sentencing decisions. Therefore, it has been argued that the media reporting of sentences simplifies the functioning of the criminal justice process (Roberts 1992). Consequently, if people gain knowledge of the criminal justice system through the media, their understanding and knowledge of issues may be limited. There has been, however, little systematic attempt to evaluate how the media report youth crime and what the public perception of youth crime is.

An important first step is to assess the media image of youth crime, and how it differs from an "official" or a statistical image of youth crime. From these two sets of images of youth crime, it may be possible to ascertain which image corresponds with the public's image of youth crime. The comparison of images of youth crime based upon the media, statistical and legal reports, and public perceptions may help us understand the perception that the public has of youth crime and youth justice policies. For this purpose, the print medium was used and data on all newspaper reports on youth crime from the three Toronto English language daily newspapers (*Globe and Mail*, Toronto *Star*, Toronto *Sun*) were collected for two months. These data provided a range of cases that were compared to statistical descriptions of cases in Ontario reported to, and by, the police.

The youth justice system itself has the problem of selective reporting. Very few cases are ever formally reported or described in public documents in most provinces. However, *The Young Offenders Service* by Bala and Lilles (1994) provides summaries of cases which focus on the factors seen by those who work in the youth justice system as being important in determining dispositions. The range of cases illustrated in the Bala and Lilles reports on sentences were also compared to the newspaper reports and statistical reports of youth crime. In addition, a method of coding information provided in the newspaper text and the Bala and Lilles text was developed so that the types of information contained in the two sets of materials could be compared. In order to sample the public image of youth crime, a survey questionnaire was developed to help understand attitudes and beliefs about the youth justice system.

Method

Measures

Bala and Lilles Reports. The *Young Offenders Reporting Service* by Bala and Lilles provided one image of youth crime. All 51 of the reports of cases at the disposition stage of processing from the beginning of 1993 to March of 1995 were examined. The principal charge and type of offence were recorded. In addition, each sentence in the description of the case was coded to indicate whether it dealt with the disposition, charge, facts of the crime, issues surrounding the youth, or the justification for the disposition. These reports were used as a proxy measure of the way in which those involved in the youth justice system view young offender dispositions. Presumably, the editors of the series, a law professor whose speciality is young offenders and a judge (and former law professor), include material in their summaries which they believe to be important in understanding a disposition.

Newspaper Articles. The three Toronto English language daily newspapers, the *Globe and Mail*, Toronto *Star*, and the Toronto *Sun*, were examined and all articles about youth crime appearing for a two month period in mid-1995 were identified. For each of these 113 articles, the principal offence was recorded, or when an offence was not mentioned, an offence type was inferred based upon the type of crime reported. Each sentence in the 113 newspaper articles was recorded and classified into the same categories created for the Bala and Lilles reports.

Public perception survey. This survey contained questions about assessments of youth court sentences, views of youth crime, preferred sentences for specific crimes, knowledge of the *Young Offenders Act* (YOA), and preferred approaches for dealing with young offenders. In addition, a few questions about adult crime were included to compare responses from the present sample to determine if this study's sample was comparable to a larger, representative sample.

Procedure

Data Collection. In an attempt to describe the relative emphasis given to different aspects of a case from Bala and Lilles and from the newspaper reports, the full written descriptions were coded sentence by sentence. Descriptions were on the average 9.6 sentences long for the 51 Bala and Lilles reports and 12.3 sentences long for the 113 media reports. Each sentence in the case summary was coded as focusing on the Disposition, the Charge or Offence, the Facts of the Crime, Issues Surrounding the Youth, or Justification for the Disposition. For the newspaper reports, two additional categories were included: Crime in General and Results (sentences that dealt with the effects or results of the crime, including descriptions of the victim, the family of victims, or other people affected by the crime). To some degree the process of coding the sentences is subjective. For example, a statement such as "the youth showed remorse" could be coded as Issues Surrounding the Youth or as Justification for the Disposition. Thus, it was necessary to estimate the reliability of the coding. Ten Bala and Lilles reports and ten media articles were randomly chosen to compare the experimenter's coding to the coding by an independent rater. Inter-rater reliability coefficients ranged from +.83 to +.99, suggesting a high degree of reliability.

Public perception survey. Over a one week period, respondents were sought at two busy downtown Toronto locations. People were asked if they would mind taking a few minutes to fill out a questionnaire on perceptions of youth crime. Most people agreed to fill out the questionnaire and those few who refused did so apparently independently of any knowledge of the content of the questions to which they were being asked to respond. Consequently, there is no reason to assume that those who filled out the questionnaire were seriously different from those who refused. The 198 respondents were almost all Canadian residents, were evenly split by gender, and were predominately between the ages of 20 to 39.

Results

"Official" and media Images

One "official" image of youth crime is the distribution of cases going to youth court provided by the Canadian Centre for Justice Statistics (1995). In Ontario youth court cases, roughly 22% of the principal charges involve violence, 50% are property crimes, and the remaining are other *Criminal Code* offences (18%), YOA offences (7%) and other federal offences (3%) (Table 1). Characteristics of the cases are not available from official statistics. However, information about youth court cases can be found in Bala and Lilles summaries of cases. The types of cases summarized by Bala and Lilles, and presented as being relevant to those interested in youth court dispositions, provide another picture of youth crime (Table 1). The majority of cases described by Bala and Lilles (69%) are serious violent cases. This is likely to be a result of the fact that serious violent cases involve more severe dispositions and therefore are more likely to be appealed or seen as being of more interest to experts such as lawyers and judges.

Most people do not receive information about youth crime through either of these two sources. Instead they rely on the media which provides them with a very different picture of youth crime (Table 1). Out of the 113 stories in the three newspapers, 25 of the stories were about youth crime in general. A general offence from those 25 stories could be inferred because the newspaper would usually use a case as an illustration. The media focused almost exclusively (94%) on violent crime – most of it serious – presumably because serious violent crimes are of more interest to the public. If the public develops an image of youth crime from the media, the almost exclusive reporting of violence may distort the public's perception of the relative incidence of particular crimes.

Information provided. The information in the newspaper stories was compared with the Bala and Lilles summaries. To get a general sense of the focus of the two sets of texts, the number of stories which mentioned at least half a sentence

Table 1
Number and percent of principal charges of young offender cases

	Ontario Youth Court Statistics 1993-94		Bala and Lilles		Toronto Newspaper	
Charge	N	%	N	%	N	%
Violence						
Homicide	16	0.02	4	7.8	57	70.4
Attempted murder	12	0.02	0	0.0	4	3.5
Sexual assault	848	1.70	6	11.8	4	3.5
Other serious assaults[1]	1,751	3.50	5	9.8	8	7.1
Minor assault	5,543	11.08	7	13.7	13	11.5
Robbery	929	1.86	8	15.7	15	13.0
Other	1,905	3.81	5	9.8	5[*]	4.4
Total	11,004	22.00	35	68.6	106	93.8
Property						
Break and enter	5,279	10.56	8	15.7	2	1.8
Possession	4,006	8.01	1	2.0	1	.9
Theft under	8,800	17.60	0	0.0	0	0.0
Mischief	2,463	4.93	0	0.0	0	0.0
Other	4,460	8.92	1	2.0	3	2.6
Total	25,008	50.01	10	19.7	6	5.3
Other Criminal Code						
Failure to comply	361	0.72	1	2.0	1	0.9
Failure to appear	5,231	10.46	0	0.0	0	0.0
Motor vehicle	217	0.43	4	7.8	0	0.0
Other	3,133	6.26	1	2.0	0	0.0
Total	8,942	17.88	6	11.7	1	0.9
YOA						
Failure to comply with disposition	3,620	7.24	0	0.0	0	0.0
Other	2	—	0	0.0	0	0.0
Total	3,622	7.24	0	0.0	0	0.0
Other federal offences[2]	1,432	2.86	0	0.0	0	0.0
Overall total	50,008	100	51	100	113	100

1 Aggravated assault, assault with a weapon or causing bodily harm, and causing bodily harm with intent.
2 Mostly drug offences (1201 of the charges).
* Two general crime stories were placed in the "other" category because they were about many violent offences and thus could not be specifically categorized.

Table 2
Percent of reports that contain some information in various categories and the average number of sentences describing this information

	Bala and Lilles percent reported	Average number of sentences	Newspaper percent reported	Average number of sentences
Disposition	100.0*	1.79 (n=51)**	13.6*	1.29 (n=12)**
Charge	98.0*	0.87 (n=50)	68.2*	1.06 (n=60)
Facts of the crime	84.3*	2.88 (n=43)	96.6*	4.91 (n=85)
Youth	76.5*	3.42 (n=39)	36.4*	3.42 (n=32)
Justification for disposition	74.5*	2.57 (n=38)	1.1*	1.00 (n=l)
Crime in general	0.0*	—	45.5*	5.00 (n=40)
Results/Impact on victim	0.0*	—	69.3*	4.43 (n=61)
Total number of stories		n=51		n=88

* $p < .05$ (Bala and Lilles vs. newspaper % reporting at least 0.5 of a sentence)
** n's refer to number of stories with at least 0.5 of a sentence in the text

pertaining to each of the various categories were counted (Table 2). The 25 "crime in general" stories from the media are not contained in this analysis.

There was a difference in focus between Bala and Lilles and the newspapers. Bala and Lilles focused significantly more on the youth, and significantly less on the facts of the crime than the newspapers did. The newspapers rarely gave any information about the justification for the disposition. Indeed, only one sentence from one story was devoted to justifying a disposition during this two month period. Hence, the public received little information about sentencing. Whereas Bala and Lilles focus more on the youth and the circumstances surrounding the youth, the newspapers had a broader focus which placed more emphasis on the impact of the crime on others. As a consequence, the public are not only getting little information about sentencing, they also receive little insight into circumstances surrounding the young offender. If judges and lawyers need the information summarized by Bala and Lilles to understand the case and arrive at a disposition, then the public must have limited understanding because so little information is relayed to them.

In addition to the number and percent of stories which focus on various aspects of youth crime, the mean number of sentences devoted to each category (where it was mentioned) provides an indication of the degree of detailed information available to readers or users of the reports. Table 2 shows that when the youth is mentioned at all, Bala and Lilles devote the same mean number of sentences to the youth as the newspapers do. The newspapers only mention the youth in 36% of the stories while the Bala and Lilles reports mention the youth in 77% of the stories. Quite obviously, Bala and Lilles on average devote more sentences, in more stories, to the justification of the disposition than the newspapers do. The newspapers are also devoting more sentences, in more stories, to the facts of the crime, crime in general, and the impact of the crime on others. Consequently, newspaper readers are getting a different view of youth crime from that which is provided to judges and lawyers for understanding and arriving at dispositions.

Using the Bala and Lilles descriptions as an indication of the relative importance of the different types of information for those making decisions, we can see that those involved in the decision making process focus on the charge, the youth, the disposition, and the justification of the disposition. Readers of the newspaper, on the other hand, receive more emphasis on the facts of the crime, crime in general, and the impact of the crime on others. We can now turn to how the public views youth crime, and see how their views relate to the information they receive from the newspapers.

Survey

Three questions on adult crime used on the survey were the same as or very similar to an earlier study which used a representative sample of the Canadian public (Doob and Roberts 1983; 1988). Results from the present survey are similar to the national sample employed in the earlier study. For example, 78% of the respondents from the earlier survey believed that adult sentences were not severe enough compared to 73% in this study. Seventy-four percent greatly overestimated violent crime compared to 70% in this study. Sixty-seven percent believed that the murder rate has increased compared to 74% in this study. It appears that the sample of people in this survey gave responses which were quite similar to those given in national surveys (Roberts 1992; 1994). Thus, although the present sample is not ideal, *there is no reason to believe its non-representativeness is a serious concern for interpreting and generalizing the results.* In particular, most of the important findings in this study relate to the relationships between variables, not to the absolute responses to a single question.

For analytical purposes, the sample was divided into two groups: the 12% of respondents who felt the sentences handed down in youth court were too severe or about right (labelled "about right" in the tables that follow), and the 88% of respondents who felt the sentences were too lenient or much too lenient (labelled "too lenient" in the tables). In an attempt to understand people's evaluation of youth court sentences, respondents were asked what kind of cases they were thinking about when they evaluated the severity of youth court dispositions. Those people who felt that the sentences were too lenient were more likely than those who felt that the sentences were about right to be thinking of repeat offenders and violent offences (Table 3). Those people who believed that the sentences handed down in youth court were about right were mainly thinking about first time property offenders, or more generally, all young offenders.

General punitive attitudes. Although not statistically significant, there was a trend in the direction of harsher sentences being suggested by those who thought that youth court was too lenient ($p > .10$). Those who believed that youth court sentences were too lenient were somewhat less likely

Table 3
The type of offender and offences people are thinking about when they evaluate youth court sentences

Evaluation of youth sentences	All cases or no violence	Violence and/or repeat	Row total
About right	20 83.3%	4 16.7%	24 100%
Too lenient	66 38.4%	106 61.6%	172 100%

Chi-Square = 15.51, (df=1), $p < .001$

Note: cell entries contain numbers and row percentages

to want a fine or probation for a first time property offender, and were more likely to want a higher proportion of those convicted of a minor assault to receive a prison disposition compared to those who believed youth court sentences were about right. It appears that the belief that sentences are generally too lenient is not very tightly tied to punitive beliefs about specific types of cases. More important, perhaps, is the finding that many of those who indicate that youth court sentences are too lenient do not favour custodial sentences for minor offences.

Knowledge of the YOA. People who believed sentences were too lenient were slightly, but not significantly (p = .07), more inclined than those who believed sentences were about right to underestimate the percent of minor assaults which result in a prison disposition. Generally, however, the belief that sentences are about right or too lenient was not tied to systematic differences in knowledge. Knowledge of the provisions of the YOA was quite low within the sample. Only 6% thought that the maximum term of imprisonment for a minor assault was as much as two years. In fact, 54% thought that the maximum term of imprisonment for a minor assault was six months. Only 14% thought that a 17-year-old could be transferred to adult court for any offence and only 20% thought that the minimum age of transfer was as low as 14 years old. More important was the finding that there was no hint of a difference between those who viewed sentences as too lenient and about right on these knowledge questions(3).

Other criminal justice beliefs. If opinions about leniency of youth court sentences are not strongly linked to preferred dispositions for specific groups of young offenders and appear to be unrelated to knowledge about the YO*A*, then the views of leniency in the youth justice system may relate to other general criminal justice beliefs. Indeed, respondents viewed the youth justice system in the same way that they viewed the adult justice system. Those who believed that youth sentences were too lenient also believed adult sentences were too lenient (Table 4 – top panel).

Another related general belief was that violence constitutes a large amount of crime. Those who believed that youth sentences were too lenient were more likely to overestimate the amount of violence in adult crime (Table 4 – middle panel). In addition, those who believed sentences for youths were too lenient were also more likely to believe that violence had increased in the past five years (Table 4 – bottom panel). Thus, it appears that people's beliefs about youth sentences are related to other general beliefs about the criminal justice system and crime in general, and not as closely related to differences in punitiveness on specific offences or to systematic knowledge about youth justice issues.

Separate youth justice system

Fifty-seven percent of those who felt that the sentences handed down in youth court were too lenient also opposed having a separate youth justice system to deal with youth crime. Only 14% of those who felt that sentences were about right opposed a separate youth justice system (chi-square = 12.95, df=l, $p < .001$). Not surprisingly, the relationships between "opposing a separate youth justice system" and other variables were similar to the relationships between views of leniency of the

Table 4
Relationship between evaluation of youth court sentences and general criminal justice beliefs

	Evaluation of youth sentences		
Evaluation of adult sentences	About right	Too lenient	
About right	17 77.3%	27 16.4%	Chi-Square = 40.02, (df = 1), $p < .001$
Too lenient	5 22.7%	138 83.6%	
	100%	100%	
Estimate of % adult crimes involving violence	About right	Too lenient	
Accurate (1-20%)	10 43.5%	33 20.4%	
Over- (21-40%) estimate	6 26.1%	34 21.0%	Chi-Square = 7.78, (df = 2), $p < .05$
Large (41-100%) overestimate	7 30.4%	95 58.6%	
	100%	100%	
Change in amount of adult violent crime	About right	Too lenient	
Much more violence	5 22.7%	86 51.8%	
Slightly more violence	7 31.8%	51 30.7%	Chi-Square = 10.73, (df = 2), $p = .004$.
No change/less	10 45.5%	29 17.5%	
	100%	100%	

Note: cell entries contain numbers and column percentages.

youth court and these same other variables. The one exception was that those who opposed a separate youth justice system held significantly more punitive attitudes about specific types of cases than did those who favoured a separate youth justice system. Eighty-five percent of those who favoured a separate youth justice system preferred a fine or probation for a first time break and enter, while only 68% of those who opposed a separate youth justice system preferred a fine or probation for a first time break and enter (chi-square = 6.81, df = 1, p = .009). Moreover, only 31% of those who favoured a separate youth justice system wanted most of those convicted of a minor assault to receive a prison disposition, while 54% of those who were opposed to a separate youth justice system wanted most of those convicted of a minor assault to receive a prison disposition (chi-square = 7.94, df = 1, p = .004). Once again, it is worth noting that many of both groups did *not* want prison dispositions for these types of cases.

Opposing or favouring a separate youth justice system was apparently unrelated to the level of knowledge of the *YOA*. In addition, all of the differences in the criminal justice beliefs of those who opposed or favoured a separate youth justice system were consistent with the differences in the general criminal justice beliefs of those who considered youth sentences too lenient versus those who believed youth sentences were about right.

Conclusion

This study illuminates many issues surrounding public perception and knowledge of youth crime and the *YOA*. One can start with the finding that most respondents (88%) indicated that they believed that the *YOA* was too lenient. Thus, on the surface, it might appear that the approach of increasing sentences would increase public satisfaction with the *YOA*. Although most respondents indicated that they believed the *YOA* was too lenient, they were thinking of the relatively unusual cases – those involving serious, violent, repeat offenders. The few people who believed that sentences handed down in youth court were about right were thinking of the more common cases before the courts – those involving non-violent offences or all young offenders generally. These findings show that it is extremely important to determine the type of offender and offence the public has in mind when evaluating a general response from the public that the youth court is "too lenient". This finding is consistent with previous research findings at the adult level (Doob and Roberts 1988). Those wanting "harsher" youth court sentences may want this change for a *minority* (violent, repeat offenders) of youth court cases. Therefore, if there were to be any policy concern about the *YOA* in response to public opinion, the concern should focus on serious violent cases, not all cases in general. This finding is consistent with Stalans and Henry (1994) who argue that in the United States the automatic legislative transfers to adult court in some states are too simplistic. These authors found that people wanted different dispositions for young people when they were given more specific information about the young offenders. The public appears to be quite sophisticated in their analysis of cases if they are given the chance.

Given that there was a significant relationship between believing youth court sentences are too lenient and opposing a separate youth justice system, it would appear that perceived leniency in youth court sentences plays an important role as to whether or not one will favour a separate youth justice system. Therefore, addressing the perception of general leniency of the youth justice system may create broader support for the concept of a separate youth justice system. Clearly, research in this area, with a truly representative sample of Canadians, is needed to illuminate these important relationships and issues.

Most respondents had inaccurate knowledge of the *YOA*. This lack of information by the public is particularly important when one realizes that the public may be influencing policy making without any substantive knowledge of the youth justice system. In most cases, the public believes the Act to be more lenient then it actually is. This reinforces the notion that politicians must be careful when evaluating a general response from the public that youth court is "too lenient". Considering the public lacks knowledge of the *YOA*, one must ask: "too lenient compared to what?"

The lack of information the public has on the *YOA* may be due, in part, to the lack of information available to the public in the newspapers. The comparison between the information provided in the newspaper and the information provided from legal reports yielded some interesting findings. The Bala and Lilles legal reports focused significantly more on the youth and significantly less on the facts of the crime than the newspapers did. The newspapers seldom reported youth court dispositions. These results are compatible with results from the content analysis of news media coverage of adult sentencing stories by the Canadian Sentencing Commission (1987) where it was found that many of the news reports about adult crime did not contain the reason for the sentence. The results from this study indicate that there is even less information available about youth court dispositions and the sentencing process for youths. For example, only one newspaper in a two month period reported a justification for a disposition. As a consequence, the public is receiving almost no information about the sentencing process for youths.

The Bala and Lilles legal reports also contained significantly more information about the youth than did the media. This means that the public receives little information about the circumstances surrounding the young offender. If it is thought that judges and lawyers need this type of information contained in the Bala and Lilles summaries to understand a case and a disposition, it would be reasonable to expect that the limited information provided to the public by the newspaper would leave them with little possibility of understanding the crime and the sentencing process.

Although the media's role is traditionally thought to include informing the public in the area of youth justice, as in other areas of criminal justice, there appears to be a serious failure to do so. If politicians are going to base policy reform on public opinion, more accurate information needs to be relayed to the public, most obviously through the media. The irony of the current lack of information is that if youth court sentences were increased, few members of the public would know since dispositions are so rarely reported.

One question which then arises is how the public develops *any* beliefs in the absence of information. It may be that there is more information available through the media on adult cases and people are therefore generalizing from adult cases. This would explain the strong relationship between perceived leniency in youth court and views on a separate youth justice system with general criminal justice beliefs. Alternatively, it is possible that statements of opinion, rather than reports of cases, drive views about the *YOA*, youth crime, and youth court dispositions. Repeated, unchallenged, assertions by various people and organizations about "leniency" in the youth justice system may drive public opinion in the absence of adequate reporting.

Roberts (1992) hypothesized that the image portrayed by the media may be particularly important in determining public perceptions of crime because the public largely gains information about crime and the criminal justice system through the media. In the present study, almost all (94%) of the newspaper stories about youth crime were about violence. Thus, if public perception is developed through media information, it is not surprising that the public has distorted perceptions of the relative frequencies of particular crimes and little understanding and knowledge of the *YOA*. During a two month period, the three Toronto newspapers (combined) reported sentences for youths in a total of 12 non-representative stories. Seven of the 12 stories involved serious violence while the other 5 involved peculiar cases of arson, break and enters, and theft over $1000. In those same two months in Ontario, a reasonable estimate would be that over 5000 cases received dispositions. Judges almost invariably give some explanation for their dispositions. In contrast, only one newspaper, out of three Toronto papers, produced a story which mentioned a justification for a disposition. That story devoted one sentence to the justification. One cannot blame the members of the public then for having little knowledge of youth court activities, since they almost never get any information about them.

Notes

1. The preparation of this article was made possible by a research grant from the Social Sciences and Humanities Research Council of Canada to A.N. Doob.
2. In actuality, it is not that simple. Generally, if a young person has remained "crime-free" for five years, depending upon the offence and disposition, the record may be cleared.
3. The difference between the percents for the two groups varied from two to four points.

References

Bala, Nicholas and Heino Lilles
1994 Young Offenders Service. Vol. 3. Toronto: Butterworths.

Canadian Centre for Justice Statistics
1995 Youth Court Statistics. Ottawa: CCJS, Statistics Canada.

Canadian Sentencing Commission
1987 Sentencing Reform: A Canadian Approach. Ottawa: Ministry of Supply and Services Canada.

Doob, Anthony N.
1985 The many realities of crime. In A.N. Doob and E.L. Greenspan (eds.), Perspectives in Criminal Law. Aurora, Ontario: Canada Law Books Inc.

Doob, Anthony N. and Julian Roberts
1983 An Analysis of the Public's View of Sentencing. Ottawa: Department of Justice. Canada.

Doob, Anthony N. and Julian Roberts
1988 Public punitiveness and public knowledge of the facts: Some Canadian Surveys. In N. Walker and M. Hough (eds.), Public Attitudes to Sentencing. Aldershot: Gower.

Doob, Anthony N., Voula Marinos, and Kimberly Varma
1995 Youth Crime and the Youth Justice System in Canada: A Research Perspective. Toronto: Centre of Criminology, University of Toronto.

Ericson, Richard V., Patricia Baranek, and Janet Chan
1987 Visualizing Deviance: A Study of News Organization. Toronto: University of Toronto Press.

Fedorowycz, Ouest
1994 Homicide in Canada. Juristat. Vol 15(11). Ottawa: Canadian Centre for Justice Statistics.

Liberal Party of Canada
1993 (Released April, 1993: Updated August, 1993) A Liberal perspective on crime and justice issues. Ottawa: Liberal Party of Canada.

Roberts, Julian
1992 Public opinion, crime, and criminal justice. In M. Tonry (ed.), Crime and Justice: A Review of Research. Chicago: University of Chicago Press.

Roberts, Julian
1994 Public Knowledge of Crime and Justice: An Inventory of Canadian Findings. Technical Report Prepared for the Department of Justice Canada #TR1994-15e. Ottawa: Department of Justice.

Stalans, Loretta J. and Gary T. Henry
1994 Societal views of justice for adolescents accused of murder. Law and Human Behaviour 18: 675-696.

PART FIVE

Trends and Issues in Youth Injustice

CHAPTER TWENTY-TWO

Young people's understanding and assertion of their rights to silence and legal counsel[1]

Rona Abramovitch,
Michele Peterson-Badali
University of Toronto
Toronto, Ontario
and ***Meg Rohan***
University of Waterloo
Waterloo, Ontario

OVER THE PAST SEVERAL DECADES THERE HAS BEEN A SUBSTANTIAL increase in public concern for children's constitutional rights. While the child welfare movement in the late 19th and early 20th centuries focused on children's rights to be nurtured, more recently the focus has shifted to their right to self-determination. In North America, juvenile criminal legislation has paralleled this movement. The earlier orientation that viewed delinquents as wayward children in need of guidance has been replaced by a "rights and responsibilities" stance which argues that young people must be held legally accountable for their actions and, therefore, afforded the due process protections that are given to adults.

The assumption underlying the extension of rights to young people is that they are capable of making meaningful use of them. From a cognitive standpoint, this requires that young people are aware that they possess these rights, know what they mean, and understand and appreciate the context-specific issues surrounding the exercise of their rights. For example,

---

Canadian Journal of Criminology/Revue canadienne de criminologie, January/janvier 1995, pp. 1–18.

in the legal domain, meaningful use of the right to legal counsel demands that young people understand not only that they have this right and that it means that they can have a lawyer, but also that the legal process is adversarial in nature, that the role of defence counsel is to help the client regardless of his or her guilt, that the lawyer-client relationship is confidential, and so on. Meaningful use of rights also requires that individuals feel free to make choices rather than feeling coerced into a decision. Together, these elements comprise the legal standard for assessing the competence of an individual's waiver of legal rights, which states that waiver must be knowing, intelligent, and voluntary.

Although it seems clear that having rights does young people little good unless they can exercise them appropriately, there is little empirical research on the extent to which they do have the necessary ability. The research that does exist has focused mainly on youths' understanding of the rights themselves, although Grisso (1981) has also examined juveniles' reasoning about rights decisions.

In the criminal law domain, several American studies have examined young people's understanding of their due process rights, specifically the rights to legal counsel and to silence. In a deception study involving a simulated police field interrogation, Ferguson and Douglas (1970) interviewed 90 youths, both delinquents and non-delinquents, between the ages of 13 and 17. Using several questionnaire instruments designed to assess juveniles' knowledge and beliefs about their rights, Grisso (1981) studied 10-16-year-old youths who had been detained on suspicion of a crime. Both studies found that many youths did not adequately understand their rights. Using measures based on Grisso's research, Wall and Furlong (1985) explored whether providing legal education to high-school students (16-18 years old) led to improved understanding of rights. Although most students showed good understanding of "basic" measures of knowledge (multiple-choice and true-false) following the training program, like Grisso's subjects, many demonstrated poor understanding of the function and significance of their rights and had difficulty adequately paraphrasing rights-related vocabulary.

In a Canadian study, Abramovitch, Higgins-Biss, and Biss (1993) found that while a majority of students (11-18 years old) demonstrated a basic understanding of the right to silence, they were less successful in paraphrasing the right to legal counsel. In addition to these rights, the *Young Offenders Act* provides that young people be told that they have the right to have a lawyer, parent, or other adult present with them during police questioning, and must waive this right in writing if they so decide. Although two-thirds of the students understood the basic meaning of this waiver, their understanding of its implications was poorer; only two students said that a formal statement would be obtained following the waiver, and just over half of the subjects understood that some sort of questioning would follow. This understanding improved significantly with grade.

Studies of the legal knowledge that is important to young people's use of their due process rights have found that such knowledge generally increases and becomes richer, more precise, and more abstract with age (see Cashmore and Bussey 1987; Peterson-Badali and Abramovitch 1992; Saywitz 1989; Warren-Leubecker, Tate, Hinton and Ozbek 1989). Findings also indicate that misconceptions about important legal principles (such as the presumption of innocence) may be retained well into adolescence (Peterson-Badali and Abramovitch 1992). In addition, compared to young adults, adolescents show less awareness of adversarial and due process concepts, and of important aspects of the lawyer-client relationship, such as privilege (Peterson-Badali and Abramovitch 1992).

Despite findings indicating that many young people have difficulty understanding their due process rights and some of the important legal principles underlying those rights, studies show that young people frequently waive their rights. In the Ferguson and Douglas study, 96% of subjects waived their rights. Similarly, in an archival study using juvenile court records, Grisso and Pomicter (1977) reported that over 90% of the 491 subjects waived their rights to silence and counsel.

Several factors have been examined as potential contributors to youths' decisions to assert or waive their rights. In most studies, however, these factors have been examined retrospectively or indirectly. In the cognitive domain, understanding of rights, experience with the legal system, and legal knowledge have received some attention. Vulnerability to coercion has been discussed as one of the affective variables influencing the decision to waive rights. Several situational or contextual variables have also been examined: the actual guilt of accused youths, the type of offence committed, and the degree of procedural safeguards in place for juveniles.

Abramovitch, Higgins-Biss, and Biss (1993) conducted the only study to relate understanding of rights to waiver decisions. They found that students' basic understanding of their right to the presence of a lawyer and/or other support person was related to assertion of that right: 90% of the subjects who were able to paraphrase the waiver form said that they would not sign it, while 65% of subjects who did not understand the form said that they would. When "understanding" of the right was defined in terms of subjects' ability to state the *implications* of the waiver form (i.e., that they would be questioned by police and asked to make a formal statement), very few subjects met this more stringent criterion and understanding was unrelated to the decision to assert or waive the right.

In terms of the impact of knowledge of legal concepts on rights decisions, several studies suggest that youths' difficulty understanding the principles underlying the criminal justice system, and specifically the role of defence counsel, may result in failure to assert the right to counsel. When interviewed about their previous legal experiences, Ferguson and Douglas (1970) found that 69% of their delinquent subjects indicated that they had not asked for or wanted a lawyer to represent them for their court appearances. Their reasons for this position included: "I knew I was guilty and deserved to be punished" and "I was guilty and a lawyer couldn't do anything for me". Thus, they focused on "moral guilt" rather than legal guilt. This result is also consistent with Grisso's (1981) finding that a number of juvenile offenders who had little experience with the law believed that lawyers defend the interests of the innocent, but not the "guilty". Finally, Melton (1983) suggests that most juveniles do not view lawyers as advocates because they perceive the judicial system as inquisitorial rather than adversarial. They, therefore, do not realize the importance of the lawyer's role as defence counsel.

In the only study to explicitly examine the issue of voluntariness in relation to assertion of rights, Ferguson and Douglas (1970: 51) reported that, while their delinquent subjects were generally aware of the right to silence, 29% of them "felt they had to talk to police when arrested." Sixty percent of juveniles felt that it would go against them if they remained silent, while 74% thought that it would benefit them to talk. Apparently, 55% were told by the arresting officer that willingness to talk would be held in their favour.

Age and experience with the legal system have also been related to rights decisions. In Grisso and Pomicter's (1977) archival study, almost all the juveniles who asserted their right to silence were 15 or 16 years old, and the rate of refusal increased with the number of prior offences. It is unclear, however, whether these variables reflect youths' legal and rights knowledge or their relative vulnerability to coercion.

Finally, several context-specific variables have been reported in relation to assertion of rights. Grisso and Pomicter (1977) found that more youths asserted their right to silence when charges related to offences against persons than when they concerned property. Interestingly, rates of assertion did not change as a function of increased procedural safeguards implemented by the juvenile court under study. As discussed above, Ferguson and Douglas' (1970) study indicates that youths' exercise of their right (particularly to legal counsel) may also vary depending on their "actual" guilt.

The following two studies examined factors affecting the assertion of the rights to silence and legal counsel. Study 1 examined students' understanding of their rights to legal counsel and to silence, as well as the impact of situation-specific variables – guilt and evidence – on their decision to assert or waive these rights. Previous research (Peterson-Badali and Abramovitch, in press) found that children as young as 10 years of age were sensitive to the amount of incriminating evidence in a case when making plea decisions in response to hypothetical vignettes. The research of Ferguson and Douglas (1970) and Grisso (1981) suggests that the "moral" guilt of an accused is also relevant to youths' exercise of their right to legal counsel.

Young people's use of their due process rights should not be measured against some ideal standard of capacity. A more appropriate standard is the behaviour of adults in a similar situation. Therefore, Study 2 examined university students' decisions to assert or waive their rights to silence and counsel.

Study 1

Method

Subjects

One hundred and ninety two students participated in the interviews: 24 females and 24 males from each of Grades 6, 8, 10 and 13. The mean age of subjects was 11.9 years for the Grade 6 group, 13.9 years for the Grade 8 group, 15.7 years for the Grade 10 group, and 18.4 years for the Grade 13 group. All subjects were volunteers drawn from two public schools in a suburb of Toronto, Canada. Students in each of the target grades were informed of the study in a classroom presentation made by the interviewer, and letters describing the study were sent home with students under the age of 18. Informed consent was obtained from the subject and, for subjects under age 18, from his or her parent or guardian.

Procedure

Each subject was read four brief vignettes, two of which described a theft (shoplifting and stealing from an open cash register), while the other two described vandalism incidents, one involving damage to a school building and the other to a car.[2] Order of presentation of the offences was held constant over subjects, with the crimes presented in the following order: Shoplifting, Vandalism (School), Theft, Vandalism (Car).

Each vignette depicted a series of events leading up to the arrest of the story's protagonist (matched to the subject's gender), who was taken to the police station and "read" his or her rights. At the police station, the police commented on the strength of the evidence in the case; in two of the vignettes the police said that they had a substantial amount of incriminating evidence against the accused and in the other two the evidence was said to be weak (Evidence variable). Similarly, in two of the vignettes the protagonist did commit the offence in question while in the other two he or she was innocent (Guilt variable).

The four vignettes presented to each subject consisted of the four possible Guilt-Evidence pairings (i.e., Guilty-Strong, Guilty-Weak, Innocent-Strong, and Innocent-Weak). In order to control for the possibility that subjects would form a "response set" as a result of hearing two similar vignettes in a row (e.g., in which the character was guilty), order of presentation of the Guilt and Evidence variables was counterbalanced in the following manner: half of the subjects received vignettes in which Strong and Weak Evidence stories were alternated (e.g., Guilty-Strong, Guilty-Weak, Innocent-Strong, Innocent-Weak), whereas the other half received vignettes in which the character's guilt or innocence was alternated (e.g., Guilty-Strong, Innocent-Strong, Guilty-Weak, Innocent-Weak), thus forming two "blocks" of vignettes. Within each of the two blocks, the Guilt-Evidence pairs were rotated through the four story positions so that each pair appeared in each of the four ordinal positions, yielding eight different presentation orders. At each grade level, three male and three female subjects received each of the 8 presentation orders.

The following is a sample of one of the stories in which the protagonist is guilty and the evidence is strong:

> This story is about a girl named Lee. One day, Lee went to the mall to do some shopping. On the way out, she went inside Eaton's to look around. As she was looking around, Lee saw a walkman she really wanted, but she didn't have the money for it, so she quietly slipped the walkman into her knapsack without paying for it. After Lee left the store, the security guard from Eaton's called the police and the police came and arrested Lee for stealing. At the police station, Lee overheard the police saying that there was a lot of proof that she did steal the walkman. Then, the police read Lee her legal rights. First they told Lee that she has the "right to retain and instruct counsel without delay". Then they told Lee that she "is not obliged to say anything". The police asked Lee if she understood her rights.

After the experimenter had read the first vignette, subjects were asked "what does it mean that Lee has the right to retain and instruct counsel without delay?". Regardless of the correctness of their own description, each subject was then given the same definition: "The right to retain and instruct counsel without delay means that Lee has the right to have a lawyer to help him/her decide what to do. S/he can ask for a lawyer right away". Subjects were then asked "if you were Lee, would you get a lawyer or not?". Similarly, subjects were asked "what does it mean that Lee has the right to remain silent?", and after responding were told that "the right to remain silent means that Lee does not have to say anything to the police if s/he does not want to". Subjects were then asked "if you were Lee, would you make a statement or say anything to the police or not?". Following the presentation of the next three vignettes, subjects were asked only whether they would get a lawyer and whether they would make a statement.

Coding

Subjects' responses to the questions probing their understanding of the rights to counsel and silence were divided into two categories, as follows: With respect to the right to counsel, subjects whose responses contained the statement that they could get a lawyer were scored as understanding the right, while those whose responses did not were scored as not understanding. Similarly, with respect to the right to silence, subjects were scored as understanding if their responses included either the notion that they had a choice of whether or not to speak, or the notion that what they did say could be used as evidence against them. Subjects whose responses contained neither of these statements were scored as not understanding the right to silence.

In order to obtain reliability estimates for the coding schemes described above, 40 of the 198 protocols were independently coded by a second rater. Protocols were chosen at random with the constraint that there be equal representation of grade levels and gender. Inter-rater agreement was 100% for subjects' understanding of both the right to legal counsel and right to silence statements.

Results and discussion

Data analysis

Subjects' understanding of their legal rights was analyzed using hierarchial log linear technique. This is a generalization of the chi square statistic for cross-tabulated data with more than two factors (which thus allows for an examination of interactions among factors). Hierarchical log linear analyses including Grade, Gender, Guilt and Evidence were performed for understanding of the right to counsel and the right to silence.

The data on subjects' choice to assert their rights to legal counsel and to silence involved categorical variables in a repeated measures design; it was impossible to analyze these data with traditional tests. Since the data were mainly binary (e.g., whether or not a lawyer was retained or a statement made), a statistical technique which transformed the data to allow a traditional analysis of variance was used (Murdock and Ogilvie 1968). Subjects were first formed into "macrosubjects". One "macrosubject" contained the information from eight subjects, each representing one of the eight presentation orders. The proportion of subjects in each "macrosubject" who responded positively (e.g., stated that they would obtain a lawyer) was calculated for all dependent measures and an arcsine transformation was performed. Two between-within ANOVA's analyzed responses to whether or not a lawyer would be retained, and whether or not a statement would be made. The independent variables included in these analyses were Grade, Gender, Guilt, and Evidence.

Understanding of rights

Overall, 57% of subjects understood their right to counsel. The analysis showed that understanding varied significantly with Grade (x^2 (3) = 49.65, $p < .001$). Whereas 80% of the Grade 10 subjects and 83% of the Grade 13 subjects understood their right to counsel, only 30% of the Grade 6 and 35% of the Grade 8 subjects displayed understanding. There were no other effects.

Sixty-seven percent of subjects understood their right to silence. As with their right to counsel, understanding of the right to silence increased significantly with grade (x^2 (3) = 43.37, $p > .001$); while only 33% of the Grade 6 subjects understood this right, 59% of the Grade 8's, 86% of the Grade 10's, and 89% of the Grade 13's demonstrated understanding. There were no other effects.

Overall, subjects showed similar levels of understanding of the rights to legal counsel and to silence; while a substantial majority (80-90%) of subjects over the age of 16 successfully paraphrased these rights, only a third of the youngest subjects did so. It should be noted, in this context, that our coding criteria for both rights were quite liberal. These results suggest that merely extending due process rights to young people will not ensure that they will be protected in an adult-like criminal justice system because many of the younger children lack even a basic understanding of what their rights to silence and counsel mean.

Assertion of rights

Despite comparable levels of understanding, subjects were more likely to assert the right to legal counsel (77%) than the right to silence (45%). While subjects' decision to assert the right to counsel was not grade-related, their assertion of the right to silence was ($F(3,16) = 10.6$, $p < .005$). Twenty-four percent of the Grade 6 subjects, 44% of the Grade 8's, 56% of the Grade 10's, and 54% of the Grade 13's said that they would not make a statement. Post-hoc analyses indicated that all pairwise differences were significant (z's > 1.87, p's < .05), with the exception of the comparison between Grades 10 and 13. Thus, approximately three-quarters of the youngest students and half of the subjects in all other grades responded that they *would* make a statement when questioned by the police. This result is particularly telling in light of the fact that subjects were students responding to hypothetical situations, and thus were not influenced by the emotional and situational pressures which would undoubtedly colour the decision of a young person actually charged with crime.

Subjects' decision to assert their rights to legal counsel and to silence was also influenced by salient legal variables – guilt and evidence. With respect to the right to counsel, significant main effects of both Guilt and Evidence were qualified by a Guilt by Evidence interaction ($F(1,16) = 5.84$, $p >$ .05). Subjects were particularly likely to state that they would retain a lawyer when the character was innocent of the crime, but the incriminating evidence was nonetheless strong (89%). Post-hoc tests indicated that this condition was significantly different from the other three: innocent-weak evidence (76%), guilty-strong evidence (75%), and guilty-weak evidence (69%). There was also a significant but uninterpretable interaction between age, gender, guilt and evidence ($F(3,16) = 3.71$, $p <$ .05).

With respect to the right to silence, a significant main effect of Evidence ($F(1,16) = 5.26$, $p < .05$) revealed that subjects were more likely to say they would remain silent if the evidence against them was strong (47%) than if the evidence was weak (41%). A significant main effect of Guilt was qualified by a Grade by Guilt interaction, (F (3,16) = 9.22, $p < .01$), which indicated that the effect of the guilt manipulation was limited to the older subjects. In Grades 6 and 8, subjects' decision to assert their right to silence differed little depending on whether the story character was innocent or guilty (20% versus 28%, respectively, for Grade 6 subjects and 40% versus 48%, respectively, for Grade 8 subjects). However, in Grades 10 and 13, a much greater percentage of subjects stated that they would remain silent when the character was guilty (66% and 82%, respectively) than when he or she was innocent (45% and 36%, respectively). Post hoc tests confirmed that the Guilt effects were significant for the Grade 10 and 13 subjects ($z = 2.99$, $p < .01$, and $z = 7.67$, $p < .00001$ respectively).

There was also a significant three-way interaction between Guilt, Evidence, and Gender ($F(1,16) = 6.46$, $p < .05$). While both males and females were more likely to assert their right to silence when the story character was guilty than when he or she was innocent, for the males this was particularly true when the evidence was strong, while for the females this was particularly true when the evidence against them was weak. Post hoc comparisons indicated that none of the pairwise gender differences was significant.

It is likely that subjects' decision about whether to assert their rights was influenced, at least in part, by their understanding of those rights. Unfortunately, procedural limitations made formal analysis of this hypothesis impossible. Subjects were presented with paraphrased definitions of the rights to silence and counsel after giving their own definitions but before making their decisions. It is impossible to know whether their original understanding of the rights was changed as a result of this additional information, and what effect this may have had on their choice to assert their rights. Future studies will examine the relationship between subjects' initial understanding of the rights to silence and counsel and decisions to assert those rights.

Study 2

Method

Subjects

Seventy-two adults (39 females, 33 males) participated. All subjects were undergraduate university students in an introductory psychology course who participated in the study for course credit. Subjects ranged in age from 18 to 24 years, with a mean age of 19.8 years.

Procedure

Subjects were presented with the four vignettes used in Study 1. The procedure was also the same as in Study 1 except that subjects in this study were not asked to provide definitions for the right to counsel and right to silence statements. Because the sample size was much smaller than in Study 1, each macrosubject (comprised of 8 individual subjects) contained both male and female subjects, and thus analyses did not include gender as a variable.

Results and discussion

Assertion of rights

Overall, 78% of the adult subjects stated that they would assert their right to counsel, a rate of assertion almost identical to the students in Study 1 (77%). As in Study 1, subjects' assertion of their right to counsel was influenced by Guilt ($F(1,8) = 32.82$, $p < .001$), but the effect was in the opposite direction; adult subjects were more likely to state that they would get a lawyer when the story character was guilty (88%) than when he or she was innocent (65%). This result suggests that the adult students may have a more accurate understanding of the role of defence counsel (i.e., that lawyers can be useful advocates when one has committed a crime) than that of the subjects in Study 1. The fact that subjects saw less need to have a lawyer when the story character was innocent than when he or she was guilty suggests that they are still somewhat naive about the need for due process protection in the context of the legal process.

Overall, 60% of subjects stated that they would assert their right to silence. This rate of assertion is very similar to that of the Grade 10 (56%) and Grade 13 (54%) students in Study 1. The only variable to significantly affect subjects' decision to assert their right to silence was Evidence ($F(1, 8) = 88.01$, $p < .001$). As was the case with the students in Study 1, the adult subjects were more likely to assert their right to silence when the evidence was strong (82%) than when the evidence was weak (38%). Unlike the students in Study 1, the assertion rate of the adult students did not vary as a function of Guilt.

General discussion

Subjects in both studies were more likely to assert the right to legal counsel than the right to silence. The substantial numbers who stated that they would waive their right to silence is particularly telling in light of the fact that subjects were responding to hypothetical situations, and thus were not influenced by the emotional and situational pressures which would undoubtedly colour the decision of a person charged with an offence. Indeed, the data from previous studies (Ferguson and Douglas 1970; Grisso and Pomicter 1977) suggest that the percentage of subjects in Study 1 who stated that they would assert their right to silence represents an overestimate of what happens in the real world. The same likely applies to the assertion of the right to legal counsel.

Students' decision to assert their rights to legal counsel and to silence was also influenced by salient legal variables – guilt and evidence. This suggests that children as young as 11 years of age are able to consider relevant legal factors in making rights-related choices. The present finding is consistent with previous research (Peterson-Badali and Abramovitch in press) which indicated that children as young as 10 use legal criteria (e.g. evidence) in making plea decisions.

Not surprisingly, the subjects in Study 1 were more likely to assert their rights to silence and to counsel when the evidence was strong than when it was weak. The effect of moral guilt on their assertion of rights differed according to the particular right in question. Subjects were more likely to assert their right to silence when the story character was guilty than when he or she was innocent, which is consistent with the notion that people feel less need of legal protection under conditions of moral innocence. For the adults in Study 2, however, the story character's guilt or innocence had no effect on their assertion of the right to silence. In this regard, the adults seem to be somewhat less "naive" about the legal system. With respect to asserting their right to counsel, the younger subjects and the adult subjects behaved quite differently. The subjects in Study 1 were more likely to assert their right to legal counsel when the character was innocent than when he or she was guilty. This may be a result of their perceptions of defence counsel. For example, as discussed earlier, Grisso (1981) found that a third of juvenile subjects who had little experience with the legal system believed that the role of the defence counsel is to protect the interests of only the innocent. In addition, Ferguson and Douglas (1970) found that many of their delinquent subjects had not retained counsel because they were "guilty". The adults' decision with respect to retaining counsel was the opposite – they were more likely to assert this right when the story character was guilty. This may reflect a belief in the inherent "fairness" of the legal system.

It could be argued that the decision whether or not to assert one's rights to legal counsel or silence should not be influenced by situational factors such as guilt and evidence, as these considerations could jeopardize one's legal position. Legal professionals would assert that it is naive to assume that it is safe to make a statement simply because one is innocent of a crime, or that one's innocence or guilt makes one any more or less in need (or deserving) of legal representation. It is interesting that both youth and adult subjects were sensitive to these situational factors, although not always in the same way. This may reflect a shared "sophistication" in terms of reasoning, along with a lack of sophistication regarding the workings of the legal system.

It was also the case that the rate of assertion of rights was not very different when comparing the older youths in Study 1 with the adults in Study 2. The younger subjects in Study 1 were less likely to assert their right to silence and also less likely to demonstrate even a very basic understanding of their rights to silence and counsel. Although we were not able to test the relation between understanding and assertion directly, it is likely that such a relation exists (Abramovitch, Higgins-Biss, and Biss 1993). Understanding of rights is not likely the sole determinant of assertion; although understanding of both rights was at about the same level, subjects were more likely to assert their right to counsel than to silence. In any case, merely extending due process rights to young people will not ensure that they will be protected in an adult-like criminal justice system because many younger children lack even a basic understanding of their rights to silence and counsel.

The subjects in these studies are not a representative sample and certainly not representative of actual offenders. Not only were the subjects in our studies school children and college students rather than young offenders, they were also not charged with a crime or in a police station being questioned by a police officer. They were asked to respond to a hypothetical situation by a non-threatening research assistant. It is likely, therefore, that performance in these studies represents an optimal understanding of the issues and that in the real world even fewer individuals would assert their rights.

This is compounded by the fact that understanding is only one of a number of factors that may contribute to people's decisions to assert or waive rights. Previous research (e.g. Ferguson and Douglas 1970) has indicated that, even when a relation between understanding and assertion of rights exists, understanding is only one of a number of factors that may contribute to people's decisions to assert or waive rights. Ferguson and Douglas have indicated that important factors such as experience with the legal system and feelings of coercion influence young people's decisions, and the current studies found that variables such as moral innocence or guilt of an offence and amount of incriminating evidence may also (perhaps inappropriately) affect decisions.

At the least, it would seem that rights should be explained in detail in simple language, the possible consequences of giving up the rights should be outlined, and young people should be questioned to make sure they understand what is involved. As just noted, it is not only a matter of understanding vocabulary or the basic meaning of what they have been told. It would entail more than merely putting existing warnings into simpler language. An iterative and interactive communication process would also have to be in place to evaluate understanding. Grisso (1981) has advised that changing the language used might only lead to false belief that understanding has been enhanced. At the extreme, it might be required that rights only be presented to young people in the presence of a lawyer and that young people not be "allowed" to waive their rights without first conferring with a lawyer. This would afford youths a large measure of protection but may not be seen as a very practical solution. A different, but also extreme solution would be to simply remove the options entirely and not take statements from young people.

Whatever the option, it is likely that improving youths' understanding of the rights *themselves* is not enough. Attempts designed to afford youths protection in a justice system with a "due process" orientation must measure young people's capacity against a broader definition of understanding involving, among other things, the principles of our criminal justice system upon which the rights are based.

Notes

1. This research was supported by a grant from the Social Sciences and Humanities Research Council. We wish to thank Michal Perlman and Michelle Von Burnschot for their assistance in carrying out the study. Requests for reprints should be sent to Rona Abramovitch, who is at the Department of Psychology, Erindale College, University of Toronto, Mississauga, Ontario, L5L 1C6.
2. The offences described in the vignettes were developed in consultation with a lawyer specializing in juvenile law, and two of the vignettes (Shoplifting and Vandalism-School) were used in a previous study

(Peterson-Badali and Abramovitch, in press). Subjects did not appear to have difficulty understanding them.

References

Abramovitch, R., K. Higgins-Biss, and S. Biss
1993 Young persons' comprehension of waivers in criminal proceedings. Canadian Journal of Criminology 35: 309-322.

Cashmore, J. and K. Bussey
1987 Children's conceptions of the witness role. In J.R. Spencer, G. Nicholson, R. Flin, and R. Bull (eds.), Children's Evidence in Legal Proceedings. Cambridge: J.R. Spencer.

Ferguson, A.B. and A.C. Douglas
1970 A study of juvenile waiver. San Diego Law Review 7: 39-54.

Grisso, T.
1981 Juveniles' Waiver of Rights: Legal and Psychological Competence. New York: Plenum.

Grisso, T. and C. Pomicter
1977 Interrogation of juveniles: An empirical study of procedures, safeguards, and rights waiver. Law and Human Behavior 1: 321-342.

Melton, G.
1983 Child Advocacy: Psychological Issues and Interventions. New York: Plenum Press.

Murdock, B.B., Jr. and J.C. Ogilvie
1968 Binomial variability in short-term memory. Psychological Bulletin 70: 256-260.

Peterson-Badali, M. and R. Abramovitch
1992 Children's knowledge of the legal system: Are they competent to instruct legal counsel? Canadian Journal of Criminology 34: 130-160.

Peterson-Badali, M. and R. Abramovitch
In press Grade related changes in young people's reasoning about plea decisions. Law and Human Behavior.

Saywitz, K.
1989 Children's conceptions of the legal system: "Court is a place to play basketball". In S.J. Ceci, D.F. Ross, and M.P. Toglia (eds.), Perspectives on Children's Testimony. New York: Springer Verlag.

Wall, S. and M. Furlong
1985 Comprehension of Miranda rights by urban adolescents with law-related education. Psychological Reports 56: 359-372.

Warren-Leubecker, A., C. Tate, I. Hinton, and N. Ozbek
1989 What do children know about the legal system and when do they know it? In S.J. Ceci, D.F. Ross, and M.P. Toglia (eds.), Perspectives on Children's Testimony. New York: Springer Verlag.

CHAPTER TWENTY-THREE

Recidivism in youth court: An examination of the impact of age, gender, and prior record[1]

Melanie Kowalski
and ***Tullio Caputo***
Department of Sociology and Anthropology
Carleton University
Ottawa, Ontario

> Few, if any, pieces of Canadian legislation have been the subject of such sustained public criticism as the Young Offenders Act, and the 'reform' of the Act has been a major priority for the Liberal Government. The YOA has been attacked by critics coming from very different perspectives, from the law and order right for not being 'tough enough' and from the 'therapeutic left' for failing to do enough to rehabilitate adolescent offenders (Bala, 1994:643).

THE *YOUNG OFFENDERS ACT* (YOA) HAS BEEN THE SOURCE OF MUCH public debate and criticism since it was introduced in 1982. One of the main areas of contention involves sentencing practices in youth court. Some critics (Lescheid and Gendreau 1986) have argued that youth court dispositions are too severe and much harsher than they had been under the previous legislation, the *Juvenile Delinquents Act* (JDA). Others, most notably the media and some 'law and order' politicians, have voiced strong concerns that youth court dispositions are not severe enough. These critics point to a rising youth crime

---

Canadian Journal of Criminology/Revue canadienne de criminologie, January/janvier 1999, pp. 57–84.

rate and an apparent increase in serious offences by young people as evidence of the system's failure to prevent crime and protect the public.

In response to these concerns, researchers have analyzed youth court sentencing outcomes. Current dispositions have been compared, where possible, with those given under the JDA. Little research, however, has focused on the dispositions imposed upon repeat offenders. This represents a serious gap in the literature, since previous studies have found that a small number of repeat offenders account for a large proportion of the serious crimes committed by young offenders in any jurisdiction (Wolfgang, Figlio, and Sellin 1972). Better knowledge about the treatment of repeat offenders by the youth justice system would, therefore, contribute to the current debate over dispositions under the YOA.

This report presents the results of an analysis which examines youth court dispositions of first-time and repeat offenders, in order to examine whether first-time offenders are treated more leniently than recidivists. In addition, the relationship between type of disposition and several key variables in the sentencing process is examined. These variables include seriousness of the current offence, gender, and age of the offender.

To begin, this report reviews previous research on the impact of different variables on youth court dispositions. The second section outlines the research design of the current study. The findings are then presented, followed by a discussion of the implications of this research.

Factors influencing sentencing decisions

According to Platt (1995: 12), sentencing determination remains one of the most difficult functions a court fulfills. The court considers mitigating factors such as a guilty plea, demonstrated remorse, restitution, and evidence of good character, as well as aggravating factors such as criminal record, evidence of premeditation, extent of violence, damage or loss, impact on the victim, and participation with others.

Roberts (1997) examined the role of criminal record in the sentencing practice. Although, based on an American and adult experience, the arguments apply equally to young offenders. Roberts (1997) found that there are various weighting schemes that are considered by the courts to determine the seriousness of the prior criminal conduct. These weighting schemes included assigning a greater weight to crimes of violence; to weight felonies more heavily than misdemeanors and more serious felonies more heavily than less serious felonies and to address concerns of the problem of persistent petty offenders.

Kueneman and Linden (1983) also conducted a study that examined the influence of prior record and sentencing. Their study was based upon a random sample of 1,000 cases selected from all cases before the Winnipeg Juvenile Court during 1979. In their study, they found that under the JDA prior record was a consistent predictor for type of disposition. They also noted clear indications that prior record resulted in more severe dispositions. Beaumount and LeBlanc (1986) discovered similar patterns. They found that having a previous record tripled the likelihood of receiving a custodial disposition. They also found that being detained in custody while awaiting trial was highly related to being sentenced to some type of institution. Having previously experienced institutionalization was found to be an important factor in determining the sentence in a study by Hoge, Andrews, and Leschied (1993). This factor, along with current offence, appeared to be important in predicting whether a custodial disposition was imposed.

Similar results were reported by Doherty and deSouza (1995) who looked at recidivism in youth court, for 1993-94. They found a strong and consistent relationship between the severity of youth court dispositions and the number of prior convictions. Ten percent of all first-time offenders received a custodial disposition, compared to 60% of all offenders with three or more prior convictions. Moyer (1992: 11) notes, "In every jurisdiction for which recidivism data are available, the larger the number of prior convictions, the lower the likelihood that the young offender will receive a non-custodial disposition."

Young (1989) found that appellate courts give sentences based on the length of the last sentence awarded to the offender, ensuring that the current sentence is marginally longer than the previous one without reference to the current offence. Young (1989: 97) states that,

> ... it must be recognized that cumulative sentencing can result in the imposition of grossly disproportionate sentences because the offender's last sentence may have been for a significantly more serious offence than the current one, or may have been imposed by a judge with a more punitive approach to sentence than the current sentence judge.

Carrington and Moyer (1995: 155) found that young offenders with a prior record were much more likely to receive custodial dispositions than first-time offenders regardless of the nature of the current offence. They concluded that,

> Although the *Young Offenders Act* itself may be offence oriented, the actual choices made by youth court judges between custodial and non-custodial dispositions suggest that their main concern in this decision was protection of society through control and deterrence, with rehabilitation a secondary interest; and that these concerns were put into practice by orientating the decision primarily towards the offender's prior record.

The studies discussed above have shown that prior record is a major factor in the sentencing decision. The influence of offender characteristics is discussed in the sections that follow. We begin with a consideration of the impact of gender on sentencing decisions.

The relationship between youth court disposition and gender

The specific gender differences related to sentencing under the YOA are no longer as obvious as they were under the JDA

(Reitsma-Street 1993: 453). For example, the Kueneman and Linden (1983) study mentioned previously indicated that males were more likely to receive a harsher disposition than females. The major difference they found was that females were more likely to receive an adjournment. Carrington and Moyer (1995) found that the apparent leniency toward females by the criminal justice system is often a result of females being more likely than males to have been found guilty of serious offences and to be less likely than males to have criminal records.

Research examining recidivism indicates that male recidivists are more likely than their female counterparts to receive a custodial disposition. According to Doherty and deSouza (1995), 24% of all dispositions for male youth involved custody compared with 11% of all dispositions for females. The problem is, of course, that findings such as these are not adequate to determine if there are actual differences in the way males and females are treated in youth court. These findings do not take into account the nature of the offence or the characteristics of the offender (Doob, Marinos, and Varma 1995: 113). Thus, for example, research indicates that female youth appear before the courts with fewer charges than male youth (Doherty and deSouza 1995). As well, Doherty and deSouza (1995) report that 44% of male youth were repeat offenders compared to 33% of females. In addition, statistics for 1995-96 show that females were convicted for more minor infractions than their male counterparts. This included charges for the following: theft under $5,000 (26%) and minor assault (15%). In contrast, males represented 18% of those convicted of theft under $5,000 and 10% of those convicted of minor assault.

The relationship between youth court disposition and age

One might expect that age will be positively related to disposition, since younger offenders might be seen as less of a threat than older ones. On the other hand, some observers argue that since younger offenders may be more amenable to treatment than adults, the courts might respond more vigorously to these individuals (Kucneman and Linden 1983: 225).

Carrington and Moyer (1995) found that differences in the actual proportions of custodial dispositions between younger and older defendants almost entirely disappeared when other case characteristics were controlled. They suggest that actual differences by age were not due to the lenient treatment of younger offenders but to a tendency for older offenders to have committed more serious offences (Carrington and Moyer 1995: 153). This finding is consistent with the findings reported by Doherty and deSouza (1995) which showed that older youth receive more custody dispositions than younger offenders.

The study

Based on the research reviewed above, the following hypotheses informed the current study:

(a) young offenders with a prior record will be punished more harshly than first-time offenders who commit the same offence;
(b) there will be a positive association between number of prior convictions and the severity of the disposition;
(c) female repeat offenders will receive custodial sentences less often than male repeat offenders who have committed the same type of offence, and
(d) younger offenders will be treated more leniently than older offenders who have committed the same offence.

The data for the current study were obtained from the Youth Court Survey (YCS) database for the fiscal year 1995-96. The objective of the YCS is to assemble a national database of statistical information on the primary court processes in Canada's youth justice system. The survey is intended to generate information for *Criminal Code* and other federal statute charges heard in youth courts involving persons aged 12 through 17 years.

In this study, data come from all of Canada except Nova Scotia. Data for Nova Scotia were not included because of a division of responsibility in their youth court. In Nova Scotia, one government department is responsible for 12- to 15-year-olds who have committed a crime, while a different government department deals with young offenders who are 16 and 17 years of age. This split responsibility makes it impossible to link data on offences committed with youth court dispositions. On the other hand, data from Ontario will be included, making this the first study in which a recidivism file will be completed with Ontario data.

The data for the present study consist of youth court cases reaching disposition in the 1995-96 fiscal year. The unit of analysis that is investigated is the 'case'. A 'case' is defined as one or more charges[(2)] against a young person brought before a youth court with the same date of disposition[(3)]. Identifiers used to link charges to cases are the coded name, gender, date of birth, date of first appearance, and the court location code. The most serious charge in each case was then selected in order to characterize it by offence type. Tables describing cases use case counts as the unit of analysis.

Recidivists are defined as people who are re-convicted after being previously convicted in court (Canadian Centre for Justice Statistics 1990). In order to determine whether or not a young person was a recidivist, all individuals found guilty of an offence during the 1995-96 fiscal year were matched with those convicted earlier, as far back as 1991-92, to determine the total number of prior charges resulting in a conviction for each offender.

Due to limitations in the method used to identify and associate young persons and their prior convictions, these data on recidivism represent a conservative estimate of the number of young persons re-offending. Variations in youth court practices, the undetected use of aliases, and the movement of offenders among provinces and territories may have resulted in some cases involving recidivists being categorised as those of first-time offenders. As well, the YCS does not consider any previous participation by youth in Alternative Measures or other diversion programs sponsored by either the police or the courts. It must also be noted that Ontario data for 1991-92 consist of only 85% of the province's caseload. The approach used to assess the relationship between sentencing patterns of first-time and repeat offenders was to calculate the proportion of custody verses non-custody dispositions received by youth in court cases classified by different offence and offender characteristics.

Findings

To illustrate current sentencing patterns under the YOA, the Canadian Centre for Justice Statistics publishes information each year on youth court dispositions. Dispositions possible for young offenders under the YOA (those from 12 to 17 years inclusive) include absolute discharge, fines, restitution, community service orders, probation, open custody, secure custody, or some combination of these. For the sake of simplicity, this study concentrated on the proportion receiving custody dispositions, which represents the most severe sentence available under this legislation.

Examining youth court dispositions in Canada for 1995-96, we find that of the 47,088 cases (excluding YOA and *Criminal Code* post-dispositional administrative offences) adjudicated, 25% received a custodial disposition as the most severe component of their sentence.

Repeat offenders represent a substantial proportion of the youth court caseload. Forty percent of these cases involved youth with prior convictions: 20% had one prior conviction, 10% had two prior convictions and 10% had three or more prior convictions.

Table 1 represents a male-female and age group comparison of first-time and repeat offenders. Male youth were more likely to be repeat offenders. Of the male youth who were convicted 42% were repeat offenders, compared with 30% of female offenders. Males were also twice as likely to be persistent offenders (3 or more prior convictions) as were

Table 1
Male-female and age group comparison by number of prior convictions, Canada, 1995-96.

	Male- female comparison				Age group comparison[1]						Total cases	
	Males	%	Females	%	12 –13	%	14 -15	%	16-17	%	N=	%
First-time offenders	22,391	58%	5,807	70%	4,279	78%	10,871	63%	12,553	53%	28,198	60%
One prior conviction	8,031	21%	1,549	19%	889	16%	3,562	21%	5,101	22%	9,580	20%
Two prior convictions	3,914	10%	542	6%	236	4%	1,519	9%	2,694	11%	4,456	9%
Three or more prior convictions	4,403	11%	451	5%	117	2%	1,325	8%	3,288	14%	4,854	10%
Total repeat offenders	16,348	42%	2,542	30%	1,242	22%	6,406	37%	11,083	47%	18,890	40%
Total Cases	38,739	100%	8,349	100%	5,521	100%	17,277	100%	23,636	100%	47,088	100%

(1) The age category 'unknown' has been excluded.

females. Eleven percent of the males convicted had three or more prior convictions compared to 5% of females in this category.

It was not surprising that the proportion of repeat offenders increases with age. The data indicated that the proportion of repeat offenders increased with age from 22% of twelve and thirteen-year-olds to 47% of sixteen and seventeen-year-olds.

Repeat offenders were convicted in court for a larger proportion of property crimes than for violent crimes compared to first-time offenders. Twenty-eight percent of first-time offenders were convicted of violent offences compared to 24% of repeat offenders. In addition, 54% of first-time offenders were convicted of property offences compared to 59% of repeat offenders.

The prior record of the offender

It has been hypothesized that young offenders with a prior conviction will be punished more harshly than first-time offenders who commit the same offence. In table 2, the proportion of custody cases is shown for first-time and repeat offenders. The results show that young offenders with a prior criminal record are more likely to be sentenced to custody than are first-time offenders. Twelve percent of first-time offenders received custodial dispositions. Forty-four percent of repeat offenders received custodial dispositions. When examining the number of prior convictions, results indicated that proportions of dispositions involving a form of custody is positively associated with the number of prior convictions. Custody dispositions were ordered for 32% of all repeat offenders with one prior conviction, 47% for all young persons with two prior convictions, and 65% of young persons with three or more prior convictions. The data show that first-time offenders were more likely to receive open custody (8%) than secure custody (5%). Overall, repeat offenders received an equal proportion of secure custody (22%) and open custody (22%) dispositions. Repeat offenders with three or more prior convictions were

Table 2
Percentage distribution of dispositions by number of prior convictions, Canada, 1995-96.

Disposition	First-time offender	%	One prior conviction	%	Two prior convictions	%	Three or more prior convictions	%	Total repeat offenders	%
Secure custody	1,324	5%	1,201	13%	1,020	23%	1,921	40%	4,142	22%
Open custody	2,199	8%	1,841	19%	1,096	25%	1,194	25%	4,131	22%
Total custody	3,523	12%	3,042	32%	2,116	47%	3,115	65%	8,273	44%
Total non-custody	24,743	88%	6,553	68%	2,354	53%	1,642	35%	10,549	56%
Total cases	28,266	100%	9,595	100%	4,470	100%	4,757	100%	18,822	100%

more likely to receive secure custody (40%) compared to open custody (25%).

To conclude that young offenders with a prior conviction will be punished more harshly than first-time offenders is indeed a true relationship, spuriousness must be considered. If the original relationship between the number of prior convictions and dispositions were spurious due to gender, age, or offence, then the original relationship would disappear when these control variables were added. To examine if there is a true relationship between prior record and disposition, the number of prior convictions and the type of disposition were examined while statistically controlling for gender, age, and type of offence.

Prior record and gender of the offender

The data show (table 3) that when gender is controlled, the association between the number of prior convictions and dispositions remains constant. That is, for both male and female young offenders the proportion of custody dispositions increases monotonically with the number of prior convictions. Results indicated that 14% of male first-time offenders received custody dispositions compared to 67% of males with three or more prior convictions. Similarly, 8% of female first-time offenders received a custody disposition compared to 48% of females with three or more prior convictions. Both male and female repeat offenders found guilty of three or more convictions were more likely to receive secure custody. Data show that 42% of male repeat offenders with three or more convictions received secure custody compared to 25% receiving open custody. Similarly, although a very small difference, 25% of females with three or more convictions receive secure custody compared to 24% who were given open custody. Therefore, the gender of a young offender has no effect on the original relationship between the number of prior convictions and the seriousness of the disposition. The results show that, overall, female offenders received custody dispositions less often than male offenders.

Table 3
Percentage distribution of dispositions by number of prior convictions, controlling for gender, Canada, 1995-96.

Disposition	First-time offender		One prior conviction		Two prior convictions		Three or more prior convictions		Total repeat offenders	
	Males	Females	Males	Females	Males	Females	Males	Females	Males	Females
Secure custody	1,194 5%	130 2%	1,076 13%	125 8%	941 24%	79 15%	1,811 42%	110 25%	3,828 23%	314 12%
Open custody	1,854 8%	345 6%	1,570 20%	271 17%	982 25%	114 21%	1,090 25%	104 24%	3,642 22%	489 19%
Total custody	3,048 14%	475 8%	2,646 33%	396 26%	1,923 49%	193 36%	2,901 67%	214 48%	7,470 46%	803 32%
Total non-custody	19,401 86%	5,342 92%	5,400 67%	1,153 74%	2,006 51%	348 64%	1,414 33%	228 52%	8,820 54%	1,729 68%
Total cases	22,449 100%	5,817 100%	8,046 100%	1,549 100%	3,929 100%	541 100%	4,315 100%	442 100%	16,290 100%	2,532 100%

Age and prior record of the offender

The original relationship between prior convictions and dispositions was not influenced by the age of the offender. Results indicated (table 4) that for all age groups, first-time offenders received a smaller proportion of custody dispositions compared to repeat offenders. Custody dispositions were given to 10% of 12- and 13-year-old first-time offenders compared to 38% of repeat offenders. Twelve percent of first-time offenders aged 14 and 15 years old received custody dispositions compared to 44% of repeat offenders in this age category while the comparable percentages for 16 and 17-year-olds were 13% and 44% respectively. Open custody was ordered more often for most age groups. Those most likely to receive a greater proportion of secure custody dispositions include 14-16-year-olds with three or more prior convictions and 17-year-olds with two or more prior convictions. These results show that the youth justice system does not treat younger offenders more leniently than older offenders.

The seriousness of the current offence[4] and prior record

The purpose of this analysis was to determine whether repeat offenders received harsher dispositions than first-time offenders who committed the same type of offence. Major offence categories were controlled to examine whether the seriousness of offence had an effect on dispositions given to both first and repeat offenders. Offences were grouped to include the major offence categories. These include violent, property, other *Criminal Code*, total drug crimes and other federal statute offences (please see appendix 1 for a detailed list of violations within each crime category).

In table 5, the proportion of custody dispositions is shown by number of prior convictions, controlling for violent, property, other *Criminal Code*, and total drug offences. Results show that for each type of offence, repeat offenders were more likely to receive larger proportions of custody dispositions than were first-time offenders. Of all first-time offenders who were found

Table 4
Percentage distribution of dispositions by number of prior convictions, controlling for age[1], Canada, 1995-96.

Disposition	First-time offender			One prior conviction			Two prior convictions			Three or more prior convictions			Total repeat offenders		
	12-13	14-15	16-17	12-13	14-15	16-17	12-13	14-15	16-17	12-13	14-15	16-17	12-13	14-15	16-17
Secure custody	90	424	719	65	426	702	34	312	667	37	473	1,402	136	1,211	2,771
	2%	4%	6%	7%	12%	14%	14%	21%	25%	32%	36%	43%	11%	19%	25%
Open custody	338	855	907	231	757	850	74	458	563	37	409	747	342	1,624	2,160
	8%	8%	7%	26%	21%	17%	31%	30%	21%	32%	31%	23%	28%	25%	19%
Total custody	428	1,279	1,626	296	1,183	1,552	108	770	1,230	74	882	2,149	478	2,835	4,931
	10%	12%	13%	33%	33%	30%	46%	51%	46%	63%	67%	65%	38%	44%	44%
Total non-custody	3,851	9,592	10,927	593	2,379	3,549	128	749	1,464	43	443	1,139	764	3,571	6,152
	90%	88%	87%	67%	67%	70%	54%	49%	54%	37%	33%	35%	62%	56%	56%
Total cases	4,279	10,871	12,553	889	3,562	5,101	236	1,519	2,694	117	1,325	3,288	1,242	6,406	11,083
	100%	100%	100%	100%	100%	100%	100%	100%	100%	100%	100%	100%	100%	100%	100%

(1) The age category 'unknown' has been excluded.

Table 5

Percentage of custody dispositions by number of prior convictions, controlling for violent, property, other Criminal Code, and total drug crimes, Canada, 1995-95.

Major offence category	First-time offender	%	One prior conviction	%	Two prior convictions	%	Three or more prior convictions	%	Total repeat offenders	%
Violent crime	1,248	16%	938	42%	593	57%	814	71%	2,345	53%
Property crime	1,658	11%	1,631	29%	1,207	46%	1,898	67%	4,736	43%
Other Criminal Code	423	15%	350	29%	254	41%	323	54%	927	39%
Total drug crime	193	10%	122	25%	62	32%	80	45%	264	31%
Total custody cases[(1)]	3,523	12%	3,042	32%	2,116	47%	3,115	65%	8,273	44%

(1) Includes other federal offences.
Note: The above data has been extracted from several individual tables. Thus, proportions do not total 100%.

guilty of a violent crime, 16% received a custody disposition. In contrast, 53% of repeat offenders who committed a violent crime received a custody disposition.

The seriousness of the offence has also been shown to affect the Court's decision to issue a custody disposition. Both first-time and repeat offenders received a larger proportion of custody dispositions for violent crimes than for all other major offence categories. Sixteen percent of first-time offenders found guilty of a violent offence were given dispositions involving custody. In contrast, only 10% of first-time drug offenders were given a custodial sentence. Similarly, youth with one prior conviction received 42% of custody dispositions for violent crimes compared to 25% of first-time offenders for drug crimes, those with two or more convictions (57% versus 32%) and three or more prior convictions (71% versus 45%). This suggests that judges take both factors into consideration.

Table 6 demonstrates that when examining what type of custody was received, first-time and offenders with one prior record had a higher proportion of open custody dispositions compared to secure custody. Repeat offenders with two or more prior convictions had a greater proportion of secure custody dispositions.

The same relationship was found when examining all major offence categories. Results indicated that type of offence does affect sentencing decisions for repeat offenders. Seriousness of the offence was related to receiving a custody disposition. Violent crimes committed by repeat offenders were more likely to result in a custody disposition than other major offence categories. Youth convicted of violent offences received the largest proportion of custody dispositions followed by property crimes, other *Criminal Code* offences, drug offences, and other federal statute offences. Regardless of type of offence we can conclude, however, that when controlling for type of offence, repeat offenders receive a larger proportion of custody dispositions compared to first-time offenders.

This analysis has been extended by controlling for type of offence and gender. Table 7 shows the proportion of guilty

Table 6
Percentage of cases with a violent crime as the most significant charge receiving a custodial disposition as a function of the number of prior convictions, Canada, 1995-96.

Type of custody	First-time offender	%	One prior conviction	%	Two prior convictions	%	Three or more prior convictions	%	Total repeat offenders	%
Secure custody	492	6%	381	17%	291	28%	548	48%	1220	28%
Open custody	756	10%	557	25%	302	29%	266	23%	1125	26%
Total custody cases	1248	16%	938	42%	593	57%	814	71%	2345	53%
Total cases	7888	100%	2213	100%	1035	100%	1143	100%	4391	100%

Table 7
Percentage distribution of guilty findings by number of prior convictions, offence type, and gender, Canada, 1995-96.

Major offence category	First-time offender		One prior conviction		Two prior convictions		Three or more prior convictions		Total repeat offenders	
	Males	Females	Males	Females	Males	Females	Males	Females	Males	Females
Violent crime	6,071 27%	1,817 31%	1,780 22%	433 28%	888 23%	147 27%	997 23%	146 33%	3,665 22%	726 29%
Property crime	12,303 55%	3,050 52%	4,880 61%	811 52%	2,353 60%	270 50%	2,640 61%	197 45%	9,873 61%	1,278 50%
Other Criminal Code	2,209 10%	708 12%	925 11%	264 17%	497 13%	118 22%	508 12%	89 20%	1,930 12%	471 19%
Total drug crime	1,743 8%	235 4%	450 6%	40 3%	190 5%	6 1%	168 4%	10 2%	808 5%	56 2%
Total cases[1]	22,449 100%	5,817 100%	8,046 100%	1,549 100%	3,929 100%	541 100%	4,315 100%	442 100%	16,290 100%	2,532 100%

(1) Includes other federal statutes.

findings by number of prior convictions, offence type, and gender. The distribution of male and female offenders indicates that females in general, are convicted of a larger proportion of violent crimes compared to males. It is important to recognise the small caseload of females compared to male offenders. Results indicate that among those without a prior record, 31% of cases involving females were convicted of violent crimes compared to 27% of male cases. Similarly, 29% of female repeat offenders were convicted of a violent crime compared to 22% of male repeat offenders. Interestingly, the results show that female offenders convicted of violent crimes received custody dispositions in smaller proportions than male offenders.

Both male and female offenders, however, received increasingly harsher dispositions from youth court as the number of prior convictions increased. The data show (table 8) that 18% of male first-time offenders who were convicted of a violent crime received a custody disposition versus 56% of male repeat offenders. Ten percent of female first-time offenders found guilty of a violent offence were given a custody disposition versus 42% of all female repeat offenders. Male repeat offenders found guilty of a violent offence received a greater proportion (56%) of custody than non-custody dispositions. This same relationship was not found for repeat female violent offenders.

A similar relationship was found for all other major offence categories. For example, for all offences committed by young offenders, both male and female repeat offenders received a larger proportion of custody dispositions than first-time offenders. We can conclude that the offender's current offence and gender did have an effect on the relationship between number of prior convictions and dispositions. That is, youth were more likely to receive custody dispositions for violent crimes followed by property crimes, other *Criminal Code*, and then total drug crimes. The results also indicated that male offenders were more likely to receive a custody disposition compared to female offenders.

Extending this analysis a little further, both offence and age were controlled. Results demonstrate (table 9) that, for all

Table 8
Percentage of custody dispositions by number of prior convictions, controlling for gender and violent, property, other Criminal Code, and total drug crimes, Canada, 1995-96.

Major offence category	First-time offender		One prior conviction		Two prior convictions		Three or more prior convictions		Total repeat offenders	
	Males	Females	Males	Females	Males	Females	Males	Females	Males	Females
Violent crime	1,071 18%	177 10%	782 44%	156 36%	523 59%	70 48%	739 74%	75 51%	2,044 56%	301 42%
Property crime	1,467 12%	191 6%	1,481 30%	150 19%	1,127 48%	80 30%	1,804 68%	94 48%	4,412 45%	324 25%
Other Criminal Code	329 15%	94 13%	272 29%	78 29%	211 43%	43 36%	283 56%	40 45%	766 40%	161 34%
Total drug crime	180 10%	13 6%	111 25%	12 30%	62 33%	— —	75 45%	5 50%	248 31%	17 30%
Total custody cases (1)	3,048 14%	475 8%	2,646 33%	396 26%	1,923 49%	193 36%	2,901 67%	214 48%	7,470 46%	803 32%

(1) Includes other federal statutes.
Note: The above data has been extracted from several individual tables. Thus, proportions do not total 100%.
— Amount too small to be expressed.

Table 9

Percentage of custody dispositions by number of prior convictions, controlling for age and violent, property, and other Criminal Code crimes, Canada, 1995-96.

Major offence category	First-time offenders			One prior conviction			Two prior convictions			Three or more prior convictions			Total repeat offenders		
	12-13	14-15	16-17	12-13	14-15	16-17	12-13	14 -15	16-17	12-13	14-15	16-17	12-13	14-15	16-17
Violent crime															
Total custody	11%	15%	19%	44%	42%	42%	59%	59%	56%	63%	70%	73%	49%	52%	55%
Total cases	1591	3188	2953	287	860	1063	66	400	568	41	344	755	394	1604	2386
Property crime															
Total custody	8%	10%	12%	27%	30%	28%	37%	47%	46%	67%	67%	67%	33%	41%	44%
Total cases	2354	6125	6616	523	2179	2980	148	877	1596	66	809	1957	727	3865	6533
Other Criminal Code															
Total custody	18%	10%	11%	33%	30%	26%	62%	48%	35%	33%	67%	53%	39%	42%	36%
Total cases	257	6125	1654	72	2179	705	21	877	384	9	809	429	102	3865	1518

Note: (1) Total drug and other federal offences have been excluded due to small caseload.
(2) The above data has been extracted from several individual tables. Thus, proportions do not total 100%.

age groups who have committed a violent crime, repeat offenders received a larger proportion of custody dispositions. The differences between custody dispositions for all age groups also almost entirely disappeared when violent crime was added as a control, with the exception of youth with three or more prior convictions. This suggests that the age of the offender does not affect the court's decision to give a custody disposition for violent crimes. Repeat offenders aged 14 through 17 who had committed a violent crime received a larger proportion of custody compared to non-custody dispositions (52% aged 14 and 15 and 55% aged 16 and 17). Results showed that, for other major offence categories and for all age groups, repeat offenders received a larger proportion of custody dispositions compared to first-time offenders. With a few exceptions, other major offence categories also demonstrate that the age of the offender was not related to disposition. That is, there was no tendency to treat younger offenders more leniently.

The final analysis controlled for all three variables (age, gender, and offence). The data show that, for all age groups who committed violent crimes, both male and female repeat offenders received a larger proportion of custody than did first-time offenders. Repeat male offenders aged 12 through 15 had a larger proportion of open custody compared to secure custody dispositions for violent offences. Male offenders aged 16 and 17 had a larger proportion of secure custody than open custody dispositions (34% versus 23%). All dispositions given to male repeat offenders, for all age groups, included a larger proportion of custody dispositions compared to non-custody dispositions.

Similar relationships were found when all other major offence categories were examined. Repeat offenders of all age groups for both male and female offenders received a larger proportion of custody dispositions than did first-time offenders. For all other major offence categories, male repeat offenders aged 16 and 17 received a larger proportion of secure custody compared to open custody dispositions. Female repeat offenders aged 12 and 13, received a larger proportion of custody dispositions for property offences and other *Criminal Code* offences than did female repeat offenders 14 through 17 years of age. Female repeat offenders aged 16 and 17 also had a larger proportion of secure versus open custody, but the difference was marginal.

In conclusion, results demonstrated that age, gender, and offence do not explain the relationship between the number of prior convictions and dispositions. This study has shown that severity of disposition is affected by the number of prior convictions, gender, and seriousness of the offence, while age did not contribute substantially to this relationship.

Conclusion

The purpose of this study was to examine how the youth justice system responds to repeat offenders. This was done by comparing sentencing patterns for first-time and repeat offenders. This study is unique in that it incorporates data from Ontario for the first time. This is important since Ontario accounts for approximately 40% of the national youth court caseload. Also, unlike previous studies which have focussed on repeat offenders, this study examined dispositions by number of prior convictions, in addition to conducting a simultaneous examination of the impact of age, gender, and seriousness of the offence.

The major finding of this study is that judges sentence repeat offenders more harshly than they do first-time offenders charged with the same offence. This finding is relatively consistent with previous research that has examined variables predicting youth court dispositions. Importantly, one variable consistently stood out as a determining factor in sentencing. In the analysis outlined above, the prior record of the offender was found to have an effect regardless of the offender's age, gender, or the seriousness of the current offence. Repeat offenders were more likely to receive a custody disposition than first-time offenders. Furthermore, the proportion of dispositions involving a form of custody was positively associated with the number of prior convictions.

Another factor related to the nature of the disposition was the seriousness of the offence. That is, youth were more likely to receive a custody disposition for violent crimes followed by property crimes, and then other major offence categories. This suggests that the seriousness of the offence was related to the type of the dispositions being given in youth court.

Consistent with Carrington and Moyer (1995), this study found that gender was related to custody dispositions. Males with or without a prior conviction were more likely to receive a custody disposition than females.

Previous studies have reported mixed conclusions regarding the impact of age, such that, some researchers have found seriousness of disposition to increase with age, while others have found no consistent relationship (Kueneman and Linden 1983; Carrington and Moyer 1995; Doherty and deSouza 1995). The results of this study have shown that the differences between age groups almost entirely disappeared when number of prior convictions and seriousness of the offence were controlled. This suggests that the age of the offender does not affect the court's decision to give custody dispositions.

While public concern regarding youth court dispositions are typically viewed as being too lenient on young offenders, this study has shown this is not the case. The youth justice system has been shown to give harsher dispositions where appropriate. That is, custody dispositions were given most often to serious offences as well as to persistent repeat offenders.

Better knowledge of how the youth justice system responds to young offenders would enhance public confidence. Dissemination of information would also play a crucial role. By allowing the public access to information about youth crime, they would become more aware of how the youth justice system really does treat young offenders.

This study has contributed to filling the gap in the literature on dispositions given to repeat offenders. There is a need for more research in the area of custodial sentence lengths. With the dramatic increase in the proportion of custody dispositions given to repeat offenders, it would be interesting to expand on Doherty and deSouzas' study (1995) to determine whether repeat offenders are also receiving longer sentence lengths, compared to first-time offenders who have committed the same offence, and whether this is proving to be beneficial in preventing youth from re-entering into the justice system. Interestingly, in a recent study Sprott and Doob (1998) found that an increase in prison rates does not have a positive effect on decreasing crime rates. Although this study is based on adults, it should be noted the importance of using sentencing options other than custody as a method of reducing crime rates. Although alternative measures and diversion programs in Canada are geared towards first-time offenders, consideration should be given to whether these programs may be useful in preventing youth with prior records from re-entering the justice system.

Appendix 1

Description of crime categories:

Violent crime: Murder; Manslaughter; Attempted murder; Aggravated sexual assault; Sexual assault/weapon; Sexual assault; Rape/indecent assault; Aggravated assault; Assault with a weapon; Cause bodily harm/intent; Minor assault; Unlawfully cause bodily harm; Assaulting peace officer; Other assaults; Robbery; Dangerous use of weapon; Possession of a weapon; Other weapon offences; Infanticide and other related; Kidnapping/hostage taking; Extortion; Other sexual offences; Criminal negligence.

Property crime: Break and enter; Arson; Taking a vehicle without consent; Theft over $1,000; Theft under $1,000; Theft unspecified; Theft other; False pretences; Forgery; Fraud; Other fraudulent transactions; Possession of stolen property; Mischief/damage.

Other *Criminal Code*: Impaired operation; Escape custody; Unlawfully at large; Failure to appear; Breach of recognizance; Failure to comply; Attempt/accessories/conspiracy; Disorderly conduct/nuisances; Abduction; Procuring; Bawdy house; Soliciting; Other motor vehicle offences; Gaming and betting; Against the administration; Currency offences; Exposure/nudity; Public morals, Public order; Offences against the person; Other *Criminal Code*.

***Narcotic Control Act* and *Food and Drugs Act*:** Importing/exporting; Trafficking in narcotics; Possession of narcotics; Failure to disclose Rx; Cultivation; Trafficking in drugs; Possession of drugs; Other FDA.

***Young Offenders Act*:** Failure to comply with a disposition; Failure to comply with undertaking; Contempt against youth court; Assist/interfere/other.

Notes

1. We gratefully acknowledge comments by Glen Doherty, Denyse Carrière, John deVries, Julian Roberts and the Journal's two anonymous reviewers.
2. Charge is defined as an accusation against a young person which has been formally and fully processed in youth court.
3. All numbers have been generated using a case definition based on the date of disposition. In contrast, the Youth Court Survey is based on cases defined as a set of charges first presented to the court on the same date. A set of charges first presented to the court as one case does not necessarily end up as a case at dispositions, since some may not reach disposition, some may be separated into another case, and some may be merged with charges which began a separate case. As a result, the numbers employed in this analysis do not correspond to the figures presented in the Youth Court Survey publications from the Canadian Centre for Justice Statistics.
4. All offence types have been controlled for this analysis. The findings show the same results, therefore, for sake of simplicity, the results shown in this report include only major offence categories.

References

Bala, Nicholas
1994 The 1995 *Young Offenders Act* amendments: Compromise or confusion? The Ottawa Law Review 26(3): 643-675.

Beaumount, H. and M. LeBlanc
1986 Les decisions des juges d'un tribunal de la jeunesse en milieu urbain. Canadian Journal of Criminology 29: 153-170.

Canadian Centre for Justice Statistics
1990 Recidivists in Youth Courts: An Examination of Repeat Offenders Convicted in 1988-89. Ottawa: Statistics Canada.

Carrington, Peter and Sharon Moyer
1995 Factors affecting custodial dispositions under the *Young Offenders Act*. Canadian Journal of Criminology 37(2): 127-162.

Doherty, Glen and Paul deSouza
1995 Recidivism in Youth Courts 1993-94. Juristat 15(16).

Doob, Anthony, Voula Marinos, and Kimberly Varma
1995 Youth Crime and the Justice System in Canada. Toronto: Centre of Criminology, University of Toronto.

Hoge, Robert, Don Andrews, and Alan Leschied
1992 An investigation of the factors associated with probation and custody dispositions in a sample of juveniles. In Toward Safer Communities: Violent and Repeat Offending by Young People. London: London Family Court Clinic.

Kueneman, R. and R. Linden
1983 Factors Affecting Dispositions in the Winnipeg Juvenile Court. In R.R. Corrado, Marc LeBlanc, and Jean Trépanier (eds.), Current Issues of Juvenile Justice. Toronto: Butterworths.

Leschied, A.W. and P.G. Gendreau
1986 The declining role of rehabilitation in Canadian Juvenile Justice: Implications of underlying theory in the *Young Offenders Act*. Canadian Journal of Criminology 28(3): 315-322.

Moyer, Sharon
1992 Recidivism in Youth Courts 1990-1991. Juristat 12(2).

Platt, Priscilla
1995 Young Offenders Law in Canada. Canada: Butterworths Canada Ltd.

Reitsma-Street, Marge
1993 Canadian youth court charges and dispositions for females before and after implementation of the *Young Offenders Act*. Canadian Journal of Criminology 35(4): 437-458.

Roberts, Julian
1997 The role of Criminal Record in the Sentencing Process. In M. Tonry (ed.), Crime and Justice: A Review of Research. Chicago: University of Chicago Press.

Sprott, Jane and Anthony Doob
1998 Understanding provincial variation in incarceration rates. Canadian Journal of Criminology 46(2): 305-322.

Wolfgang, Marvin, Robert Figlio, and Thorsten Sellin
1972 Delinquency in a Birth Cohort. Chicago: The University of Chicago Press.

Young, Alan
1989 Appellate court sentencing principles for young offenders. In Lucien Beaulieu (ed.), Young Offender Dispositions. Toronto: Wall and Thompson Inc.

CHAPTER TWENTY-FOUR

What's intermediate about 'intermediate' sanctions?: The case of young offender dispositions in Canada[1]

Voula Marinos
Centre of Criminology
University of Toronto
Toronto, Ontario

THE CONCEPT OF "INTERMEDIATE SANCTIONS" HAS BECOME increasingly popular in the literature on punishment. Intermediacy in punishment has been defined as a range of punishments between the two extreme poles of probation and imprisonment. Recent strategies of penal reform in the United States and Canada have called for an increased use of "intermediate sanctions" (Morris and Tonry 1990; Department of Justice Canada 1991; Byrne, Lurigio, and Petersilia 1992; Smykla and Selke 1995; Tonry and Hamilton 1995). For example, Morris and Tonry (1990) argue that in the United States, probation and prison have become overused in the 1980's and 1990's, and that the fiscal and prison crowding crises require attention. Thus, what is needed, they argue, is a range of meaningful sanctions between probation and prison (Morris and Tonry 1990: 3).

Intermediacy in punishment has become an important penal strategy in Canada. First, sentencing legislation requires that judges use imprisonment only when necessary for both adults and young offenders. For adults, amendments to the *Criminal Code,* which came into effect in September 1996,

---

Canadian Journal of Criminology/Revue canadienne de criminologie, October/octobre 1998, pp. 355–375.

specify that sanctions other than imprisonment should be considered for all offenders (sections 718.2 (c) & (d)). In sentencing young offenders, the *Young Offenders Act* instructs judges to impose the least restrictive means possible in the circumstances. Thus judges are to consider numerous ways of dealing with the youth other than imprisonment (see section 24 (1.1) (b) and (c)). Second, we have also seen the development of new sanctions such as conditional sentences of imprisonment for adult offenders (section 724 of the *Criminal Code*) which are consistent with the rationale of 'intermediacy'. This analysis explores the imposition of 'intermediate' sanctions for young offenders in Canadian youth courts for 1994-5, and suggests an explanation for the combination of an intermediate sanction and custody.

The imprisonment–denunciation nexus

While decreasing the use of imprisonment and increasing the use of intermediate sanctions are important goals in sentencing, it is critical to inquire into the sensibilities[(2)] and purposes of different sanctions. Analyses of penal changes over time suggest that the values and meanings underlying punishment have led to the development and demise of particular penal practices (Beattie 1986; Braithwaite 1989). Doob and Marinos (1995) argue that different sanctions have different meanings across time and place and serve a variety of purposes. Thus, they suggest that certain intermediate sanctions, though punitive, may not be seen as capable of serving particular purposes for some offences.

Proposals to replace imprisonment with intermediate sanctions have not considered adequately the broader purposes of different sanctions in different contexts. It is assumed that fines and community service orders, for instance, are highly flexible and can be made equivalent to sentences of imprisonment for a variety of offences by increasing the size of these sanctions (Morris and Tonry 1990; Smykla and Selke 1995; Tromblay 1990). In fact, there is some evidence to suggest that the meanings and purposes of punishments may pose limits on interchangeability. A study of the public's sensibilities about fines and imprisonment in Canada revealed that regardless of severity, fines were not seen as accomplishing the traditional sentencing goal of denunciation as effectively as imprisonment. For some circumstances, namely violent or sexual offences, members of the public saw the need to denounce the crime, and believed that this could be accomplished most effectively through imprisonment (Marinos 1997).

Over time, imprisonment has been constituted and coupled with the expressive purposes of punishment – the goals of denunciation and general deterrence. The courts, media, criminal justice agencies and others are active participants in constituting 'punishments' and reproducing meanings and sensibilities about their usefulness. In examining a range of special commission and committee reports in Canada, for instance, it is apparent that there has been an increasing reliance on conceptualizing and interpreting imprisonment as being effective in expressing condemnation of criminal behaviour. Beginning with the Ouimet Committee Report in 1969, to the Federal Government Task Force Report in 1977, we see how imprisonment has been actively linked with denunciation and general deterrence to symbolize the condemnation of 'criminals', while non-institutional punishments have been linked to providing opportunities for, and reformation of the 'socially responsible' offender (see Ekstedt and Griffiths 1988: 56; Ouimet 1969; Law Reform Commission 1975; MacGuigan Subcommittee 1977; Task Force 1977). As the rationale of rehabilitation lost its credence and academic doubt increased about achieving general deterrence through sentencing (Canadian Sentencing Commission 1987: 138; Doob, Marinos and Varma 1995: 65-83), decisions to impose imprisonment are most likely to be linked with denunciation (Manson 1997: 290-3).

Short sentences of custody, in particular, may be relied upon by the courts in communicating messages about crime and punishment. Manson (1997) argues that the only purpose for imposing a short sentence of imprisonment is to express denunciation. Using mandatory 14-day custodial sentences for impaired driving as an example, he argues that "[t]he rationale for the short mandatory sentence is its expressive denunciatory message: "Impaired driving is a crime." As with all short sentences, any presumption of incarceration is not based on general deterrence" (Manson 1997: 292). In a recent sentencing decision in Ontario, Judge David Cole argued that, in a case of robbery and in the particular circumstances of three first-time, youthful adult offenders, a minimum short period of custody (90 days) was required in order to express denunciation. After this denunciatory component was accomplished, the judge sentenced the offenders to substantial hours of community service (*R.* v. *Visanji*).

The study on public perceptions of fines and imprisonment (Marinos 1997) and the link between imprisonment and denunciation suggests that punishment is multidimensional. The present analysis suggests that it is inaccurate to assume that sanctions are highly fluid, flexible 'things' which can be made equivalent by simply focusing on severity. Garland (1990; 1991), for instance, argues that there are various dimensions to punishment – moral, political, economic, and cultural – and to evaluate punishment in merely instrumental terms is both misguided and unproductive. The nature of the offence for which the offender is being punished seems to be a critical aspect of understanding the sensibilities about different sanctions. Thus, there are limits to the fluidity and flexibility of sanctions and the extent to which they can be "equivalent" on all dimensions. 'Intermediate' sanctions may not be "intermediate" on certain dimensions.

Understanding the use of 'intermediate' sanctions in youth courts

Understanding that there are both qualitative and quantitative dimensions to punishment has important implications for examining the use of intermediate sanctions in Canadian youth courts. The concept of "intermediacy" suggests that sanctions can be placed along a single continuum of severity – from most to least severe. The model of the single continuum is useful in highlighting a *range* of individual sanctions, as well as shifting our attention away from imprisonment – away from notions such as "alternatives" or "non-custodial" sanctions.(3) The continuum model is problematic in reinforcing the view that sanctions only differ on a dimension of severity (Doob and Marinos 1995; Marinos 1997). In fact, research on perceptions of intermediate sanctions has generally focused on comparing punishments by their severity (Tremblay 1988; Petersilia and Deschenes 1994; Harlow, Darley, and Robinson 1995).

The limitations of conceptualizing punishment as a single continuum of severity has important implications for our understanding of young offender dispositions. Statistics published by the Canadian Centre for Justice Statistics (hereafter CCJS) demonstrate that as the "most significant disposition", intermediate sanctions are infrequently imposed by youth courts across Canada (see, for example, CCJS, 1994-5, Table 8). In examining statistics for 1994-5 (CCJS, Table 8), it is apparent that custody (secure and open combined) and probation are heavily used: they are the "most significant dispositions" in 34.1% and 48.2% of cases respectively. All other sanctions – those which may be considered "intermediate" – are imposed in only 19.2% of all cases given dispositions in youth courts across Canadian provinces (n = 73,969 cases). Hence, from published statistics of the "most significant disposition", we would conclude that custody and probation are both frequently imposed compared to intermediate sanctions.

It is critical to point out that the conclusion of the apparent low use of intermediate sanctions (19.2% of all cases) relates to the way in which youth court dispositions are presented. On the one hand, the published statistics on youth court dispositions are informative in outlining in an easily understandable manner the varying use of sentencing options by youth court judges. On the other hand, the published statistics obscure the extent to which intermediate sanctions are imposed. In the published statistics by CCJS, the dispositions handed down in a "case" are typically categorized by the single "most significant" disposition. The range of punishments available are ranked along a single continuum – from most severe to least severe in a specified invariant order. Thus, if a young offender was sentenced to open custody, probation, and a fine, a count would appear under open custody as it is defined by CCJS as the "most severe" of these three. In this same example, the result is that the published statistics underestimate the use of intermediate sanctions such as a fine. All intermediate sanctions that are combined with probation are counted under the rubric of the sanction deemed "most significant" (probation), and thus underrepresenting their actual use. Thus, the published statistics on youth court dispositions underrepresent the imposition of intermediate sanctions as 19.2%.

A number of important questions arise, then, from the discussion of the multiple dimensions of punishment and the limitations of published statistics of young offender dispositions in Canada. How frequently are intermediate sanctions imposed? For which offences are intermediate sanctions used alone and in combination with imprisonment? What do intermediate sanctions accomplish? What is the purpose of combining an intermediate sanction with custody? Moyer's recent analysis (1996) of youth court dispositions addressed combinations; however, the findings were not linked to the broader purposes or sensibilities about punishment.

By examining combinations of dispositions, it is possible to assess the purposes of the use of custody and intermediate sanctions. Research on young offender dispositions reveals concerns about the increasing use of short sentences of custody since the introduction of the *Young Offenders Act* (Doob 1992). In a study of six provinces, Doob revealed that youth courts increased the proportion of cases getting short sentences of three months or less and youth courts are apparently handing down fewer very long sentences (1992: 81-82). Unfortunately, the published statistics on young offender dispositions do not provide information on the offences for which these short sentences are imposed, nor whether short custodial sentences are handed down alone or in combination with other sanctions. In fact, statistics for 1994-5 demonstrate that sentences of imprisonment of thirty days or less make up over one-quarter of custodial sentences imposed in youth courts (CCJS, 1994-5: Table 6; Markwart 1992). Doob (1992: 83) concludes his analysis by suggesting that "[a] more detailed analysis and a clearer statement of *purpose* of dispositions under the present legislation are necessary in order to evaluate these trends" (emphasis added). An examination of the use of intermediate sanctions is not only important in and of itself, but it will likely shed light on the purpose of imposing them along with short custodial sentences.

Method

Since the focus of the present analysis was to understand the use of intermediate sanctions for young offenders in Canada, it was critical to explore the *combinations* of dispositions handed down in youth courts. As mentioned earlier, the Canadian Centre for Justice Statistics presently publishes statistics on the "most significant disposition" handed down for each case disposed of in youth courts. Each case is associated with a single disposition ordered from the most to the least serious disposition, starting with custody (secure followed by open), probation, fine, compensation, pay purchaser, compensation in kind, community service order, absolute discharge, and "other" (CCJS, 1994-5: Table 8). While this is useful for many purposes, it has the unfortunate effect of burying combinations of dispositions.

Data on young offender dispositions were obtained from CCJS in a form in which cases were aggregated according to whether they included each of the possible dispositions listed in section 20(1) of the *Young Offenders Act*. In addition, because of the importance of custody and the high frequency of short custodial sentences (Doob 1992; Markwart 1992), CCJS provided a special code on whether or not the case included a total (open plus secure) custodial sentence of 1-30 days, 31-180 days, and 181 days and more.(4) It was important to know the total length of custody because it related to the theory that the lack of denunciatory power of intermediate sanctions could be compensated by being attached to a short term of imprisonment. Thus, cases involving custodial sentences were described as having a total custody length of 1 to 30 days, 31 to 180 days, and 181 days and over – described as "short", "medium" and "long" total custodial terms.

For the purposes of this analysis, intermediate sanctions were considered to be a fine, restitution, compensation, pay purchaser, compensation in kind, community services, and "other". Thus, custody, probation, detain for treatment, prohibition/seizure/forfeiture, absolute discharge, and suspend driver's license were not included in the measure of an intermediate sanction. The data also included the type of offence as described in Tables 3 and 8 in CCJS statistics (1994-5).

Findings

The use of 'intermediate' sanctions

In examining the use (alone and in combination) of all dispositions (n= 73,969 cases), probation is imposed most frequently, in 65.4% (48,381) of all cases, and custody is imposed in 34.1% (25,214) of all cases.(5) Intermediate sanctions were imposed in 42.9% (31,714) of all convicted cases. In contrast, the published "most significant disposition" statistics by CCJS revealed that intermediate sanctions were the "most severe" sentencing options imposed in only 15.8% of the cases (CCJS, 1994-5: Table 8). Thus, an examination of *combinations* of dispositions is important in understanding the actual overall use of intermediate sanctions.

For a selected number of relatively high frequency violent, property, drug, and administration of justice offences (constituting over 90% of sentenced cases in youth court), Table 1 reveals that intermediate sanctions are imposed quite often

Table 1
The use of 'intermediate' sanctions, alone and in combination with other sanctions, for selected offences

Most significant charge	Received 'intermediate' sanction	Did not receive 'intermediate' sanction	Total	N
"Serious" offences				
Aggravated assault & Assault with weapon	41.8%	58.2%	100%	2 180
Assault	41.7%	58.3%	100%	7 311
Sexual assault	22.6%	77.4%	100%	879
Robbery	34.3%	65.7%	100%	1 332
Break and enter	45.4%	54.6%	100%	10 196
Possession weapon	36.8%	63.2%	100%	1 303
Trafficking drug or narcotic	63.9%	36.1%	100%	1 098
"Medium" serious offences				
Theft over	42.3%	57.7%	100%	2 524
Vehicle theft	44.1%	55.9%	100%	1 065
"Less serious" offences				
Theft under/Poss. stolen property	47.8%	52.2%	100%	15 894
Mischief property	56.0%	44.0%	100%	4 055
Possession drug or narcotic	51.2%	48.8%	100%	2 047
Offences against administration of justice				
Escape custody/ Unlawfully at large	7.5%	92.5%	100%	1 899
Other administration of justice offences [1]	34.4%	65.6%	100%	14 992
All other cases	49.2%	50.8%	100%	7 194
Total	42.9%	57.1%	100%	73 969

(1) This category of offences "other administration of justice offences" – is largely made up of the offences of "failure to comply with disposition" and "failure to appear". It also includes "breach of recognizance", "failure to comply with probation order", "offence against the administration of justice", "failure to comply with undertaking", and "contempt against youth court".

for all offences except for escape custody/unlawfully at large. In examining the range of intermediate sanctions, it becomes clear that community service is the most popular, imposed in over two-thirds of cases in which at least one intermediate sanction is used (67.23%). Fines, on the other hand, are imposed in only 19% of all cases receiving at least one intermediate sanction.

Table 2 presents the extent to which custody and probation are used in comparison to intermediate sanctions. The findings demonstrate that, when intermediate sanctions are imposed, they are typically attached to probation. Standing on their own, there is a relatively low use of 'intermediate' sanctions as "intermediate" – imposed without prison or probation in only 14.2% of the cases.

Short "denunciatory sentences" and 'intermediate' sanctions

For certain types of offences – violent, sexual, or serious property – denunciation is an important purpose in sentencing a young offender.[6] For the less serious instances of these offences (e.g., where the role of the particular offender was minor or where the particular offence was relatively minor), denunciation may still be seen as being important, but a custodial sentence may be seen as inappropriately harsh. One way to resolve this conflict is to impose a very short custodial sentence (e.g., a total sentence of 30 days or less) and combine it with the "appropriate" intermediate sanction (e.g., a community service order). If this logic is correct, then in instances where denunciation is important, one would expect intermediate sanctions to be more likely combined with short custodial sentences than with longer ones where, presumably, the custodial sentence is seen as being the appropriate punishment.

Table 3 demonstrates that for offences requiring expressions of condemnation – violent, sexual and serious property – one or more intermediate sanctions are more likely to be combined with short custodial sentences rather than

Table 2
The use of 'intermediate' sanctions alone and in combination with prison and probation

Use of intermediate sanctions	Percentage (%)	N
Intermediate sanction only	14.2%	10 485
Intermediate sanction and probation only	25.8%	19 105
Intermediate sanction and custody only	0.6%	432
Intermediate sanction and custody and probation only	2.3%	1 692
Subtotal: Intermediate sanction alone or combined with other sanction	42.9%	31 714
No intermediate sanction	57.1%	42 225
Total	100%	73 969

long. This finding is consistent with the theory of the lack of denunciatory power of intermediate sanctions. In looking at the offence of aggravated assault/assault with a weapon in Table 3, we see that of those who received a short custodial sentence, the proportion that received an intermediate sanction with "short" custody was 17.2%. This is greater than the proportion that received an intermediate sanction along with a medium (9.8%) or long (3.9%) custodial sentence. In contrast, the effect is not the same for minor offences such as theft under/possession of stolen property: for each custody length, the proportion receiving intermediate sanctions with a short (8.8%), medium (8.0%), or long (9.2%) custodial sentence did not vary substantially.

The findings shown in Table 3 reveal that for "serious" and "medium serious" offences receiving different custody lengths – aggravated assault/ assault with a weapon, assault, sexual assault, robbery, break and enter, possession of a weapon, theft over $1,000, trafficking of drugs or narcotics, and vehicle theft – intermediate sanctions were more likely to be attached to a

Table 3
The proportion of those cases that received a short, medium or long custodial sentence that also received an 'intermediate' sanction

Offences	Short custody %	(N)[1]	Medium custody %	(N)[1]	Long custody %	(N)[1]
"Serious" offences						
Aggravated assault/ Assault with weapon	17.2%	(233)	9.8%	(429)	3.9%	(154)
Assault 9.9%	(825)	6.9%	(728)	4.5%	(89)	
Sexual assault	17.9%	(56)	3.8%	(157)	9.9%	(131)
Robbery	20.0%	(135)	12.6%	(341)	10.8%	(369)
Break and enter	20.5%	(987)	12.1%	(2373)	10.0%	(912)
Possession weapon	7.0%	(129)	5.5%	(201)	3.7%	(54)
Trafficking drug or narcotic	17.0%	(106)	11.5%	(183)	4.9%	(41)
"Medium serious" offences						
Theft over	13.4%	(284)	9.8%	(634)	8.0%	(200)
Vehicle theft	10.1%	(109)	8.0%	(100)	0.00%	(10)
"Less serious" offences						
Theft under/ Possession stolen property	8.8%	(1760)	8.0%	(1861)	9.2%	(314)
Mischief property	14.5%	(351)	11.4%	(315)	12.5%	(40)
Possession drug or narcotic	6.5%	(169)	9.0%	(67)	5.6%	(18)
Offences against administration of justice						
Escape custody/ Unlawful at large	2.4%	(1078)	3.9%	(559)	4.8%	(62)
Other administration of justice offences[2]	5.6%	(4515)	3.8%	(2085)	6.3%	(223)
All other offences	10.2%	(689)	7.3%	(855)	4.3%	(282)
Total 8.8%	(11426)	8.1%	(10888)	8.2%	(2899)	

(1) N's in parentheses refer to the number of people from which each percentage is based.
(2) See Note 1 in Table 1.

short period of custody than long. In contrast, for less serious offences receiving custody such as possession of stolen property, theft under $1,000, mischief to property, and possession of drugs or narcotics, the likelihood of receiving an intermediate sanction did not vary substantially with custody length. Administration of justice offences not only had a low overall use of intermediate sanctions, but they also were equally likely to be attached to each length of a custodial sentence. It is important to point out that the range of selected offences accounts for 90.3% of the total sentenced cases in 1994/5 (n = 73969 cases, total) and 93% (n = 24214 cases, total) of those who received custody.

Discussion

The use of 'intermediate' sanctions for young offenders

The assumption that sanctions serve multiple purposes, and that they are not highly fluid, flexible entities appropriate for a variety of offences and offenders led to the present inquiry of combinations of dispositions in youth courts across Canada. Recent literature (Department of Justice Canada 1991: Annex 1; Morris and Tonry 1990; Petersilia and Deschenes 1994) and legislation to increase the use of intermediate sanctions assumes that sanctions can be made equivalent across a range of offences as long as they are roughly similar in severity or punitiveness. In contrast, poststructuralist writings on penality and penal reform conceptualize 'punishment' as dispersed, fluid, and multidimensional (Foucault 1977; Garland; 1985; 1990; McMahon 1993), and suggest that punishment and penal reform are far more complex than simply focusing on the severity of sanctions. The very term *penality*, in fact, acknowledges that 'punishment' refers to the "whole of the penal complex, including its sanctions, discourses and representations, rather than simply stressing institutional practices" (Garland 1985: x). Thus, while one might expect that sanctions are easily interchangeable across a range of offences and offenders, the present analysis suggests that there are some limits to the fluidity and flexibility of (criminal justice) sanctions.

In order to understand these limits, the social and cultural contexts of crime and punishment must be addressed. The nature of the offence for which the offender is being punished, as well as modern sensibilities about what is 'appropriate' and 'civilized' are important elements of these contexts. Garland (1990: 214) highlights the role of modern sensibilities in structuring the practices of contemporary penal systems:

> But penal measures will only be considered at all if they conform to our conceptions of what is emotionally tolerable. The matter-of-fact administration of most penal policy is possible because it relies upon measures which have already been deemed tolerable and the morality of which can be taken for granted... I do not mean by this that governments and penal authorities always take care to search their consciences, or put morality before expediency in their use of punishments – clearly they do not. But political decisions are always taken against a background of mores and sensibilities which, normally at least, will set limits to what will be tolerated by the public or implemented by the penal system's personnel.

The analysis of dispositions reveals that youth courts across Canada seem to be using intermediate sanctions quite differently for different kinds of offences. In general, the findings of the present analysis demonstrate that the nature of the offence and purposes of punishment are important considerations in understanding the use of intermediate sanctions and imprisonment. The analysis of combinations of dispositions reveals that they are imposed across a range of high frequency violent, property, drug, and administration of justice offences – between 22% to 63% of these cases (Table 1). It was expected, however, that intermediate sanctions would more likely be imposed for property offences than violent and sexual offences. Consistent with this expectation, there were differences found in the use of intermediate sanctions among offences such as mischief to property (56.0%) and theft under/ possession of stolen property (47.8%), compared to possession of a weapon (36.8%), robbery (34.3%), and sexual assault (22.6%) (see Table 1).

Some authors have suggested that part of the importance of the conceptualization of "intermediate sanctions" – and moving away from notions like "alternatives to imprisonment" or "non-custodial sanctions" – is that individual sanctions are imposed alone, as important sanctions on their own. For example, Morris and Tonry (1990: 11) argue that both fines and community service orders should be taken seriously as credible sanctions and used more frequently, "standing alone or as part of a punishment package". While intermediate sanctions – community service in particular – are imposed fairly frequently, they may not be seen by youth court judges as being capable of accomplishing what they want to accomplish on their own. Rather, when intermediate sanctions are imposed, they are predominately attached to probation (Table 2). In light of the finding that community service is the most commonly imposed intermediate sanction, it is likely that, at least in part, probation provides a mechanism for supervising these young offenders.

The lack of denunciatory power of 'intermediate' sanctions and the use of short custody

As mentioned earlier, an examination of combinations of dispositions is particularly important in trying to understand the purpose of *short* periods of custody for young offenders. Some authors have highlighted the denunciatory and expressive functions of short periods of custody, while attributing incapacitative and/or rehabilitative purposes to long periods of incarceration for young offenders. Thus, it becomes particularly interesting to inquire into those cases that received a short period of custody that also received an intermediate sanction (Table 3). The findings in Table 3 are consistent with the theory that intermediate sanctions lack denunciatory power and, therefore, must be tied to a short custodial sentence when denunciation is seen as important. These results are also consistent with a broader assumption that sanctions serve various purposes according to the nature of the offence and offender, and that intermediate sanctions may not be as effective in accomplishing denunciation as imprisonment (Doob and Marinos 1995; Marinos 1997). In the present context, there has been concern expressed by members of the public that sentences for violent offences are not severe enough and that there is a need for increased accountability of young offenders under the *Young Offenders Act* (Sprott 1996). One way to accomplish denunciation and accountability when custody, per se, is not seen as being justified is to impose an intermediate sanction along with a short custodial sentence.

One might suggest that the trend towards short custodial sentences (Doob 1992: 24; Markwart 1992: 267; Doob *et al.* 1995: 139) is caused by a general desire to impose "short sharp shocks" on young offenders. A simple "short sharp shock" explanation does not adequately fit the data, however, because it suggests nothing about the pattern of combinations of custody with other sanctions. It also might be possible to explain the variation in the frequency of custodial sentences and intermediate sanctions by "just proportionality". As the seriousness of the offence increases, so too does the length of custody. A proportionality model does not suggest an explanation about why intermediate sanctions should be attached to custody in the pattern revealed in Table 3.

Accomplishing denunciation without incarceration is obviously a challenge for the youth justice system as it is for the adult criminal justice system. In the adult system, this problem is being articulated in the context of the conditional sentence of imprisonment. For example, the Ontario Court of Appeal in *Wismayer* (1997: 33) attempted to uncouple the link between imprisonment and denunciation through the imposition of a conditional sentence of imprisonment for a sexual assault. Justice Rosenberg argued that "I cannot accept that a conditional sentence of imprisonment is unavailable where the paramount consideration is denunciation of the offender's conduct". In this case for the Ontario Court of Appeal, denunciation was accomplished through the imposition of strict conditions of house arrest, monitored by the offender's parents. It may be possible, then, to decrease the use of some sentences of short custody for young offenders through more creative conditions of community supervision (such as house arrest). While efforts must be made in the courts to uncouple the nexus between imprisonment and denunciation, it is also necessary to acknowledge the limits of our sensibilities. It seems that we value autonomy and security of the person to the extent that only imprisonment, in some circumstances, meets this expectation of punishing offenders.

The findings may explain the increased use of short sentences of custody since the introduction of the *Young Offenders Act* (Doob 1992). It is possible that judges are reacting to public disapproval about youth crime and young offenders' sentences, and this might explain the increase in short sentences of custody for young offenders. As the public demanded "denunciation" and strong statements about crime through sentencing, this was being accomplished increasingly by combining a short custodial sentence with an intermediate sanction.

In the (adult) case referred to earlier (*R.* v. *Visanji* [1997]), Judge Cole explained the purpose of short custody – ninety days – combined with an intermediate sanction for three first-time youthful adult offenders convicted of robbery:

> ... I have decided that it would be consistent with Parliament's direction that judges are to reduce the use of incarceration, expressed in ss. 718.2(d) and (e) of the *Code* to impose community service as a *substitute* for additional imprisonment, once the *minimum* denunciatory period of 90 days incarceration has been satisfied (emphasis added) (417).

In the case noted above, the judge found that a conditional sentence of imprisonment – even with the mandatory and optional conditions which could be imposed – would be "insufficient to meet the principles of denunciation" (406). The "appropriate minimum" term of custody was required to fulfill the denunciatory portion of the sentence for robbery, which then allowed the judge to impose community service as a substitute for additional incarceration as well as restitution to the victim. It is also interesting to note that the judge saw this particular robbery – committed by first-time youthful adult offenders causing some physical and psychological harm to the victim – as being appropriate for an intermediate sanction, but also requiring a short denunciatory sentence of custody.

Conclusion

Understanding the combination of custody and intermediate sanctions is important because it may help explain the relatively frequent use of custody for relatively minor offences. As provisions under the *Young Offenders Act* specifically relate to imposing custody only when necessary, it is critical to inquire into the variations in the use of intermediate sanctions and the purposes of different punishments. A focus on the combination of custody and intermediate sanctions is useful in exposing the qualities and complexities of punishment. The imposition of 'intermediate' sanctions for young offenders does not seem to be related to what is seen as an 'intermediate' crime. Furthermore, when one considers that 15.4% of *all* dispositions handed down in 1994/5 involved a period of custody of 30 days or less, and that short dispositions constituted 45.3% of all custodial dispositions handed down to young offenders in 1994/5, it is important to consider whether there might be a more sensible way of accomplishing the relevant goals of sentencing.

Notes

1. The research and preparation of this paper were supported by a Social Sciences and Humanities Research Council of Canada grant to A.N. Doob. I would like to thank him for his suggestions on numerous drafts of this paper. I would also like to thank Kelly Hannah Moffat and Greg T. Smith for their helpful comments.

2. The term "sensibilities" refers to the feelings, values, and sentiments which are associated with, and support attitudes about different sanctions, and what it means to punish.
3. While terms like "alternatives to imprisonment" or "non-custodial punishments" are useful in shifting attention away from imprisonment, they reinforce it as *the* reference point of punishment. It is also noteworthy to point out that it is quite common to hear people use the term "sentenced" as the way to describe imprisonment: if an offender is not "sentenced" then he or she did not receive imprisonment. The association between sentencing and imprisonment is another example of the prison-punishment nexus – the ways in which "punishment" is connected to imprisonment.
4. Note that total (open and secure) custodial sentences were actually coded as 1 to 29 days, and 30 days, but then were pooled as total length of custody from 1 to 30 days. We wish to thank Denyse Carriere and Glen Doherty for their work in providing the data on youth court dispositions for Canada, 1994-5, in a form which showed multiple dispositions and total length of custody.
5. In all analyses that follow, I examined the 73,969 cases in Canada in 1994-5 where there was a finding of guilt.
6. *R.* v. *H. (S.R.)*, for example, stated that secure custody may be imposed for reasons other than protection of the public, including factors such as general deterrence and "the expression of society's abhorence of certain crimes". The Ontario Court of Appeal held that "... the abhorence of society of certain crimes must be taken into account by the youth court both when deciding whether there should be a period of custody and when deciding whether that custody should be open or secure or a combination of both" (at 50-1). A number of adult cases also have linked denunciation as an important purpose of sentencing violent and sexual offences, see *R.* v. *M.(C.A.)*, and *R.* v. *M.(G.)*.

References

Beattie, John
1986 Crime and the Courts in England, 1600-1800. Princeton: Princeton University Press.

Braithwaite, John
1989 Crime, Shame and Reintegration. Cambridge: Cambridge University Press.

Byrne, James. M., Arthur J. Lurigio, and Joan Petersilia
1992 Smart Sentencing: The Emergence of Intermediate Sanctions. Newbury Park, CA: Sage.

Canadian Centre for Justice Statistics
1994-5 Youth Court Statistics. Ottawa: Minister of Industry, Science and Technology.

Canadian Sentencing Commission
1987 Sentencing Reform: A Canadian Approach. Ottawa: Supply and Services Canada.

Department of Justice Canada
1991 Intermediate Sanctions. Ottawa: Department of Justice Sentencing Team.

Doob, Anthony N.
1992 Trends in the Use of Custodial Dispositions for Young Offenders. Canadian Journal of Criminology 34: 75–84.

Doob, Anthony N. and Voula Marinos
1995 Reconceptualizing punishment: Understanding the limitations on the use of intermediate sanctions. The University of Chicago Law School Roundtable 2(2): 413–33.

Doob, Anthony N., Voula Marinos, and Kimberly Varma
1995 Youth Crime and the Youth Justice System in Canada: A Research Perspective. Toronto: Centre of Criminology, University of Toronto.

Ekstedt, John W. and Curt T. Griffiths
1988 Corrections in Canada: Policy and Practice. Toronto: Harcourt Brace.

Foucault, Michel
1977 Discipline and Punish. New York: Springer.

Garland, David
1990 Punishment and Modern Society: A Study in Social Theory. Chicago: Clarendon Press.

Garland, David
1991 Sociological Perspectives on Punishment. In Michael Tonry (ed.), Crime and Justice: A Review of Research. Chicago: University of Chicago Press.

Garland, David
1985 Punishment and Welfare: A History of Penal Strategies. London: Aldershot.

Harlow, Robert E., John M. Darley, and Paul. H. Robinson
1995 The severity of intermediate penal sanctions: A psychophysical scaling approach for obtaining community perceptions. Journal of Quantitative Criminology 11: 71–95.

Law Reform Commission of Canada
1975 Working Paper II: Imprisonment and Release. Ottawa: Information Canada.

MacGuigan, M. (Chairman)
1977 Report to Parliament by the Sub-Committee on the Penitentiary System in Canada. Ottawa: Supply and Services Canada.

McMahon, Maeve
1993 Persistent Prison? Rethinking Decarceration and Penal Reform. Toronto: University of Toronto Press.

Manson, Allan
1997 Finding A Place for Conditional Sentences. 3 Criminal Reports (5th): 283–300.

Marinos, Voula
1997 Equivalency and interchangeability: The unexamined complexities of reforming the fine. Canadian Journal of Criminology 39: 27–50.

Markwart, Alan
1992 Custodial sanctions under the *Young Offenders Act*. In R.R. Corrado, N. Bala, R. Linden, and M. LeBlanc (eds.), Juvenile Justice in Canada: A Theoretical and Analytical Assessment. Toronto: Butterworths.

Morris, Norval and Michael Tonry
1990 Between Prison and Probation: Intermediate sanctions in a Rational Sentencing System. New York: Oxford University Press.

Moyer, Sharon
1996 A Profile of the Juvenile Justice System in Canada: Report to the Federal-Provincial-Territorial Task Force on Youth Justice. Ottawa: Federal-Provincial-Territorial Task Force on Youth Justice.

Ouimet, R. (Chairman)
1969 Report of the Canadian Committee on Corrections – Toward Unity: Criminal Justice and Corrections. Ottawa: Supply and Services Canada.

Petersilia, Joan and Elizabeth P. Deschenes
1994 What punishes? Inmates rank the severity of prison vs. intermediate sanctions. Federal Probati*on* 58(1): 3-8.

R. v. *M. (C.A.)* (1996) 105 C.C.C. (3d) 374 (S.C.C.).
R. v. *M. (G.)* (1992) 77 C.C.C. (3d) 310 (Ont. C.A.).
R. v. *H. (S.R.)* (1990) 56 C.C.C. (3d) 46 (Ont. C.A.).
R. v. *Visanji* (Ont. Prov. Div.) 9 C.R. (5th) 388 (Cole Prov. J.).
R. v. *Wismayer* (Ont. C. A.) 115 C.C.C. (3d) 18.

Smykla, John O. and William L. Selke
1995 Intermediate Sanctions: Sentencing in the 1990s. Cincinnati, OH: Anderson Publishing.

Sprott, Jane
1996 Understanding public views of youth crime and the youth justice System. Canadian Journal of Criminology 38: 271-90.

Task Force on the Creation of an Integrated Canadian Corrections Service
1977 The Role of Federal Corrections in Canada. Ottawa: Supply and Services Canada.

Tonry, Michael and Kate Hamilton
1995 Intermediate Sanctions in Overcrowded Times. Boston, Mass.: Northeastern University Press.

Tremblay, Pierre
1988 On Penal Metrics. Journal of Quantitative Criminology 4: 225-45.

CHAPTER TWENTY-FIVE

Risk for court contact and predictors of an early age for a first court contact among a sample of high risk youths: A survival analysis approach

David M. Day[1]
Hincks-Dellcrest Centre
Toronto, Ontario

CONSIDERABLE RESEARCH CONDUCTED OVER THE PAST HALF CENTURY has sought to identify the early factors that are associated with the development of criminal behaviour. This research is predicated on the promising proposition that the early identification of risk factors will lead to the development of effective prevention and intervention strategies for children who are at risk for delinquency or who currently present with antisocial tendencies. The social benefits derived from such research in terms of prevention of antisocial and violent behaviour in children and youth as well as the savings in monetary costs associated with both the commission of delinquent acts as well as incarceration and treatment are tremendous (Kazdin 1987; Wierson, Forehand, and Frame 1992).

One of the most consistent findings of this research is that children who evince an early age of onset for aggressive and antisocial behaviour are at high risk for juvenile delinquency and adult criminality (Farrington, Loeber, Elliot, Hawkins, Kandel, Klein, McCord, Rowe, and Tremblay 1990; Loeber and Dishion 1983; Osborn and West 1978; Tolan 1988). An age of onset prior to 12-15 years substantially increases the likelihood that an individual will continue to offend, diversify

Canadian Journal of Criminology/Revue canadienne de criminologie, October/octobre 1998, pp. 421–446.

his or her offending behaviour, and be represented among the 5% to 10% of youth who become chronic offenders. For example, Frechette and LeBlanc (1987) found that boys who committed their first offence prior to age 12 to 13 years committed twice as many offences based on an annual rate of self-reported offending than those who started later. Osborn and West (1978) reported that 61% of those individuals who committed an offence prior to age 14 had a conviction before age 25, compared with 36% with an age of onset in their late teens. Similarly, Moffitt, Caspi, Dickson, Silva, and Stanton (1996) found that 43% of males in their New Zealand sample who had an age of onset for conduct problems during childhood (the "life-course persistent" group) had a court record by age 18 and 25% had been convicted for a violent offence. In contrast, 30% of males with an age of onset for conduct problems during adolescence (the "adolescent-limited" group) had a court record by age 18 and 8% had been convicted for a violent offence.

The early starter model

The early starter model of the development of delinquency and criminal behaviour provides a theoretical framework with which to account for these empirical findings (Loeber 1990; Moffitt 1993; Moffitt *et al.* 1996; Patterson, Capaldi, and Bank 1991; Snyder and Patterson 1987). According to Patterson *et al.* (1991), there are two unique and separate pathways through which delinquent behaviour may develop. The early starter trajectory, with an age of onset for antisocial behaviour problems in childhood, is characterized by high rates of aggressive and "coercive" family experiences. These experiences at home are thought to provide an early training ground for the kinds of aggressive and antisocial interactions with peers and other adults that place children on a developmental pathway towards a career as antisocial adolescents and adults. Moreover, children with an early age of onset for antisocial behaviours have been found to experience a large number of risk factors that disrupt many facets of their lives including their academic and social development (Kazdin 1987; Loeber 1990).

The late starters evince conduct problem behaviours in late childhood or early adolescence, at which time the deviant peer group, rather than the family, plays a greater role in the individual's involvement in delinquent activity (Patterson, DeBaryshe, and Ramsey 1989). The late starters are considered to be at lower risk for more serious and protracted criminal histories and experience fewer risk factors than early starters.

In summary, the theoretical and empirical research reviewed above highlights the role of age of onset as a risk factor for serious delinquent activity. This research gives rise to serious concerns about the developmental outcomes of children who experience an early age of onset for conduct problem behaviours, as these children appear to evince high levels of risk for a range of maladaptive outcomes, including contact with the justice system.

A difficulty in interpreting these findings, however, is that much of the research is based on samples that have been drawn from the general community rather than high risk children and youths who present with clinical levels of disturbance. Differences in the developmental outcomes of these samples may be expected given their range of risk factors and life experiences. For example, in reviewing studies on the effectiveness of clinical treatment programs, Weisz, Weiss, and Donenberg (1992) have shown that outcomes are generally more positive for nonreferred than referred children. Nonreferred children have lower levels of disturbance, experience problems affecting fewer aspects of their lives, and are not representative of clients seen in conventional clinical practice. While there is a need for longitudinal research on delinquency with samples from both the general community and clinical settings, the literature is marked by a dearth of follow-up studies using more seriously disturbed children and youth. This methodological shortcoming has implications for the generalizability of the criminal outcomes of children and youth who are at risk for juvenile delinquency to those who manifest the highest levels of risk, that is, those who present for treatment with serious conduct problem behaviours.

For example, Robins (1966) reported that 70% of 260 male patients referred for conduct disorder during their childhood had been arrested for at least one non-traffic crime and 44% had been arrested for a major crime in the United States. In contrast, the general consensus in the literature for at-risk, community-based samples suggests that between 20% and 45% of such adolescents will be arrested at least once by age 18 (Snyder and Patterson 1987; Wolfgang, Figlio, and Sellin 1972). Farrington and West (1981) reported that 20% of boys raised in a working class area of London, England were convicted as juveniles between their 10th and 17th birthdays and 30% were convicted up to age 21 (Farrington 1978). Patterson, Reid, and Dishion (1992) reported that 37% of their sample of boys from high crime neighborhoods in Oregon were arrested at least once by age 15. Indeed, prevalence rates reported in the extant literature may themselves be confounded by the level of clinical disturbance of their samples. Moffitt *et al.* (1996), for example, reported that the families of 55% of their life-course persistent group had sought treatment. Moreover, most of these studies are limited to examining outcomes for males to the exclusion of reporting outcome data for females at risk for juvenile delinquency.

The present study

The present study is a long-term follow-up of the court contact and criminal behaviour of a sample of high risk, clinic-referred youths. The youths were admitted, when they were between the ages of 6 and 12 years, into the Under 12 Outreach Project (ORP), a 12-week specialized treatment program for children under the age of 12 years who have had, or are at risk of having, police contact as a result of delinquency. The follow-up period for this study was 4 to 11 years from the time of their admission into the ORP. The objectives of the study were to determine the prevalence and incidence of court contacts among this high risk sample and identify the best set of predictors of an early age for a first court contact. Considerable research has shown that the factors that contribute to an early age of onset for criminal behaviour include family, peer, school, and personal difficulties. Indicators for nine risk factors addressing these areas were developed, based on data derived from the children's clinical files from their admission into the ORP. It was expected that each risk factor would have significant explanatory power in the predictive equation.

This study extends the previous research in three important respects. First, a clinical, rather than a community, sample of high risk youths was followed-up. Second, the results are presented using survival analysis to determine the probability of a youth having court contact by a given age. Third, the results are presented by sex to examine the risk for court contact for males and females, separately.

Method

Participants

The sample was derived from an initial pool of 292 children who were admitted between 1985 and 1992 into the ORP. The ORP is provided by Earlscourt Child and Family Centre, a children's mental health center in a large metropolitan Canadian city and is based on a behavioural-systems model of the development and treatment of aggression and antisocial behaviour. The program consisted of three components adapted from established interventions for children: (a) group problem-solving and self-control skills training, (b) group parent training and family counselling, and (c) individual befriending (i.e., "Big Brother/Sister" type of relationship).

The main admission criterion to the ORP was police contact within six months prior to the referral. Although the police have no legal recourse with children under the age of 12 years in Canada, according to the *Young Offenders Act* (YOA), referrals were made by special arrangement with the Youth Bureau of the Toronto Police Service. Children who had no police contact but were rated by their parents as within the clinical range on the Delinquent scale of the Child Behavior Checklist (CBCL) (Achenbach and Edelbrock 1983), indicating behaviour problems more serious than 98% of same age and sex peers, were also eligible for admission. Examples of items on this scale are "Destroys things belonging to his/her family," "Truancy, skips school," and "Vandalism." Exclusion criteria included over the age of 12 years at the time of referral, out of the Metropolitan Toronto catchment area, had developmental delays, and was already receiving intensive treatment (e.g., day treatment, residential care).

Of the initial pool of admissions, 203 met the study's criterion of eligibility, that is, 12 years of age or older as of December 31, 1992. There were 173 boys (85.2%) and 30 girls (14.8%) and their mean age at the time of admission was 9.9 years (*SD* = 1.3). As of October, 1996, the end of the follow-up period, the youth ranged in age from 15 to 22 years with a mean of 17.6 years (*SD* = 1.9).

As indicated in Table 1, the majority of the sample was referred to the program by the Toronto Police Service for a range of behaviours including stealing/theft, fighting, assault, arson, and vandalism. Moreover, given that police contact is typically a fortuitous or chance occurrence (Patterson *et al.* 1991), having police contact likely reflects the high rate of antisocial behaviour in which these children were engaging (Patterson *et al.* 1992; Dunford and Elliot 1984). Finally, many of the children were experiencing problems at school as 42% had repeated a grade and 40% were in a special class for behavioural problems or a learning disability.

With regard to the parents/household, as indicated in Table 1, 45.8% of the children were living in single-parent households. In 56.5% of the families, the responding parent (the mother in 85.3% of the households) had a grade school education and 63% of the families with 3 or more children under the age of 19 years living at home had an annual household income of $24,000 or less. Lastly, 83.7% of the families had contact with a social service agency before coming to the ORP and 50% had had contact with a child welfare agency.

Table 1
Characteristics of the sample

Variable	f[a]	%
Child variables		
Sex		
Boys	173/203	85.2%
Girls	30/203	14.8%
Had police contact	151/192	78.6%
Year of referral		
1985	3/203	1.5%
1986	41/203	20.2%
1987	37/203	18.2%
1988	37/203	18.2%
1989	32/203	15.8%
1990	19/203	9.4%
1991	27/203	13.3%
1992	7/203	3.4%
Referral source		
Police	123/194	63.4%
School	20/194	10.3%
Parent	12/194	6.2%
Social agency	21/194	10.8%
CAS	13/194	6.7%
Other	5/194	2.6%
Reason for referral		
Stealing/theft	95/195	48.7%
Assault	10/195	5.1%
Sexual assault	5/195	2.6%
Break & enter	10/195	5.1%
Running away	8/195	4.1%
Fighting	10/195	5.1%
Arson	12/195	6.2%
Truancy	2/195	1.0%
Vandalism	9/195	4.6%
Other	34/195	17.4%
Parent/Household variables		
Marital status		
Married	71/168	42.3%
Common-law	20/168	11.9%
Separated	27/168	16.1%
Widowed	5/168	3.0%
Divorced	22/168	13.1%
Single	23/168	13.7%
Language spoken at home		
English	160/195	82.1%
Portuguese	18/195	9.2%
Italian	2/195	1.0%

Vietnamese	3/195	1.5%
Other	12/195	6.2%
Highest level of education received by respondent		
Grade school	74/131	56.5%
High school	38/131	29.0%
College	15/131	11.5%
University	4/131	3.1%
Income level		
Less than $13,000	47/127	37.0%
$13,000-$24,000	37/127	29.1%
$24,000-$30,000	16/127	12.6%
$30,000-$40,000	8/127	6.3%
More than $40,000	19/127	15.0%
Source of income		
Wages and salary	89/144	61.8%
Unemployment insurance	2/144	1.4%
Government assistance	51/144	35.4%
Other	2/144	1.4%

Note: [a] Denominators differ because of missing data on some variables.

Measures and procedure

Predictor variables

Indicators for nine predictor variables were developed, based on data derived from the children's clinical files. Information, coded by a research assistant, was gathered from standardized clinical measures such as the CBCL (Achenbach and Edelbrock 1983) and TRF (Achenbach and Edelbrock 1986) and from demographic questionnaires and various school, agency, and clinical reports[(2)]. The nine predictors were: (a) family stressors, (b) history of child abuse, (c) peer problems, (d) delinquent peers, (e) school problems, (f) behavioural problems, (g) the age at the time of ORP admission, (h) the child's likeability rating at the time of admission, and (i) whether the reason for referral involved a violent or nonviolent behaviour.

Scales were developed as indicators for five of these predictor variables. The items comprising the scales and the scale properties are presented in Table 2. With the exception of the history of abuse scale, the scales were found to have adequate reliability. As well, while it was not possible to examine the validity of the scales in detail, they did meet the criterion for face validity.

The scales were created by summing relevant items derived from the clinical file. Except for the items that made up the likeability scale, the items comprising the scales were dichotomous in nature, i.e., 0-1. The likeability scale, derived from the Interviewer Impression Form (IIF), which was completed as part of the screening procedure for admission into the program, consisted of 12 items, rated on a 5-point scale by the ORP Children's Group Leader. Examples of items on this scale are, "This child was cooperative during the interview," "To what extent were you able to develop rapport with this child?," and "How much did you like this child as an individual?" A low score denoted less likeability. The history of abuse scale was based on official reports from a child welfare agency rather than parent-reported or self-reported incidents. The indicator for the variable, delinquent peers, was based on the response to one item in the codebook. The Delinquent scale of the CBCL was used to measure delinquent behaviour problems and the reason for referral was categorized for each child as either violent (e.g., sexual assault, assault, fighting) or nonviolent (e.g., stealing, break and enter, arson, vandalism).

Coder reliability. Inter-rater agreement between two coders was determined on a random sample of 18 files. Reliability was defined as the percentage of agreement between the two raters for each variable (Agreements ÷ Agreements + Disagreements x 100). Agreements for each variable ranged from 27.8% to 100%, with a mean agreement rate of 88.7% for all variables. Variables were dropped from the analyses that had a less than 70% agreement rate between the two coders and for which 50% or more of the data were missing. This procedure resulted in the loss of 12 variables for less than 70% agreement and 2 variables for missing data.

Follow-up court data

The court data were derived from records obtained from the Ministry of Community and Social Services (MCSS) for Phase

Table 2
Risk factor scales

Scale and items	N of items	M	SD	Coefficient Range	Alpha
Family stressors	11	2.2	1.9	0-8	.63
Financial problems					
Housing problems					
Problems with the law					
Alcohol problems					
Marital problems					
Health problems					
Parental depression					
Other psychiatric problems					
Drug abuse					
Family violence					
CAS contact					
School problems	7	3.6	2.1	0-7	.72
Academic problems					
Behavioral problems at school					
Type of class (regular/other)					
Repeated a grade					
Problems with teacher					
Disruptive in class					
Disruptive in the schoolyard					
Peer problems	2	.49	.71	0-2	.51
No or few positive friends					
Does not get along well with peers					
History of abuse	4	.31	.61	0-3	.32
Physical abuse					
Sexual abuse					
Emotional abuse					
Neglect					
Likeability scale	12	2.5	.72	1.3-4.5	.87
Cooperative					
Shy and withdrawn					
Positive attitude towards clinician					
Good social skills					
Antisocial attitude					
Easy to develop rapport					
Honest in responding to questions					
Comfortable with and not threatened by questions					
Attractive physical appearance					
Child seems satisfied with home life					
Child seems well-supervised by parents					
How much the clinician liked the child					

I young offenders (ages 12 to 15) and the Ministry of the Solicitor General and Correctional Services (MSGCS) for Phase II young offenders (ages 16 to 17) and adult offenders (over 17 years). The records were obtained over a three year period, beginning in May, 1993 and ending in October, 1996, and were gathered both retrospectively, for those youths who were entered into the ministries' database systems prior to 1993, and prospectively, over the course of the follow-up period.

It is important to note that the ministries' databases were developed to meet "operational" objectives, that is, to monitor individuals who come under their "supervision" within a ministry facility (e.g., jail or detention centre). As such, they were not established as criminal justice databases, although some of the data are derived from court records. The criteria for entering an individual into each database are such that they may also be used to monitor court appearances and related sentencing information (e.g., charges, dispositions, length of sentences). In this regard, the ministries' databases were used to monitor the study participants' court appearances, arising from the commission of a criminal offence or set of offences.

Moreover, individuals often have multiple court appearances arising from one set of charges. In the present study, one court contact was counted for each offender, for each court date that was set for a charge or set of charges for which a prior court date had not been set. In this way, the number of court contacts reflected repeated offending, that is, court contacts resulting from different sets of offences, rather than multiple court appearances arising from the same charge or set of charges.

Given the restricted nature of young offender records in Canada, according to the YOA, access to the follow-up data was obtained through a court order provided to this author, signed by a youth court judge. The court order consisted of a number of provisions designed to ensure the anonymity of the records and to restrict the use of the data. Steps were taken to ensure that the identifiable information in the records was kept privileged. This author was responsible for coding the data from the offender records.

For each offender, a range of information was coded from the offender record. The results are presented here for only some of the variables and included: (a) the total number of court contacts, (b) the total number of charges, (c) the age at the time of the first contact, (d) the seriousness rating for the most serious charge ever, and (e) the offender type (i.e., property, violent, other), based on *all* of the documented offences that the youth had ever committed, not just the most serious offence. The seriousness ratings were from the MSGCS's Statistical Reporting System User Manual (1995) and ranged from 1 to 20 where 1 = most serious and 20 = least serious.

Concerns about the use of official records versus self-report measures as an indicator of criminal activity and recidivism have been raised in the literature (e.g., Dunford and Elliot 1993). As Farrington (1987: 39) noted, "official records include the worst offenders and the worst offences. Self-reports have the advantage of including undetected offences, but the disadvantages of concealment and forgetting". Others have reported a high degree of concordance between self-report delinquency and official records (Moffitt *et al.* 1996). For example, Farrington, Ohlin, and Wilson (1986: 29) noted that "crimes that have been recorded are also reported by the subjects". It is acknowledged that criminal activity should ideally be measured by both methods. For the present study, official records provided an objective indicator of not only the rate of court contact, but the nature and severity of the offences as well.

Results

The results are organized in three sections. First, the findings for the follow-up data are presented in descriptive terms. Second, the results for the survival analysis are presented for males and females, separately. Survival analysis allows for the examination of the proportion of participants who have survived an event (i.e., not arrested) over the course of the follow up period. Survival analysis is concerned with addressing the question of "when," or the timing of an event, in this case "the juvenile's entrance into the justice system" (Luke 1993: 208), and not simply "whether" an event occurs by a particular point in time (Singer and Willett 1991). Third, the results of the Cox regression analyses are presented to identify the best set of risk factors for males and females that predicts age for a first court contact.

Rate of court contact and pattern of offending behaviour

The results indicated that 98 youths, or 48.3%, had at least one court contact during the follow-up period. Approximately half of the males (88/173) and one third of the females (10/30) had at least one court contact, a difference that was only marginally significant, x^2 (1, N = 203) = 3.1, p < .06, likely reflecting the high risk nature of the sample. The number of court contacts among the offenders ranged from 1 to 23 with a mean of 4.1 contacts per offender (SD = 4.5) and a mode of 1. The number of charges ranged from 1 to 65 with a mean of 10.0 charges per offender (SD = 12.7) and a mode of 2.

With regard to the frequency of their court contacts, 32.7% were first offenders, 37.8% had two to four court contacts, and 29.6% had five or more court contacts. There was no significant difference across the three categories by sex, x^2 (2, N = 98) = 2.5, p < ns.

Consistent with other studies, the group of chronic offenders was responsible for 69% of the court contacts (279/404) and 75% of the total charges incurred by the entire sample (641/856). As shown in Table 3, these offenders also had their first court contact at a significantly younger age, had a longer career length, and engaged in more serious offences than either first offenders or offenders who had two to four court contacts.

With regard to their pattern of offending, 49.4% were property offenders only (e.g., theft, vandalism), 13.8% were violent offenders only (e.g., robbery, assault, sexual assault), 33.3% were versatile offenders (i.e., engaging in both property and violent offences), and 3.4% committed other types of offences exclusively (e.g., trafficking, possession of drugs). There was no significant difference in offending type by sex, x^2 (2, N = 87) = .36, p < ns.

Table 3
One-way analyses of variance by offender type based on the frequency of court contacts

	1 contact		2-4 contacts		5 or more contacts		F (df)
	M	SD	M	SD	M	SD	
Age at first contact[1]	15.8_a	1.4	15.1_a	1.5	13.8_b	1.6	12.5 (2,95)
Career length in years	0.0_a	.2	1.6_b	1.3	3.6_c	1.8	58.9 (2,95)
Seriousness rating[2]	7.6_a	3.8	7.0_a	3.7	4.1_b	2.6	8.3 (2,84)

Note: 1) In years.
2) Lower values denote more serious offences. Seriousness ratings are for the most serious offence ever committed.
3) All values in rows with different subscripts are significantly different at the .05 level. By post-hoc Scheffe tests of means.
4) All F values are significant at the .001 level.

Survival analysis

Although 49% of the sample went on to have at least one court contact at some point during the follow-up period, it is also important to examine the cumulative rate of survival, or, conversely, the rate of court contacts (the "target event") over the "risk period" (between the ages of 12 and 22 years). The "survival time" for this study was the number of years from turning 12 years of age to the age of the first court contact.

Moreover, 53.7% of the youths remained under the age of 18 years for the duration of the follow-up period, and so were still eligible for youth court contact at the end of this study. Survival analysis allows for the examination of the rate of court contact for those youths who were 18 years or older. Ideally, the present study would continue to follow-up the sample for three more years, when they all will turn 18 years or older. Follow-up periods, such as they are, however, are sometimes arbitrarily determined or based on circumstances beyond the control of the researcher (Singer and Willett 1991). To be sure, longer follow-up times provide more complete information on the "censored" cases, that is, those cases that have not had an event during the follow-up period, and so provide better data. At the same time, "longer data collection periods have their own disadvantages, including higher costs and increased attrition" (Singer and Willett 1991: 273).

The survival functions for males and females are presented in Figure 1. The results indicated that males were at higher risk of having court contact (less likely to survive) during the follow-up period than females. The probability that a randomly selected male would "survive" to age 18 was 34.3%. Conversely, a male had a 65.7% chance of having a court contact by the time he turned 18 years of age. The probability that a female would survive to age 18 was 62.1%. Conversely, a female had a 37.9% chance of having a court contact by the time she turned 18 years of age. A log-rank test indicated that these survival functions were not significantly different, x^2 (1, N = 203) = 3.4, $p < .08$. Given the magnitude of the difference between males and females, this nonsignificant effect may have been due to the relatively small number of females in the sample, and the corresponding lack of power to detect a difference when one exists. At the same time, the results may also reflect the high risk nature of the sample and suggests that contact with the justice system represents a potential long-term outcome for both seriously disturbed boys and girls. The median survival time, which is the age at which half of the sample had had court contact, was, for males and females, respectively, 5.4 years, or about age 15, and 10+ years, or age 22+.

Figure 2 displays the hazard rate by sex, or conditional probability that a youth will have a court contact at a given age, given that he or she has not had court contact by the

Figure 1
Survival functions for males and females

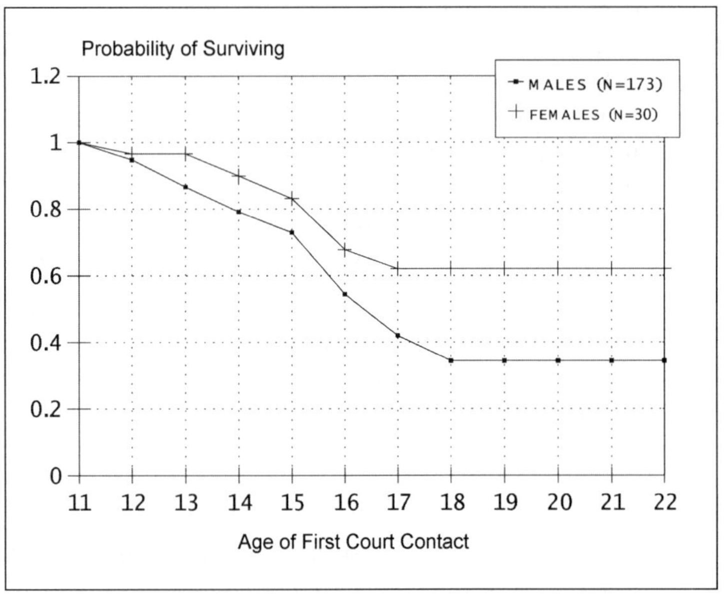

Figure 2
Hazard rates for males and females

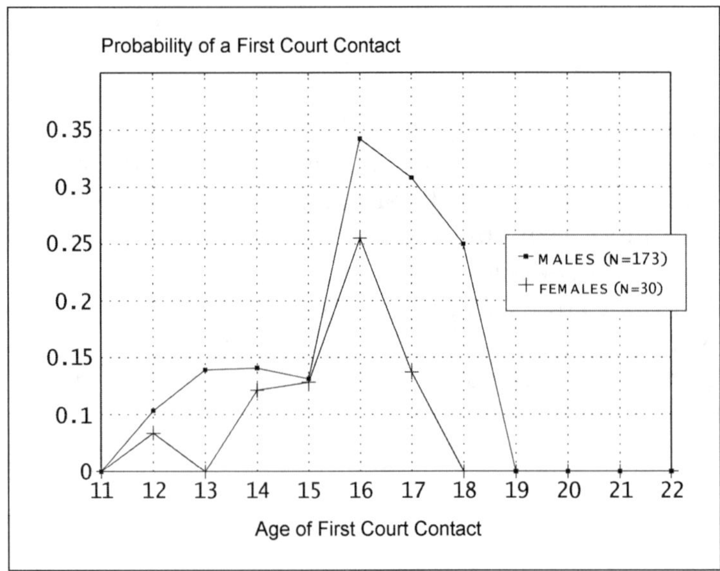

beginning of the interval. "[W]hereas the estimated survival rate tells us how many people have survived up to some time point, the estimated hazard rate tells us the event rate for any particular person within a specific time interval, assuming they have survived to that time interval" (Luke 1993: 220).

As shown in Figure 2, there was no difference in the peak age period by sex. Age 16 years represents the age at which the largest percentage of both males and females in this sample had their first court contact, representing the age of greatest risk. However, the steeper incline for males between the ages of 12 and 15 years indicated that they were "quicker off the mark" than females to enter the juvenile justice system.

Predicting an early age for a first court contact

Separate Cox regression models were estimated for males and females to examine the relation between the predictor variables and survival time, that is, time to first court contact (i.e., the hazard function). Cox regression, also called Cox proportional hazards models, tests the degree to which the set of predictors affects the hazard rate. In the present models, the nine predictor variables were entered in a forward stepwise order to maximize the probability of the Wald statistic.

The results of the Cox regression analysis for males indicated that only the likeability scale entered the equation (B = -.53, $p < .04$, Odds Ratio = .59), yielding a statistically significant model, $x^2(1, N = 105) = 4.5$, $p < .03$. Males with a lower likeability score had a higher hazard rate, resulting in a quicker time to first court contact than males with a higher likeability score.

The results for females indicated that a history of abuse was the only variable that entered the equation (B = 2.1, $p < .04$, Odds Ratio = 8.33), yielding a statistically significant model, $x^2(1, N = 21) = 6.1$, $p < .01$. Females who had experienced more abuse, either physical or sexual, had a higher hazard rate, resulting in a quicker time to first court contact, than females who had experienced less abuse.

Discussion

The aim of this study was to follow-up the court contact and offending behaviour of a clinical sample of high risk youths whose antisocial behaviour began before age 12 years. The results indicated that 48.3% of the sample had had court contact by the end of the follow-up period. To put this figure into perspective, the rate was: (a) substantially higher than the 5.3% that was reported for the general population of adolescents, aged 12 to 17 years, in Ontario who were seen in youth court in 1996/97 (Canadian Centre for Justice Statistics 1998); (b) slightly higher than the 20% to 45% rates that are often reported for at-risk, community-based samples (Snyder and Patterson 1987; Wolfgang, Figlio, and Sellin 1972); and (c) lower than the 70% rate reported by Robins (1966) for her clinical sample. In this regard, the prevalence of court contact for this clinical sample may be considered low. This may be due either to the fact that the youth had been in a treatment program for children with conduct problem behaviours or that the follow-up period was too short to detect all of the offenders, as about half of the sample was under 16 years of age, the peak age for court contacts.

Moreover, survival analyses indicated that the risk for court contact by age 18 was 65.7% and 37.9% for males and females, respectively. These findings suggest that there is a high likelihood that the developmental outcomes for a large number of children with conduct problem behaviours, particularly boys, who are seen at children's mental health centers will involve contact with the justice system.

It is of interest to note that, although the rate of court contact in the present study was substantially higher than the rate of court contact for adolescents, in general, the peak age for a first court contact did not differ from the peak age at which youth have court contact (although not necessarily for their *first* court contact). According to Snyder and Patterson (1987), Tolan (1988), and Wolfgang *et al.* (1972), the peak age for a youth to be arrested is 15 to 17 years. This is consistent with the age range at which the number of juveniles who appeared in youth court in Ontario in 1996-1997 peaked, before dropping off (Canadian Centre for Justice Statistics 1998). Moreover, for many of these Ontario youths, this age likely corresponds to the age of their first court contact. For the present sample, 27.6% of the youths had their first court contact at the age of 16.

At the same time, 24.5% of the present sample had their first court contact at either 12 or 13 years of age. This figure was nearly twice as high as reported for the general population of offenders in Ontario in 1996/97. During this period, 12- and 13-year-old adolescents accounted for 12.7% of the total number of offenders who appeared before youth courts (Canadian Centre for Justice Statistics 1998). This finding is particularly disconcerting as the probability of a second arrest given the first is .54; the likelihood of a third arrest given the second is .65 and a fourth given the third is .72 (Wolfgang *et al.* 1972). The high rate of court contact at an early age is also consistent with Moffitt *et al.* (1996) who reported significantly higher rates of self-reported delinquency between the high risk, early onset youth and the low risk, adolescent-onset youth at ages 13 and 15 years, but not age 18.

Finally, Cox regression analyses were performed to identify the best set of variables, based on information derived from the children's clinical files, that predicts an early age of first court contact. The results indicated that the clinician's rating of the child's likeability was a significant predictor for males. This finding is consistent with previous studies of adults' ratings of the likeability of children in relation to treatment outcomes (e.g. Cowen, Lorion, and Wilson 1976; Gesten, Cowen, and Wilson 1979).

To account for the relationship between the boys' likeability rating and subsequent court contacts, it is hypothesized that the likeability rating is related to the youth's demeanor, a factor that has been identified in the literature as influencing police officers' decisions when dealing with offenders. As Worden, Sheppard, and Mastrofski (1996: 324) noted, "[o]ne of the most consistently replicated and widely accepted findings about police behaviour is that police tend to sanction suspects who display a disrespectful demeanor toward the police", characterized by acts of overt hostility, resistance, and noncompliance. Rutter and Giller (1984: 21) reported that, in a study of 47 cases, "an unfavourable attitude by the juvenile when interviewed was associated with an increased likelihood of being taken to court rather than cautioned".

An assumption of this hypothesis is that the rate of actual (versus official) delinquency was equivalent across the entire sample, such that the determination of charging (i.e., resulting in court contact) or not charging (i.e., cautioning) was, in part, based on the police officer's (and, indeed, other members' of the youth justice system) perception of the offender's personal characteristics. This assumes that the prevalence rate of delinquent behaviour among this entire sample was higher than that reflected in their rate of court contact. Indeed, Sparks, Genn, and Dodd (1997) observed that official records constitute only about one tenth of self-reported offences. Unfortunately, the lack of self-report delinquency data in this study precludes empirically testing this assumption. It would be important in future research to examine the predictive power of the likeability characteristic on court contact status, controlling for the rate of self-reported delinquency.

The finding of the predictive relationship between likeability and an early age for a first court contact also highlights a methodological issue concerning the use of court records as an outcome indicator of criminal activity. Court contact is mediated by a variety of factors including the age of the offender, prior arrest history, severity of offending behaviour, and so forth. An additional set of factors that comes into play in influencing a police officer's decision about how to deal with a young offender concerns the offender's demeanor, factors that, for the arresting officer, are more personal-based than policy-based. Research that uses court contact as an outcome measure should take into account these mediating variables that affect court contact status.

In a similar vein, Hoge, Andrews, and Leschied (1995) reported that extralegal factors, such as the juvenile offender's antisocial attitudes, may be implicated in court decisions about referrals to open custody facilities. They found that young offenders who had less serious offence convictions, but who presented with criminal and antisocial attitudes and values, were subjected to more serious dispositions than young offenders who displayed more prosocial attitudes. It would be of interest to examine the likeability rating of the present study in relation to the youths' dispositions. It would be expected that, as Hoge *et al.* found, demeanor would play a role in decisions made about the young offender, beyond the context of police contact and well into the justice system.

The model for females revealed that a history of abuse was the single best predictor of early first court contact. This finding is consistent with a large number of studies that have demonstrated a relationship between a history of abuse and a range of negative outcomes for females, including high rates of delinquency. A number of theories have been developed to account for this finding. In reviewing the empirical and theoretical research, Robinson (1994), for example, focused on four aspects of abuse that may lead to delinquency: (a) girls' sense of a betrayal of trust by the perpetrator and other adults and persons of authority, (b) self-blame and guilt as a result of self-stigmatization, (c) survival by running away and committing crimes of survival, and (d) their struggles with powerlessness. The results pertaining to females must be interpreted with caution given the relatively small sample size and the small number who had had court contact.

Lastly, the lack of predictive effects for most of the risk variables was surprising. Perhaps, as suggested by Visher, Lattimore, and Linster (1991), variables that predict early delinquency are less useful in predicting continued criminal behaviour. In keeping with this notion, it is hypothesized that the family, school, and peer variables were not *directly* related to continued criminal behaviour, but were *indirectly* related through their association with either the likeability rating, for males, or child abuse, for females. This hypothesis is consistent with developmental models of delinquency that are conceptualized as path models (e.g., Patterson *et al.* 1989), where the effect of early risk factors such as family problems (exogenous variable) are related to the development of subsequent risk factors such as school and peer problems (endogenous variables), which themselves lead to delinquency (endogenous variable). To be sure, the results of the present study need to be replicated with another sample.

Study limitations

A number of limitations of the study need to be addressed. First, due to budgetary constraints, it was not possible to account for the censored cases in terms of the reasons for which they did not have court contact. It may have been that, due to various circumstances, they were not in a position to have had court contact that would have been detected for this study. Some of these youths may have moved out of the province (and may have had court contact elsewhere) or they may be deceased. Without accurate data to account for these cases, it was not possible to determine how much of an effect these youths have had on the results. Either way, the effect would be to underestimate the observed prevalence rates.

Second, the rate of court contact among these youths may have been affected by various factors of the justice system. For example, receiving a harsh disposition such as incarceration in a secure custody facility, as a result of committing more serious offences or having a longer criminal record or an antisocial attitude, would have led to fewer opportunities for further court contact. Further research on court contacts should attempt to account for the effects due to the nature and duration of the dispositions received.

Third, the results concerning the type of offender and seriousness of the offences were affected by differences in the nature of the data received from the two ministries, due to differences in their respective computerized databases. Information received from the MSGCS for Phase II and adult offenders was very detailed and included charges for which the individual was sentenced, as well as expired remand charges. Information received from the MCSS for Phase I offenders was less comprehensive and was generally provided in summary form, that is, dispositions received and the corresponding charges. Therefore, in terms of both counting the total number of charges for each youth and classifying the offenders by offender type, more data were provided for Phase II and adult offenders than for Phase I offenders. The findings pertaining to these outcome data should be interpreted with this caveat in mind.

Finally, the variables used to develop the predictive models were risk factors. This study was not able to include variables that would be considered protective factors to identify those characteristics that contribute to desisting from further antisocial behaviour. Although a large number of youths in the sample had court contact, many did not. As well, not all of these youths were chronic offenders, although they all had an early age of onset for antisocial behaviour. Further research should examine the protective variables that allow high risk children to remain outside of the justice system or to have only limited involvement.

Conclusion

In conclusion, the high risk for court contact among the present sample points to the need, in an effort towards crime prevention, for effective early identification and intervention programs for certain children and their families. As Crittenden (1995: 391) stated, "developmental pathways... are best conceptualized as pathways with changing probabilities of outcome rather than fixed continuities or specific outcomes". As such, they are open to influence and change. Practitioners need to work with children who may be difficult to manage, who get into trouble a great deal at home, in school, or in the community, or who "turn others off" with their antisocial attitude and posturing, as these distressed children have a high likelihood of becoming juvenile offenders. Investing in high-quality, evidence-based, multifaceted services today will yield tremendous personal and financial gains in the future.

Notes

1. This study was conducted while the author was at Earlscourt Child and Family Centre and was supported with a grant from the Trillium Foundation. I wish to thank Leena Hrynkiw-Augimeri, Laryssa Tyson, Jennifer MacLeod, Ann Hunt, and Alex Minevich for their assistance with this research. I am also grateful to his Honour Judge James P. Felstiner, Jan Perfect of the Ministry of the Solicitor General and Correctional Services and Mark Trumpour and Brendan Stacey of the Ministry of Community and Social Services. Requests for reprints should be addressed to Dr. David M. Day, Hincks-Dellcrest Centre, 1645 Sheppard Avenue West, Toronto, Ontario, M3M 2X4, email day@scar.utoronto.ca
2. A copy of the codebook and dictionary is available from the author.

References

Achenbach, Thomas M. and Craig S. Edelbrock
1983 Manual for the Child Behavior Checklist and Revised Behaviour Profile. Burlington, VT: University Associates in Psychiatry.

Achenbach, Thomas M. and Craig S. Edelbrock
1986 Manual for the Teacher's Report Form and Teacher's Version of the Child Behavior Checklist. Burlington, VT: University Associates in Psychiatry.

Canadian Centre for Justice Statistics
1998 Youth. Court Statistics: 1996-1997. Ottawa, Ontario: Statistics Canada.

Cowen, Emory L., Raymond P. Lorion, and Alice B. Wilson
1976 Knowing, liking, and judged problem severity in relation to referral and outcome measures in a school-based intervention program. Journal of Consulting and Clinical Psychology 44: 317-329.

Crittenden, Patricia M.
1995 Attachment and psychopathology. In Susan Goldberg, Roy Muir, and John Kerr (eds.), Attachment Theory: Social, Developmental, and Clinical Perspectives. Hillsdale NJ: The Analytic Press.

Dunford, Franklyn W. and Delbert S. Elliott
1984 Identifying career offenders with self-reported data. Journal of Research in Crime and Delinquency 21: 57-86.

Farrington, David P.
1978 The family backgrounds of aggressive youths. In Lionel A. Hersov, Michael Berger, and David Shaffer (eds.), Aggression and Antisocial Behavior in Children and Adolescence. New York: Pergamon.

Farrington, David P.
1987 Early precursors of frequent offending. In James Q. Wilson and Glenn C. Loury (eds.), From Children to Citizens: Families,

Schools, and Delinquency Prevention. New York: Springer-Verlag.

Farrington, David P., Rolf Loeber, Delbert S. Elliott, J. David Hawkins, Denise B. Kandel, Malcolm W. Klein, Joan McCord, David C. Rowe, and Richard E. Tremblay
1990 Advancing knowledge about the onset of delinquency and crime. In Benjamin B. Lahey and Alan E. Kazdin (eds.), Advances in Clinical Child Psychology. New York: Plenum.

Farrington, David P., Lloyd Ohlin, and James Q. Wilson
1986 Understanding and Controlling Crime: Toward a New Research Strategy. New York: Springer-Verlag.

Farrington, David P. and David J. West
1981 The Cambridge study in delinquent development. In Samuel A. Mednick and Andre E. Baert (eds.), Prospective Longitudinal Research. Oxford: Oxford Press.

Fréchette, Marcel and Marc LeBlanc
1987 Délinquances et Délinquants. Chicoutimi, Québec: Gaétan Morin.

Gesten, Ellis L., Emory L. Cowen, and Alice B. Wilson
1979 Competence and its correlates in young normal and referred school children. American Journal of Community Psychology 7: 305-313.

Hoge, Robert D., Don A. Andrews, and Alan W. Leschied
1995 Investigation of variables associated with probation and custody dispositions in a sample of juveniles. Journal of Clinical Child Psychology 24: 279-286.

Kazdin, Alan E.
1987 Treatment of antisocial behavior in children: Current status and future directions. Psychological Bulletin 102: 187-203.

Loeber, Rolf
1990 Development and risk factors of juvenile antisocial behavior and delinquency. Clinical Psychology Review 10: 1-41.

Loeber, Rolf and Thomas Dishion
1983 Early predictors of male delinquency: A review. Psychological Bulletin 94: 68- 99.

Luke, Douglas A.
1993 Charting the process of change: A primer on survival analysis. American Journal of Community Psychology 21: 203-246.

Ministry of the Solicitor General and Correctional Services
1995 Statistical Reporting System User Manual. North Bay, Ontario: Statistical Services, Correctional Services Division.

Moffitt, Terrie E.
1993 "Life-course persistent" and "adolescent-limited" antisocial behavior: A developmental taxonomy. Psychological Review 100: 674-701.

Moffitt, Terrie E., Avshalom Caspi, Nigel Dickson, Phil Silva, and Warren Stanton
1996 Childhood-onset versus adolescent-onset antisocial conduct problems in males: Natural history from ages 3 to 18 years. Development and Psychopathology 8: 339-424.

Osborn, S.G. and David J. West
1978 The effectiveness of various predictors of criminal careers. Journal of Adolescence 1: 101-117.

Patterson, Gerald R., Deborah Capaldi, and Lew Bank
1991 An early starter model for predicting delinquency. In Debra J. Pepler and Ken H. Rubin (eds.), Development and Treatment of Childhood Aggression. Hillsdale, NJ: Earlbaum

Patterson, Gerald R., Barbara D. DeBaryshe, and Elizabeth Ramsey
1989 A developmental perspective on antisocial behavior. American Psychologist 44: 329-335.

Patterson, Gerald R., John B. Reid, and Thomas J. Dishion
1992 Antisocial Boys. Eugene, OR: Castalia.

Robins, Lee N.
1966 Deviant Children Grow Up. Baltimore: Williams and Wilkins.

Robinson, Robin A.
1994 Private pain and public behaviors: Sexual abuse and delinquent girls. In Catherine K. Riessman (ed.), Qualitative Studies in Sociological Research. Newbury Hill, CA: Sage.

Rutter, Michael and Henri Giller
1984 Juvenile Delinquency: Trends and Perspectives. New York: Guilford Press.

Singer, Judith D. and John B. Willett
1991 Modeling the days of our lives: Using survival analysis when designing and analyzing longitudinal studies of duration and the timing of events. Psychological Bulletin 110: 268-290.

Snyder, James and Gerald R. Patterson
1987 Family interaction and delinquent behavior. In Herbert C. Quay (ed.), Handbook of Juvenile Delinquency. New York: Wiley.

Sparks, Richard F., Hazel G. Genn, and David J. Dodd
1977 Surveying Victims. Chichester: Wiley.

Tolan, Patrick H.
1988 Delinquent behaviors and male adolescent development: A preliminary study. Journal of Youth and Adolescence 17: 413-427.

Visher, Christy A., Pamela K. Lattimore, and Richard L. Linster
1991 Predicting the recidivism of serious youthful offenders using survival models. Criminology 29: 329-366.

Weisz, John R., Bahr Weiss, and Geri R. Donenberg
1992 The lab versus the clinic: Effects of child and adolescent psychotherapy. American Psychologist 47: 1578-1585.

Wierson, Michelle, Rex L. Forehand, and Cynthia L. Frame
1992 Epidemiology and treatment of mental health problems in juvenile delinquents. Advances in Behavior Research and Therapy 14: 93-120.

Wolfgang, Marvin E., Robert M. Figlio, and Thorsten Sellin
1972 Delinquency in a Birth Cohort. Chicago, IL: University of Chicago Press.

Worden, Robert E., Robin L. Shepard, and Stephen D. Mastrofski
1996 On the meaning and measurement of suspects' demeanor toward the police: A comment on "demeanor and arrest." Journal of Research in Crime and Delinquency 33: 324-332.

CHAPTER TWENTY-SIX

Get tough or get smart? Options for Canada's youth justice system in the twenty-first century

John H. Hylton
Associate Editor
Canadian Journal of Criminology
and Executive Director,
Canadian Mental Health Association
Regina, Saskatchewan

THIS ISSUE OF THE CANADIAN *JOURNAL OF CRIMINOLOGY IS* DEVOTED to a review of Canada's Young *Offenders Act* (YOA). There are several reasons for dedicating an entire issue to an analysis of the YOA:

- Without a doubt, the YOA represents one of the most significant pieces of social policy legislation enacted in Canada during this generation, perhaps this century;
- While many articles about youth justice have appeared in the Journal over the years, 1994 marks the tenth anniversary of the YOA. Therefore, the Journal's editors felt a thorough evaluation of the Act was due; and
- As this issue of the Journal goes to press, sweeping reforms to address a number of controversial provisions of the YOA are under consideration. Since one of the important objectives of the Journal is to bring high quality research and analyses to bear on key justice policy and practice issues, a special issue on the YOA seemed particularly timely.

Canadian Journal of Criminology/Revue canadienne de criminologie, July/juillet, pp. 229-246.

While it is beyond the scope of any special issue of the Journal to provide comprehensive coverage of all the important questions pertaining to a given topic, the Journal does see thematic issues as an opportunity to provide broad and balanced coverage on important concerns of the day. In this case, we were fortunate to receive articles addressing many of the most factious aspects of the Act from leading Canadian experts - scholars, policy analysts, and practitioners.

As always, we invite the comments of our readers.

How did we get here?

The articles in this special issue focus on contemporary problems arising from the YOA, and the way it has been implemented. By way of introduction, however, it is useful to trace briefly some of the history leading up to the adoption of this legislation.

Canada's system of youth justice dates from the mid-1800's. Prior to this time there was very little by way of an organized justice system in Canada. During this period, however, a more formal system began to emerge.

There is little evidence that law or practice differentiated among offenders on the basis of age during this period, except for very young children. Rather, offenders were usually subjected to the same laws, the same adjudication processes, and the same punishments, whether adults or youth.

The historical record is replete with references to young people being housed in correctional facilities with adult criminals. In addition, like adults, it appears many young offenders were subjected to all manner of corporal and capital punishment for offences that would be considered minor by today's standards (Griffiths and Verdun-Jones 1994).

Beginning in the mid-1800's, specific legislation for young offenders began to emerge. For example, *An Act for the Establishment of Prisons for Young Offenders* was passed in 1857. It provided for two reformatories for young offenders to be built in Upper and Lower Canada. In this same year, *An Act for the*

Speedy Trial and Punishment of Young Offenders was passed to institute bail provisions and reduce pre-trial detention. Later in the 1800's, a number of provinces, particularly Ontario, developed specific legislation and programs to deal with youth in conflict with the law. In 1867, the *British North America Act* imposed a certain order on criminal justice and child welfare matters by clarifying the respective responsibilities of federal and provincial governments.

The *Juvenile Delinquents Act* (JDA), adopted in 1908, was the first comprehensive juvenile justice legislation in Canada. The main features of the Act included:

- The establishment of a separate youth justice system, complete with courts, probation services, and reformatories;
- Provisions for hearings that were closed to the public;
- Provisions requiring that parents be notified about proceedings under the Act; and
- Requirements that juvenile delinquents be held separate from adults.

The JDA provided for one all-encompassing offence of "delinquency". A person found to have violated federal, provincial, or municipal laws was guilty of a "delinquency". Even those who were truant from school, or who exhibited "sexual immorality or any similar form of vice", could be subjected to the provisions of the Act.

The JDA did not distinguish between neglected and delinquent youth, but, rather, adopted a child welfare approach to youth crime. It required the youth justice system to priorize the needs of young persons above other considerations. Instead of focusing on punishment, or the protection of society, the "parens patriae" philosophy of the Act required the state to act as a benevolent parent (Caputo and Goldenberg 1986). This philosophy was explicitly set out in the Act itself:

> This Act shall be liberally construed in order that its purposes may be carried out, namely, that the care and

> custody of a juvenile delinquent shall approximate as nearly as may be that which should be given by his parents, and that as far as practicable every juvenile delinquent shall be treated not as a criminal, but as a misdirected child, and one needing aid, encouragement, help, and assistance.

The events leading up to passage of the JDA are the subject of varying interpretations. Some have suggested that the development of a youth justice system must be understood in the context of the emergence of capitalism in late 19th century Canadian society. These analysts contend that capitalism disrupted traditional social support systems, including the family, and resulted in the marginalization of youth. In turn, this resulted in higher levels of youth crime and heightened community pressure to "do something" about the problem (Alvi 1986; West 1984; Platt 1969).

Others have suggested the adoption of the JDA was part of a much broader trend to extend social support services to troubled youth and families around the turn of the century. These analysts point out that while growing youth crime was widely perceived to be a problem, so too were the conditions faced by youth in the justice system (e.g., harsh penalties, and the incarceration of young people with "hardened" adult criminals). Since these problems were believed to be correctable through state intervention, reformers pushed the state to develop a separate justice system that would intervene in the lives of troubled youth and families to provide needed services (Griffiths and Verdun-Jones 1994).

Whatever the origins of the JDA, it is remarkable that such significant public policy legislation remained in effect, virtually unchanged, for nearly 75 years. The longevity of the Act can be attributed to the widespread public, political, and stakeholder support that it enjoyed up until the 1960's.

Concerted attempts to reform the JDA began with the 1965 report of the Federal Committee on Juvenile Delinquency in Canada. This was followed by a rapid succession of controversial legislative proposals in 1967, 1970, 1975, 1977.

Most notable among these was a proposed Act Respecting Young Offenders and to Repeal the Juvenile Delinquents Act in 1970, and "Young Persons In Conflict With The Law" proposals circulated in 1975. The YOA was first introduced in 1977, although it was remodelled several times before finally being adopted in 1982.

The criticisms of the JDA were many, and some were damning. Critics claimed:

- The "parens patriae" philosophy of the Act placed too much emphasis on the needs of young persons, and not enough on society's right to be protected from crime; the child welfare approach also did not properly recognize the importance of punishment in the deterrence of criminal behaviour;
- Although called for in the JDA, treatment services were not always available in many areas of the country, and even when available, they were not necessarily effective in reducing recidivism;
- By failing to punish or treat young offenders, they were neither deterred nor rehabilitated. Therefore, the JDA actually contributed to an escalating crime problem among youth;
- The child welfare philosophy of the JDA resulted in inadequate sentencing options being made available to the courts. A frequently cited example was the twenty-five dollar maximum fine available under the JDA;
- The JDA allowed different provinces to adopt vastly different approaches to implementation. Therefore, there was little uniformity across the country. Perhaps the most widely cited example was the differences among provinces respecting the age limits for applying the Act;[1]
- The JDA failed to provide due process rights. Most hearings were informal, and they did not adhere to the usual rules of evidence that, for example, would normally prohibit the admissibility of hearsay

evidence. In addition, accused were not always allowed to cross-examine witnesses, or even be present at hearings affecting them. Furthermore, there was no assurance of legal representation. And the JDA provided only limited rights to have decisions reviewed or appealed;

- The all encompassing offence of "delinquency" was widely criticized for a number of reasons. By lumping all offences into one category, critics claimed there was a failure to distinguish between serious criminal offences and other matters that were not crimes at all.[2] Often, little or no relationship could be detected between the seriousness of the offence and the disposition of the court. Moreover, critics claimed that by classifying all offences as delinquencies, the accountability of youths for their acts was diminished; and
- Once matters were dealt with by the courts, the social welfare administrators had far too much discretion to affect the lives of youth, and they were insufficiently accountable to the courts or society for the exercise of this discretion. The system effectively provided child welfare authorities with a form of indeterminate sentencing.

As one observer remarked (West 1984: 33):

> The vagueness of this legislation, its lack of due process, the inclusion of a wide range of status offenses (for example, truancy), and wide dispositional powers left the treatment of juveniles open to administrative arbitrariness, and subsequently allowed much of its humanitarian potential to be undermined in its implementation.

Three important influences contributed to (or at least justified) the end of the JDA epoch:

- A new era of "rights" was ushered in by the *Canadian Charter of Rights and Freedoms*. The JDA was incapable of meeting some of the standards embodied in the Charter;

- Public and political attitudes about crime, and about youth, evolved in directions that were antithetical to the key underlying principles of the JDA. In particular, critics believed the JDA was incapable of addressing the punishment, deterrence, youth accountability, and societal protection responsibilities of a modern youth justice system;
- Proponents of the JDA, and others who wanted to retain a treatment focus, were effectively neutralized — by evidence of abuse in institutional treatment settings, by dramatic examples illustrating the consequences of failing to extend due process rights, and by numerous illustrations showing the evils of unchecked discretion by social welfare authorities. In addition, in the then emerging tide of nihilism in the correctional rehabilitation field known as the "nothing works" philosophy (Martinson 1974), proponents were unable to satisfy critics that treatment was efficacious.

Although the JDA might have survived a while longer, perhaps with some amendment, its demise was more or less assured by the adoption in 1982 of the *Canadian Charter of Rights and Freedoms.* It was no mere coincidence that the YOA was adopted in the same year as the Charter. Because of the absence of due process rights in the JDA, and a number of other deficiencies, it was widely believed the Act could not withstand a Charter challenge, and would be struck down by the courts. Of particular concern was the difficulty reconciling Charter guarantees for "equality before the law" with JDA provisions that allowed youth of different ages to be treated differently from province to province.

A "New Deal" for young offenders?

After nearly twenty years in the making, a new *Young Offenders Act* was finally passed by Parliament in 1982 with the unanimous support of the Liberal, Progressive

Conservative, and New Democratic Parties. The Act was proclaimed in April 1984, although provinces were given an additional year to prepare for the new uniform age provisions.

The most important provision of the YOA may be briefly summarized as follows:[3]

- A system of separate and specialized youth courts and correctional programs is maintained;
- A statement of principles setting out the philosophy of the Act is provided. In sentencing decisions, and in decisions to transfer young offenders to adult court, youth courts are required to balance the needs of young offenders with youth accountability, and public protection;
- All provinces are required to comply with a uniform age range (from 12 to 17 years) for determining the application of the Act;
- Those under twelve are not to be dealt with by the criminal justice system, but, rather, by child welfare authorities according to provincial child welfare legislation;
- Unlike the JDA, the YOA is clearly criminal law. It only addresses violations of federal criminal law statutes, not provincial, municipal, or status offences;
- Young offenders, like adult offenders, are now charged with a specific offence, not a delinquency, and the standards of proof are the same as in adult courts;
- A wide array of sentencing options, from closed and open custody to probation, compensation, restitution, community service, and many other programs, are made available to the court;
- The authority of child welfare authorities in the administration of sentences is significantly diminished. Instead, most decisions are now made by the youth court;
- Extensive new due process rights (for example, rights to counsel, rights to participate in hearings, rights to have dispositions reviewed, etc.) are provided for; and

- A detailed legal and administrative structure, covering such matters as the appointment of officials, the designation of programs and facilities, pre-trial procedures, alternative measures, dispositional reviews, and the creation and use of records is prescribed by the Act.

Despite a twenty-year gestation period, however, the YOA was controversial from the beginning, and it has remained so. Initial criticisms focused on the new philosophy embodied in the Act. On the one hand, the punishment and deterrence advocates, including the law enforcement community, claimed the Act was "too soft" because it required some attention be paid to the needs of offenders, offered the option of treatment, and failed to arrest rising rates of youth crime. The rehabilitation advocates, on the other hand, pointed to skyrocketing custody rates following the implementation of the Act, and pointed out that there was often a failure to provide needed treatment services. For them the Act was "too hard". These would prove to be recurrent themes.

But there were other criticisms. Provinces complained the federal government was not providing the necessary financial resources to effectively implement the Act. Provinces were criticized for failing to implement some of the Act's more progressive provisions. Many involved on the front lines of service delivery found the Act complex and cumbersome to administer.

Two rounds of amendments to the YOA were introduced in 1986 and 1992. Although many technical modifications were introduced in both rounds, a number of substantive amendments were also introduced. In 1986, these included:

- A new provision allowing for pre-trial placements to be made with a responsible adult. This was introduced in order to deal with a perceived over-reliance on pre-trial detention;
- Failure to comply with a disposition of the youth court became a new and separately punishable offence. The

three year maximum sentence was extended in the case of youths who committed a subsequent offence while still under sentence for a previous offence;

- To deal with public concerns about being adequately protected, new provisions were included to allow for the publication of identifying information about dangerous young offenders who were at large; and
- The *Criminal Code* was amended to strengthen provisions prohibiting adults from counselling young people to commit criminal acts.

In 1992, substantive amendments included:

- Increasing the maximum disposition for first or second degree murder from three to five years;
- In order to encourage transfers to adult court in certain instances, new provisions were introduced to shorten the length of time to parole eligibility for young offenders convicted of murder in adult court; and
- The standard used in assessing transfers to adult court was modified to make considerations relating to the protection of society paramount.

Despite the two rounds of amendments, the Act remains controversial, and for many of the same reasons expressed a decade ago. And after extensive analyses of the Act covering a ten year period (e.g., Beaulieu 1989; Clark and O'Reilly-Flemming 1993; Corrado, Bala, Linden, and LeBlanc 1992; Hudson, Hornick, and Burrows 1988; Leschied, Jaffe, and Willis 1991; Platt 1989), there is still little consensus on how it should be reformed.

The debate is intense, and public. During the 1993 federal election campaign, for example, youth justice was a federal campaign issue for the first time in Canadian history. The Liberal, Conservative, New Democratic, and Reform parties all called for more of a "get tough" approach.

As this issue of the Journal goes to press, proposals for reforming the YOA continue to be widely discussed, and it now appears likely a further round of amendments will be forthcoming. On June 2, 1994, the federal Minister of Justice made good on the Liberal Party's campaign promises (Liberal Party of Canada 1993). A package of amendments to the YOA was tabled in the House of Commons that would place even more emphasis on the protection of society, and even less on the rehabilitation of young offenders (Howard 1994). Key proposals include:

- Increasing the maximum sentence for first degree murder from five to ten years in custody;
- Increasing the maximum sentence for second degree murder from five to seven years;
- Increasing the minimum amount of time (from five to ten years) that young offenders convicted of murder in the adult court system must serve before becoming eligible for parole;
- Removing some restrictions on access to records of young offenders so that information about their backgrounds can be made more widely available; and
- Requiring young offenders accused of serious crimes (murder, attempted murder, aggravated assault) to convince a youth court judge that they should not have their trials in adult court.

These proposals are to be put before the Commons Justice Committee, with amendments to the Act expected in the Fall of this year.

These changes, if enacted, would represent a further significant shift in emphasis towards more punishment for young offenders. Yet, a number of critics have been quick to condemn the proposals as too soft. The Reform Party and law enforcement interests, for example, have already expressed disappointment. They would have liked to have seen other changes, including:

- The extension of the maximum sentence provisions (currently reserved for murder) to other offences;

- Lowering the minimum age, perhaps to ten years from the current twelve years;
- Lowering the maximum age from the current eighteen years to, perhaps, sixteen or seventeen;
- Providing for the automatic cases, for example, those violent offence; and transfer to adult court in some involving murder, or a second
- Special provisions to deal with dangerous young offenders.

These proposals, which go far beyond those contained in the government's package, should not be regarded as far-fetched. A number of prestigious organizations, including the Canadian Association of Chiefs of Police have recently endorsed some of these ideas. Interest groups will continue to lobby the government, and they will have a new forum at their disposal – the Commons Justice Committee. Moreover, the media have mounted nothing short of an all out assault on the Act, and the barrage will no doubt continue in advance of and during debates in Parliament that will follow. We may yet see some of these additional proposals incorporated into the package of amendments.

An overview of the special issue

It is against this backdrop of historical evolution and current controversy that six articles by leading analysts are presented in this special issue of the Journal. Below, a brief synopsis of these papers is provided.

Professor Nicholas Bala ("What's wrong with YOA bashing?") suggests that many of the criticisms of the YOA, including those from the "get tough" right and the "return to rehabilitation" left, are simplistic, and mask important distinctions between the law, the interpretation of the law, and choices about how to implement the law. He cautions that there are limits to what any law can accomplish, and suggests that those who expect the law to alter patterns of criminal behaviour are being unrealistic. Such beliefs, he points out, ignore the complex social etiology of youth crime.

Bala also feels that proponents who feel the YOA can assure effective rehabilitation are being unrealistic. While he acknowledges that rehabilitation may be beneficial in some instances, he cautions that treatment should not be oversold, especially in cases where young offenders have demonstrated a pattern of serious offending.

While pointing out the limits of law, Bala nonetheless feels that a number of improvements to the YOA are worthy of consideration. Among his proposals: a review of the lower age limit (at least in some instances), a review of the costs and benefits of extending legal rights and protections to youth that are beyond those available to adults, allowing judicial discretion around the admission of statements given to police, allowing more flexibility regarding publication of identities and access to records, developing sentencing guidelines, tightening up the use of pre-trial detention, and more standardization of provincial implementation of the Act, particularly with regard to alternative measures.

In their paper, Carrington and Moyer ("Interprovincial variations in the use of custody") examine one of the most controversial aspects of the YOA — the use of custody. The authors point out that custody rates are affected by discretionary decisions at each stage of the justice system. They then proceed to analyze the relative contribution of decisions made at each of these steps.

Variation among the provinces in the use of custody under the YOA is examined using 1990 data from the Uniform Crime Report. Significant variations in the per capita use of custody are evident. These differences are found to be primarily related to variations in charge rates, and in the length of custodial dispositions issued by the courts. Differences between jurisdictions in the use of pre-trial diversion, in the outcome of adjudication, and in the type of disposition selected by the courts were less important explanations of overall differences in custody rates. The authors urge further analyses of the police response to youth crime, and of the factors that influence the length of custodial dispositions.

Leschied and Gendreau ("Doing justice in Canada"), well-known for promoting the use of rehabilitation programs in the youth justice system, concentrate their analysis of the YOA on what they view to be the two most controversial aspects of the Act — the use of custody, and access to treatment services. They note that the YOA was accompanied by a dramatic increase in the use of custody, and a dramatic decline in the provision of treatment services. They question whether this approach will result in effective control of youth crime.

The authors point out that there are treatment strategies that have proved to be effective in reducing recidivism rates, but the youth justice system has not taken adequate account of the relevant research. They believe that rehabilitation programs should be more fully utilized. They call for amendments to the YOA's statement of principles, so that more emphasis can be placed on the provision of treatment services, and they question the reasonableness of requiring consent to treatment from young offenders who may adhere to anti-social values and beliefs.

Clark and O'Reilly-Fleming ("Out of the carceral straight jacket") examine the contentious issue of offenders under the age of twelve. Using a survey of twenty-seven police forces, they provide data to show that offending among this age group is not common, and serious offences involving violence are a rarity. Nonetheless, relying on their experience in Ontario, they believe that current approaches to responding to under twelves is inadequate, and may even lead to the creation of persistent offenders.

The authors call for the development and implementation of an action plan for under twelves that would focus on early intervention, family involvement, and the fostering of effective problem solving skills among high risk youth. Effective measures to deal with under twelves, they suggest, could constitute an important crime prevention strategy.

In his paper ("Youth offenses — adult consequences"), Judge Beaulieu carefully reviews the provisions of the YOA as they apply to the transfer of young offenders to adult court. He suggests that these provisions require scrutiny because they require that decisions about transfers be made before the case is adjudicated. Therefore, all the facts about a case cannot be known when a transfer decision is made.

Beaulieu points out that, at present, the YOA requires that transfer decisions be partly based on the assumption that the Crown will be able to prove the charge. Thus, in a system founded on a presumption of innocence, the transfer provisions must assume guilt. He suggests that the Act be amended to allow transfer considerations only after there has been a finding or a plea of guilt.

In the final paper, Corrado and Markwart ("The need to reform the YOA") provide a wide ranging review of the YOA. They document the public and law enforcement critique that the Act is "too soft", and point out that this view is not shared by many academics who, preoccupied with rising custody rates, have been concerned to demonstrate that the Act is "too hard". While the two schools of thought appear completely at odds, the authors point out that both critiques may have validity.

Corrado and Markwart's careful examination of crime trends leads them to conclude that there has been a real and substantial increase in youth crime in recent years, at least in some areas of the country. These increases, they feel, are not statistical abberations that can be explained by changes in police charging practices following the implementation of the YOA, as some have claimed. Furthermore, they point out that there have been cases, often sensationalized by the media, where young offenders accused of serious crimes have got off on technicalities, or received lenient sentences. Furthermore, they suggest that because there have been few long sentences under the YOA, and not many offenders have been transferred to adult court, there may be some validity to the public's view that the Act is "too soft".

At the same time, the authors point out that sentences in youth court are often longer and more punitive than many realize. In fact, they present data to show that there has been a doubling or more of custody rates since the YOA was implemented. Furthermore, while custody is being justified for deterrent and punitive reasons, they also show that it is being justified for non-violent offenders on rehabilitation grounds. Because many offenders are being sentenced to custody, albeit for shorter periods, the authors suggest there is some validity to the view that the Act is "too hard".

Corrado and Markwart call for a number of reforms. They feel the Act provides too much discretion, and a complete lack of guidance and direction on how discretion should be used. They believe that the attempt to balance irreconcilable principles in the Act results in a muddled philosophy and inconsistent practices. They propose more certain and onerous provisions for serious offenders in order to restore public confidence in the Act. But they also urge a revisiting of welfare-based approaches to youth justice that would provide greater flexibility and informality, place greater emphasis on the provision of support services, and create stronger links between the justice and child welfare systems. They further propose the adoption of sentencing guidelines, and suggest that cost-sharing be used to entice provinces to provide effective early intervention and rehabilitation programs.

How tough is tough enough?

In this brief historical sketch and overview of current issues, the broad trends in Canadian youth justice over the past three decades are clearly evident. Canada has been moving away from a system of youth justice based on the needs of young offenders, and towards a system that gives greater weight to youth accountability, deterrence, and the protection of society.

The trend first became evident in the 1960's, when growing disenchantment with the JDA began to set in. A number of legislative proposals for reform followed during the 1960's and 1970's. A watershed event was the replacement of the JDA with the YOA in 1982.

Since 1982, there has been further evidence of this trend. As Corrado and Markwart (1992) have pointed out, the amendments to the YOA have continued to shift youth justice towards a model based on crime control principles. Despite this, the public remains skeptical about the effectiveness of the system, and still further measures to toughen the Act are now under active consideration.

Particularly since the introduction of the YOA, there has been a marked increase in the use of punitive sanctions for young offenders (Doob 1992; Markwart 1992). Despite this, there is no evidence that crime rates are being held down. While this could be taken as evidence that the "crime control" approach is not working, instead, it is used by crime control advocates to push for even stronger punitive measures. All of this begs the question: how tough is tough enough?

It has been well established in this country and elsewhere that punishment is not an effective deterrent, and that prisons are not very good at either deterring or rehabilitating offenders (e.g., Leschied and Vark 1989). Yet, the youth justice system appears all too ready to place more and more young offenders into custody, while, at the same time, it often neglects even the most basic needs for alternative programs or rehabilitation services.

While there may well be a role for punishment, or at least incapacitation, for some serious young offenders who pose a threat to society, the blanket toughening of the youth justice system over the past decade has not effectively discriminated between these offenders and others, with the result that many non-violent perpetrators are routinely incarcerated for relatively minor infractions. It seems likely that further changes to the Act, if they are along the lines currently being contemplated, will have much the same effect. Perhaps it is time to consider not just punishing more, but punishing smarter (Gendreau, Paporrozi, Little, and Goddard 1993).

The current debate is an emotional one, replete with pleas from victims of violent crimes, a concerted lobby by law enforcement interests, and extensive political posturing. In this climate, a rational examination of the issues is difficult. Yet, the development of cost-effective solutions to the pressing problems facing the nation ought to be a priority. Otherwise, policy formulation amounts to little more than pandering to public outcry. In the drive to transform the youth justice system into one that more closely approximates the adult system, it is well to remember that the adult system is also not held in very high esteem by the same constituencies that seek to make the youth system more like it.

Perhaps too much is expected of the YOA. Perhaps prevention and rehabilitation are largely beyond its purview. If Canada is serious about preventing crime and protecting the public, perhaps it needs a whole host of social development programs that would address the more basic needs of youths, children, and families. Perhaps we need a clear plan to differentiate among types of crimes and offenders. Some will say we have no money to undertake such liberal initiatives. Then again, there seems to be no shortage of resources for custody.

Notes

1 In Saskatchewan, for example, a 16-year-old would be tried as a juvenile delinquent, whereas in neighbouring Manitoba, the same person committing the same act would be tried in adult court, up until their eighteenth birthday. In other provinces, sixteen-year-olds were considered youth, but seventeen-year-olds were considered adults. At times, different age limits had applied to males and females;

2 The fact that so-called "status offenses" could land a young person before the juvenile courts was widely criticized. These "offenses", involving such matters as sexual immorality and truancy, were only offences if committed by a young person. The same act committed by an adult, however, was not an offence under any statute. Beyond claims of "age discrimination", critics pointed out that these provisions were often used by child welfare authorities to exert social control over disadvantaged young women (West 1984).

3 For a more complete description of the provisions of the *Young Offenders* Act, see Solicitor General of Canada (1986), Archambault (1986), and Hylton (1983; 1985).

References

Alvi, Shahid
1986 Realistic crime prevention strategies through alternative measures for youth In Dawn H. Currie and Brian D. MacLean (eds.), The Administration of Justice. Saskatoon: University of Saskatchewan, Department of Sociology.

Archambault, O.
1986 Young Offenders Act: Philosophy and principles. In R.A. Silverman and J.J. Teevan (eds.), Crime In Canadian Society. Toronto: Butterworths.

Beaulieu, Lucien (ed.)
1989 Young Offender Dispositions: Perspectives on Principles and Practice. Toronto: Wall and Thompson.

Caputo, T.C. and Sheldon Goldenberg
1986 Young people and the law: A consideration of luddite and utopian responses. In Dawn H. Currie and Brian D. MacLean (eds.), The Administration of Justice. Saskatoon: University of Saskatchewan, Department of Sociology.

Clark, Barry and Thomas O'Reilly-Fleming (eds.)
1993 Youth Injustice: Canadian Perspectives. Toronto: Canadian Scholars' Press.

Corrado, R.R., Nicholas Bala, Rick Linden, and Marc LeBlanc (eds.)
1992 Juvenile Justice In Canada: A Theoretical and Analytical Assessment. Toronto: Butterworths.

Corrado, R.R. and A. Markwart
1992 The evolution and implementation of a new era of juvenile justice in Canada. In R.R. Corrado, Nicholas Bala, Rick Linden, and Marc LeBlanc (eds.), Juvenile Justice In Canada: A Theoretical and Analytical Assessment. Toronto: Butterworths.

Doob, Anthony N.
1992 Trends in the use of custodial dispositions for young offenders. Canadian Journal of Criminology 34: 35-50.

Gendreau, P., M. Paporrozi, T. Little, and M. Goddard
1993 Does "punishing smarter" work? An assessment of the new generation of alternative sanctions in probation. Forum on Corrections Research 5: 31-34.

Griffiths, Curt T. and Simon Verdun-Jones
1994 Canadian Criminal Justice, 2nd edition. Toronto: Harcourt Brace.

Howard, Ross
1994 Youth rehabilitation loses priority. Toronto: Globe and Mail. June 3, p. A1.

Hudson, J., J.P. Hornick, and Barbara A. Burrows
1988 Justice and the Young Offender in Canada. Toronto: Wall and Thompson.

Hylton, John H.
1983 The juvenile justice system: Implications of new young offenders legislation. Social Work Papers 17: Summer.

Hylton, John H.
1985 Judging young offenders. Policy Options 6 (2): 25-28.

Leschied, A. and L. Vark
1989 Assessing Outcomes of Special Need Young Offenders. London: Family Court Clinic.

Leschied, A., P. Jaffe, and W. Willis
1991 The Young Offenders Act: A Revolution In Canadian Juvenile Justice. Toronto: University of Toronto Press.

Liberal Party of Canada
1993 Creating Opportunity: The Liberal Plan for Canada. Ottawa: Liberal Party of Canada.

Martinson, Robert
1974 What works? Questions and answers about prison reform. The Public Interest 35: 22-54.

Markwart, Allan
1992 Custody sanctions under the Young Offenders Act. In Raymond R. Corrado, Nicholas Bala, Rick Linden, and Marc LeBlanc (eds.), Juvenile Justice In Canada: A Theoretical and Analytical Assessment. Toronto: Butterworths.

Platt, Anthony
1969 The Child Savers. Chicago: University of Chicago Press.

Platt, Priscilla
1989 Young Offenders Law In Canada. Toronto: Butterworths.

Solicitor General of Canada
1986 The Young Offenders Act: Highlights. Ottawa: Supply and Services Canada.

West, W. Gordon
1984 Young Offenders and the State: A Canadian Perspective on Delinquency. Toronto: Butterworths.